Lecture Notes in Computer Science   2544

Edited by G. Goos, J. Hartmanis, and J. van Leeuwen

T0233042

Springer
Berlin
Heidelberg
New York
Barcelona
Hong Kong
London
Milan
Paris
Tokyo

Subhash Bhalla (Ed.)

Databases in Networked Information Systems

Second International Workshop, DNIS 2002
Aizu, Japan, December 16-18, 2002
Proceedings

 Springer

Series Editors

Gerhard Goos, Karlsruhe University, Germany
Juris Hartmanis, Cornell University, NY, USA
Jan van Leeuwen, Utrecht University, The Netherlands

Volume Editor

Subhash Bhalla
University of Aizu
Database Systems Laboratory
Aizu-Wakamatsu, Fukushima 965-8580, Japan
E-mail: bhalla@u-aizu.ac.jp

Cataloging-in-Publication Data applied for

A catalog record for this book is available from the Library of Congress.

Bibliographic information published by Die Deutsche Bibliothek
Die Deutsche Bibliothek lists this publication in the Deutsche Nationalbibliografie;
detailed bibliographic data is available in the Internet at http://dnb.ddb.de

CR Subject Classification (1998): H.2, H.3, H.4, H.5, C.2

ISSN 0302-9743
ISBN 3-540-00264-2 Springer-Verlag Berlin Heidelberg New York
-

Springer-Verlag Berlin Heidelberg New York
a member of BertelsmannSpringer Science+Business Media GmbH

http://www.springer.de

© Springer-Verlag Berlin Heidelberg 2002
Printed in Germany

Typesetting: Camera-ready by author, data conversion by PTP-Berlin, Stefan Sossna
Printed on acid-free paper   SPIN 10871631   06/3142   5 4 3 2 1 0

Preface

Information systems in healthcare and public utility services depend on computing infrastructure. Many research efforts are being made in related areas, such as mobile computing, web-based computing, and information extraction and handling. Government agencies in a few countries also plan to launch many facilities in education, healthcare, and information support as e-government initiatives. In this context, Information Interchange Management has become an important research field. A number of new opportunities have evolved in design and modeling based on the new computing needs of users. Database systems play an important role in supporting networked information systems for access and storage aspects.

The second international workshop on Databases in Networked Information Systems (DNIS) 2002 was held on December 16–18, 2002 at the University of Aizu in Japan. The workshop program includes research contributions and invited contributions. A view of research activity in Information Interchange Management and related research issues was provided in the session on this topic, with an invited contribution by Prof. Gio Wiederhold. The workshop session on Web Data Management had an invited paper by Prof. Tosiyasu L. Kunii. The workshop session on Data Management Systems included a contributed invited paper by Prof. Joachim Biskup. The two sessions on Networked Information Systems included invited contributions by Prof. Masaru Kitsuregawa and Dr. Umeshwar Dayal. I would like to thank the members of the program committee for their support and all authors who considered DNIS 2002 for their research contributions.

The sponsoring organizations and the organizing committee deserve praise for the support they provided. A number of individuals contributed to the success of the workshop. I thank Prof. P.C.P. Bhatt, Prof. J. Biskup, Prof. D. Agrawal, Prof. Krithi Ramamritham, Dr. S. Grumbach, Prof. Sushil Jajodia, and Prof. M. Kitsuregawa for providing continuous support and encouragement.

The workshop received invaluable support from the University of Aizu. I thank Prof. Nikolay Mirenkov, Head of Department of Computer Software, for making this support available. I express my gratitude to the members and chairman of the International Affairs Committee for supporting the workshop proposal. Many thanks are also due to the faculty members at the university for their cooperation and support.

September 2002   Subhash Bhalla

Organization

The DNIS 2002 international workshop was organized by the Database Systems Laboratory, University of Aizu, Aizu-Wakamatsu City, Fukushima, PO 965-8580, Japan.

Executive Committee

Honorary Chair: T.L. Kunii, Hosei University, Japan
Program Chair: S. Bhalla, University of Aizu, Japan
Organizing Chair: Qun Jin, University of Aizu, Japan
Executive Chair: N. Bianchi-Berthouze, University of Aizu, Japan

Program Committee

D. Agrawal, University of California, USA
N. Bianchi-Berthouze, University of Aizu, Japan
S. Bhalla, University of Aizu, Japan
P.C.P. Bhatt, IIIT Banglore, India
J. Biskup, University of Dortmund, Germany
L. Capretz, University of Western Ontario, Canada
M. Capretz, University of Western Ontario, Canada
U. Dayal, Hewlett-Packard Laboratories, USA
S. Grumbach, INRIA, France
S. Jajodia, George Mason University, USA
Q. Jin, University of Aizu, Japan
M. Kitsuregawa, University of Tokyo, Japan
A. Kumar, Pennsylvania State University, USA
J. Li, University of Tsukuba, Japan
K. Myszkowski, Max-Planck-Institut fuer Informatik, Germany
G. Mansfield, Tohoku University, Japan
K. Ramamritham, IIT Bombay, India
P.K. Reddy, IIIT Hyderabad, India
V. Savchenko, Hosei University, Japan
M.V. Sreenivas, Sylantro Systems, USA

Additional Reviewers

P. Veltri, INRIA, France
S. Zhu, Center for Secure Information Systems, George Mason University, USA
P. Bottoni, University La Sapienza of Rome, Italy
S. Ramanujam, University of Western Ontario, Canada

Sponsoring Institution

International Affairs Committee, University of Aizu,
Aizu-Wakamatsu City, Fukushima, PO 965-8580, Japan.

Table of Contents

Information Interchange and Management Systems

Information Systems That also Project into the Future 1
    Gio Wiederhold

A Design Methodology for Workflow System Development 15
    Jaehyoun Kim, C. Robert Carlson

Adding Valid Time to XPath 29
    Shuohao Zhang, Curtis E. Dyreson

Communication Deadlock Detection of Inter-organizational Workflow
Definition 43
    Jaeyong Shim, Dongsoo Han, Hongsoog Kim

Web Data Management Systems

Web Information Modeling: The Adjunction Space Model 58
    Tosiyasu L. Kunii

Advanced Storage and Retrieval of XML Multimedia
Documents 64
    Jérôme Godard, Frédéric Andres, Kinji Ono

A New Query Processing Scheme in a Web Data Engine 74
    Zhiqiang Zhang, Chunxiao Xing, Lizhu Zhou, Jianhua Feng

An Approach to Modelling Legacy Enterprise Systems 88
    Janet Lavery, Cornelia Boldyreff

Data Management Systems

Explicit Representation of Constrained Schema Mappings for
Mediated Data Integration 103
    C. Altenschmidt, J. Biskup

Xeena for Schema: Creating XML Data with an Interactive Editor 133
    Mark Sifer, Yardena Peres, Yoelle Maarek

Coding and Presentation of Multimedia for Data Broadcasting with
Broadcasting Markup Language 147
    Hun Lee, Gun Ho Hong, Ha Yoon Song, Sang Yong Han

A Proposal for a Distributed XML Healthcare Record 161
    Francesco Barbera, Fernando Ferri, Fabrizio L. Ricci,
    Pier Angelo Sottile

Networked Information Systems: Applications

Some Experiences on Large Scale Web Mining 173
    Masaru Kitsuregawa, Iko Pramudiono, Yusuke Ohura, Masashi Toyoda

An Approach for Distance Learning via Internet and Its Evaluation 179
    Tomoyuki Sowa, Kotaro Hirano

A Graph Based Approach to Extract a Neighborhood Customer
Community for Collaborative Filtering.............................. 188
    P. Krishna Reddy, Masaru Kitsuregawa, P. Sreekanth,
    S. Srinivasa Rao

An Interactive Programming Environment for Enhancing Learning
Performance.. 201
    Mungunsukh Jambalsuren, Zixue Cheng

Networked Information Systems: Implementations

Business Operation Intelligence 213
    Fabio Casati, Umeshwar Dayal, Ming-Chien Shan

Peer-to-Peer File Sharing with Integrated Attribute Descriptions
in XML and an Embedded Database Engine.......................... 225
    Shuichi Takizawa, Qun Jin

In Search of Torrents: Automatic Detection of Logical Sets Flows
in Network Traffic... 239
    Koide Kazuhide, Glenn Mansfield Keeni, Shiratori Norio

Dynamic Location Management with Caching in Hierarchical
Databases for Mobile Networks 253
    Chang Woo Pyo, Jie Li, Hisao Kameda, Xiaohua Jia

An Experimental Study on Query Processing Efficiency of
Native-XML and XML-Enabled Database Systems 268
    Atakan Kurt, Mustafa Atay

Author Index 285

Information Systems That Also Project into the Future

Gio Wiederhold

Computer Science Department. Stanford University,
Gates Computer Science Building 4A, Stanford CA 94305-9040.
1 415 725-8363 / 725-2588
http://www-db.stanford.edu/people/gio.html
gio@cs.stanford.edu

Abstract. We study requirements to make information systems used for decision-making support effective. Lacking today is support for projection within these systems: the action that a decision maker initiates has effects in the future, and these must be assessed. Information systems however, focus on the past, and leave projection to be performed either by the decision makers intuition, or to a variety of tools that are not well integrated. After enumerating needed functions, we present concepts needed for an adequate infrastructure.
We then describe some research that has demonstrated a capability for integrating output from spreadsheets and other simulations into information systems. We close by indicating research and development direction that should be pursued to make the vision of information systems that can also project into the future a reality.

1   Introduction

An important objective of our information systems is to provide support to decision makers, so that the actions they initiate will be well informed and optimal within the bonds of our knowledge. A focus for the last 8 or so years has been integration of information from diverse sources. Technologies as middleware [Charles:99] and mediation [WiederholdG:97], has greatly increased the breadth of information an reduce the fraction of missing information. Historical records, now part of many databases, has increased the reach of the timelines [DasSTM:94], sometimes back to the period when electronic records were first collected. When data arrive continuously new approaches to extract information out of streaming. Data mining increases the depth of the search, and provides insights into relationships and functions for projecting into the future [BettiniWJ:96]. All these technologies are being integrated into the information systems we are building now, although each topic is still of active research interest.

Does that mean that the decision maker is well served by information systems? An answer to this question can be obtained by seeing decision makers in action: they rarely use our information systems directly. They do rely on information from them, collected by staff, summarized, and often placed into reports. These reports contain tables of alternative conditions and results, and often on-line pointers to spreadsheet used to justify those results. The ability of word-processing documents to contain active spreadsheets has become a valued capability, more so than the ability to access

S. Bhalla (Ed.): DNIS 2002, LNCS 2544, pp. 1–14, 2002.
© Springer-Verlag Berlin Heidelberg 2002

databases. Dozens of books on this topic are on the market and sell well [MooreWW:01]. In situations where the amount of data is modest and relatively static, files associated with spreadsheets have supplanted the use of database technology, and extensions to allow sharing of such files are being developed [FullerMP:93].

Fig. 1. Information and Decision making

Unless information systems can narrow the gap between the past and the future this isolation of the information gathering and information using disciplines is not likely to change. Our vision is then one where decision makers can move seamlessly from the past to the future (Fig.1). Given that the focus in the past has been on past data, we will here focus on information that is obtained by using tools that project into the future [Wiederhold:99].

2   Projective Services for Decision Makers

In order to provide decision makers with effectively projective capabilities a number of computation functions are needed. These in turn will require additional infrastructure capabilities in our information systems. The results that these function s compute replace on the whole the results that information systems obtain by accessing databases for past, recorded data. The computational predictive functions we discuss and the infrastructure capabilities needed have already been demonstrated in isolation. The intellectual sources are in the planning sciences, in simulation technology, databases, software composition, workflow management and the distributed extensions of all of these. However, their integration has not yet been achieved.

2.1 Predictive Computations

Basic to this our vision is access to a variety of information sources that try to predict the future. Prediction invariably requires computation, but the computational models vary widely. Just like databases, instances are differentiated by content, but the tools used in diverse application areas overlap a great deal. Existing sources for predictions are spreadsheets, more formal discrete simulations, computations based on continuous equations, some dynamic programming formulations, all of them aided at times by published projections of economists, and environmental scientists, and even politicians whose models are not open to inspection.

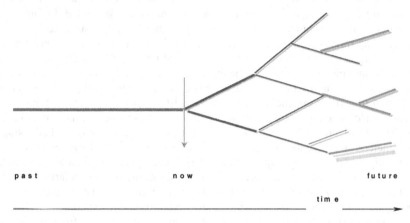

Fig. 2. Past information and future projections

Published projections appear in print and now often on the web [FishwickH:98]. The results are generally at a high level of abstraction since they are intended for a broad audience, and most be combined with local an domain specific information in order to become actionable information for decision makers. For instance, projections of future inflation rates must be combined with capital reserves, cash flow, production capacities, personnel information, purchase and sales rates in order to project corporate performance. Datamining over past data can provide a source for future projections as well, given an assumption that the past is an adequate predictor of the future.

The spreadsheet is the most common tool used in business for computation. When used for projection typically columns are assigned for timepoints that reach into the future, and rows handle the variety of given, intermediate, and result values at each timepoint.

A typical example is a budget projection, with estimates of income, sales, and as well as on product, personnel, and interest costs. The parameters for future income are often based on past growth, while costs include published projections. Published parameters can be loaded through import interfaces, although we find that in the majority of cases they are entered by cutting and pasting from the source data. Internal parameters, as production factors are most commonly hidden within the spreadsheet's formulas, although the parents which require frequent modification may be assigned to initial cells, to allow easy reassessment of alternative futures. Results are again either extracted through standard interfaces, or by cutting and pasting. Many interfaces are used to drive graphic presentation, with curves plotting results over future points in time, but not well suited to integartion. Complex spreadsheets are often created by experts, and the actual decision maker will never change the formulas, but only enter alternate values for selected parameters. Such parameters may represent values under control of the decision maker, say investments, or values that represent external risks, say prices of input commodities.

Discrete simulations have a similar computational model, but deal with larger scale cases. Here the provider and the user are more explicitly separated. Future values are computed at determined points in time, perhaps days, but may be aggregated to longer, say monthly, periods to satisfy the needs of the decision maker. An example we have used is a business model for a gas station, which included seasonal factors. Specific models are common in health care, in order to predict outcome for various patient types and treatments. The result presentation in this models is already oriented towards convenient presentation at future points in time, often 1, 3, and 5 years hence. A disincentive to their use of detailed discrete simulations in health care is the cost of entering data, since a patient may have to be described using many parameters. Computations may explicitly compute risks, by being carried out at low and high ranges of input parameters, and then statistically summarized. Computational performance becomes also a concern, since predictions are only of value if they are produced much faster than real-time. There will be carefully designed input formats for variables that drive alternative outcomes, and the results will be placed directly in reports or databases. If parameters from mined data are used then the predicted results will often mirror the mined data at a high level of abstraction.

Continuously executing simulations provide up-to-date results continuously, refining results and projecting them as far into the future as their computational capabilities permit. They must also be constantly re-initialized with new data observations. Weather prediction is the most familiar example. Here computational resources become limiting. Probabilities are routinely produced, although not always well understood. What does 60% chance of rain mean? Here the individual decision maker has little control, the results are intended for a wide audience. The user can only select the date and place for the prediction, and if the output must be integrated with further computation one has to resort to cut-and-paste or screen-scraping. On long-range flights we can often observe a specialized simulation of this type, computing the expected arrival time of the aircraft at its destination, which aggregates flight parameters, weather predictions, and landing conditions. Some automotive navigation systems try to provide a similar function, but as of today cannot acquire expected road conditions.

Functional simulations have been used mainly where little detail is available. Here the predictions are based on differential equations, initialized from parameters based on fitting prior observations. Since these observations are due to prior results, rather than based on a detailed model of underlying relationships they have to applied with extreme care. An early, well known example were the projections about future world energy and food needs and resources, estimated by the Club of Rome for over 20 years [vanDieren:95]. Recent examples include the modeling of global warming and, on a smaller scale, the expectations about Internet commerce [SA:97]. Stability of the projections can be estimated by varying input parameters within bounds of likelihoods. The ranges of resulting values at the projected points can then be reduced to risk factors; however, for complex models an assessment of all combinations becomes computationally extravagant. Computing with little real data means that much uncertainty remains and can seriously affect the value of the results [BenHaim:01]. In these models the decision maker will have little influence, and can only enter the future pint-in-time and observe the results.

Interpolation is a secondary function needed for effective support of decision making. The points in time where existing, general prediction tools provide results may not match the point in time of interest of the decision maker. When published data are used or intermediate results have been stored in databases or files the points-in-time are also preselected. In those cases projected results must be adjusted to the decision makers framework. In many cases simple linear interpolations between the prior point and the next point suffice. If the differences a relatively major a second-order interpolation may be needed. Similarly, measures of risks or uncertainties around that number must be interpolated. Here reducing the information to statistical variances, and then applying their mean to the interpolated value produces credible results.

Extrapolations are much more risky. Going more than a few intervals beyond the last predicted value is generally unwise, and using complex functions induced from prior points is especially risky. We have seen many business extrapolations during the Internet bubble that provided results that did not make sense of they had been placed in a more global model [PerkinsP:00]. Perhaps short range simulations can be combined explicitly with long range simulation, larger granularity to minimize risks.

Computational comparison of alternatives is needed by decision makers who have investigated more than one alternative. Now for each point in time multiple results exist, so that for that point a series of values should be displayed, each value clearly labeled with the assumptions that led to the result. If the set of alternatives is complete, then the sum of probabilities at any point in time should be equal to 1.0, allowing some validation of the model used to describe the possible futures. Reports that are manually produced commonly show graphs of results under different conditions, but do not support comparative computations.

A tree of alternatives will be needed if at successive points in time new decision can be made or external factors can affect outcomes (Fig. 3). Game trees are familiar to all scientists, but grow rapidly when at each point in time more than a few alternatives must be considered. if, say five alternatives exist at 10 successive points in time the tree will have grown to nearly 10 million branches. Low probability paths must to be pruned, both for the sake of the presentation and to reduce computational effort. Now the sum of probabilities over all alternatives shown at a point in time will be less than one, but preferably not much less. Labeling the branches of the tree so that their ancestry is clear will be challenge. Effective reasoning in this space becomes complex [Winslett:88]. Alternate sequences of events may combine, creating DAGs. There is a high volume of a literature on dealing with trees in planning, a recent contribution is [DomshlakB:02], but little connection to data-oriented practice.

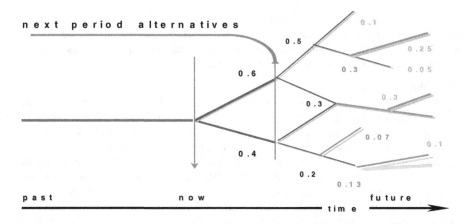

Fig. 3. A tree of alternatives

Attaching outcome values is another function needed to complement many simulations. If the decision are purely business then financial measures suffice. Outcomes are the profits and losses at the terminal nodes in the planning tree. These outcomes can be substituted back along the branches to the current time, perhaps with corrections to net present values. At each node the sum of the set of results of its alternatives should be available. When simulations are used to also assess the risks or likelihood of various alternatives the decision maker may need to augment that final values of the outcomes: one outcome may have a large expected gain, but an intolerable risk, others modest gains and little risk. When dealing with other metrics, as human welfare, then setting the relative values of the outcomes at these periods requires much insight, and perhaps interviews with the patient to assess their utility function [ChajewskaEa:98].

2.2 Infrastructure Requirements

From the summary of needed functions we perceive that information systems cannot tightly integrate all the candidate functionalities to support decision making. We will need interfaces for the information sources, and means to store and access their results.

   Since the world changes which each passing time interval we also need a capability to rapidly recompute predictions.

Interfaces are needed to support interaction with any and all of the candidate methods that predict future information. In Section 3 we will describe an initial experiment with such a language, modeled om SQL, where the schema defines the variables accessible to the decision maker and the SELECT statement is replaced with a PREDICT statement which retrieves both the value and a variance. Other interface choices are certainly feasible. Of importance is that we cannot conceive the major extension we foresee can be managed in a tightly integrated approach.

Storage for Alternative Futures has to be provided. Alternative futures have not been integrated into today's information systems. These systems have focused on past information, with the assumption that there is only one truth.

If the predicted alternative results branch out into bushy trees available storage systems will be severely challenged. Databases being developed to handle XML hierarchies should be able to cope with some of the requirements, including the labeling of time points and provenance [Connolly:97]. DAGs are not that easily handled, although they would reduce the breadth of the trees. Overall, the volumes to be stored should be modest in terms of database technology, since only results will need to be stored. Storing large amounts of predictive information is of little value, since most predictions will be invalidated one the next point-in-time is reached and alternatives that once were feasible, are closed forever.

Effective presentation has to be supported so that the decision maker can effectively investigate the results at any point in time, together with its likelihood. The most likely or valuable alternatives must be shown. In planning textbooks and demonstration exercises the number of alternatives shown is limited, and easily presented [Tate:96]. When the choices become complex a clear presentation becomes harder. Summarization will often be needed [DeZegherGeetsEa:88]. Some advanced spreadsheet programs allow graphing from multiple sequential sheets to show alternatives. Temporal seamlessness is desirable, so that data from the past, stored in databases are obtained in the same way as the projections into the future. Dialing forwards or backwards should create a trail that can be easily visualized.

The probability of any alternative path must always be stored and shown to the decision maker. When predictive systems do not provide probabilities or certainties directly ancillary estimates can be computed, based on an expert's assessment of the credibility of the source or by comparing past predictions with actual observations. For past data one would expect the certainty to be one, but since probabilities are inherent in the information system we envisage, *that aint necessarily so* [GershwinH:34].   For instance, intelligence data may well be labeled with uncertainties, and those uncertainties would be carried forward into the projections. Uncertainties also exist in past data sources, and here technology transfer from the projected models to needs in historical databases may occur [GarciaMolinaBP:92].

Composition of probabilities and uncertainties is still an open question. While statistical measures are composable, the semantics associated with the various risks encountered in decision making differ. We have used probability whenever statistical methods seem adequate and certainty when the focus is on the decision maker [DeyS:96]. Once systems as we visualize here are used in practice it is likely that new insights and computational approaches will develop.

Recomputation of the entire set of predicted results should be easy and fast. Conceptually, recomputation is needed whenever a time interval of the smallest contributing source has been passed. That might be every week, every day, every hour, or every minute. It need not be more frequent than the decision maker needs results, but deferring recomputation to the time of need would make for a very poor system response. Many optimizations can be devised to deal with specific situations, including automatic selective recomputation. Results from maintaining warehouses might be useful here [ZhugeEa:95]. To support the process the entire task must be effectively encoded. The capabilities of automated workflow models might be exploited [GaudiotB:91].

2.3 Summary

We can now recapitulate our initial vision. Information systems are being extended to encompass wider access and analysis capabilities to provide more information for decision makers.   However, the decision maker has to plan and schedule actions beyond the current point-in-time. Simulation tools are required for projecting the outcome at some future time of the decisions that can be made today. Many tools are available for projections, ranging from back-of-the envelope estimates, spreadsheets, business-specific simulations, to continuous simulations, as used for weather forecasting. These tools provide information which is complementary to the information about the past provided by databases, and help in selecting the best course-of-action [LindenG:92].

The need for integrating information systems and projection has been felt primarily in military planning [McCall:96] and in health care [GustafsonEa:01] two fields where decision maker can not afford to have long delays between information processing and acting on the results.

Any implementation will require cooperation of specialists in distinct fields, and a willingness to learn about the methods and paradigms used by others. The task is of a scale that building a tightly integrated system is not feasible. On the other hand, we believe that relatively simple advances can provide convincing demonstrations, since most of the computational components exist already.

3 An Interface Implementation

We indicated that a crucial component for a system that can present past and future information is an interface to the variety of predictive services . We have demonstrated such a system, using concepts from SQL, calling it SimQL [Jiang:96]. Experiments with SimQL have demonstrated that a single interface, using a style that is easy to understand can indeed be used to drive and return predictive information from multiple sources.

3.1 Language

To introduce the language we provide an example in SQL which retrieves weather information from a historical database and corresponding SimQL statement that retrieves weather predictions, with their results:

```
        SQL
SELECT Temperature, Cloudcover, Windspeed, Winddirection FROM  WeatherDB
            WHERE Date = 'yesterday' AND Location = 'ORD'.
                ---> {75, .30, 5, NW}
        SimQL
PREDICT Temperature, Cloudcover, Windspeed, Winddirection FROM  WeatherSimulation
            WHERE Date = 'tomorrow' AND Location = 'ORD'.
                ---> { (75, .8), (.30,.8), (5, .8), (NW, .8) }
```

The weather simulation in our demonstration case was accessed via a wrapper [HammerEa:97].

Note that there are two aspects of SQL that SimQL mimics:

1. A *Schema* that describes the accessible content to an invoking program, its programmers, and its customers. A SimQL schema is a view, providing access only to the input and output parameters of the simulation. The computational complexity is hidden.

2. A *Query Language* that provides the actual access to information resources.

Using familiar interface concepts simplifies the understanding of customers and also enable seamless interoperation of SimQL with existing database tools in supporting advanced information systems.   There are some significant differences in accessing past data and computing information about the future:

1) Not all simulation information is described in the schema. Simulations are often controlled by hundreds of variables, and mapping all of them into a schema to be accessed by the decision maker is inappropriate. In SQL similar subsetting is achieved thorough the view mechanism. In SimQL only those variables that are needed for querying results and for controlling the simulation are externally accessible. The rest will still be accessible to the simulation developer by direct interaction with the forecasting tools. Defining the appropriate schema require the joint efforts of the developer, the model builder, and the customer.

2) The SimQL schema and query languages differentiate between IN, OUT, and INOUT variables, restricting the flexibility seen in SQL relational access.

3) Unlike SQL views, which are supported by real underlying SQL tables having static data, SimQL models only keeps information about interfaces to wrapped simulations, which can change constantly.

4) Predictions always incorporate uncertainty. Thus, measures of uncertainty are always reported with the results; the OUT variable in SimQL has two parts in the form of (value, uncertainty).

5) We do not expect to need persistent update capabilities in SimQL. Model updates are the responsibility of the providers of the simulations. The queries submitted to SimQL supply temporary variables that parameterize the simulations for a specific instance, but are not intended to update the simulation models.

We were able to demonstrate SimQL by adapting an exsting SQL compiler.

3.2 System Design

Components of the demonstration system include four component types

1. a compiler for a. the SimQL schema statements that during execution link the queries via the wrappers to the prediction tools and   b. the SimQL query language, which generates code to access wrapped forecasting resources.

2. a repository containing the schemas for the wrapped resources, identifying input and output parameters for each.

3. a wrapper generation tool to bring existing forecasting tools, as simulations, spreadsheets, and dynamic web sources into compliance
4. The actual forecasting tools, note that we only access pre-existing predictive tools.

Wrappers are used to provide compatible, robust, and 'machine-friendly' access to their model parameters and execution results [HammerEa:97]. Our wrappers also convert the uncertainty associated with simulation results (say, 50% probability of rain) to a standard range (1.0 - 0.0) or may estimate a value if the simulation does not provide a value for its uncertainty.

3.3 Experiments

Our experiments used diverse simulations as sketched in Figure 4.. They were wrapped to provide information to our SimQL interfaces for schema generation and querying.
a. Two spreadsheets containing formulas that projected business costs and profits into the future. Inputs were investment amounts, and results were made available for years into the future.
b. A short-range weather forecast available from NOAA on the world-wide web. Temperature and precipitation results were available for major cities, with an indication of uncertainty, which rapidly increased beyond 5 days.
c. A long-range agricultural weather forecast for areas that overlapped with the cities. The initial uncertainty here was quite high, but increased little over a period of a several months.
d. A discrete simulation of the operation of a gasoline station, giving required refill schedules and profits.

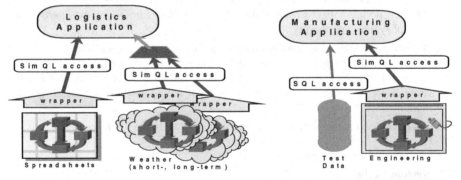

Fig. 4. Examples of Experiments with SimQL, demonstrating commonality

Combining b. and c. in an application allowed us to report weather data with minimal uncertainty over a wide range. Details of the prototype are given in [WiederholdJG:98] and on our webpages.

4 Research Questions

The focus of traditional database technology has been highly reliable and consistent services for operational systems. As decision-making support has become more important, the constraints due to this emphasis have restricted the services needed for effective decision-making support. There are many research opportunities, from tool development for understood issues to conceptual research to deal with new issues that arise in the integration of predictive capabilities into information systems.

The hardest issues appear in providing the infrastructure and presentation capabilities. While there are many good examples for modest effort, they don't appear to scale well to the volume of data and complexity of models that an integration of systems will allow.

Storage of predicted results. For database specialists the immediate question is: why not store all predictive data that is obtained in databases, and query those? Our response here is at least twofold:

a.   the information produced is transient, and becomes invalid after each interval. While database technology deals well with simple updates, here the change process differs greatly. The relative frequency of updates to read request, in databases typically greater than 1:5 is likely to be much lower and could be 5:1.

b.   current databases do not deal with the bushy data created by alternative futures.

However caching technology may help in improving response times. Caching should consider the volatility of the results. The volatility will depend on the soyurces being used, and may be easier to manage than in a setting where updates are not manageable.

Recomputation. Recomputation of the predictions should be automatic, but must be optimized with respect to the users needs. Caching and recomputation of results are alternatives that must be balanced. Recomputaion may also be needed if parametrs used in prediction change, pehaps as a result of ongoing datamining [SalatianH:99] .

Interoperation. Interoperation with past information is essential to realize the vision. Information systems must integrate past, present, and simulated information, providing a continuous view. The source data will have different temporal granularities, and simulated results must be computed to coincide with expected future events. Complementary research includes stream technology, which dynamically extracts information from continuous data streams [MotwaniEa:01].

Probability and Uncertainty. Important research into uncertainty processing has not been applicable in the traditional database model [Pearl:88]. There have been multiple definitions of uncertainty and their range of applicability is not clear [BhatnagarK:86]. The information systems that process forecast results will have to take uncertainty explicitly into account, so that the decision-maker can clearly weigh risks versus benefits. By supplying data about the future that have intrinsic uncertainties developers will be forced to deal with the issue explicitly.

By explicitly considering the utility of various outcomes modeling, greater support can be provided to decision makers. Pruning of the tree can reduce the alternatives faced by the decision maker to a manageable number say about 7 at a time [Miller:56]. Some planning models are intended to automatically select optimal actions. That assumes that the model has all, and perfect information, and does not seem to be an acceptable approach in the military and healthcare domains we are familiar with [Wiener:93]. When the assessment involves multiple attributes that are mutually non-commensurate human decision making will be important to strike a balance.

Incorporation of risk balancing. Balancing benefits versus risk when selecting alternatives is another task that seems to be hard to automate. There are examples in financial investments, as in hedge funds [Zask:00], and in healthcare, both using the beta function [DavidianC:87].

5 Conclusion

We have presented requirements for effective support of decision making by integrating predictive capabilities, as provided by spread sheets and other simulation tools, into information systems. An interface language, SimQL, combined with wrappers technology, has provided an initial positive answer to one of the research questions: are these simulations similar enough that a common interface is feasible.

More experiments are needed to further demonstrate the feasibility of the vision. Establishing scalable infrastructure technology and good interfaces for the decision maker will require substantial efforts over time. Better tools will improve decision making in situation where the decsion make is overwhelmed with past information and simply choses an approach that has worked before or recent experience [HammondKR: 98].

Not all prediction will look into the future. Already, when historic records are a bit out-of-date, planners routinely make undocumented projections to extrapolate to the current situation and obtain an approximate current picture as sketched in Figure 5. Predicting values for the current time when the source databases that are not fully up-to-date, can be of great value to decision-makers.

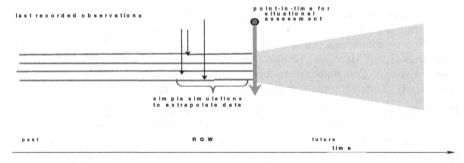

Fig. 5. Projection of integrated information to the current state

In discussing our vision the hardest problem appears not to be conveying the general concept, but the breaking down the barriers between communities which focus on building better simulations and those that want to build better databases. We are convinced that there integration, even if not perfect will be more significant for our customers than the achievements which can be created in isolation.

Acknowledgments. The experimental research was supported by DARPA DSO, Pradeep Khosla was the Program Manager; and awarded through NIST, Award 60NANB6D0038, managed by Ram Sriram. Continuing support is provided at Stanford Civil Engineering by the Product Engineering Program at NIST. The prototype of the SimQL compiler was written and tested by Rushan Jiang. The original SQL compiler adapted for SimQL was written by Mark McAuliffe, of the University of Wisconsin - Madison, and modified at Stanford by Dallan Quass and Jan Jannink. James Chiu, a Stanford CSD Master's student, provided and wrapped the gas station simulation.

References

[BenHaim:01] Yakov Ben-Haim: Information-Gap Decision Theory: Decisions Under Severe Uncertainty ; Academic Press, 2001.

[BettiniWJ:96] C. Bettini, X.S. Wang, and Sushil Jajodia: "Testing complex temporal relationships involving multiple Granularities and its application to Data Mining"; Proc. ACM SIGMOD/PODS 1996, ACM, pp.67-78.

[BhatnagarK:86] Bhatnagar and L.N. Kanal: "Handling Uncertain Information: A Review of Numeric and Non-numeric Methods"; in Kanal and Lemmer(eds.): Uncertainty in AI, North-Holland publishers, 1986.

[Charles:99] John Charles: "Middleware Moves to the Forefront"; IEEE Computer Magazine, Vol.32 no.5, May 1999, pages 17-19.

[ChajewskaEa:98] U. Chajewska, L. Getoor, J. Norman, & Y. Shahar. Utility Elicitation as a Classification Problem. Uncertainty in Artificial Intelligence, Madison, Wisconsin, 79-88. Morgan Kaufmann, 1998.

[Connolly:97] Dan Connolly (ed.): XML: Principles, Tools, and Techniques; O'Reilly, 1997.

[DasSTM:94] A.K. Das, Y. Shahar, S.W. Tu, and M.A. Musen: "A temporal-abstraction mediator for protocol-based decision support"; Proceedings of the Eighteenth Annual Symposium on Computer Applications in Medicine, Washington DC, Hanley & Belfus 1994, pp.320-324.

[DavidianC:87] Marie Davidian and Raymond Carroll: Variance Function Estimation; Jo. American Statistical Ass. vol 82, 1987 pp.1079-1092

[DeyS:96] Debabrata Dey and Sumit Sarkar: "A probabilistic relational model and algebra"; ACM Transactions on Database Systems (TODS), Vol.21 No.3, Sep. 1996, pp: 339 - 369.

[DeZegherGeetsEa:88] IsabelleDeZegher-Geets, Andrew G. Freeman, Michael G. Walker, Robert L. Blum, and Gio Wiederhold: "Summarization and Display of On-line Medical Records"; M.D. Computing, Vol.5 No.3, March 1988, pp.38-46.

[DomshlakB:02] Carmel Domshlak and Ronen I. Brafman: "Structure and Complexity of Planning with Unary Operators"; Proceedings of the Sixth International Conference on Artificial Intelligence Planning & Scheduling (AIPS-02); 2002.

[FishwickH:98] Paul Fishwick and David Hill, eds: 1998 International Conference on Web-Based Modeling & Simulation; Society for Computer Simulation, Jan 1998, http://www.cis.ufl.edu/~fishwick/webconf.html.

[GarciaMolinaBP:92] Hector Garcia-Molina, D. Barbara, and D. Porter: "The Management of Probabilistic Data"; IEEE Transactions on Knowledge and Data Engineering, Vol. 4, No. 5, October 1992, pp. 487-502.

[GaudiotB:91] J.-L. Gaudiot and L. Bic (eds.): Advanced Topics in Data-Flow Computing; Prentice-Hall, 1991.

[GershwinH:34] Ira Gershwin and DuBose Heyward: Porgy and Bess; 1934, Act II, scene 2.

[GustafsonEa:01] David Gustafson, P. Johnson, T. Molfenter, T. Patton, B. Shaw, and B. Owens: "Development and Test of a Model to Predict Adherence to a Medical Regimen"; Journal of Pharmacy Technology, in press 2001.

[HammerEa:97] J. Hammer, M. Breunig, H. Garcia-Molina, S. Nestorov, V. Vassalos, R. Yerneni: "Template-Based Wrappers in the TSIMMIS System"; ACM Sigmod 26, May, 1997.

[HammondKR: 98] John S. Hammond, Ralph L. Keeney, and Howard Raiffa: "The Hidden Traps In Decision Making"; Harvard Business Review, September-October 1998, pp. 47-58.

[Jiang:96] Rushan Jiang: Report on the SimQL project; submitted to Prof. Wiederhold, CSD Stanford, August 1996.

[LindenG:92] Ted Linden and D. Gaw 1992: "JIGSAW: Preference-directed, Co-operative Scheduling," AAAI Spring Symposium: Practical Approaches to Scheduling and Planning, March 1992. <x>

[McCall:96] Gene McCall (editor): New World Vistas, Air and Space Power for the 21st Century; Air Force Scientific Advisory Board, April 1996, Information Technology volume, pp. 9. <x>

[MooreWW:01] Jeffrey H. Moore (Editor), Lawrence R. Weatherford, Larry R. Weatherford: Decision Modeling with Microsoft(R) Excel (6th Edition); Prentice Hall; ISBN: 013017789X; 6th edition, 2001.

[Miller:56] George Miller: "The Magical Number Seven Two"; Psych.Review, Vol.68, 1956, pp.81-97.

[MotwaniEa:02] Rajeev Motwani, Jennifer Widom, Arvind Arasu, Brian Babcock, Shivnath Babu, Mayur Datar. Gurmeet Manku, Chris Olston ; Justin Rosenstein, and Rohit Varma: Query Processing, Approximation, and Resource Management in a Data Stream Management System; Stanford CSD Report, August 2002, http://dbpubs.stanford.edu/pub/2002-41

[Pearl:88] Judea Pearl: Probabilistic Reasoning in Intelligent Systems; Morgan-Kaufman, 1988.

[PerkinsP:00] Anthony B. Perkins and Michael C. Perkins: The Internet Bubble: Inside the Overvalued World of High-Tech Stocks -- And What You Need to Know to Avoid the Coming Shakeout; HarperBusiness, 2000. <x>

[SA:97] Scientific American Editors: The Internet: Fulfilling the Promise; Scientific American March 1997.

[SalatianH:99] Apkar Salatian and Jim Hunter: "Deriving Trends in Historical and Real-Time Continuously Sampled Medical Data"; Journal of Intelligent Information Systems, Vol. 13 No. 1/2, pp.5-8, 1999.

[Tate:96] Austin Tate (ed.): Advanced Planning Technology, AAAI Press, May 1996.

[VanDieren:95] Wouter Van Dieren, Editor: Taking Nature Into Account: A Report to the Club of Rome; Springer-Verlag, 1995.

[Wiederhold:99] Gio Wiederhold: "Information Systems that Really Support Decision-making; in Ras & Skowron: Foundations for Intelligent Systems, Springer LNAI 1609, pp. 56-66.

[WiederholdG:97] Gio Wiederhold and Michael Genesereth: "The Conceptual Basis for Mediation Services"; IEEE Expert, Intelligent Systems and their Applications, Vol.12 No.5, Sep-Oct.1997. <x>

[WiederholdJG:98] Gio Wiederhold, Rushan Jiang, and Hector Garcia-Molina: "An Interface for Projecting CoAs in Support of C2; Proc.1998 Command & Control Research & Technology Symposium, Naval Postgraduate School, June 1998, pp.549-558.

[Wiener:93] Lauren Ruth Wiener: Digital Woes: Why We should Not Depend on Software; Addison-Wesley Publishing Company. 1993.

[Winslett:88] Marianne Winslett: "Reasoning about Actions using a Possible Models Approach"; Proc 7th National AI Conference, AAAI'88, Morgan Kaufmann Publishers, San Mateo CA., 1988, pp. 89-93.

[Zask:00] Ezra Zask: "Hedge Funds, an Industry Overview"; The Journal of Alternative Investments, Winter 2000.

[ZhugeEa:95] Yue Zhuge, Hector Garcia-Molina, Joachim Hammer, and Jennifer Widom: View Maintenance in a Warehousing Environment; Proc. ACM SIGMOD, May 1995, pages 316-327.

A Design Methodology for Workflow System Development

Jaehyoun Kim[1] and C. Robert Carlson[2]

[1]Department of Computer Education
Sungkyunkwan University, Seoul, Korea
jhkim@comedu.skku.ac.kr
[2]Department of Computer Science
Illinois Institute of Technology, Wheaton, Illinois 60187, U.S.A
carlson@iit.edu

Abstract. In every business organization, procedures are established to improve the efficiency, consistency, and quality of work. In this paper, we propose a design methodology for workflow application. It begins with an initial analysis phase (i.e., use case analysis) to capture requirement specifications, and ends with a workflow schema to be executed by a workflow management system. It incorporates workflow technology to support business process modeling that captures business processes as workflow specifications. Also, it employs a multi-step design approach to workflow schema generation, resulting in workflow schema at different levels of abstraction.

1 Introduction

A workflow information system requires the information architecture to identify the flow of information throughout the business lifecycle of an enterprise that supports each business process. Having done this for each business process, the resulting database design is a network of shared data that supports all aspects of the business lifecycle of an enterprise. Thus, the business processes play a key role in the design approach to workflow information system.

Many workflow models have been proposed in the literature. They include the object-oriented workflow process model [8], Generalized Process Structure Grammars (GPSG) [7], workflow models in [2, 3, 6, 9, 13] and the conceptual workflow schema proposed by Meyer-Wegener et al [12]. Little effort has been made to develop design methodological approaches for workflow applications [1]. Such an approach should not only guide designers through the requirement specification and design steps so that the design process can be understood easily, but also make it possible to generate a workflow schema easily and the code to support the business process.

For the conceptual workflow model in Casati F. et al [3], a workflow schema has been defined as a coordinated set of work tasks (or activities) that are connected to carry out a common goal based on a predefined sequence of execution. It possible for each workflow schema to be instantiated in several instances of the workflow schema (i.e., cases). The schema differs from Meyer-Wegener et al [12] in that it defines a

S. Bhalla (Ed.): DNIS 2002, LNCS 2544, pp. 15–28, 2002.

directed graph and involves more technical information, such as exceptions that Meyer-Wegener et al [12] handles in later design. However, the process of building the workflow schema is not described.

The conceptual workflow schema proposed by Meyer-Wegener et al [12] uses an intermediated description and schema to define a workflow schema that is independent of a particular workflow management system. This approach is designed to cover functional, behavioral, informational, operational and organizational perspectives. It main contribution is providing a set of operations to adapt the hierarchy of tasks, and to add or remove the task types. However, it is limited to functional and behavioral perspectives so far.

The UML (Unified Modeling Language) has become a widely adopted approach to software development. It allows developers to visually describe an application. It is independent of the development process, and will be effective if it is applied to a good software engineering process [5].

In this paper, we describe a methodology for developing workflow systems based on use case analysis, interaction diagram generation, use case integration, object model generation and multi-level workflow schemas. Applying design units [10] to the workflow design process, we can improve maintainability, traceability, testability and modularization throughout the development process. Also, these design units provide multiple options to modularize workflow specification in terms of small pieces, i.e., work units, and facilitate the generation of different levels of workflow schema. Consequently, workflow schema specification can be specified at different levels of abstraction. That is, a higher level of abstraction can help management control a business process while lower levels of abstraction are required to capture exactly what is required in order to implement a workflow.

This paper is organized as follows. In section 2, we briefly describe a design methodology for workflow application. In section 3, we introduce an *Order Processing* application to illustrate the design methodology.

2 A Design Methodology for Workflow Applications

Figure 1 illustrates the steps of the proposed workflow design methodology. These steps include use case analysis, interaction diagram generation, object model generation, design unit generation, use case integration, and multi-level workflow schema generation. Based on the workflow schema created in this process, the designers are provided with a mechanism to automatically generate code [11]. Our discussion here will be limited to those steps required for object model and workflow schema generation as these are needed to support workflow queries.

When treating these steps as separate activities, designers can concentrate on different concerns one at a time and encapsulate design experience specific to that step. As a consequence, designers can produce modular and reusable designs, and obtain a framework for workflow schema design.

The methodology begins with a use case analysis step to capture user requirements. Based on the user specified scenarios produced in the use case analysis step, the designer creates workflow-based interaction diagram(s) for each use case.

Designers then can apply design unit analysis to the workflow-based interaction diagrams. The various design units [11] allow software engineers to develop well-structured and easily testable code. The details of this step will not be included in the discussion since its primary value has to do with code and test plan generation and neither database design nor query support. To integrate the identified use cases, once all workflow-based interaction diagrams have been created, the designers have to identify precondition and postcondition states for each use case. The information will form the input to the use case integration algorithm. At the same time, the designers can apply two other algorithms to workflow-based interaction diagrams. Using these algorithms, the workflow-based interaction diagrams can be automatically converted to multi-level workflow schemas. In addition, an object model can be generated based on the service objects in the workflow-based interaction diagrams by using the layered architecture pattern [3]. The final step involves the generation of code which is discussed in Kim's thesis [11].

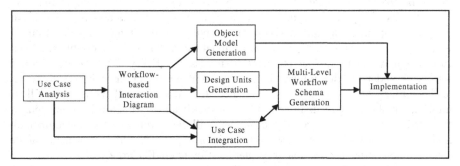

Fig. 1. A Design Methodology for Workflow Applications

3 Application of the Workflow Design Methodology

Upon completion, a multi-level workflow schema can be produced. The workflow schema provides a framework for the workflow application. In this section, we will illustrate the application of the methodology to workflow-oriented design. An "Order Processing" workflow example will be used to create top and middle levels of workflow schema.

3.1 Use Case Analysis

Use cases define basic business processes the system needs to handle. They represent the functions of a system, which the system must support from the user's point of view.

An "Order Processing" workflow example, involving five actors (i.e., customer, secretary, order handler, accounting clerk and workhouse worker) and seven use cases (i.e., "place order", "process order", "confirm", "notify out-of-stock", "invoice & payment", "assemble" and "delivery"). The following descriptions apply to the scenarios identified in Figure 2.:

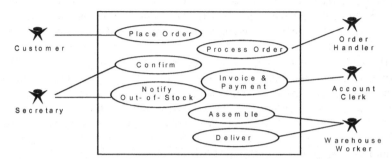

Fig. 2. A Use Case Diagram for Order Processing Application

***Place an Order* Use Case**: A customer browses an electronic Catalog looking for items to buy. To place an order, the customer selects the order item(s) that he/she intends to purchase, and then the system will put the order item(s) in an "electronic shopping cart". In other words, a provisional customer order is established. The customer may update his/her purchases if necessary. Every time when a customer selects or updates order information, he/she will get an order summary to review his/her order. Once the order is completed, the customer will be asked to fill out information about credit, mailing, and delivery. If all information is completed and the credit card is approved, the customer will be given an acknowledgment of receiving this order as well as the customer's prov.order #. Otherwise, the customer has to complete the information or reenter a different credit card #.

***Process Order* Use Case**: An order handler retrieves a provisional customer order to process the order. Processing consists of checking whether the items requested are in stock. If an item is in stock according to the product inventory file, then a reservation hold is placed on that item. Also, a customer order file is established which contains available order item(s). If not, then an item-not-available-notice (i.e., an available list) will be generated which contains unavailable order item(s). When all items have been processed, the order handler will be given an order summary.

***Confirm* Use Case**: When a secretary selects a customer order file, the system generates a confirmation letter automatically for that customer. The confirmation letter is reusable. For different customers, the system just needs to change the customer name and ordered item information by retrieving related data from its database. Once the confirmation letter is generated and examined by the secretary, then it will be sent by e-mail.

***Notify Out-of-Stock* Use Case**: When a secretary selects an unavailable list, the system generates an out-of-stock letter automatically for that customer. The out-of-stock letter is reusable. For different customers, the system just needs to change the customer name and their unavailable order items information by retrieving related data from the database. Once the out-of-stock letter is generated and examined by the secretary, then IT will be sent by e-mail.

***Invoice & Payment* Use Case**: When an accounting clerk selects a customer order file, the system generates an invoice automatically for that customer. After the accounting clerk examines the invoice, he/she will request the payment. The system changes the amount based on the customer's order and then displays the payment amount to the accounting clerk. Also, the system will print out the invoice and payment information.

Assemble **Use Case**: When a warehouse worker selects a customer order file, he/she will be provided the order list of items that need to be packed. Once the products have been packed, the warehouse worker needs to record this information, which leads the system to update the inventory. Finally, the warehouse worker will be notified that the inventory has been updated.

Deliver **Use Case**: When a warehouse worker has finished packing, then the system will schedule a delivery date for that order. Once a warehouse worker submits the delivery information, such as the track #, then the system will record the delivery information, which terminates the whole "order processing" workflow.

3.2   Construct Workflow-Based Interaction Diagrams

Based on the scenarios provided in section 3.1, the designer can construct the workflow-based interaction diagrams shown in Figures 3 and 4. Figures 3 and 4 represent workflow-based interaction diagrams for *Place an Order* and *Process Order* use cases. Space dose not permit a discussion on interaction diagrams for *Confirm, Invoice & Payment, Notify Out-of-Stock, Assemble,* and *Deliver* use cases. The brace { in the left side of Figures 3 and 4 represents the range of a dialogue unit.

3.3   Applying Design Units to Workflow-Based Interaction Diagrams

As noted earlier, the primary value of this step has to do with code and test plan generation and neither query support nor database design.

3.4   Use Case Integration

It is necessary to integrate the use cases that we have identified during the use case analysis phases in order to capture the global system behavior of the specific business process. The resulting integration is a use case dependency diagram, which can be regarded as the top level of THE workflow schema showing the dependencies amongst the use cases. To integrate these use cases, after all the workflow-based interaction diagrams have been created, the designers have to identify pre- and post-condition state(s) for each use case. A use case integration table will be provided for the designers to analyze and collect the information on each use case name and its pre- and post-condition state(s). Table 1 shows the use case integration for the use cases in the "Order Processing" example. The default precondition state for the initial use case has been defined as blank. For the rest of the use cases, each of them may have one or more precondition and postcondition states. For example, the use case "Notify Out-of-Stock" has the precondition state name "Order Rejected". This information will form the input for the use case integration algorithm in order to generate high-level workflow process schema automatically. This high-level workflow process schema makes it easier for designers to track workflow or larger-scale business scenarios that cross many use cases shown in Figure 5.

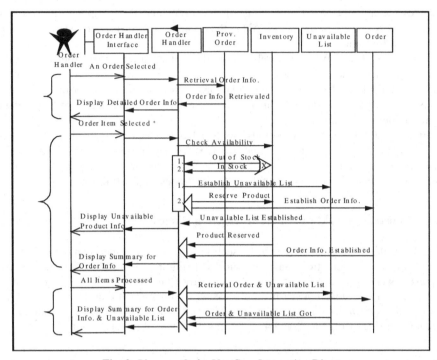

Fig. 3. *Place an Order* Use Case Interaction Diagram

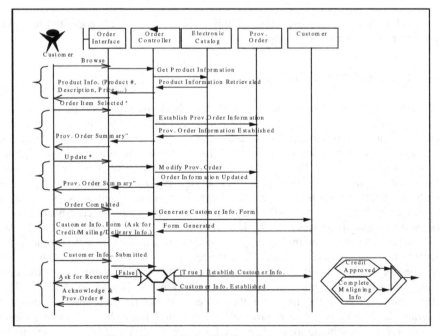

Fig. 4. *Process Order* Use Case Interaction Diagram

Table 1. Use Case Integration Table

Precondition State	Use Case Name	Postcondition State
	Place Order	Prov. Order Taken
Prov. Order Taken	Process Order	Order Rejected or Order Taken
Order Rejected	Notify Out- of Stock	Notification Sent
Order Taken	Confirm	Confirmation Letter Sent
Confirmation Letter Sent	Invoice & Payment	Payment Paid
Payment Paid	Assemble	Packed
Packed	Deliver	Delivered

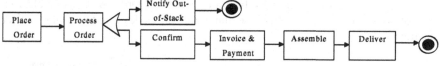

Fig. 5. A Use Case Integration Diagram based on Table 1.

3.5   Multi-level Workflow Schema

Since a workflow process model can become quite complex, we propose a multi-level approach consisting of the following four levels:

Workflow level: Each workflow corresponds to a particular business lifecycle. It integrates the workunits defined by the business life cycle.

Use case level: A use case describes a workunit initiated by an actor. Each use case schema is made up of a number of dialogue units.

Dialogue level: Each dialogue is a sequence of method executions bounded by input from an actor and the response to that actor. It is composed of a collection of state units. Each external event initiated by an actor initiates a dialogue.

State unit level: A state unit consists of an event/function (or event/decision) pair. An event can be either an external event initiated by an actor or an internally triggered event. A function at this level is a simple function, which describes a single step in the workflow process model. It also can be regarded as an action and executed by a single agent that can be a person, an object, or a machine.

This four-level workflow structure provides a framework to hierarchically decompose workflow application processes. In addition, this four-level workflow structure leads to multi-level workflow schemas that provide abstraction of workflow at different levels. Higher levels of abstraction can help management follow or control a business process. Lower levels of abstraction are required to capture exactly what is required in order to implement a workflow. Three algorithms [4] have been proposed so that the designers can automatically generate a multi-level workflow schema without a great deal of manual processing. The first algorithm helps designers integrate use cases and establish the top level of workflow schema. The second algorithm helps designers generate more detailed workflow schema that is the decomposition of each use case at the top level. The third algorithm focuses on the details of the implementation of a workflow.

Figure 6 shows an example of a multi-level workflow schema based on the workflow-based interaction diagrams in section 3.2. The top level represents the *Order Processing* workflow. It is a use case dependency diagram, which shows the integration of seven use cases and their dependencies. The middle level illustrated the content of each use case at the top level in term of events and complex functions (or decisions). For example, the "Process Order" use case has three dialogues. The first dialogue unit is composed of event "An Order Selected" and the complex function "Retrieval Order Information". The second dialogue unit contains the event "Order Item Selected" and the complex function "Check Availability". This event may occur more than once since it is marked with "+". The third dialogue unit has the event "All Items Processed" and the complex function "Retrieval Order & Unavailable List". The bottom layer details each dialogue unit at the middle layer in terms of events and functions.

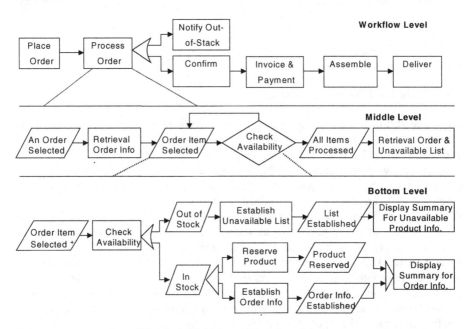

Fig. 6. A Multi-Level Workflow Schema

3.6   Object Model Generation

Based on the object classes we have identified in the workflow-based interaction diagrams, we can generate an object model for the workflow application. We will use the layered architecture pattern [3] where the architecture is divided into three layers: interface layer, control layer, and service layer. The interface layer will contain all the interface objects, each of which will call a control object. The control layer has all the control objects for the system. A control object will call one or more service objects when it receives an event from the interface object or service object(s). Therefore, this layer provides a behavioral aspect that can be detailed in workflow-based interaction diagrams through events and functions. The service layer contains service objects that provide various services, such as information perspective, and shoe how service objects are shared across multiple use cases. Figure 7 illustrates an object model based on the objects in the workflow-based interaction diagrams that were generated in section 3.2.

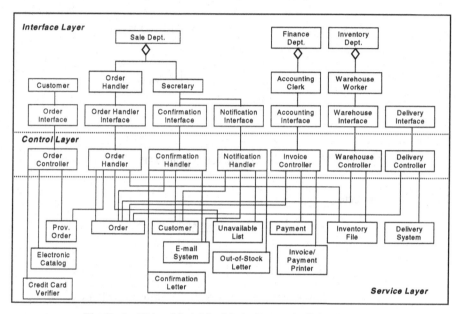

Fig. 7. An Object Model for "Order Processing" Application

3.7   Relationship with Data Views and (Workflow) Query

The design methodology of workflow applications that we just illustrate up to this points leads to a multi-level workflow schema. This schema can provide several advantages. During the development, it allows different audiences to communicate with each other. These audiences include customers/managers, designer and developers. After the completion, it supports different users' perspectives, such as workers, managers, and executives. Meanwhile, the resulting workflow schema may support database views and process queries, if the workflow has been integrated with the database. In this section, we will illustrate the relationship between the produced workflow schema and data views/ workflow queries. The views associated with each (use case) state, and some possible process queries will be introduced here.

Data Views:
Figure 8 shows the top level of the multi-level workflow schema. Each sub-workflow process (i.e., use case unit) is followed by one or more states, each of which is

associated with a data view. Each state will be represented by a dot. There are eight states in Figure 8. We will illustrate the data view with each state by using Figure 9 to Figure 16.

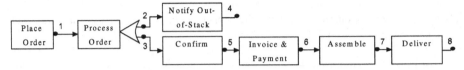

Fig. 8. An Example of Top Level of Multi-Level Workflow

State 1: Prov. Order Taken

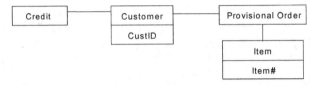

Fig. 9. A Data View Associated with State 1 Named "Prov. Order Taken"

State 2: Order Rejected

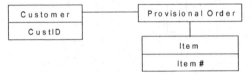

Fig. 10. A Data View Associated with State 2 Named "Order Rejected"

State 3: Order Taken

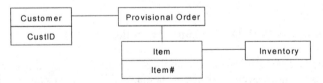

Fig. 11. A Data View Associated with State 3 Named "Order Taken"

State 4: Notification Sent

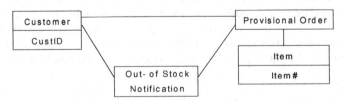

Fig. 12. A Data View Associated with State 4 Named "Notification Sent"

State 5: Confirmation Letter Sent

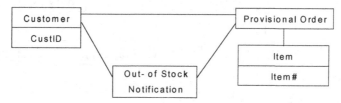

Fig. 13. A Data View Associated with State 5 Named "Confirmation Letter sent"

State 6: Payment Paid

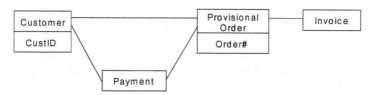

Fig. 14. A Data View Associated with State 6 Named "Payment Paid"

State 7: Packed

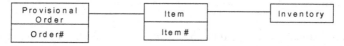

Fig. 15. A Data View Associated with State 7 Named "Packed"

State 8: Delivered

Fig. 16. A Data View Associated with State 8 Named "Delivered"

Workflow Queries:

Collectively, the data views described above form the composite database design shown in Figure 17. The numbers indicate the order in which new data objects are created. They also define the "information trail" produced by the Ordering Process Workflow schema.

The following process query uses this information trail to resolve the query.

(1) Query: Retrieve the "currently available" information produced by "Ordering Process" workflow process about the customer whose customer ID is "1000"
SELECT *
FROM Ordering Process (Customer)
WHERE Customer.CustId = 1000

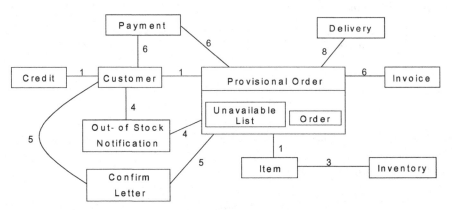

Fig. 17. Composite Database Design with Information Trail

The workflow schema defined by the Ordering Process is used by the query processor to resolve this query. The SCOPE of "retrieved information" will vary with time. For example, at the point in time when the customer submits credit/mailing/delivery information and gets order # back from the system (i.e., the place order process is finished), this query will produce information from the following data schema:

Once the provisional order issued by the customer ID 1000 has been processed by the order handler, the unavailable item list, ordered items, or both will be generated. The following data schema will be available to solve this same query:

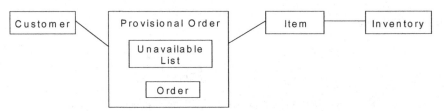

When the secretary receives the ordered items or unavailable item list, the confirmation letter or out-of-stock notification will be generated, respectively. The following data schema will be available to solve this same query:

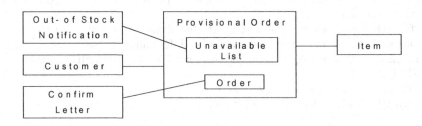

When the account clerk receives the order information, an invoice will be generated and the customer will be charged by the total amount of the invoice. The following data schema will be available to solve this same query:

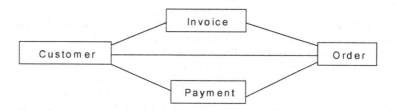

(2) Query: Retrieve the information produced by the "Ordering Process" workflow process for all orders for which payment has been made.
SELECT *
FROM Ordering Process (*)
WHERE EXIST PAYMENT

This query will produce information based on the following data schema:

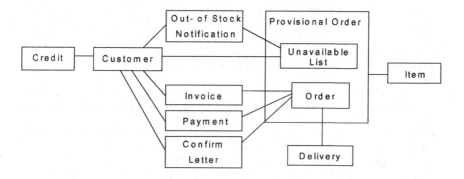

4 Conclusion

The main contribution of the paper is to develop a conceptual framework for workflow application design that will able the workflow designer to model complex business processes in a simple and straightforward manner. It incorporates workflow technology to support business process modeling that captures business processes as workflow specification. Guidelines are provided for workflow designers to follow systematically. We intend to limit our approach to production workflow since production workflow involves repetitive and predictable business processes.

References

1. Baresi, L., Casati, F., Casati, S., Fugini, M. G., Mirbel, I., and Pernici, B., "WIDE Workflow Development Methodology",
    (http://dis.sema.es/projects/WIDE/Documents/) Accessed Jan. 6, 2000.
2. Carlson, C. R., and Kim, J., *Object-Oriented Modeling and Design*, Lecture Notes, Computer Science Department, Illinois Institute of Technology, Chicago, IL. 2001.
3. Casati, F., Grepen, P., Pernici, B., Pozzi, G., and Sanchez, G., "WIDE: Workflow Model and Architecture", *CTIT Technical Report 96-19*, University of Twente, 1996.
4. Chen, P., *A Use Case Driven Object-Oriented Design Methodology for the Design of Multi-Level Workflow Schemas*, Ph.D. Thesis, Illinois Institute of Technology, 2000.
5. Colbert, E., "Applying Methods, Process, and Tools to Your Software Development Lifecycle," *Seminar Presentation Sponsored by the Aonix Corp.*, June 1999.
6. Eder, J., Groiss, H., and Nekvasil, G., "A Workflow System based on Active Databases", Chroust G., and Benczur A. (eds.): *Proc. Connectivity-94: Workflow Management – Challenges, Paradigms and Products*, CON 1994, Oldenbourg, Linz, Austria, pp. 249-265, 1994.
7. Glance, N. S., Pagani, D. S., and Pareschi, R., "Generalized Process Structure Grammars (GPSG) for Flexible Representations of Work," in *Proc of CSCW'96*, Boston, pp. 180-189, November 1996.
8. Inamoto, A., "Object-Oriented Model Driven Workflow Process Analysis", *Japan/USA Symposium on Flexible Automation*, Vol. 2, pp. 1317-1324, 1996.
9. Kappel, G., Rausch-Schott, S., and Retschitzegger, W., "Coordination in Workflow Management Systems – A Rule-Based Approach", 1997, in: Conen, W. and Neumann, G. (eds.): *Coordination Technology for Collaborative Applications – Organizations, Processes, and Agents*, Springer, New York, NY. Pp. 99-120, 1998.
    (http://www.ifs.uni-linz.ac.at/ifs/research/publications/papers97.html) Accessed August 20, 1999.
10. Kim, J., and Carlson, C. R., "Design Units - *A Layered Approach for Design Driven Software Development*," Information and Software Technology, Elsevier Science, Vol. 43, Issue 9, pp. 539-549, August 2001.
11. Kim J, *A Layered Approach to Automatic Code Generation and Testing Based on Design Units*, Ph.D. Thesis, Illinois Institute of Technology, 2000.
12. Meyer-Wegener K., and Bohm, M., "Conceptual Workflow Schemas", *Proceedings: Cooperative Information Systems*, Edinburgh, Scotland, pp. 234-242, September 1999.
13. Ngu, A. H., Duong, T., and Srinivasan, U., "Modeling Workflow Using Tasks and Transactions", *in Proceedings of Seventh International Workshop on Database and Expert Systems Applications*, Zurich, Switzerland, pp. 451-456, September 1996.

Adding Valid Time to XPath

Shuohao Zhang and Curtis E. Dyreson

School of Electrical Engineering and Computer Science
Washington State University
Pullman, WA, United State of America
(szhang2, cdyreson)@eecs.wsu.edu

Abstract. In this paper we extend the XPath data model and query language to include valid time. XPath is a language for specifying locations within an XML document. We extend XPath's data model by adding to each node a list of disjoint intervals or instants that represents the valid time. The valid time for a node is constrained to be a subset of the valid time for a node's parent. We extend the XPath query language with an *axis* to access nodes in a valid-time *view* of the valid time for a node. The view is a calendar-specific formatting of the valid time in XML. By rendering the time in XML, we can reuse non-temporal XPath to extract the desired information within a valid-time axis. The extension is fully backwards-compatible with XPath.

1 Background

The World Wide Web ("web") is the largest and most frequented network of information resources. The majority of the documents on the web conform to the HyperText Markup Language (HTML) [1] but the Extensible Markup Language (XML) [2] is expected to replace HTML as the next-generation markup language for web documents and data. There are several proposed query languages for XML such as Quilt [3], XQL [4], XML-QL [5], and XQuery [6], which is a W3C recom-mendation. XPath [7] is a subset of XQuery (and of several other recommendations by the W3C, e.g., XSLT [8]). XPath is a language to locate information in an XML document. Every XQuery query contains XPath expressions [9]. XPath operates on a tree-like data model, which is a logical-level data model of an XML document. XPath is a compact, expression-based grammar with a non-XML syntax.

XPath currently lacks temporal semantics. Time is pervasive in the real world. All events happen at some point of time, all objects exist for some interval of time, and most relationships among events and objects evolve over time. Interest in supporting and incorporating time in database systems led to the research area of temporal databases, which has been a quite active area for about twenty-five years [10]. Temporal database research has identified (at least) three dimensions of time: valid time, transaction time and user-defined time. *Valid time* concerns the time in the modeled reality. It is the time when an event occurs or an object is true in the real world. *Transaction time* concerns the system time instead of the real world time. It is the database time

S. Bhalla (Ed.): DNIS 2002, LNCS 2544, pp. 29–42, 2002.

when an object is stored in the database. These two dimensions are orthogonal. *User-defined* time is the time in the world that the user specifies. It is an un-interpreted attribute domain of time.

In this paper we extend the XPath data model to include valid time. There have been few papers on this research topic. Grandi and Mandreoli present techniques for adding explicit valid-time timestamps to XML documents [11]. Amagasa et al. propose a temporal extension of the XPath data model [12]. In their data model, valid-time timestamps are added to each edge. In contrast, we extend nodes with valid time. Dyreson was the first to establish a transaction-time XPath data model with special transaction-time axes, node tests and constructors [13].

There are two primary contributions of this paper. First, we propose that a valid time be presented in a *valid-time view*. The view is a calendar- and query-specific rendering of the valid time as a virtual XML document. We observe there are many different calendars each with their own representation of time, and even in a single calendar, the representation of time needs to be flexible. Second, we extend XPath with a *valid-time* axis. The role of the axis is both to provide users with a query language mechanism for accessing valid times and to keep wild-card queries from exploring the valid time. In our model, valid times are isolated in their own dataspace.

As an example, consider the XML document "bib.xml" shown in Fig. 1. The document contains data about publishers and the books they publish. The valid times of the <book> elements are shown in Table 1. The valid times indicate when the book facts represented in the document are true. A user wants to select only the book elements that are valid before the year 2000, where 2000 is a year in the Gregorian calendar. In XPath, the book elements can be located with the following expression.

```
/descendant-or-self::book
```

But how are the valid times reached? In our model the valid-time axis serves to locate the valid time(s) formatted as a virtual XML document as sketched in Fig. 3 (note that XPath's abbreviated syntax is used to find the books).

```
//book/valid::time
```

The valid axis contains a list of every element in the valid-time view. The time node test selects only the <time> elements. The times have been located but how can we view the year? We know that the Gregorian calendar view has a <year> element that contains the year data as shown in Fig. 4, so we can locate that information as follows.

```
//book/valid::time/descendant-or-self::year
```

We could also shorten the expression to directly locate the year information.

```
//book/valid::year
```

Finally, we are interested in determining if the some year comes before 2000. The predicate can be expressed as follows.

```
//book/valid::year[text() &gt; 1999]
```

One important point to observe is that the query

```
//*/time
```

is very different from the following query.

```
//*/valid::time
```

The former locates all <time> child elements in the document whereas the latter locates only times in the valid-time views. The valid-time axis ensures that all nodes in the valid-time view are isolated from wild-card queries. Furthermore, (non-temporal) XPath can be reused to search within the valid-time view for calendar-specific information.

The remainder of this paper is organized as follows. In the next section a data model for valid-time XPath is developed. The data model extends the information set for a node with a list of times. XPath is then extended with the valid-time axis to query the times and valid-time views to support multiple calendars. The paper concludes with a brief discussion of future work.

2 Data Models

In this section, we briefly outline a data model for valid time. We first present some time-related concepts that serve as background for this research. We then discuss a data model for XML (XPath) and finally extend that data model to support valid time by adding valid time to the nodes in the data model. In the next section we extend XPath with the ability to query the valid-time information.

Time Background

A simple image of time is a directed line. The time-line could be isomorphic to the rational numbers, the real numbers, or the integers, resulting in a *continuous*, *dense* or *discrete* model, respectively [14]. Each point on the line represents a time *instant* and the segment between two points represents a time *interval*. A time *constant* is a pair of times, (b_i, e_i). In a time instant constant, $b_i = e_i$, whereas in an interval constant $b_i \leq e_i$. We assume, without loss of generality, that time is bounded in our model. The starting and ending instants are called *beginning* and *forever* [15].

The XPath Data Model

A well-formed XML document is a collection of nested *elements*. An element begins with a start tag and ends with a paired end tag. Between the tags, an element might contain *content* that is either a text string or other elements. The XPath data model is commonly assumed to be an ordered tree. The tree represents the nesting of elements within the document, with elements corresponding to nodes, and element content comprising the children for each node. Unlike a tree, the children for a node are *ordered* based on their physical position within the document. The XPath recommendation [7] does not provide a formal model.

Below we give one possible data model that omits details extraneous to the aims of this paper.

Definition [XPath data model] . The *XPath data model, D*, for a well-formed XML, *X*, is a four-tuple $D(X) = (r, V, E, I)$ where,

- *V* is a set of nodes of the form (i, v) where *v* is the node identifier and *i* is an ordinal number such that for all $(i, v), (j, w) \in V$, *v* starts before *w* in the text of *X* if and only if $i < j$.

- *E* is a set of edges of the form (v, w) where $v, w \in V$. Edge (v, w) means that *v* is a parent of *w*. In terms of *X*, it represents that *w* is in the immediate content of *v*. There is an implied ordering among the edges; edge (v, y) is before edge (v, z) if $y < z$ in the node ordering.

- The graph (V, E) forms a tree.

- *I* is the information set function which maps a node identifier to an *information set*. An information set is a collection of properties that are generated during parsing of the document. For example, an element node has the following properties: *Value* (the element's name), *Type* (element), and *Attributes* (a set of name-value pairs, in XPath, attributes are unordered).

- $r \in V$ is a special node called the root. Note that *r* is the data model root rather than the document root. The document node is the first element node of the document. A document may also contain processing instruction nodes or comment nodes that precede the document root.

Fig. 2 depicts a fragment of the data model for the XML document "bib.xml" shown in Fig. 1. For brevity, not all the information is included in this figure. Each node is represented as an oval and the corresponding ordinal number is inside it. Each edge is represented as a straight line and the first three levels of edges are shown beside the corresponding lines. Note that the ordinal number of a node is unique in a document while that of an edge is not. This is because the node ordinal numbers reflect the order of all the nodes in the whole document, while the edge ordinal numbers only differentiate edges that emanate from the same node.

The information in the data model of "bib.xml" is sketched below (part of which is not displayed in Fig. 2).

$V = ((0,\&0),(1,\&1),...,(28,\&28))$

$E = ((\&0,\&1),(\&1,\&2),(\&1,\&12),...,(\&27,\&28))$

$I = ((\&0, (Value=root, Type =root, Attributes="")),$

  $(\&1, (Value=db, Type =element, Attributes="")),$

  $(\&2, (Value=publisher, Type =element, Attributes="")),$

  $(\&3, (Value=name, Type =element, Attributes="")),$

  $(\&4, (Value="ABC", Type =text, Attributes="")),$

  $...$

  $(\&4, (Value="59.99", Type =text, Attributes="")))$

$r = (0,\&0)$

Valid-Time XPath

We have established the data model for XPath. But this data model contains no support for time. To define the data model we first need a uniform representation scheme. Usually, a node is valid at a point of time or an interval of time. But more generally, a node could be valid at several points and (or) intervals of time, e.g., a *temporal element* [15]. A combination of valid-time constants should be allowed. We therefore define the valid time of a node to be a list of time constants.

```
<db>
   <publisher>
      <name>ABC</name>
      <book>
         <isbn>1234</isbn>
         <title>book1</title>
         <price>19.99</price>
      </book>
   </publisher>
   <publisher>
      <name>XYZ</name>
      <book>
         <isbn>2345</isbn>
         <title>book2</title>
         <price>29.99</price>
      </book>
      <book>
         <isbn>5678</isbn>
         <title>book5</title>
         <price>59.99</price>
      </book>
   </publisher>
</db>
```

Fig. 1. The document "bib.xml"

Definition [node valid-time representation]. The *valid time* of a node in an XML document is represented as a list of time constants, $[t_1, t_2,...,t_n]$, where each t_i ($i = 1,...,n$) represents a time constant when the node is valid.

- Each time constant $t = (b_i, e_i)$ is either a time interval or a time point.
- All and only the time constants when the node is valid are included in this list.
- Any two time constants do not overlap, no matter if they are time intervals or time points, i.e., $(b_i, e_i) \cap (b_j, e_j) = \varnothing$, $\forall i \neq j$, $1 \leq i, j \leq n$.
- These time constants are ordered by the valid time contained in each of them, i.e., $b_{i+1} \leq e_i$, ($i = 1,...,n-1$).

It is required that the time constants in any valid-time list be disjoint. Otherwise, the constraint cannot be satisfied that these time constants are ordered. For example, time intervals (1,3) and (2,4) cannot be ordered; neither can time interval (1,3) and time point (2,2). Order is important in an XML document.

We are now in a position to define a valid-time XPath data model.

Definition [valid-time XPath data model]. The *valid-time XPath data model*, D_{VT}, for a well-formed XML document, X, is a four-tuple $D_{VT}(X) = (r, V, E, I)$.

- V is a set of nodes of the form (i, v, t) where v is the node identifier, i is an ordinal number and t is a valid time such that the following two conditions hold.
  1   For all (i, v, t), $(j, w, s) \in V$, v starts before w in the text of X if and only if $i < j$.
  2   For all $(i, v, t) \in V$ and its children (i_1, v_1, t_1), (i_2, v_2, t_2),…, $(i_n, v_n, t_n) \in V$, $t_1 \cup t_2 \cup … \cup t_n \subseteq t$.
- E, I, and r are the same as the non-temporal XPath data model.

Every node in the valid time data model is associated with the valid time that represents when the node is valid. A node's valid time constrains the valid time of other nodes in the model. No node can exist at a valid time when its parent node is not valid. The following things can be further inferred from the data model definition,

- The valid time of any node is a superset of the union of the valid times of all its children.
- The valid time of any node is the superset of the union of the valid times of all its descendants.
- The valid time of the root node is the superset of the union of the valid times of all the nodes in the document.

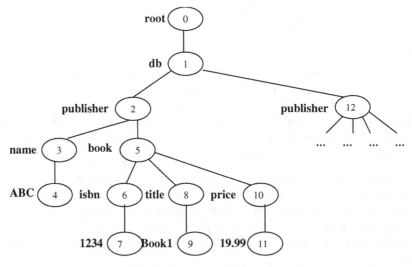

Fig. 2. The data model for "bib.xml"

In the valid-time XPath data model, only nodes have valid time information. The edge set E is the same as it is in the non-temporal data model. It does not mean that edges are not associated with valid time information, rather the valid time information is implied since only nodes can have information in an XML data model. The valid time of an edge is in fact determined by the valid time of the nodes at the edge's two ends. An edge can only exist at the time when both nodes are valid. For an edge $(n, v, w) \in E$ that emanates from the parent node (i, v, t_i) to the child node (j, w, t_j), its valid time $t = t_i \cap t_j$. Since $t_j \subseteq t_i$ (as mentioned above in the data model definition), the valid time of an edge is always the same as the child node: $t = t_j$.

We again use the XML document "bib.xml" shown in Fig. 1 as an example. The only difference here is the node set V and therefore only some nodes are shown (other components are identical to those described previously). Table 1 shows the time information for the "book" nodes in "bib.xml". The node set, V, containing the three "book" nodes is given below.

$V = ((0, \&0, t_0),\dots,(5,\&3, t_5),\dots,(15,\&15, t_{15}),\dots,(25,\&25, t_{22}),\dots)$

$t_5 = [(\text{"Jan 31,1999"}, now)]$

$t_{15} = [(\text{"Jan 31,2000"}, \text{"Dec 31, 2000"}), (\text{"Jan 1, 2001"}, now)]$

$t_{22} = [(\text{"Jan 31,2002"}, now)]$

The important thing to note is that the valid time information must satisfy the constraint in the data model definition. For example, the valid time of the root node, t_0, should be a superset of the union of the valid times of all the nodes in "bib.xml".

Table 1. Valid-time information for "book" elements in "bib.xml"

Book (ISBN)	Valid time
1234	[("Jan 31,1999", now)]
2345	[("Jan 31,2000", "Dec 31, 2000"), ("Jan 1, 2001", now)]
5678	[("Jan 31,2002", now)]

3 Querying Valid Time

In this section we present extensions to XPath to query the valid time information. The semantics is *unsequenced*. In a sequenced semantics a query would (logically) be evaluated in every valid-time snapshot simultaneously. Sequenced queries often do not have explicit valid-time constraints. We extend XPath with an axis to locate the valid time for a node. The valid time can be *viewed* as an XML document in any calendar that the user has defined.

Review of XPath

An XPath expression is a sequence of steps. Each step may have four portions, a *context*, an *axis*, a *node text* and some *predicates*. The *context* is the starting point of the evaluation. The *axis* specifies a certain relationship between the nodes selected by the axis step and the context node. For example, a child axis selects the nodes that have a "child" relationship with the context node, i.e., each selected node is a child of the context node. The *node test* specifies the node type of the nodes selected by the axis step. The symbol ": :" is used to syntactically separate a node test from an axis. A *predicate*, enclosed in square brackets, further filters a node sequence, retaining some nodes and discarding others. There can be zero or more predicates in one step. The nodes selected after the axis and the node test are finally evaluated against the predicates in the order that they appear in the step. A simplified syntax for a step in XPath is given below.

```
axis::node test[predicate₁]…[predicateₙ]
```

Below is an example of an expression that locates all the <book> elements that are children of a <publisher> element.

```
/descendant-or-self::publisher/child::book
```

The first step starts at the data model root, and locates all publishers by following the descendant-or-self axis to every node, and then applying a node test to keep only publishers. The second step finds the children relative to each publisher and keeps only those children that happen to be books.

Valid-Time Axis

The valid time axis of a node contains the valid-time information of the node as if it had originated from an XML document. The goal is to provide *flexible* representation for the valid time of a node in XML, and to provide the means by which users can customize their view of the valid time. In this section, the concepts of a *valid-time view* and *default valid-time view* are introduced, followed by the definition and syntax of the valid-time axis. We also address a specific problem of how different calendars can be used in views desired by different users.

An axis returns a list of nodes relative to the context node. The valid-time axis returns a list of nodes that forms the valid-time information of the context node. The valid time of a node can be viewed as an XML document.

Definition [node valid-time view]. A valid-time list can be viewed as an XML document. Let v be a node in the data model tree of an XML document. The valid-time view, V, is a mapping from the valid time for v to an XML data model, X, denoted $V(v) = X$.

Each node has a corresponding view containing its valid time information. A node valid-time view of a node x is shown in Fig. 3. The root node in the view serves as a handle that the user can use to access the valid time information. Each time in the valid-time list is denoted as a `<time>` element. The content of the `<time>` element is unique to the view (specific examples are given later in this chapter).

It is assumed that each node in an XML document has a corresponding valid-time view. These views are created and maintained by the system that stores the XML document. The user should be able to query the views to extract the desired valid-time information of the nodes.

```
<validTime>
  <time>
    view of t₁
  </time>
  <time>
    view of t₂
  </time>
    ...
  <time>
    view of tₙ
  </time>
</validTime>
```

Fig. 3. A node valid-time view document

Fig. 3 does not show what is exactly contained in each view. To be a valid XML document, each view must contain XML. The user, often the creator of the valid-time view documents, can define specific views. For example, Fig. 4, shows the valid-time view in the commonly used Gregorian calendar. "Year", "month" and "day" element nodes are nested under "begin" and "end" of each view; text nodes representing the "year", "month" and "day" information are further nested.

```
<time>
  <begin>
    <day>31</day>
    <month>1</month>
    <year>2000</year>
  </begin>
  <end>
    <day>31</day>
    <month>12</month>
    <year>2000</year>
  </end>
</time>
```

Fig. 4. A valid-time view in Gregorian calendar

Though the valid-time view can be user-defined, it is useful to have a default valid-time view provided by the system. The default valid-time view uses the system time, commonly seconds from the origin, to represent the "begin" and "end" time points. Therefore, a text node is nested under any "begin" or "end" node in the default valid-time view document. This default view has several advantages. Because the system time is commonly used in computer systems to represent time, a valid-time view can be more easily created by the computer system. It is also easy to compare since the system time is represented as a number. Time information can be easily extracted because there is no additional sub-tree under the "begin" and "end" nodes.

The default valid-time view for t_1 is shown in Fig. 5, where b_1 and e_1 are represented with the system time. The default valid-time view is used when there is no user-defined view.

```
<time>
  <begin>
    b₁
  </begin>
  <end>
    e₁
  </end>
</time>
```

Fig. 5. The valid-time view is used in a valid-time axis

Definition [valid-time axis]. The *valid-time axis* selects the list of nodes that forms a document-order traversal of the *valid-time view*.

Syntax [valid time axis]. `v/valid` specifies the valid-time axis of the node v.

From the definition, the nodes in the valid time axis is ordered in document order traversal of the valid-time view. Since the `<time>` elements in the valid-time view are ordered by the actual time they represent, these `<time>` elements selected by the valid time axis are also in this order.

Multi-calendar Support

The valid time is the real world time, which may be represented in various calendars used by people in different regions. It should not be restricted to any fixed type of representation. The most commonly used calendar in computer systems is Gregorian calendar. In this section, the study of Chinese calendar helps us understand the multi-calendar support in valid time axis.

The Chinese calendar is based on a combination of lunar and solar movements. The lunar cycle is about 29.5 days hence a lunar year consisting of 12 months is approximately 12 x 29.5 = 354 days. So a lunar year is about 11 days shorter than a solar year. In order to "catch up" with the solar calendar a leap month is inserted once every few years. To be precise, there are seven leap months, called an intercalary month, in each nineteen-year cycle. This is the same as adding an extra day on a leap year in Gregorian calendar. This is why, according to the solar calendar, the Chinese New Year falls on a different date each year.

Let us consider the example document "bib.xml" (shown in Fig. 1). The valid time in Table 1 is represented in Gregorian calendar. However, there are other calendars that are widely used by people in different regions. For instance, we can also represent the valid time in Chinese calendar as shown in Table 2. For the convenience of the readers to convert between the two calendars, Table 3 lists the recent Chinese new-year days (the first day of a year in Chinese calendar) in Gregorian calendar. A book element is valid from its publishing date to current time (denoted *now*). Therefore, if the speci-fied calendar is Gregorian calendar, then the valid time of the book element with ISBN "1234" is [("Jan 31,1999", "*now*")]. Similarly, its valid time in Chinese calendar is [("Month 12, Day 19, Year Wu-yin (Cycle 78)", "*now*")]. They are lists both consisting of one time constant. The corresponding node valid-time views are shown in Fig. 6 and Fig. 7.

Table 2. Publishing date in different calendars

Book (ISBN)	Publishing date	
	Gregorian	Chinese
1234	Jan 31,1999	Cycle 78, Year Wu-yin, Month 12, Day 15
2345	Jan 31,2000	Cycle 78, Year Ji-mao, Month 12, Day 25
5678	Jan 31,2002	Cycle 78, Year Xin-si, Month 12, Day 19

Table 3. Recent Chinese new-year days in Gregorian calendar

Year in Chinese calendar		Chinese new-year day in Gregorian calendar
Chinese name	Western name	
癸未	Gui-wei	February 1, 2003
壬午	Ren-wu	February 12, 2002
辛巳	Xin-si	January 24, 2001
庚辰	Geng-chen	February 5, 2000
己卯	Ji-mao	February 16, 1999

The special symbol "*now*" should be interpreted into a form that conforms to the corresponding beginning time. For example, if the beginning node has three child nodes, "year", "month" and "day", then the sub-tree starting from the end node should be like that shown in Fig. 7.

```
<validTime>
  <time>
    <begin>
      <day>31</day>
      <month>Jan</month>
      <year>1999</year>
    </begin>
    <end>
      now
    </end>
  </time>
</validTime>
```

Fig. 6. A node valid-time view in Gregorian calendar

```
<validTime>
  <time>
    <begin>
      <day>19</day>
      <month>12</month>
      <year>Wu-yin(Cycle 78)</year>
    </begin>
    <end>
      now
    </end>
  </time>
</validTime>
```

Fig. 7. A node valid-time view in the Chinese calendar

```
<end>
  <day>now</day>
  <month>now</month>
  <year>now</year>
</end>
```

Fig. 8. A possible representation of "now"

Before a user queries an XML document, he or she should be informed of what type of calendar is supported. This may be specified in the document itself (as a processing instruction for example) or in the schema that the document that it must conform to. The user is then able to specify which calendar to use in the query. A proposed syntax for specifying calendar is given below.

Syntax [calendar in valid time axis]. v/valid("calendar") specifies that the calendar to use in the valid time axis of v is "calendar".

It is the responsibility of a system to provide the user with a list of supported calendars. For instance, it may support Gregorian calendar, Chinese calendar and Russian calendar. The system should verify if a calendar required by the user is available. It may also use a default calendar (which should probably be Gregorian calendar) since some users may not be interested in a specific calendar.

Examples

Below are some simple examples of using the valid-time axis to query within the default view of the valid time.

v/valid::day selects all the day nodes in the axis.

v/valid::time[2] selects the second time node in the axis. It contains the second time constant during which the context node was valid. Note that here [2] is an abbreviated syntax for [position()=2].

v/valid::begin[1] selects the first begin node in the axis. It contains the time point when the context node first became valid.

If a user has knowledge of a valid-time view, such as that of the Gregorian calendar, then they can make node tests such as v/valid("Gregorian")::year, and v/valid("Gregorian")::month.

4 Conclusions

This paper presents a simple scheme to add valid-time support to XPath. The support results in an extended data model and query language. Adding a list of valid times to each node extends the data model. A valid-time axis is added to the query language to retrieve nodes in a view of the valid time for a node. The benefit of adding an axis to reach valid-time information is that the nodes cannot be reached with existing axis (such as the descendant axis). Hence, the extension is fully backwards compatible with XPath. The valid-time view is a formatting of the valid time in XML. This allows XPath to be reused to query within a valid-time axis. Multiple calendars are supported through different valid-time views.

In future, we plan to extend XPath with temporal predicates and aggregates. We can add temporal predicates to permit some reasoning about the valid-time information, e.g., the complete set of predicates found in *Allen's temporal logic* [16]. We are also exploring operations to perform temporal aggregates, e.g., moving-window averages. Finally, implementation is an immediate goal. We plan to extend Xalan, which is Apache's XPath processing engine, with the valid-time axis and view.

References

[1]   Dave Raggett, Arnaud Le Hors, and Ian Jacobs, *HTML 4.01 Specification,* W3C Recommendation, 24 December 1999, <http://www.w3.org/TR/html4/> (30 April 2002).

[2]   Tim Bray, Jean Paoli, C. M. Sperberg-McQueen, and Eve Maler, *Extensible Markup Language (XML) 1.0 (Second Edition),* W3C Recommendation, 6 October 2000, <http://www.w3.org/TR/REC-xml> (30 April 2002).

[3]   Don Chamberlin, Jonathan Robie, and Daniela Florescu, *Quilt: an XML Query Language for Heterogeneous Data Sources,* Proceedings of WebDB 2000, Available at <http://www.almaden.ibm.com/cs/people/chamberlin/quilt.html>(30 April 2002).

[4]   J. Robie, J. Lapp, and D. Schach, *XML Query Language (XQL),* <http://www.w3.org/TandS/QL/QL98/pp/xql.html> (30 April 2002).

[5]   Alin Deutsch, Mary Fernandez, Daniela Florescu, Alon Levy, and Dan Suciu, *A Query Language for XML,* <http://www.research.att.com/~mff/files/final.html> (30 April 2002).

[6]   Scott Boag, Don Chamberlin, Mary F. Fernandez, Daniela Florescu, Jonathan Robie, Jérôme Siméon, and Mugur Stefanescu, *XQuery 1.0: An XML Query Language,* W3C Working Draft, 20 December 2001, <http://www.w3.org/TR/xquery> (30 April 2002).

[7]   James Clark, and Steve DeRose, *XML Path Language (XPath) Version 1.0,* W3C Recommendation, 16 December 1999, <http://www.w3.org/TR/xpath> (30 April 2002).

[8]   Michael Kay, *XSL Transformations (XSLT) Version 2.0,* W3C Working Draft, 20 December 2001, <http://www.w3.org/TR/xslt20> (30 April 2002).

[9]   Ashok Malhotra, Jim Melton, Jonathan Robie, and Norman Walsh, *XQuery 1.0 and XPath 2.0 Functions and Operators,* W3C Working Draft, 20 December 2001, <http://www.w3.org/TR/xquery-operators/ > (30 April 2002).

[10] Vassilis J. Tsotras and Anil Kumar. Temporal database bibliography update. *ACM SIGMOD Record,* 25(1):41-51, March 1996.

[11] F. Grandi and F. Mandreoli, The Valid Web: it's Time to Go, Technical Report 46, TimeCenter, Aalborg, Denmark, December 1999.

[12] T. Amagasa, Y. Masatoshi, and S. Uemura, A Data Model for Temporal XML Documents, Database and Expert Systems Applications, 11th International Conference, DEXA 2000, pages 334-344, London, UK, September 2000.

[13] Curtis E. Dyreson, Observing Transaction-time Semantics with TTXPath, *Proceedings of the Second International Conference on Web Information Systems Engineering (WISE2001),* December 2001, Kyoto, Japan.

[14] Richard T. Snodgrass, *The TSQL2 Temporal Query Language,* Kluwer Academic Publishers, 1995.

[15] Christian S. Jensen, Curtis E. Dyreson (editors), et al, *The Consensus Glossary of Temporal Database Concepts—February 1998 Version,* February 1998, <http://www.cs.auc.dk/~csj/Glossary/download/1399ch52.ps> (30 April 2002).

[16] J. F. Allen, Maintaining Knowledge about Temporal Intervals, *Communications of the Association of Computing Machinery,* 26, No. 11, November 1983, page 832-843.

Communication Deadlock Detection of Inter-organizational Workflow Definition

Jaeyong Shim, Dongsoo Han, and Hongsoog Kim

School of Engineering, Information and Communications University
58-4 Hwaam, Yusong, Daejon, South Korea
{jaeyong7, dshan, kimkk}@icu.ac.kr

Abstract. As the needs for interconnections of processes in different companies or departments are so increasing and companies try to realize business processes across organizational boundaries, the correctness issues of inter-organizational workflow definition is getting more important. In this paper, we develop community process definition language(CPDL) for inter-organizational workflow specification. It is devised to analyze correctness of inter-organizational workflow definition and especially it is used to detect latent communication deadlocks. A new communication deadlock detection technique in the context of inter-organizational workflow definition is developed on CPDL using the set based constraint system. Any inter-organizational workflow languages that can be translated into CPDL can detect its communication deadlock using the technique of this paper.

1 Introduction

Nowadays, the needs for interconnections of processes in different companies or departments are so demanding and companies try to realize business processes across organizational boundaries. Several research works have been done to resolve the inter-organizational operability for virtual business process[10][11][12]. When an inter-organizational workflow is activated, several local workflow instances might be in running state simultaneously. Tasks in each local workflow are executed in parallel on different workflow environments and interoperate by exchanging messages for input and output parameters. In that case, we say that the local workflows forms *p-to-p composition* in this paper. Because the execution of an activity is started along the control path of workflow definition and data exchange specification, if there is incongruity between control paths of local workflows and data path of inter-organizational workflow, tasks in p-to-p composition can be blocked permanently. We define this situation as *communication deadlock* of inter-organizational workflow. The control path and data path in inter-organizational workflow instance create dependent relations and the permanent blocked state is caused by *cyclic dependence* among tasks.

Detecting inter-organizational workflow process fallen into deadlock situation at runtime is difficult and it usually requires high computing and networking overhead. The deadlock problem may cause a long lasting workflow process to

S. Bhalla (Ed.): DNIS 2002, LNCS 2544, pp. 43–57, 2002.

be invalid because the business process instance in deadlock situation must be canceled in general. In the case of B2B application, an agreement made by companies may be broken because of the deadlock problem. Therefore, it is desirable to statically detect the latent deadlock problem in inter-organizational workflow definition before the real execution and remove it completely.

The latent communication deadlock is mostly resulted from mistakes or lack of considerations for various situations that might be encountered at runtime. Because inter-organizational workflow definition is usually large-scale and intricate, it is not reasonable to put all the responsibility for detecting deadlock comprising definition on only workflow designers. An automatic way to find the set of tasks being likely fallen into deadlock situation at runtime and to notify them to the designer is required.

Communication deadlock is a kind of conventional issues of operating system and parallel and distributed systems. To resolve it, many studies have been done taking static or dynamic analysis approaches. Large number of the analysis methods use the theories of graph[15] and petri-net[16] for verifying parallel program and deadlock detection or avoidance mechanism. Analogously, in the workflow analysis researches, most of analytic verification method for workflow definition adopt petri-net[7] and directed graph.

In this paper, to statically(before runtime) find the deadlock problem, we propose a set based deadlock detection method. We adopt set constraint system[3] approach that is used to analyze runtime properties of programs. And, we develop *Community Process Definition Language(CPDL)* that is an expanded version of Structured Workflow Definition Language (SWDL)[13] to accommodate interoperation of business community. Differently from other researches, we use set expressions for the semantics of language constructs and inference rules to find deadlock. It gives simple but more intuitive understanding rather than the computational algorithms of other approaches. Moreover, it opens the opportunity for having uniform framework to resolve other problems such as resource conflict analysis and exception analysis of workflow. We ascribe it to the uniformity of set based constraint system.

This paper is organized as follows. In section 2, we introduce a community process definition language that is a target of our analysis. Section 3 describes communication deadlock problem that can be in community process definition. The details of analysis method to detect communication deadlock is presented in section 4. Section 5 summaries similar studies to this paper and finally, we conclude our study in section 6.

2 Community Process Definition Language

We have developed the Community Process Definition Language (CPDL) as target language for simple and clear description for our deadlock detection method. It focuses on control flow perspective and in part data flow perspective of inter-organizational workflow. Like SWDL, control structures of CPDL are similar to those of structured programming languages. The benefit of using them is ob-

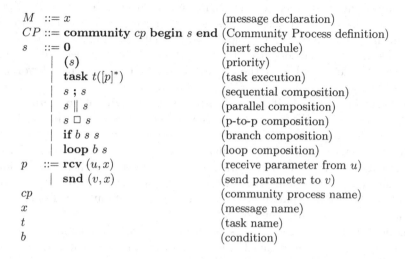

$$
\begin{array}{lll}
M & ::= x & \text{(message declaration)} \\
CP & ::= \textbf{community } cp \textbf{ begin } s \textbf{ end} & \text{(Community Process definition)} \\
s & ::= \mathbf{0} & \text{(inert schedule)} \\
& | \ (s) & \text{(priority)} \\
& | \ \textbf{task } t([p]^*) & \text{(task execution)} \\
& | \ s \ ; \ s & \text{(sequential composition)} \\
& | \ s \parallel s & \text{(parallel composition)} \\
& | \ s \ \square \ s & \text{(p-to-p composition)} \\
& | \ \textbf{if } b \ s \ s & \text{(branch composition)} \\
& | \ \textbf{loop } b \ s & \text{(loop composition)} \\
p & ::= \textbf{rcv } (u, x) & \text{(receive parameter from } u) \\
& | \ \textbf{snd } (v, x) & \text{(send parameter to } v) \\
cp & & \text{(community process name)} \\
x & & \text{(message name)} \\
t & & \text{(task name)} \\
b & & \text{(condition)}
\end{array}
$$

Fig. 1. Abstract Syntax of CPDL

vious in guiding designers to define correct workflow expressions [13]. Figure 1 shows the abstract syntax of CPDL. CPDL contains only minimum features that are indispensable to represent control flow patterns and task declarations with parameter information, such as message name, destination, and source of messages.

2.1 Control Flow Expression

Various workflow languages with a variety of expressive power have been developed to meet the requirements of workflow users. Control structure of workflow is one of the features bringing the variety of workflow languages. W.M.P. van der Aalst[14] systematically classified the control flow expressions in the name of *workflow pattern*. CPDL does not have all control structures that are directly mapped to each workflow pattern respectively but has basic syntactic elements for them. All the advanced workflow patterns can be specified by composing the basic control flow elements. Each syntactic element is explained in the below.

- Sequential composition: Sequential execution is the most basic control flow pattern of workflow and it specifies the dependency between consecutive task schedules explicitly. "$s_0; s_1$" indicates that schedule s_1 should be activated after the completion of schedule s_0.
- Parallel composition: Parallel composition is used to specify that a single thread of control splits into two threads which are executed in parallel within the same workflow environment, allowing tasks in different threads to be executed concurrently and their order of execution is decided arbitrarily by the system situation. The AND-split(another name of parallel composition) element must be paired with another basic workflow pattern AND-join which is

assumed implicitly specified in CPDL. That is, two activated threads of workflow connected by parallel composition are converged into a single thread in synchronized manner. So, "$s_0 \| s_1$" means that two threads of workflow s_0 and s_1 are executed concurrently within the workflow instance and converged into a single thread after the processing of the two segments of workflows are completed.

- Branch composition: "**if** b s_0 s_1" corresponds to XOR-split pattern of workflow and it does the same role as the if-then-else control structure in programming languages. This operator is used when one of two branches needs to be taken according to the evaluation of the transition condition b. To keep the language as structured form, like the case in the parallel composition, a branch composition implicitly has its corresponding XOR-join element indicating the two alternative branches get together without synchronization at the end of the branch composition.

- Loop composition: "**loop** b s" is used to specify that the community schedule s is repeated while b is true. The loop construct, presenting iteration pattern, of CPDL is a structured cycle containing only one entry point and one exit point. Many workflow models and commercial workflow systems support arbitrary loop allowing multiple entry and exit points, but it can typically be converted into structured cycles connected by basic control flows.

- P-to-p composition: As community process definition usually integrate several workflows of different organizations to describe interoperations, p-to-p composition operator is devised to specify organizational borders among them. Its semantic is very similar to parallel composition but the split control threads of p-to-p composition are individual and local workflows that will be running in different organizations respectively at runtime.

- Priority: "()" is used only to bundle up a group of workflow expressions to modify the precedence relations between operators inside of the bundle and adjacencies to it. To clarify the semantic of control flow in community process definition, we define the precedence relations between pairs of operators as follow:

$$; \; > \; \| \; \doteq \; \mathbf{if} \, b \; \doteq \; \mathbf{loop} \, b \; > \; \square$$

where we use the notation $a < b$ to specify a yields precedence to b and $a \doteq b$ for the precedence of a and b is the same. Besides, the sequence of equal precedence operators follows left-associative association rule.

2.2   Task Declaration

To make a definition of workflow interaction, each step of workflow must be specified. Syntactic elements of CPDL concerning with the task declaration are in the below.

- Inert schedule: This element is used to specify that there is no task to be activated. The inert task is developed to keep the expressive power without losing the structural nature of CPDL.

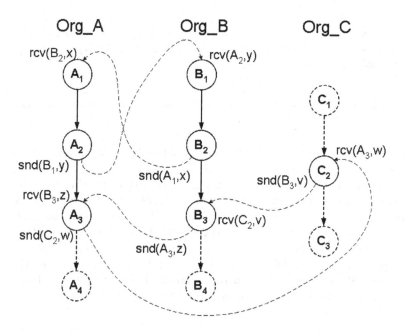

Fig. 2. An p-to-p composition of three local workflows

– Task execution: "**task** $t(p_1, \ldots, p_n)$" denotes that the execution of a task t. A task may have zero or more input parameters, denoted by $\mathbf{rcv}(u, x)$(i.e. before the task to be started, it must receive message x from task u), and output parameters, denoted by $\mathbf{snd}(v, x)$(i.e. after the task is finished, it sends its output x to task v). As community process definition concentrates on inter-organizational workflow interactions, parameter denotations present message interchange between tasks included in respective organizations. For a task to be activated, it must receive all the input parameters from its predecessor tasks through the communication facilities provided by workflow system. After the task is processed with the parameters, output parameters are generated and sent to its successor tasks. Input parameters may block the processing of a task until all the parameters are ready but snd(v,x) is performed in asynchronous manner. The task is an abstraction of an activity and workflow declaration. At the time of localization of community process definition, the task can be treated as local workflow definition or activity of the organization. It is useful to preserve the independency of organizations in predefined linking approach for inter-organizational workflow.

2.3 Example

Figure 2 shows a simple community process comprising three local workflows of different organizations(in this case Org_A, Org_B and Org_C). Task name is

> **task** $A_1(\text{rcv}(B_2,\text{x}))$; **task** $A_2(\text{snd}(B_1,\text{y}))$; **task** $A_3(\text{rcv}(B_3,\text{z}), \text{snd}(C_2,\text{w}))$
> □ **task** $B_1(\text{rcv}(A_2,\text{y}))$; **task** $B_2(\text{snd}(A_1,\text{x}))$; **task** $B_3(\text{rcv}(C_2,\text{v}), \text{snd}(A_3,\text{z}))$
> □ **task** $C_2(\text{rcv}(A_3,\text{w}), \text{snd}(B_3,\text{v}))$

Fig. 3. CPDL example of p-to-p composition of three local workflows

written in upper case letters with subscript number and message name is in lower case letters. Sequential workflows, such as $(A_1; A_2; A_3)$, $(B_1; B_2; B_3)$ and (C_2), are executed in parallel, and they interact with each other by exchanging messages named v, w, x, y and z. The tasks denoted by dotted circle (such as A_4, B_4, C_1 and C_3) are not a part of community process definition. They are created during process localization stage, at that time each organizations integrate the community process with its local workflow that does not interact with other organization's workflows. Figure 3 shows CPDL expression representing the community process definition of Figure 2. This example will be referred again in next section to explain communication deadlock problem.

3   Communication Deadlock

Several tasks in a community schedule of p-to-p composition could be activated concurrently and might exchange messages. At that situation, a task could be *blocked* by some reasons. The delivery delay of input messages is one of such reasons. A blocked task can start its processing upon receiving all messages that are specified in parameter lists. If a task does not receive all the input parameters, it does not change its status and that of its community process either. On the other hand, a task is said to be in *sleep* when its predecessors are not completed yet. A sleeping task can start execution upon completion of its preceding tasks. Based on the definitions, we define the communication deadlock of community process instance. A community process instance CP is in *deadlock* state if and only if
(1) Except completed tasks, all tasks in a CP are either blocked or sleep-state;
(2) There is no message in transit between tasks in the CP.
A task is in *deadlock* also if it is in a deadlocked community process instance.

Above deadlock state is difficult to be detected while the community process is in processing and thus it can bring serious problems to inter-organizational business and virtual enterprise. In that sense, if a community process definition comprises latent deadlock problem, it should be eliminated or revised correctly before the real execution. The *latent deadlock* is a problem existing in community process definition that it has the possibility to lead the process into deadlock situation at runtime. To explain how to statically detect latent deadlock in a process definition, we define some terminologies. They are useful to figure out the latent communication deadlock of inter-organizational workflow definition.

Definition 1. (Explicit Dependence)

Assume that s and t are tasks in a single organization's workflow of a community process definition. If s is a predecessor of t and t is a successor of s in the definition, t is *explicitly dependent* on s. In the example Figure 2, B_2 is *explicitly dependent* on B_1 in Org_B's workflow.

Definition 2. (Implicit Dependence)

Assume that task s and task t are contained in respective organization's local workflows of a community process definition. If t is defined to receive messages, as input parameters, from s and s is defined to send messages, as output parameters, to t, t is *implicitly dependent* on s. For example, in Figure 2, B_3 is *implicitly dependent* on C_2 by message v.

Definition 3. (Conjunctive Parameters)

Assume that task t has a set of input parameters $\{i_1, i_2, \ldots, i_n\}$. If t remains blocked until all input parameters are received and it can start execution after receiving all the input parameters, they are called *conjunctive parameters*.

The deadlock problem of community process definition can be formally modeled using a wait-for-graph(WFG)[5] which is a useful mathematical model for representing task dependency. A WFG is classified into a class of directed graphs. The vertices of this graph are used to model tasks of community process. Directed edges in the graph represent dependence relations between tasks. Both of the dependence relations(i.e. explicit and implicit dependence) can be represented by directed edges in WFG. When a vertex has outgoing edges, it represents one or both of the two cases, that is, a task having precedent tasks and a task having input parameters. A community process definition has *latent deadlocked tasks* if it satisfies all the properties described in the below:

(1) If any task in community process definition has input parameters, they are conjunctive parameters.
(2) The WFG presenting the explicit dependences and implicit dependences between tasks of community process definition has a cycle.

Although not all of the community process definitions satisfy the first condition, we can easily transform them to satisfy the condition by introducing new dummy tasks. Thus the first condition does not restrict the range that the analysis can cover.

4   Analysis

To detect communication deadlock in a community process definition, we adopt a set constraint system that is typically used to analyze runtime properties of programming languages. Set based analysis technique largely consists of two phases. One is set constraints generation phase and the other one is constraints solving phase[3]. The first phase concentrates on setting up set constraints from a community process definition by applying derivation rules. Once the constraints set is created, the second phase tries to find a minimal solution from the set constraints by applying constraints solving rules.

$$se ::= \mathcal{X}_i \qquad \qquad \text{set variable}$$

$$|\quad \phi \qquad \qquad \quad \text{empty set constraint}$$

$$|\quad task(t) \qquad \quad \text{constraint for task execution}$$

$$|\quad send(t,d,m) \quad \text{constraint for sending message}$$

$$|\quad receiv(t,o,m) \text{ constraint for receiving message}$$

$$|\quad seq(\mathcal{X}_i,\mathcal{X}_i) \quad \text{constraint for sequential composition}$$

$$|\quad p2p(\mathcal{X}_i,\mathcal{X}_i) \quad \text{constraint for p-to-p composition}$$

$$|\quad arrow(s,t) \quad \text{constraint for data dependency of community}$$

$$|\quad deadlock(s,t) \text{ constraint for comm. deadlock}$$

Fig. 4. Syntax of Set Expression

4.1   Set Constraints for Analysis of CPDL

The constraint is an expression unit to describe runtime properties of community process definition. Every syntactic element of CPDL has a set variable and each set variable has constraints, called *set constraints*, used to approximate the runtime behavior of syntactic element of it. The set constraint is of the form $\mathcal{X} \supseteq se$ where $\mathcal{X}$ is a set variable and se is a set expression. The constraint indicates that the set $\mathcal{X}$ must include the set se. Each element of set expression has partial information on task dependence that is necessary to detect communication deadlock.

The set expression can be a set variable, empty set and several notations such as $task(t)$, $send(t,d,m)$, $receiv(t,o,m)$, $p2p(X_i,X_j)$ and $seq(X_i,X_j)$ that are constructed by syntax element of CPDL at constraints generation time. Semantics of these set expressions naturally follows from their corresponding language constructs. $task(t)$ means that task t is executed. The second notation $send(t,d,m)$ means that task t sends message m to destination task named d. On the contrary, $receiv(t,o,m)$ means that task t waits for message m from task o. The fourth expression $p2p(X_i,X_j)$ means that set variable X_i and X_j are connected by p-to-p composition, that is, two schedules are executed in different process instances at runtime and they could interact one another. The last expression $seq(X_i,X_j)$ denotes that two schedules having set variables X_i and X_j respectively are executed sequentially.

At set constraints solving phase, two set expressions can be generated, such as $arrow(s,t)$ and $deadlock(s,t)$. Constraint solving rules decide semantics of these set expressions. If task s waits for data from task t(i.e. implicit dependence) or task s is preceded by t(i.e. explicit dependence), constraint solving rules construct the set expression $arrow(s,t)$. This set expression represents the directed edge of wait-for-graph model. It represents dependent relations between tasks. Set expression $deadlock(s,t)$ means that task s and t are dependent on one another to be active. If we can find the set expression $deadlock(s,t)$ in result set of constraints, we can conclude that the community process definition of the result has possibility of falling into permanent blocked state. Figure 4 illustrates the syntax of set expressions.

$$[\text{NULL}] \quad \mathbf{0} \triangleright \phi \qquad [\text{BRACE}] \quad \frac{s \triangleright \mathcal{C}}{(s) \triangleright \mathcal{C}}$$

$$[\text{TASK}] \quad \begin{array}{l} \mathbf{task}\ t\ (\ \mathbf{rcv}(o_1, n_1), \cdots, \mathbf{rcv}(o_n, n_n), \\ \qquad \mathbf{snd}(d_1, m_1), \cdots, \mathbf{snd}(d_n, m_n)\ ) \\ \triangleright \{\mathcal{X} \supseteq task(t), \quad \mathcal{X} \supseteq receiv(t, o_1, n_1), \cdots, \mathcal{X} \supseteq receiv(t, o_n, n_n), \\ \quad \mathcal{X} \supseteq send(t, d_1, m_1), \cdots, \mathcal{X} \supseteq send(t, d_n, m_n)\} \end{array}$$

$$[\text{SEQ}] \quad \frac{s_0 \triangleright \mathcal{C}_0 \quad s_1 \triangleright \mathcal{C}_1}{s_0\ ;\ s_1 \triangleright \{\mathcal{X} \supseteq \mathcal{X}_{s_0}, \mathcal{X} \supseteq \mathcal{X}_{s_1}, \mathcal{X} \supseteq seq(\mathcal{X}_{s_0}, \mathcal{X}_{s_1})\} \cup \mathcal{C}_0 \cup \mathcal{C}_1}$$

$$[\text{PAR}] \quad \frac{s_0 \triangleright \mathcal{C}_0 \quad s_1 \triangleright \mathcal{C}_1}{s_0\ \|\ s_1 \triangleright \{\mathcal{X} \supseteq \mathcal{X}_{s_0}, \mathcal{X} \supseteq \mathcal{X}_{s_1}\} \cup \mathcal{C}_0 \cup \mathcal{C}_1}$$

$$[\text{P2P}] \quad \frac{s_0 \triangleright \mathcal{C}_0 \quad s_1 \triangleright \mathcal{C}_1}{s_0\ \square\ s_1 \triangleright \{\mathcal{X} \supseteq \mathcal{X}_{s_0}, \mathcal{X} \supseteq \mathcal{X}_{s_1}, \mathcal{X} \supseteq p2p(\mathcal{X}_{s_0}, \mathcal{X}_{s_1})\} \cup \mathcal{C}_0 \cup \mathcal{C}_1}$$

$$[\text{IF}] \quad \frac{s_0 \triangleright \mathcal{C}_0 \quad s_1 \triangleright \mathcal{C}_1}{\mathbf{if}\ c\ s_0\ s_1 \triangleright \{\mathcal{X} \supseteq \mathcal{X}_{s_0}, \mathcal{X} \supseteq \mathcal{X}_{s_1}\} \cup \mathcal{C}_0 \cup \mathcal{C}_1}$$

$$[\text{LOOP}] \quad \frac{s \triangleright \mathcal{C}}{\mathbf{loop}\ c\ s \triangleright \{\mathcal{X} \supseteq \mathcal{X}_s\} \cup \mathcal{C}}$$

Fig. 5. Constraint Generation Rules : $\triangleright$

4.2 Construction of Set Constraints

Figure 5 illustrates the derivation rules, $\triangleright$, to generate set constraints for every expression of CPDL. The set variable $\mathcal{X}$ is for the community schedule to which the rule applies and the subscripted set variable $\mathcal{X}_s$ is for the community schedule s. The relation "$s \triangleright \mathcal{C}$" represents that "constraints $\mathcal{C}$ are generated from community schedule s". The meanings of each rule are as follows.

Rule [NULL] denotes that inert schedule does not have any constraint and [BRACE] denotes that set constraints of parenthesized schedules (s) are the same as those of s. Rule [TASK] extracts information on task execution and data flow among tasks from the arguments declaration of task. It generates a set of corresponding set constraints, such as $\mathcal{X} \supseteq task(t)$, $\mathcal{X} \supseteq receiv(t, o, m)$ and $\mathcal{X} \supseteq send(t, d, m)$. Rules [P2P] and [SEQ] make set constraints $\mathcal{X} \supseteq p2p(X_{s_0}, X_{s_1})$ and $\mathcal{X} \supseteq seq(X_{s_0}, X_{s_1})$ respectively and inclusion relation between set variables. The other rules of constraints generation are for propagating set constraints to outer block. By this propagation rules, runtime properties implied in the set constraints of sub-expression can be held in the set variable of current expression.

During analysis, community definition are recorded in a syntax tree, in which each node represents an operation as you can see in Figure 6. This syntax tree is equivalent to the example of Figure 2. Every node of syntax tree has its set variable and set constraints constructed by constraint generation rules. Set constraints generated from the syntax tree by applying constraint generation rules are presented in Figure 7.

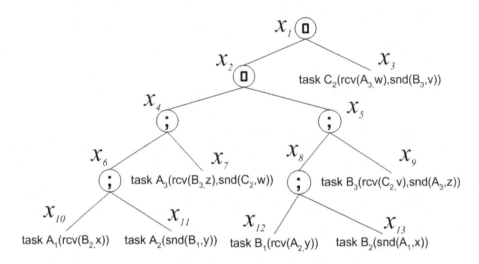

Fig. 6. Syntax Tree of CPDL Example and Set Variable for SBA

4.3   Resolving Set Constraint

In the previous subsection, we showed how to generate set constraints. This section presents how to compute the solution from the set constraints. To solve the set constraints, we derive constraint solving rules S and Figure 8 illustrates them. Each rule in S has the same form with a horizontal bar. One or more set constraints already contained are written above the bar and new set constraints are written below the bar. This structure states that if set constraints written above the bar are found then new set constraints written below it are appended to the set of constraints. Brief explanations about the meaning of each rule are in the below.

[DIST$_{p2p}$] means distribution rule of p2p-compositions, that is, $\mathcal{X}$ has two p2p-compositions of $\mathcal{V}$ and $\mathcal{Z}$ and $\mathcal{W}$ and $\mathcal{Z}$ if set variable $\mathcal{X}$ has a p2p-composition of $\mathcal{Y}$ and $\mathcal{Z}$ and set variable $\mathcal{Y}$ has a p2p-composition of $\mathcal{V}$ and $\mathcal{W}$. [ARROW$_{ctl}$] presents explicit task dependence arising from control flow

$$
\begin{array}{llll}
\mathcal{X}_1 \supseteq \mathcal{X}_2 & \mathcal{X}_1 \supseteq \mathcal{X}_3 & \mathcal{X}_1 \supseteq p2p(\mathcal{X}_2, \mathcal{X}_3) & \mathcal{X}_2 \supseteq \mathcal{X}_4 \\
\mathcal{X}_2 \supseteq \mathcal{X}_5 & \mathcal{X}_2 \supseteq p2p(\mathcal{X}_4, \mathcal{X}_5) & \mathcal{X}_3 \supseteq receiv(C_2, A_3, w) & \mathcal{X}_3 \supseteq send(C_2, B_3, v) \\
\mathcal{X}_3 \supseteq task(C_2) & \mathcal{X}_4 \supseteq \mathcal{X}_6 & \mathcal{X}_4 \supseteq \mathcal{X}_7 & \mathcal{X}_4 \supseteq seq(\mathcal{X}_6, \mathcal{X}_7) \\
\mathcal{X}_7 \supseteq receiv(A_3, B_3, z) & \mathcal{X}_7 \supseteq send(A_3, C_1, w) & \mathcal{X}_7 \supseteq task(A_3) & \mathcal{X}_5 \supseteq \mathcal{X}_8 \\
\mathcal{X}_5 \supseteq \mathcal{X}_9 & \mathcal{X}_5 \supseteq seq(\mathcal{X}_8, \mathcal{X}_9) & \mathcal{X}_9 \supseteq receiv(B_3, C_2, v) & \mathcal{X}_9 \supseteq send(B_3, A_3, z) \\
\mathcal{X}_9 \supseteq task(B_3) & \mathcal{X}_6 \supseteq \mathcal{X}_{10} & \mathcal{X}_6 \supseteq \mathcal{X}_{11} & \mathcal{X}_6 \supseteq seq(\mathcal{X}_{10}, \mathcal{X}_{11}) \\
\mathcal{X}_{10} \supseteq receiv(A_1, B_1, x) & \mathcal{X}_{10} \supseteq task(A_1) & \mathcal{X}_{11} \supseteq send(A_2, B_1, y) & \mathcal{X}_{11} \supseteq task(A_2) \\
\mathcal{X}_8 \supseteq \mathcal{X}_{12} & \mathcal{X}_8 \supseteq \mathcal{X}_{13} & \mathcal{X}_8 \supseteq seq(\mathcal{X}_{12}, \mathcal{X}_{13}) & \mathcal{X}_{12} \supseteq receiv(B_1, A_2, y) \\
\mathcal{X}_{13} \supseteq send(B_2, A_1, x) & \mathcal{X}_{12} \supseteq task(B_1) & \mathcal{X}_{13} \supseteq task(B_2) &
\end{array}
$$

Fig. 7. Set Constraints constructed by $\triangleright$

$$[\text{TRANSITIVE}_1] \quad \frac{\mathcal{X} \supseteq \mathcal{Y} \quad \mathcal{Y} \supseteq task(t)}{\mathcal{X} \supseteq task(t)} \quad \frac{\mathcal{X} \supseteq \mathcal{Y} \quad \mathcal{Y} \supseteq send(s,d,m)}{\mathcal{X} \supseteq send(s,d,m)}$$

$$[\text{TRANSITIVE}_2] \quad \frac{\mathcal{X} \supseteq \mathcal{Y} \quad \mathcal{Y} \supseteq receiv(t,o,m)}{\mathcal{X} \supseteq receiv(t,o,m)}$$

$$[\text{DIST}_{\text{p2p}}] \quad \frac{\mathcal{X} \supseteq p2p(\mathcal{Y},\mathcal{Z}) \quad \mathcal{Y} \supseteq p2p(\mathcal{V},\mathcal{W})}{\mathcal{X} \supseteq p2p(\mathcal{V},\mathcal{Z}) \quad \mathcal{X} \supseteq p2p(\mathcal{W},\mathcal{Z})} \quad \frac{\mathcal{X} \supseteq p2p(\mathcal{Y},\mathcal{Z}) \quad \mathcal{Z} \supseteq p2p(\mathcal{V},\mathcal{W})}{\mathcal{X} \supseteq p2p(\mathcal{Y},\mathcal{V}) \quad \mathcal{X} \supseteq p2p(\mathcal{Y},\mathcal{W})}$$

$$[\text{ARROW}_{\text{ctl}}] \quad \frac{\mathcal{X} \supseteq seq(\mathcal{Y},\mathcal{Z}) \quad \mathcal{Y} \supseteq task(t) \quad \mathcal{Z} \supseteq task(s)}{\mathcal{X} \supseteq arrow(s,t)}$$

$$[\text{ARROW}_{\text{dfl}}] \quad \frac{\mathcal{X} \supseteq p2p(\mathcal{Y},\mathcal{Z}) \quad \mathcal{Y} \supseteq send(s,d,m) \quad \mathcal{Z} \supseteq receiv(d,s,m)}{\mathcal{X} \supseteq arrow(d,s)}$$

$$\frac{\mathcal{X} \supseteq p2p(\mathcal{Y},\mathcal{Z}) \quad \mathcal{Y} \supseteq receiv(d,s,m) \quad \mathcal{Z} \supseteq send(s,d,m)}{\mathcal{X} \supseteq arrow(d,s)}$$

$$[\text{TRANSITIVE}_{\text{arrow}}] \quad \frac{\mathcal{X} \supseteq arrow(s,t) \quad \mathcal{X} \supseteq arrow(t,u)}{\mathcal{X} \supseteq arrow(s,u)}$$

$$[\text{DEADLOCK}] \quad \frac{\mathcal{X} \supseteq arrow(s,t) \quad \mathcal{X} \supseteq arrow(t,s)}{\mathcal{X} \supseteq deadlock(s,t)}$$

$$[\text{TRANSITIVE}_3] \quad \frac{\mathcal{X} \supseteq \mathcal{Y} \quad \mathcal{Y} \supseteq arrow(s,t)}{\mathcal{X} \supseteq arrow(s,t)} \quad \frac{\mathcal{X} \supseteq \mathcal{Y} \quad \mathcal{Y} \supseteq deadlock(s,t)}{\mathcal{X} \supseteq deadlock(s,t)}$$

Fig. 8. Constraint Solving Rules : $\mathcal{S}$

of tasks and [ARROW$_{\text{dfl}}$] shows implicit task dependence caused by data flow between tasks that belong to different local workflows. [TRANSITIVE$_{\text{arrow}}$] denotes the transitivity of task dependence relation and the other [TRANSITIVE]s propagate the constraints of current expression to super expressions. Rule [DEADLOCK] finds a pair of tasks that are dependent on one another. The detected pairs of tasks are involved in latent communication deadlock.

Our static analysis is defined to be the least model of constraints. Collected constraints for a community definition guarantee the existence of its least solution because every operator has monotonic set inclusion relation[3]. The minimum solution is computed by iterative application of constraint solving rules $\mathcal{S}$ to set of constraints $\mathcal{C}$. This iterative application is denoted by $\mathcal{S}^*(\mathcal{C})$. The iteration continues until the results of consecutive iterations coincide. Although $\mathcal{S}^*(\mathcal{C})$ certainly denotes the solution, it might include unnecessary and redundant constraints also. We can get a more concise solution by eliminating superfluous set constraints by using the function $Select(\mathcal{S}^*(\mathcal{C}))$ and its semantics is defined as follows:

$$Select(\mathcal{S}^*(\mathcal{C})) = \{\mathcal{X} \supseteq deadlock(s,t) \mid \mathcal{X} \supseteq deadlock(s,t) \in \mathcal{S}^*(\mathcal{C})\}$$

In the case of our example, when $\mathcal{C}$ is a set of constraints of Figure 2, we can get the final solution of $Select(\mathcal{S}^*(\mathcal{C}))$ as follows:

$$\{ \; \mathcal{X}_1 \supseteq deadlock(A_3, B_3), \;\; \mathcal{X}_1 \supseteq deadlock(B_3, C_2), \;\; \mathcal{X}_1 \supseteq deadlock(C_2, A_3),$$
$$\mathcal{X}_1 \supseteq deadlock(A_2, A_1), \;\; \mathcal{X}_1 \supseteq deadlock(A_1, B_2), \;\; \mathcal{X}_1 \supseteq deadlock(B_2, B_1),$$
$$\mathcal{X}_1 \supseteq deadlock(B_1, A_2), \;\; \mathcal{X}_1 \supseteq deadlock(A_2, B_2), \;\; \mathcal{X}_1 \supseteq deadlock(B_1, A_1) \; \}$$

This solution indicates that the example CPDL process in Figure 2 has two groups of tasks that may fall into communication deadlock. From the solution above, we can conclude that two task groups, such as $\{A_3, B_3, C_2\}$ and $\{A_1, A_2, B_1, B_2\}$, have the possibility to fall into deadlock state at runtime.

The time complexity of the algorithm to detect communication deadlock is $O(n^3)$ where n is the size of input expression, that is, the number of nodes in syntax tree of CPDL. The $O(n^3)$ bound is explained as follows. First, The construction of constraints is proportional to n(size of expression) and at most n^2 new constraints can be added by the constraints solving algorithm. The cost of "adding" each new constraint can be bounded by $O(n)$ because it needs n times computing to determine what other new constraints can be added when this constraint is added. Thus, the sum of the first and the second phase become $O(n) + O(n^3) = O(n^3)$.

5   Related Work

Since the late of nineties, several researches have been done to resolve the heterogeneity and interoperability. Some projects focused on the application of workflow technology to electronic commerce. The WISE[10] and COSMOS[11] studied architectures for enabling workflow process across organizational boundaries. On the other hand, the Workflow Management Coalition (WfMC) identified several models of interoperability and published e-mail MIME binding specification and recently released Wf-XML binding[2] improving the former. These proposals could be used as a concrete basis for the implementations of WfMC's interface-4.

Because business processes are getting more diverse and complex, improvements to workflow specifications are going on. Much of the developments in the expressive power of workflow specifications have been established with workflow models for business requirements, but only a few researches focus on the verification of workflow definition. H.Davulcu[1] proposed concurrent transaction logic as the language for specifying, analyzing, and scheduling of workflows. N.R.Adam[6] proposed concrete verification procedures based on Petri net and its target was checking the consistency of transactional workflows. I.B.Arpinar[20] formalized components of workflow system related to the correctness in the presence of concurrency based on set theory and graph theory and developed constraint based concurrency control technique.

Contrary to the above approaches, for transparent integration of different organization's business process, some projects conducted researches about description language and enactment service for inter-organizational workflows. The InterWorkflow[4] presented the interworkflow language and implementation of it

with experimental proof using WfMC's standard protocol. It assumes that interactions among WfMSs of organizations are predefined in one place at buildtime.
CrossFlow[9] defined XML-based contract description language to specify data
exchange between trading partners and it implemented the framework including from contract conceptual model to interaction between WfMS of the two
organizations. Its framework considers that the decision of trading partner is
performed at runtime.

In the e-commerce society, many XML-based languages are developed for
data exchange among organizations, but only small part of them consider the
process of e-commerce trading and admit control flow into XML-based standards. The BPML[22] of BPMI.org is a XML-based language for coordination of
collaborative business processes among trading partners. It involves exception
handling, transactions and rich format to enable the different types of activities.
However, these studies do not consider the correctness of specification and don't
provide verification methods tackled in this paper.

Only a few papers explicitly focus on the problem of verifying the correctness
of inter-organizational workflows. W.M.P. van der Aalst[7] and E.Kindler[8] extends the WF-net derived from Petri net to be able to verify inter-organizational
workflow definition and present the interaction between workflows in terms of
message sequence charts. XRL[21] is also Petri net based inter-organizational
workflow language focusing on workflow instance for ad-hoc interoperation. It
supports less structured and more dynamic process and provides formal methodology for verification also.

6   Conclusion

In this paper, we have proposed an inter-organizational workflow definition language, called CPDL, to accommodate predefined interoperations among workflows and adopted set constraints system to statically detect communication
deadlock. Although CPDL is lack of some features to specify practical workflow,
it has sufficient features to express control flow and data flow among tasks that
are needed to analyze deadlock problem.

The syntactic elements of CPDL provide basic workflow patterns such as
sequential composition, parallel composition, conditional branch, loop composition, p-to-p composition which are useful to comprise inter-organizational workflow interaction and task declaration with parameter information. Workflow systems of these days have their different insights into expression capability and
provide diverse ways of representing control flow constructs. However, we consider them as syntactic sugar that can be translated into compounding of basic
operators in CPDL.

Compared to other workflow analysis techniques, set based workflow analysis
employs a simple and intuitive definition of program approximation. This is motivated by a desire to separate the definition of program approximations from
the algorithms used to compute it, and leads to declarative program analysis
which is easier to understand and reason about. In contrast, most of approaches

in the literature of workflow definition analysis, such as petri-net or directed graph, provide only an implicit algorithmic definition of runtime properties approximation. The other advantage of set based analysis is that the definition of approximation is very uniform. We think that this uniformity has implications for the stability and scalability of the analysis. For instance, resource conflict analysis[13] and exception analysis[19] has same analysis process including constraints constructions and solving them. This uniformity is favorable to make a framework for the analysis of workflow definition.

A straightforward implementation of the set constraint algorithm leads to poor performance. To achieve very substantial improvements, we are studying on how to make appropriate representation schemes and minimization techniques. And, in the near future, we are planning to apply CPDL and our analysis technique to other practical inter-organizational workflow definition languages. Definition language for predefined workflow interaction is evenly necessary to both of the predefined linking approach and runtime linking approach. So, static analysis for detecting latent deadlock is useful for inter-workflow definition designer and contract designer also.

References

1. H. Davulcu, M. Kifer, C.R. Ramakrishnan and I.V. Ramakrishnan, "Logic based modeling and analysis of workflows," In ACM Symposium on Principles of Database System, June 1998.
2. Workflow Management Coalition, "Workflow Standard – Interoperability Wf-XML Binding, TC-1023", May 2000.
3. N. Heintze, "Set Based Program Analysis," Ph.D. thesis, School of Computer Science, Carnegie Mellon University, Oct. 1992.
4. Haruo Hayami and Masashi Katsumata, "Interworkflow: A Challenge for Business-to-Business Electronic Commerce," workflow handbook 2001 published in association with WfMC, pp 145–159.
5. Andrezej Goscinski, "Distributed Operating Systems – The Logical Design," Addison-wesly, pp 533–580, 1991.
6. N.R. Adam, V. Atluri and W. Huang, "Modeling and Analysis of Workflows using Petri Nets," Journal of Intelligent Information Systems, 10(2):pp.131–158, 1998.
7. W.M.P. van der Aalst, "Inter-organizational Workflows: An approach based on Message Sequence Charts and Petri Nets," Systems Analysis - Modelling - Simulation, 34(3):335–367, 1999.
8. E. Kindler, A. Martens and W. Reisig, "Inter-operability of Workflow Applications: Local Criteria for Global Soundness," Business Process Management: Models, Techniques, and Empirical Studies, Lecture Notes in Computer Science 1806 (2000), pp. 235–253. Springer-Verlag, Berlin.
9. P. Grefen, K. Aberer, Y. Hoffner and H. Ludwig, "CrossFlow: Cross-organizational Workflow Management in Dynamic Virtual Enterprise," International Journal of Computer Systems, Science, and Engineering, 15(5):277–290, 2001.
10. A.Lazacano, G. Alonso, H. Schuldt and C. Schuler, "The WISE Approach to Electronic Commerce," International Journal of Computer Systems, Science, and Engineering, 15(5):345–357, 2001.

11. M. Merz, B. Liberman and W. Lamersdorf, "Crossing Organizational Boundaries with Mobile Agents in Electronic Service Markets," Integrated Computer-Aided Enginnering, 6(2):91–104, 1999.
12. F. Casati, P. Grefen, B. Pernici, G. Pozzi and G. Sanchez, "WIDE Workflow Model and Architecture," April 1996; available online at http://dis.sema.es/projects/WIDE/Documents.
13. Minkyu Lee, Dongsoo Han and Jaeyong Shim, "Set-Based Access Conflict Analysis for Structured Workflow Definition Language," Information Processing Letters 80 (2001), Elsevier, pp. 189–194.
14. W.M.P. van der Aalst, A.H.M. ter Hofstede, B. Kiepuszewski and A.P. Barros, "Workflow Patterns," Technical report. Eindhoven University of Technology, 2002. (available at http://tmitwww.tm.tue.nl/research/patterns).
15. R. Taylor, "A general purpose algorithm for analyzing concurrent programs," Communications of the ACM, vol. 26, pp 362–376, May 1983.
16. T. Murata, B. Shenker and S.M. Shatz, "Detection of Ada static deadlocks using petri net invariants," IEEE Transactions on Software engineering, pp 314–326, March 1989.
17. S.P. Masticola and B.G. Ryder, "Static infinite wait anomaly detection in polynomial time," In Proceedings of the 1990 International Conference on Parallel Processing, vol. 2, pp 78–87, 1990.
18. C. Demartini and R. Sisto, "Static analysis of Java multithreaded and distributed applications," In Proceedings of International Symposium on Software Engineering for Parallel and Distributed Systems, pp 215–222, 1998.
19. Jaeyong Shim, Dongsoo Han and Minkyu Lee, "Exception Analysis of Structured Workflow Definition," In Proceedings of the Twentieth IASTED International Conference on Applied Informatics(AI 2002), February 18-21, 2002, Innsbruck, Austria.
20. I. B. Arpinar, U. Halici, S. Arpinar and A. Dogac, "Formalization of workflow and correctness issues in the presence of concurrency," Journal of Parallel and Distributed Databases, Vol. 7, No. 2, April 1999, pp. 199–248.
21. W.M.P. van der Aalst and A. Kumar, "XML Based Schema Definition for Support of Inter-organizational Workflow," Journal of Information Systems Research, 2002
22. Assaf Arkin, "Business Process Modeling Language(BPML)," workfing draft 0.4 of BPMI.org, March 2001.

Web Information Modeling: The Adjunction Space Model

Tosiyasu L. Kunii

Hosei University, Graduate School of Computer and Information Sciences
3-7-2 Kajono-cho, Koganei City Tokyo 184-8584 Japan
tosi@kunii.com
http://www.kunii.com/; http://cis.k.hosei.ac.jp/;
Open Source Institute, Linux Café
Linux Building, 3-13-2 Sotokanda, Chiyoda-ku, Tokyo 101-0021 Japan
linuxcafe@kunii.info; http://www.linux-cafe.jp/;
IT Institute, Kanazawa Institute of Technology
1-15-13 Jingumae, Shibuya-ku, Tokyo 150-0001 Japan

Abstract. The nature of Web information is clarified and modeled as the adjunction space model.. Practical Web information management requires Web information to be modeled in such a way that the model captures the dynamic changes, present the dynamism visually, and validate the results formally. As the mathematical ground of the model, we have adopted algebraic topology, cellular spatial structures in the homotopic framework and adjunction spaces in particular. The results have been applied successfully to typical Web information systems such e-finance and e-manufacturing to validate the advantages of our Web information modeling over the popular relational model, the entity relationship model, UML, and XML.

1 Background: The Nature of Web Information

Web information management systems are emerging as key players in the global society we live. As a matter of fact, the global society has been driven by cyberworlds on the Web. Cyberworlds are types of information worlds created on the Web with or without design [Kunii98]. The major key players of cyberworlds include e-finance that trades a GDP-equivalent a day and e-manufacturing that is transforming industrial production into Web shopping of product components and assembly factories. We can handle the complexity and the growth speed of such cyberworlds only through Web information management systems by processing them instantly as needed.

Owing to the fact the human brain dedicates the majority of the cognitive power to visual information processing, Web information management systems have to incorporate Web information visualization capability as Web graphics [Kunii2000, Kunii2002]. For Web information management systems and Web graphics to be effective to meet the needs, there are numbers of technical barriers requiring innovations beyond what we traditionally practice in database management and computer graphics. We first need to theorize Web information *per se* by modeling it [Kunii99].

S. Bhalla (Ed.): DNIS 2002, LNCS 2544, pp. 58–63, 2002.
© Springer-Verlag Berlin Heidelberg 2002

2   Web Information Modeling: What It Is and What It Is for?

Usually the business of Web information management systems is to manage information on the Web in close interaction with human cognition through information visualization via Web graphics. The business of Web graphics is to project varieties of images on graphics screens for human understanding. Human understanding of displayed images is achieved by linking displayed images in the display space to human cognitive entities in the cognitive space. Often geometrically exact display misleads human cognition by the low priority geometrical shapes that are usually not the essential information in cyberworlds. Web graphics for Web information management has to deliver the essential messages on the screen for immediate human cognition at the speed to match the cyberworld changes [Kunii2002].

Let us take simple examples.

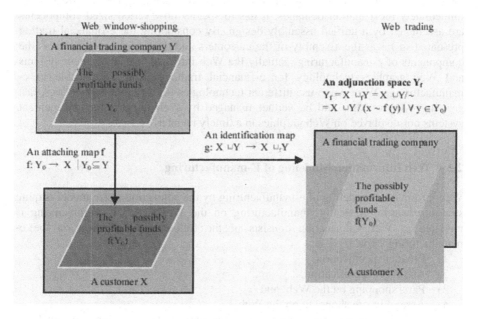

Fig. 1. Financial trading processes on the Web displayed on Web graphics.

2.1   Web Information Modeling of E-finance

Suppose in e-finance a customer X has found the possibly profitable funds Y_0 posted on the Web at the home of a financial trading company Y during Web surfing as we do window-shopping for goodies. It is a Web window-shopping process and since the customer X and the trading company Y do not yet share the funds, X and Y are disjoint as denoted by X⊔Y. Let us also suppose for generality that X and Y are topological spaces. Since the funds Y_0 are a part of the properties of the financial trading company Y, $Y_0 \subseteq Y$ holds. The processes of e-financial trading on the Web as Web trading are represented on Web graphics as illustrated in Figure 1. Then, how the customer X is related to the trading company after the funds are identified for trading? The Web information model we present here precisely represents the relation by an *attaching map* f, and also represents the situation "the funds are identified for trading" as an *adjunction space* of two disjoint topological spaces X (the customer) and Y (the financial trading company), obtained by starting from the customer X and by attaching the financial trading company Y to the customer via a continuous function f by *identifying* each point $y \in Y_0 \mid Y_0 \subseteq Y$ with its image $f(y) \in X$ so that $x \sim f(y) \mid \forall y \in Y_0$. Thus, the *equivalence* denoted by $\sim$ plays the central role in Web information modeling to compose an adjunction space as the *adjunction space model* of Web information.

The adjunction space model illustrated above is quite essential and equally applied to e-manufacturing. It requires the exactly the identical technology to manage and display the e-manufacturing processes. For e-manufacturing to be effective to immediately meet market demands, it has to specify how varied sized components are assembled by a unified assembly design. By considering the e-financial trading presented so far as the assembly of the customers and the trading companies as the components of e-manufacturing, actually the Web information management systems and Web graphics technology for e-financial trading become applicable to e-manufacturing. Were we to use different technologies for different applications, fast growing cyberworlds could be neither managed by Web information management systems nor displayed on Web graphics in a timely manner.

2.2   Web Information Modeling of E-manufacturing

Web information modeling of e-manufacturing by the adjunction space model is quite straightforward. Basically, manufacturing on the Web called e-manufacturing is modeled as Web information consists of the following information on the e-manufacturing steps:

1) Product specification,
2) Assembly specification,
3) Parts shopping on the Web, and
4) Assembly site shopping on the Web.

Each step is decomposed into finer sub steps as needed. For example, the step 1 can be decomposed into:

1.1) Product market survey on the e-market,
1.2) Product requirement derivation from the survey, and
1.3) Product specification to meet the requirements.

The core of the whole Web technology for e-manufacturing is product and assembly modeling on the Web as Web information modeling. It is shown in Figure 2 using a simple assembly case of a chair with just two components of a seat and the support, for clear illustration of the most elementary assembly modeling. In e-manufacturing as an advanced manufacturing, the product components are defined to be modularly replaceable for higher quality components shopping, and also for most effective upgrades and repair.

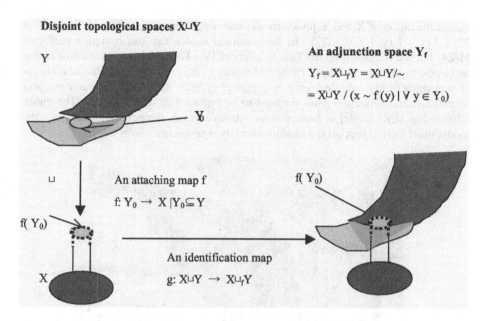

Disjoint topological spaces X⊔Y

Y

An adjunction space Y_f

$Y_f = X \sqcup_f Y = X \sqcup Y / \sim$

$= X \sqcup Y / (x \sim f(y) \mid \forall y \in Y_0)$

Y_0

⊔

An attaching map f

$f: Y_0 \rightarrow X \mid Y_0 \subseteq Y$

$f(Y_0)$

$f(Y_0)$

$f(Y_0)$

X

An identification map

$g: X \sqcup Y \rightarrow X \sqcup_f Y$

An adjunction space of two disjoint topological spaces X and Y, obtained by starting from X and by attaching Y to it via a continuous function f by identifying each point $y \in Y_0 \mid Y_0 \subset Y$ with its image $f(y) \in X$.

Fig. 2. Web information modeling of e-manufacturing: A case of modeling a chair assembly of the seat and the support.

It is clear that e-finance and e-manufacturing share the identical information modeling based on an adjunction space and equivalence.

3 Comparison with the Relational Model, the Entity Relationship Model, UML, and XML

None of the currently popular information models such as the relational model, UML, and XML have the information modularity simply because they are not based on the disjoint unions of information. Hence, modular Web information modeling based on equivalence to identify necessary information does *not* apply to any of them.

Suppose on the Web a company X is searching for a joint venture partner company, say Y. After the successful search, a joint venture (JV) is formed such that $X \sqcup Y / (x \sim f(y) \mid \forall y \in Y_0)$ via an attaching function f An attaching map f where f: $Y_0 \rightarrow X \mid Y_0 \subseteq Y$. $Y_0 \subseteq Y$ is the part of company Y running the JV with the corresponding part $f(Y_0)$ of company X. As a model, this JV model belongs to, and is exactly identical with, the adjunction space model explained so far. Now, let us suppose a company X is searching for a company, say Y, to merge and acquire (M&A) Y. After successful M&A, denoting the part Y_0 of Y ($Y_0 \subseteq Y$) merged to X, we get the union of X and Y joined by the part $Y_0 \subseteq Y$ common to that of Y such that $X \cup Y / (x \sim f(y) \mid \forall y \in Y_0)$. In the relational model, the join operation performs M&A, but the relational model fails to support JV. Union by join in manufacturing makes the product parts irreplaceable and makes it impossible to enjoy the advantages of e-manufacturing. A steel gate in Figure 3 is built by fusing the parts via join operations, and hence the parts are hard to be replaced or interchanged. The entity relationship (ER) model is basically an intuitive graph theoretical model, and the model itself fails to support the identification by equivalence. So is UML.

Fig. 3. A steel gate made by fusing components via join operations.

XML is flexible, born from bibliographic markup language SGML. It consists of nested pairs of brackets, lacking formalisms to validate the ever-expanding and complicated nesting. When the system being constructed becomes very large as usual in any practices, it falls apart by the lack of the formal and hence automated mechanism of validation.

4   Conclusions

The adjunction space model presented here as a Web information model is shown to have advantages of its generality overcoming many shortcomings of existing data models and Web information models. The researches on the implementations are underway quite well. We expect to release a prototype for initial field-testing soon.

Acknowledgements. As the advanced model its researches have been conducted for years by myself single-handed with zero financial or manpower support. The author's thanks go to Professor Subhash Bhalla for his invitation to deliver this at DNIS 2002 as a keynote.

References

[Kunii98] Tosiyasu L. Kunii and Annie Luciani, Eds., "Cyberworlds", Springer-Verlag, 1998.

[Kunii2000] Tosiyasu L. Kunii, "Discovering Cyberworlds", Vision 2000 of the January/February, 2000 issue of IEEE Computer Graphics and Applications, pp. 64-65.

[Kunii99] Tosiyasu L. Kunii and Hideko S. Kunii, "A Cellular Model for Information Systems on the Web – Integrating Local and Global Information –", 1999 International Symposium on Database Applications in Non-Traditional Environments (DANTE'99), November 28-30, 1999, Heian Shrine, Kyoto, Japan, Organized by Research Project on Advanced Databases, in cooperation with Information Processing Society of Japan, ACM Japan, ACM SIGMOD Japan, pp. 19-24, IEEE Computer Society Press, Los Alamitos, California, U. S. A.

[Kunii2002] Tosiyasu L. Kunii, "Cyber Graphics", Proceedings of the First International Symposium on Cyber Worlds (CW2002), November 6-8 2002 Tokyo, Japan, in press, IEEE Computer Society Press, Los Alamitos, California, November 2002.

Advanced Storage and Retrieval of XML Multimedia Documents[1]

Jérôme Godard, Frédéric Andres, and Kinji Ono

National Institute of Informatics,
Hitotsubashi 2-1-2, Chiyoda-ku, Tokyo 101-8430, Japan
jerome@grad.nii.ac.jp
{andres, ono}@nii.ac.jp

Abstract. Multimedia documents are more and more expressed in XML as data representation and exchange services. In this paper, we describe the data and execution models of XML Multimedia Document management as a part of the PHASME information engine. The core data model exploits the Extended Binary Graph structure (so called EBG structure); we present the storage and indexing services. The goals of the on-going project are to tackle the increase of multilingual multimedia documents within the PHASME prototype as key advances to prepare the next generation of information engines.

1 Introduction

In the age of multimedia worldwide web, XML [7] has been created as a meta-language for describing tags and the structural relationships between them. So that richly structured documents could be used over the web. In the past, HTML and SGML were not practical for this purpose. HTML has been created with a set of semantics and does not provide arbitrary structure. SGML has provided arbitrary structure, but has been too difficult to implement just for a web browser. Full SGML systems solved large, complex problems that justify their expense. Viewing structured multimedia documents sent over the web rarely carries such justifications. In order to optimize the storage and to exploit this markup, it has been become important to use an efficient repository for XML multimedia data and related to Metadata.

In this paper, we describe the architecture of the XML support inside the PHASME Information Engine, so called Application Oriented DBMS [4]. PHASME storage units are XML documents inside the core data structure (EBG structure). We base our approach on this EBG structure as it has shown its efficiency in some case studies [3,4] and we seek improvements related to the XML support both at the XML content level and at the XML content management level and the indexing support. XML content includes the structural information and the values.

[1] This research project is supported by the National Science Foundation (grant n° 9905603) and the Japanese Ministry of Education, Culture, Sports, Science and Technology (grant n° 13480108).

S. Bhalla (Ed.): DNIS 2002, LNCS 2544, pp. 64-73, 2002.

Figure 1 shows an XML multimedia document, which describes a fragment of inventory related to the Silk Road, alongside its associated syntax tree; both representations present equivalent structural properties. We simplified the syntax tree avoiding the cdata nodes. Furthermore, each node has an OID assignment (noted OID(value); e.g. OID0 for the node "inventory").

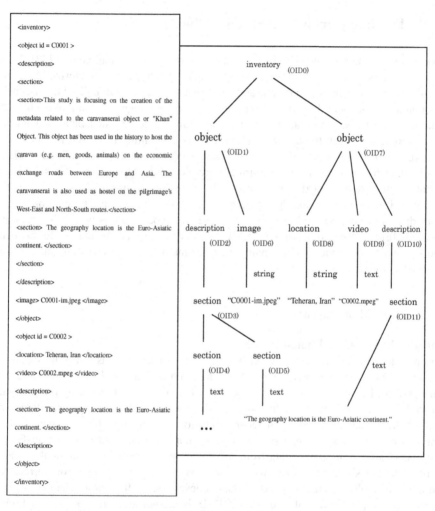

Fig. 1. XML Example

According to this equivalence, we are concerned in this paper with providing effective XML management tools. We describe the architecture of the XML support inside the PHASME Information engine. Our approach is innovative by two features. Firstly, the EBG storage processing does not require any related XML schema or any related DTDs. Secondly, it reduces the volume of stored data. An EBG structure enables to share common parts of documents between multimedia documents that are stored only once.

The remainder of this paper is organized as follows: Section 2 discusses related works. In Section 3, we describe the XML support in the PHASME Information Engine and present initial qualitative assessments related to this approach. Our conclusions are contained in Section 4.

2   XML Management and States of the Art

There are two main kinds of XML files: data-centric and document-centric [22]. Data-centric documents are using XML as a data transport. They are characterized by fairly regular structure, fine-grained data and little or no mixed content. Document-centric documents are usually documents that are designed for human consumption. They are characterized by less regular or irregular structure, larger grained data, and lots of mixed content. In fact, the document-centric view is resulting from SGML. As a general rule, data type is stored in a traditional database, such as a relational, object-oriented, or hierarchical database. Furthermore, document type can be also stored in a *native* XML database (a database designed especially for storing XML). But in the real world, with complex and heterogeneous XML files such as multimedia ones, it is very difficult to define the limit between those two types. That is why it is necessary to use hybrid systems to manipulate XML in order to keep its advantages. In this part, we will give an overview of the main and more interesting ways to store and retrieve XML documents.

2.1   Storage Management

Storing data in a Traditional DBMS
In order to transfer data between XML documents and a database, it is necessary to map the XML document structure (DTD, XML Schema) to the database schema. The structure of the document must exactly match the structure expected by the mapping procedure. Since this is rarely the case, products that use this strategy are often used with XSLT. That is, before transferring data to the database, the document is first transformed to the structure expected by the mapping; the data is then transferred. Similarly, after transferring data from the database, the resulting document is transformed to the structure needed by the application. A way to move or correct the structure of multilingual lexical XML data is described in [9]. One of the main weaknesses that imply the use of traditional DBMS is the waste of memory space. Implementation done in [14] shows that from 7,65 MB of XML documents, it requires 11,42 MB as a table-based structure; which is 50% more.

Storing data in a native XML database
It is valuable when the data is semi-structured, i.e. has a regular structure. As a result, mapping it to a relational database results in either a large number of columns with null values (which wastes space) or a large number of tables (which is inefficient). A

second reason not to use traditional DBMS is retrieval speed. Some storage strategies used by native XML databases store entire documents together physically or use physical (rather than logical) pointers between the parts of the document. This allows the documents to be retrieved either without joins or with physical joins, both of which are faster than the logical joins used by relational databases. For example, an entire document might be stored in a single place on the disk, so retrieving it or a fragment of it requires a single index lookup and a single read to retrieve the data. A relational database would require several index lookups and at least as many reads to retrieve the data. Speed is increased only when retrieving data in the order it is stored on disk. Retrieving a different view of the data will probably bring worse performance than in a relational database.

In [23], .the storage management is done through an offset space, which is an address space in secondary memory. This is an efficient way to store structures such as trees and avoids using multiple relations. An offset space is very similar to a main memory space and offers the same characteristics than UNIX file system does. We must here point out that this approach has been used from the beginning in the Phasme project [1]. Another problem with storing data in a native XML database is that most native XML databases can only return the data as XML. We must point out that using version control systems such as CVS brings the possibility to have simple transaction management.

Encoding problems

By definition, an XML document can contain any Unicode character except some of the control characters. Unfortunately, many databases offer limited or no support for Unicode and require special configuration to handle non-ASCII characters. If data contain non-ASCII characters, it has to be ensured that database and data transfer software handle these characters. A cleaning process is very often needed to make pure Unicode files. As an example, a rigorous strategy is described in [9] in the case of multilingual lexical data contained in XML files.

2.2 Retrieval Management

Indexing Issues

There are many ways to index XML document in order to use their content in a database. [15] gives an overview of two parts of XRS-II (XML Retrieval System) architecture: database search and full-text search engine. The text retrieval is performed with indexes based on term frequencies and siblings; it uses BUS (Bottom-Up Scheme) technique to index and retrieve full text. But in that case, the query must be very precise and respect the attributes definition because the database search engine manages only exact matching. Another method is described in [14]; the authors use path-based indexing to move out the tree structure into a relational table-based structure. They add to each node "regional" data that consist in some parameters defined by the position in the tree and their hierarchy. In that case, database schemas for storing XML documents are independent of the XML files structure (DTD or schema). So it makes it possible to add any kind of well-formed XML file to the database. Because of the decomposition into fixed tables, DBMS index structures can be used (e.g. B+ trees, R trees). We have to underline here XPath [20] that offers some strong and well-defined opportunities to describe XML documents without dealing directly with a tree structure.

Query languages Issues

Query languages dealing with XML are getting more complicated because they have to mix declarative and navigational features. In fact, queries are not necessary generic (i.e. a query answer does not only depend on the logical level of the data) as the separation of the logical and physical levels is not ensured with the various uses of XML. Another aspect brings some challenges: XML is ordered. It induces to fill the lack of order within database systems as it is explained in [19]. Many proposals have been done for XML query languages [6]; we shortly present the current leading solutions. XSLT allows users to transform documents to the structure dictated by the model before transferring data to the database, as well as the reverse. Because XSLT processing can be expensive, some products also integrate a limited number of transformations into their mappings. The long-term solution to this problem is the implementation of query languages that return XML, since the output has to be expressed as a tree. Currently, most of these languages rely on SELECT statements embedded in templates. This situation is expected to change when XQuery is finalized, as major database vendors are already working on implementations. Unfortunately, almost all of XML query languages (including XQuery 1.0) are read-only, so different means will be needed to insert, update, and delete data in the near term. (in the long term, XQuery will add these capabilities).

2.3 Mixed Approach: Hybrid System

Since most of data become more and more complex and heterogeneous (especially in the multimedia area), it seems interesting to mix both storing approaches described above. First, the major reason is the storing constraints (memory space, access time, declustering...), and secondly it enables to use efficient retrieving methods (indexing, query management...). In the case of a hybrid system (this the name commonly used to describe the mixed approach), it is first necessary to look at the physical organization used to store the data. [11] introduces a hybrid system called Natix that has a physical record manager that is in charge of the disk memory management and buffering. Of course, it uses a tree data model. Then it handles methods to dynamically maintain the physical structure. [15] describes how XML documents can be indexed and how the text retrieval process can be improved with the use of a mixed storage model: attributes are stored in a DBMS and the element contents and their indices are saved in files. It seems this hybrid approach is a good trade-off between performance and cost in indexing and retrieval.

3   XML Support in PHASME Information Engine

The PHASME architecture is provided in Figure 2. XML is supported under the XML plug-ins service including the document management functions (creation, manipulation, suppression, indexing). The core of the system is the execution reactor, which mediates the requests coming from external applications (XSQL query or direct document manipulation). The document-type support includes the meta-data [16] associated to each document. PHASME is being extended to support DTDs and XML Schema. The latter support will allow mapping directly XML representation information such as structural properties of documents into Extended Binary Graphs. All the vertical XML support depends heavily on the many-sorted algebra that defines XML manipulation functions. For this reason, a plug-ins defines a set of functions based on the PHASME Internal Language. A major goal in this project is to extend PHASME customizability to XML support and to optimize the implementation of such an XML support plug-ins.

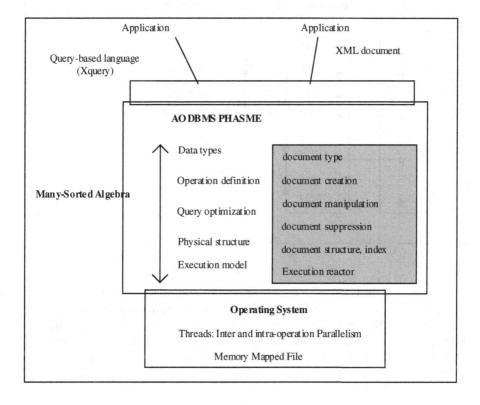

Fig. 2. XML Support inside PHASME Engine

3.1 PHASME XML Support

The PHASME storage is based on the Extended Binary Graph (EBG structure). The EBG structure is a combination of three concepts DSM [18], DBgraph [17], and GDM [12]. It ensures a compact data structure to maximize the probability that the hot data set fits in main memory.

Figure 3 shows how XML data are stored as EBGs (e.g. EBG_1, EBG_2). The left column is referred as *source*, the right column as *destination*. An EBG is a set of non-oriented arcs between items that are either oids or values. EBGs contain either fixed-size item values or variable-size item values. Each value is stored only once so data values are shared between oids when values belong to at least two different objects (e.g. OID5 and OID11 share the same value). Here, we do not include the description of the tag set for the values them-selves. The semantic tagging issues are tackled under the Linguistic DS cooperation [10].

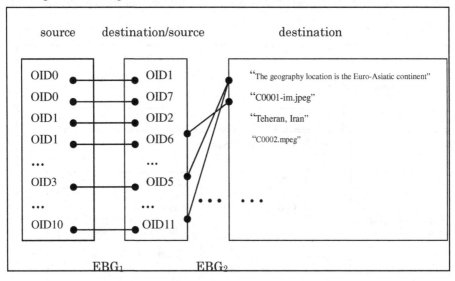

Fig. 3. Extended Binary Graph Support

Persistency is managed in an orthogonal way from the data structure point of view. So in our case, any persistent index or persistent data structures are stored directly inside EBGs. EBGs map the graph contents of documents into the main-memory. PHASME uses the mmap file mechanism, which enables to have the same data image on disks and in memory. This mapping enables to tune the granularity of the retrieval mechanism.

3.2 Execution Model

PHASME query processor includes a dynamic query optimization and execution optimization at run-time as it has been described in [5]. PHASME processing is based on the many-sorted algebra approach for query processing and optimization processing directly applied on the EBG structures. It gives a high performance layer that is customizable accordingly to workloads and to users. W3C XML algebra [21] is one issue of improvement for our system. Here, we omit a technical presentation of the EBG query processing and refer the interested reader to [4] for a comprehensive overview.

3.3 Indexing Support

The PHASME XML Indexing is based on the EBG structure. The indexing mechanisms are those available in PHASME as plug-ins, so it gives a set of indexing mechanisms and strategies available according to the characteristics of the XML contents. Indexing support follows the EBG structure's fast access. It includes the support of multi-dimension indexing such as SR-TREE [2] or signature file indexing [1]. We intend to extend the indexing to support UBTREE [13] and to improve this indexing accelerator according to EBG features. Though indexing processing in the context of EBGs is different from traditional model for XML support, it enables to tune and to customize the usage of indexing strategies according to the XML-based application requirements and workloads. The tuning/customization issue is another key point to be addressed by this project where the knowledge and the environment mining processing are two relevant domains to be investigated.

3.4 Qualitative Assessments

XML document processing can be processed either in a pipeline-based way or in a set-based way. This section will compare the alternatives. We assume that intermediate results of document querying cannot fit in memory.

Definition:
An EBG is graph G(X,A) where X= (S,D) is the set of vertices of G, A is the set of edges of G; S is the Source set and D the Destination set. The Edge (s, d, S.k) $\in$ A iff s $\in$ S, d $\in$ D, and $s_{S.k}$ = d where S.k represents the kth item of the Source set. $s_{S.k}$ corresponds to the value in the Destination set.

Processing Complexity: complex data operations are often expressed by composition of traversal operations to optimize the data access in the EBG structure. Also it has been demonstrated in [8] that pipeline-based and set-based processing strategies are equivalent for graph-based operations. Depth-first search inside the EBG has a complexity of $O(max(card(X), card(A)))$ which is similar to breast-first search complexity equal to $O(card(A))$. The processing strategies are chosen according to the index support and to the management of intermediate results. Intermediate results are inside PHASME, either materialized or either transferred in pipeline. The main advantages of the materialization are to exploit share common results and to optimize multiple accesses to the XML document set. Multi-query optimization issue is often seen as a

NP-hard problem so heuristics are necessary. This issue will be the object of a specific investigation in the context of XML document set.

4 Conclusions

In this paper, we presented the data model and the execution model of the PHASME engine for XML multimedia documents efficient processing. We showed the core of the approach, the mapping between the XML document multimedia and the Extended Binary Graph (EBG structure). We highlighted two main issues related to our research: tuning/customization and multiquery optimization. Moreover, we expect to provide a better understanding of XML processing in the context of main-memory information engine, storage and indexing. Finally, the prototype will give the opportunity of performance benchmarking in a very large scale XML data set. We will focus as future works on multi-dimensional indexing of XML multimedia documents and multilingual support. This research and project cooperate within the Digital Silk Road Initiative of UNESCO.

References

1. Andres, F., Boulos, J., Ono, K.: Accessing Active Application-oriented DBMS from the World Wide Web. In Int'l Symp. on Cooperative Database Systems for Advanced Applications, pp 232-234, Dec 1996
2. Andres, F., Dessaigne, N., Ono, K., Satoh, S.: Toward The MediaSys Video Search Engine (MEVISE). In Proc. of 5th IFIP 2.6 Working Conference on Visual Database Systems (VDB5), pp. 31-44, Fukuoka - Japan, May 10-12, 2000
3. Andres, F., Kawtrakul, A., and al.: NLP Techniques and AHYDS Architecture for Efficient Document Retrieval System. Proc. of NLPPRS'99, 5th Natural Language Processing Pacific Rim Symposium, Beijing, China, November 5-7, 1999
4. Andres, F., Ono, K.: Phasme: A High Performance Parallel Application-oriented DBMS. Informatica Journal, Special Issue on Parallel and Distributed Database Systems, Vol.22, pp. 167-177 May, 1998
5. Andres, F., Ono, K.: The Distributed Management Mechanism of the Active Hypermedia Delivery System platform. In Trans. on IEICE. VolE84-D, No.8, pp.1033-1038, August, 2001
6. Bonifati, A., Ceri, S.: Comparative Analysis of Five XML Query Languages. ACM SIGMOD Record, 29(1), pp. 68-79, March 2000
7. Bray, T., Paoli, J., Sperberg-McQueen, C.M.: Extensible Markup Language (XML) 1.0. [http://www.w3.org/TR/REC-xml]
8. Gibbans, A.: Algorithmic Graph Theory. Cambridge University Press, Ltd, 1985
9. Godard, J., Mangeot-Lerebours, M., Andrès, F.: Data Repository Organization and Recuperation Process for Multilingual Lexical Databases. Proc. of SNLP-Oriental COCOSDA 2002, pp. 249-254 , Hua Hin, Prachuapkirikhan, Thailand, 9-11 May 2002

10. Hashida, K., Andres, F., Boitet, C., Calzolari, N., Declerck, T., Fotouhi, F., Grosky, W., Ishizaki, S., Kawtrakul, A., Lafourcade, M., Nagao, K., Riza, H., Sornlertlamvanich, V., Zajac, R., Zampolli, A.: Linguistic DS, ISO/IEC JTC1/SC29/WG11, MPEG2001/M7818
11. Kanne, C., Moerkotte, G.: Efficient storage of XML data, Proc. of 16th International Conference on Data Engineering (ICDE) , page 198, San Diego, California, February 28 - March 03, 2000
12. Kunii, H.S.: Graph Data Model and its Data Language. 1990
13. Ramsak, F., Markl, V., Fenk, R., Zirkel, M., Elhardt, K., Bayer, R.: Integrating the UB-Tree into a Database System Kernel. In Proc. of VLDB Conf. 2000, Cairo, Egypt, 2000
14. Shimura, T.,. Yoshikawa, M, Uemura, S.: Storage and Retrieval of XML Documents using Object-Relational Databases. Proc. of the 10th International Conference on Database and Expert Systems Applications (DEXA'99), Lecture Notes in Computer Science, Vol. 1677, Springer-Verlag, pp. 206-217, August-September 1999
15. Shin, D.: XML Indexing and Retrieval with a Hybrid Storage Model. Knowledge and Information Systems, 3, Springer-Verlag, pp. 252-261, 2001
16. The Dublin Core Metadata Initiative, [http://dublincore.org]
17. Thevenin, J.M.: Architecture d'un Systeme de Gestion de Bases de Donnees Grande Memoire, Ph.D. Thesis of Paris VI University, 1989
18. Valduriez, P., Khoshafian, S., Copeland, G.: Implementations techniques of Complex Objects. In Proc. of the International Conference of VLDB, pp 101-110, Kyoto, Japan, 1986
19. Vianu, V.: A Web Odyssey: from Codd to XML. In Proc. of the ACM Symposium on Principles of Database Systems (PODS), 2001
20. W3C (1999): XML Path Language (XPath) [www.w3.org/TR/xpath]
21. W3C XML algebra [http://www.w3.org/TR/query-algebra/]
22. XMLdev [http://www.xml.org/xml/xmldev.shtml]
23. Yamane, Y., Igata, N., Namba, I.: High-performance XML Storage/Retrieval System. Fujitsu Sci. Tech. J., 36, 2, pp. 185-192, December 2000

A New Query Processing Scheme in a Web Data Engine⋆

Zhiqiang Zhang[1], Chunxiao Xing[2], Lizhu Zhou[2], and Jianhua Feng[2]

[1] Department of Computer Science and Technology
Tsinghua University, 100084, Beijing China
zqzhang99@mails.tsinghua.edu.cn
[2] Department of Computer Science and Technology
Tsinghua University, 100084, Beijing China
{xingcx, dcszlz, fengjh}@tsinghua.edu.cn

Abstract. The explosion of information on the web turns the search for interested information from the web into a great challenge. In this paper, we present a system called Web Data Engine-SESQ (**S**earch **E**xtract **S**tore **Q**uery) that is designed to solve this problem by integrating database techniques with search engine techniques. In contrast with traditional database systems and searching engines, SESQ is different in data model, query expression, data storage schema and the use of index.

1 Introduction

Nowadays finding relevant information from the World Wide Web (WWW) is often frustrating. Help from commonly used search engines in finding information from the web is very much limited by following facts: (1) many of the results returned from search engine are irrelevant to the decision problem, (2) results from search engines are just document's URLs. To get interested information, users have to follow these URLs and browse manually, and (3) the search condition expression is too simple to express reasonable complex requests. To address these problems, we have developed an ontology-based Web data engine, SESQ, which integrates both search engine and database techniques to support more complex search requests and get more precise results. Given a domain specified by an ontology, SESQ can (1) search the Web to find relevant web pages, (2) extract information from the web pages based on the ontology, (3) store the extracted information in a local database, and (4) provide query facilities to support the retrieval of semantically related information with rather complex query conditions. The novel features of SESQ include:

- The ability of identifying relevant data sources based on the given domain ontology.

⋆ This work was supported by National Grand Fundamental Research 973 Program of China under Grant No.1998030414.

S. Bhalla (Ed.): DNIS 2002, LNCS 2544, pp. 74–87, 2002.

- The ability of extracting data from various sources, such as HTML pages, XML documents, traditional databases, etc., encapsulating them into data objects, and storing them in local storage as a materialized view of the Web.
- A powerful visual query interface helping user to construct queries involving complex relationships among data objects.
- The ability of processing such complex queries.

In this paper, we introduce the query processing method of SESQ system. In contrast with search engine and traditional database system, SESQ is different in the aspects of the modeling of Web data [18], query expression, data storage schema, and indexing. These differences are reflected in query processing steps, basic data operation semantics, and their implementations. The remainder of the paper is organized as follows. Section 2 gives an overview of the SESQ system. Section 3 presents the method for modeling the Web data in SESQ. Section 4 describes the query expressing approach. Section 5 discusses the query processing method. Finally, in section 6 we conclude the paper with comparison of related works and discussions on future work.

2   System Overview

As shown in Figure 1, SESQ consists of five major parts: Web Data Searching Crawler (A), Information Extraction (B), Basic Data Storage Management (C), Query Processing (D), and Personal and Active Services Provider (E). The system works as follows.

User first manually enters some URLs of documents of interests. Those documents are used as training samples by extracting keyword using traditional information retrieval methods. Those keywords are sent to search engines, such as Yahoo, Google, etc. Among the returned URLs, those with higher rankings are identified as documents of interests.

The Information Extractor extracts data from retrieved documents. For semi-structured data, such as HTML, XML etc., a tool is used to train the extractor to recognize information of interests, and generate extraction rules for the Information Extractor to extract data from the source documents. The schema defined in ontology and vocabulary are used to name the data elements and encapsulate them into data instances.

Data instances obtained from this process are given unique ID, and stored locally. A basic storage manager manages these data instances. An index manager provides direct access to data instances based on give values of concepts. Since the current focus of SESQ is on using ontology, data management functions are relatively simple. User queries are issued against the local copy of the data, and processed by the query processor using optimized query execution plans. Finally, the Result Generator returns the result to user with personal manner provided by the Personal and Active Services Provider.

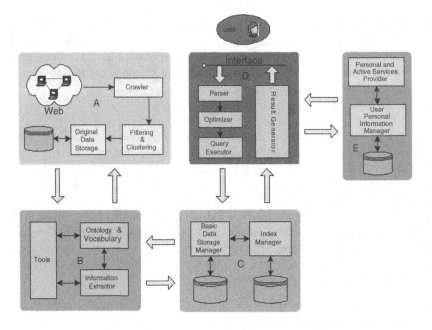

Fig. 1. The Architecture of the SESQ System

3   Domain Ontology and Conceptual Schema

In general, it is not easy to model the Web data and their relationships because (a) The dynamic nature of the Web data results in the complexity of the concept relationships. (b) It is not easy to capture the diverse complex relationships from original data sources, and (c) The property information about a concept from real data sources may be different. SESQ is intended to overcome the difficulties by introducing a simple and flexible method that uses domain ontology to model the domain at the abstract level and uses concept schema to describe the data extracted from the Web [18].

In SESQ, data objects are organized in a concept schema. Figure 2 depicts such a concept schema constructed for the domain of research papers. The given ontology on a domain defines a set of simple concepts: PAPER, RESEARCHER, JOURNAL, CONFERENCE, and UNIVERSITY denoted by rounded rectangle. In addition, there are thirteen atomic concepts, denoted by ellipse. Note an edge between an atomic concept and a simple concept indicates that the atomic concept is an attribute of the simple concept. For example, the attribute edge, (PaperTitle, PAPER), means atomic concept PaperTitle is an attribute of simple concept PAPER. A labeled edge between two simple concepts, such as [PaperDerivation, ConferenceName] represents the semantic relationship among two simple concepts 'the paper was presented at the conference'. Such as an edge is called Relationship edge.

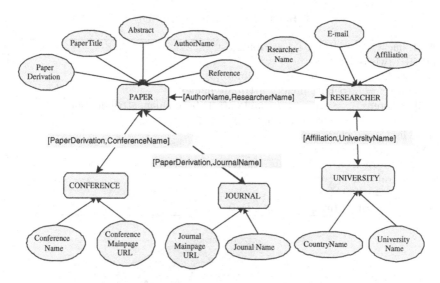

Fig. 2. The Concept Schema Example of Research Paper Domain

Observe that, relationship edge is represented by two attributes of the two participating simple concepts. They are derived from the semantic information specified in the ontology. Such semantic information includes the Semantic Inheritance Rules (SIR), which specify the concepts semantics hierarchy, the Object Property Descriptions (OPD), which define the attributes of concepts, and the Semantics Information Pairs (SIP) about attributes, which illuminate the semantic information of the attribute. Algorithms have been developed to construct the concept schema from given domain ontology [18].

4   Query Expressing

For easily expressing query requests and capturing the user query intent, we design a query method and a user-friendly visual interface. Users express their query requests with the query language CSQL(**C**onceptual **S**tructure **Q**uery **L**anguage) over the tree view schema which is simplified from the concept schema. User can design the tree view schema according to their query requests. CSQL is similar USQL [4]. Informally, the grammar of CSQL was shown in Table 1.

Following **Query1** and **Query2** of Figure 3 are expressed over the Tree view 1 and Tree view 2 respectively. To query the all information about a simple concept, the user could directly use the simple concept's name in SELECT clause. In following examples, we omit the relationship edge label pair in WHERE clause.

Query 1: *Please find the paper delivered on the conference VLDB*
　　SELECT PAPER
　　WHERE PAPER.CONFERENCE.ConferenceName = "VLDB"

Table 1. The Grammar of CSQL

⟨CSQL query⟩ :: = SELECT ⟨ attribute list ⟩
[WHERE ⟨where list⟩]
⟨attribute list⟩ :: = ⟨attribute⟩[, ⟨attribute⟩]*
⟨attribute⟩ :: = ⟨attribute prefix⟩.⟨attribute name⟩
⟨attribute prefix⟩ :: = ⟨concept variable⟩[.(attribute name, attribute name)
                                    ⟨concept variable⟩]*
⟨where list⟩ :: = ⟨where expression⟩
[⟨AND-OR⟩⟨where expression⟩]*
⟨where expression⟩ :: = ⟨attribute⟩⟨op⟩⟨compare value⟩
⟨compare value⟩ :: = ⟨value⟩
⟨op⟩ ::=⊇ | = | < | ≤ | > | ≥ |
⟨value⟩ :: = String | Integer | Float | Date

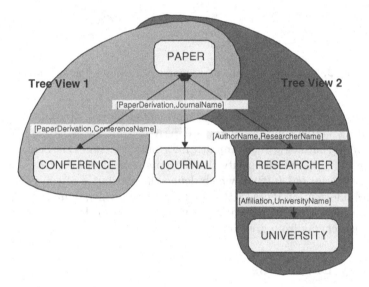

Fig. 3. The Tree Views

Query 2: *Please find the paper written by the author from a university in USA*
　　SELECT PAPER
　　WHERE PAPER.RESEARCHER.UNIVERSITY.CountryName= "USA"

5 Query Processing

In this section, we introduce the basic query processing scheme of SESQ system. We first describe the main data operations, and then describe the data storage manager and the logical index structure. And at the end, we give the main query processing steps.

5.1   Main Data Operations

SESQ supports three main operations, *Select operation*, *Project operation* and *Join operation* like relational database. Just as we mentioned in [18], in general, we view the attributes as multi-value attributes, as compared with the relational database, these operations have some different semantics.

Select Operation. *Select* allows us to choose the data in a simple concept instances. Considering the instances of the simple concept EMPLOYEE, suppose *Position* is an attribute of EMPLOYEE. In reality, one person often has more than one position, e.g. Mike is the 'Vice Board Chairman' and the 'General Manager' of the company. Let $V=\{a_1, a_2, ..., a_{|V|}\}$ is the value set of an employee's attribute *Position*. If we want to find the employee who has the title 'General Manager', we can express this query as follows,

$$\sigma_{\exists i(a_i='GeneralManager')}(EMPLOYEE), \text{ where } a_i \in V \ (i = 1, ..., |V|)$$

The selection operator σ specifies the matching condition. In general, this selection condition is very similar to the WHERE clause of SQL SELECT. For example, let *Name* be another attribute of EMPLOYEE and an employee only has one name. If we want to find the employee whose name contains string 'Brown', we can express this query as

$$\sigma_{(Name \supseteq 'Brown')}(EMPLOYEE)$$

Project Operation. The projection operator Π allows us to extract attributes of a simple concept. For example, we can find out all the *Name* and *Position* by using Π operation. The following expression

$$\Pi_{(Name, Position)}(EMPLOYEE)$$

will be evaluated over the EMPLOYEE instances. One possible returning result is {Mike, {Vice Board Chairman, General Manager}}.

Join Operation. Since the attributes are multi-values, the Join operation is more complex than relational database. Suppose *C1* and *C2* are two simple concepts, *a* and *b* are the associated attributes of *C1* and *C2* respectively. The value set of *C1.a* is $A=\{a_1, a_2, ..., a_{|A|}\}$; The value set of *C2.b* is $B=\{b_1, b_2, ..., b_{|B|}\}$. The equal join operation can be expressed as follows,

$$C1 \bowtie_{\exists i,j(a_i=b_j)} C2, \text{ where } a_i \in A, \ b_j \in B, (i = 1, ..., |A|; j = 1, ..., |B|)$$

The Join Algorithm. The semantics of join operation in SESQ system is more complex than the join operation in relational database. Here is the simple description of the equal join algorithm. Let *C1* and *C2* be two simple concepts, and *a* and *b* are the associated attributes of *C1* and *C2*.

Input: The instance ID set ID_{C1} and ID_{C2} of concepts $C1$ and $C2$ respectively.

Output: Result file.

1. First, estimate the size of $|ID_{C1}|$ and $|ID_{C2}|$, suppose $|ID_{C1}| > |ID_{C2}|$.
2. Find the $C1$ instances from the basic storage manager with instances ID set ID_{C1}, say a instance j ($j=1,...,|ID_{C1}|$), project the attribute a of instance j, and get the attribute value set $V(a)=\{a_k \mid k=1,...,|V(a)|\}$. For each value a_k in $V(a)$, use the index on attribute b to get the $C2$ instance IDs, these instances satisfy the join condition, $\bowtie_{\exists i(a_k=b_i)}$, where b_i is one member of attribute b value set $V(b)=\{b_i \mid i=1,...,|V(b)|\}$. Let this $C2$ instance ID set be $ID2_k$, then for the instance j of $C1$, get a corresponding instance ID set of $C2$,

$$RESULT_j = \bigcup_{k=1}^{|V(a)|} ID2_k$$

3. Join the $C1$ instance j with every $C2$ instance in $RESULT_j$, and put the join result into the result file.
4. End the loop until the $C1$ instance ID set ID_{C1} is empty.

5.2   Index Manager and Basic Data Storage Manager

At present, we choose the full-text index as the basic index in SESQ system. With the development of Semantic Web, there will emerge more and more data types. Other indexes, such as HASH index will be introduced. In contrast with search engines, SESQ establishes an index family, rather than a big general index. Figure 4 shows the logical index structure of research paper domain. Formally, there is an index on every attribute. This is different from database systems. The Index Manager accessing interface is shown in Figure 5. Taking the query constraint 4-tuple {*simple concept name, attribute name, operator, constraint value*} as its input, the index manager would return the instance IDs that satisfy the query constraints.

In SESQ, a basic storage manager manages simple concept data instances. The logical access unit is the data instance. SESQ creates an ID for every data instance when it is extracted. The access interface of this storage manager, shown in Figure 6, is very simple, only by instance ID. Query Plan Executor sends the instance ID to Storage Manager, and Storage Manager returns the required data instances.

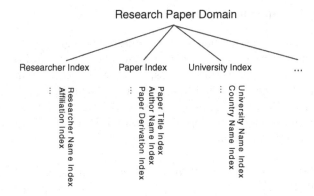

Fig. 4. Logical Index Structure of the Research Paper Domain

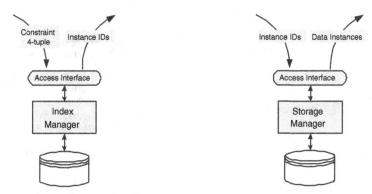

Fig. 5. Index Manager   **Fig. 6.** Data Storage Manager

5.3   Query Processing Steps

SESQ processes queries in following steps:

- First, for the query statements, it creates a preliminary operation tree. For example, for the **Query2** in section 4, its preliminary operation tree is shown in Figure 7.
- Second, prune the preliminary operation tree.
- Third, transform the operation tree, and further prune it.
- Fourth, pass the pruned operation tree to the query optimizer, then get a better query execution plan.
- At last, Query Plan Executor executes the query and returns the results.

Similar ideas with relational database [15] are adopted in step 4 and 5, such as, join ordering, and cost estimation of data operation etc. to further optimize the query execution plan.

5.4   Prune the Operation Tree

In SESQ, users can express their query requests through a friendly interface. They can use the mouse to design the tree view schema, and add the constraints on the relevant attributes. In this process, user can express a same query in different manners. For the example of **Query1** in section 4, the constraint is added on the attribute *ConferenceName* of CONFERENCE. The user can also add the constraint on the attribute *PaperDerivation* of PAPER. These two manners have the same query semantics.

Query 1': *Please find the paper delivered on the conference VLDB*
  SELECT PAPER
  WHERE PAPER.PaperDerivation = "VLDB"

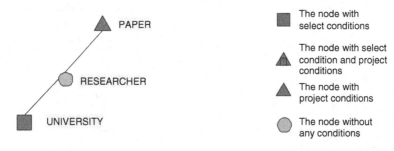

Fig. 7. The Preliminary Operation Tree of Query 2

Fig. 8. The Figure Notations

The pruning of the operation tree is performed in following steps.

First, for each attribute with the constraints, if the constraint is not on leaf nodes of the tree, and there are children nodes associated with this node through this attribute, or it is associated with the parent node through this attribute, then we could move the constraints to the son nodes or the parent node on their corresponding attributes. For example, there is a constraint on the attribute *Att* of node A in the operation tree in Figure 9(a), and it is associated with the son node B through the attribute *Att*. Hence, we can put the same constraint on the corresponding attribute of node B. This is shown in Figure 9(b). (Figure 8 gives the notations of the figures 7,9,10.)

Second, we need to estimate if all the constraints and nodes could make contribution to the query result. For example, in Figure 10(a), there is a constraint on an attribute of node A. And B is the correspondingly associated child node of A. If there is no any attributes of A in the SELECT clause, namely, users do not want to search the information of A, after moving down the constraint to node B, we could delete node A from the operation tree. This is shown in Figure 10(b).

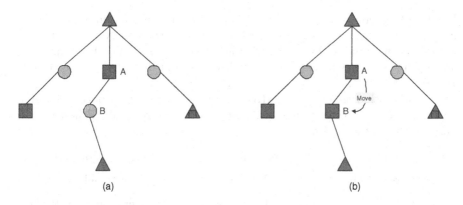

(a)   (b)

Fig. 9. Pruning Operation Tree Example 1

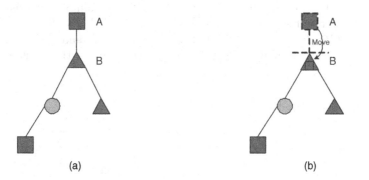

(a)   (b)

Fig. 10. Pruning Operation Tree Example 2

5.5   Transform the Operation Tree

In general, different data sources could include different parts of information
about same simple concept. For example, from data source A, we might get
the data about *ResearcherName* and *E-Mail* of RESEARCHER, and from data
source B, we might get the data about *ResearcherName* and *Affiliation* of RE-
SEARCHER. If we simply combine these data into a unified storage schema,
then there will be too many Null values in the stored data. To avoid this situation, we organize the data about same simple concept into more parts. Each
part has an Underlying Schema. We use the P_i to denote the schema of part i
or the i_{th} part, where $i=(1,...,m)$, when there is no confusion.

In general, one simple concept could have one or more than one parts. Let
$P_1,P_2,...,P_m$ be the parts of simple concept B, $INSTANCE(P_i)$ be the instance
set of part P_i, where $INSTANCE(P_i) \cap INSTANCE(P_j) = \emptyset$ ($i \neq j$, $i,j=1,...,m$).
$C_1,C_2,...,C_n$ be the child nodes of B, and A be the parents node of B in the
operation tree (See Figure 11).

$S(C_i)=\{P_j \mid P_j$ has the attribute that associates B with $C_i\}$, where
$i=(1,...,n)$, $(j=1,...,m)$, and $S(A)=\{P_j \mid P_j$ has the attribute that associates

B with A}, where $j=(1,...,m)$. $S(CON)=\{P_j \mid P_j$ has the attribute which occurs in constraint $CON\}$, where $j=(1,...,m)$, for example, the **Query 1'** in section 5.4, there is a constraint $CON=:$ PAPER.PaperDerivation = "VLDB". Suppose P_1 and P_2 are two parts of simple concept PAPER, and they all have the attribute *PaperDerivation*, then $S(CON)=\{P_1, P_2\}$.

The operation tree can be further optimized from top to bottom by eliminating those parts that do not contribute to the query result. Following steps perform this optimization.

- First, find the connectible path from A to C_1, C_2,...,C_n. For getting this goal, we get the set $\left(\bigcup_{i=1}^{n} S(Ci)\right) \cap (S(A)) = S_M$, and the elements in set $\{\{P_1, P_2, ..., P_m\} - S_M\}$ will be deleted from the operation tree. If all the elements of one $S(C_i)$ are deleted, then delete the sub-tree with the root node C_i from the operation tree. Figure 12 shown an example. In this example B have five parts, and set $S(A)=\{P_1, P_2, P_3, P_4\}$ and $S(C_1)=\{P_1, P_2\}$, $S(C_2)=\{P_2, P_3\}$, $S(C_3)=\{P_3, P_4\}$, $S(C_4)=\{P_4, P_5\}$, and $S_M=\{P_1, P_2, P_3, P_4\}$. It is clear that part P_5 makes no contribution to the query result. So P_5 is deleted.

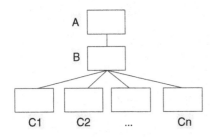

Fig. 11. The General Operation Tree

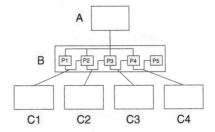

Fig. 12. One Example Tree

- Second, determine which parts are satisfied with the constraints on B. Suppose there are k constraints on B, CON_1, CON_2,..., CON_k. SESQ will evaluate following equation,

$$S(CONSTRAINT) = S(CON_1) \; op \; S(CON_2) \; op \; \cdots \; op \; S(CON_k) \quad (1)$$

Where op is the set operator $\cap$ or $\cup$.

If the $S(CONSTRAINT)$ is empty, then stop and return NULL. Otherwise, continue to evaluate the set $S(CONSTRAINT) \cap S_M$ and delete the elements in set $S_M - S(CONST RAINT)$. If all the elements of an $S(C_i)$ are deleted, then delete the sub-tree with root node C_i. If there is no constraint on B, then skip this step.

The operator op of equation (1) can be determined by following rule.

"For all the constraints with prefix 'WHERE' and 'AND', choose $\cap$, and for all the constraints with prefix 'OR', choose $\cup$"

For example, suppose there are two constraints CON_1 and CON_2 on B, $S(CON_1)=\{P_1, P_2\}$, $S(CON_2)=\{P_3\}$. If 'WHERE' and 'OR' are the prefix of CON_1 and CON_2 respectively, then we can get $S(CONSTRAINT) = S(CON_1) \cup S(CON_2) = \{P_1, P_2, P_3\}$, and $S(CONSTRAINT) \cap S_M = \{P_1, P_2, P_3\}$. In this case, we could find that the part P_4 makes no any contribution to final query result, because the data instances in P_4 are not satisfied with the constraints on B. So P_4 is deleted from the operation tree. The sub-tree with root C_4 is deleted as well because of the deletion of P_4 and P_5. The result is shown in Figure 13.

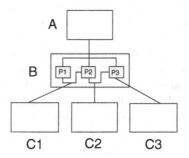

Fig. 13. The Result Tree

Note: If node B is root node of operation tree, then its parents node is NULL, and it maybe assumed $S(A)=\{P_1, P_2, ..., P_m\}$. In addition, the set $S(C_i)$ and S_M in the second step should be re-computed because the operation tree might be pruned in the first step and as a result the value of $S(C_i)$ and S_M might be changed.

6   Conclusion

There are three systems that are closely related to SESQ. The first is Webspace [17], which adopts similar ideas with SESQ method. It uses a concept-based model extended with Mirror 's framework [16] for content-based multimedia DBMS. This system only covers a part of the approach followed by SESQ. It focuses on modeling large collections of web documents based on object-oriented data model. The IR model of Webspace allows users to specify their information request in keywords. While SESQ aims at finding special domain data from the Web, integrating valuable information, modeling the domain data and supporting a flexible query. It also utilizes the domain ontology and knowledge to extract the information from various data sources, including HTML pages,

XML documents and database systems. SESQ uses enhanced ontology method to automatically establish the concept schema of special domain of web data.

The second one is Araneus [13], which focuses on the modeling of websites and using a relational approach. The web documents and hypertexts are modeled and stored using a relational data model, called ADM. This project is also concerned with handling both structured and semi-structured documents. In case of the Araneus project, this concerns the web-data modeling part. While SESQ uses concept schema approach, and stores data in XML documents rather than a database. SESQ combines concept-based search with content-based information retrieval and comes up with new query formulation techniques for data on the web.

The system Object-Web wrapper [7] focuses more on querying web-data using object-classes. The object classes define a view, which is incorporated in the search process. It is based on an intermediate object view mechanism called search views [8,9]. In case of the Object-Web Wrapper, the modeling part is left out. There the focus is more on the query process. With use of views, defined in terms of object-classes, queries can be composed to search a domain specific data collection. This work could make a contribution to SESQ information extraction. Furthermore, the SESQ Method aims at integrating conceptual modeling with information retrieval, which is also not the case there.

Others, in the field of information retrieval and integration, many work was introduced, such as SIMS [1,2], TSIMMIS [3,5], Information Manifold [11], and OBSERVER [12]. However, these systems focus only on retrieving and integrating data from multiple sources and not on the learning, exploring and understanding aspects. The goal of SESQ is to provide an environment where users can find, extract, organize the special domain data available from multiple web sources, and support user to query the data based on the data relationships among the domain concepts. In future works, we will go on refining our system to support more intelligent query.

Reference

1. J. Ambite, and C. Knoblock. Planning by Rewriting: Efficiently generating high-quality plans. Proceedings of the 14thNational Conference on Artificial Intelligence, Providence, RI, 1997.
2. Y. Arens, C. A. Knoblock, and W. Shen. Query reformulation for dynamic information integration. Journal of Intelligent Information Systems, Vol. 6, 1996, 99-130.
3. S. Chawathe, H. Garcia-Molina, J. Hammer, K. Ireland, Y. Papakonstantinou, J. Ullman, and J. Widom. The TSIMMIS Project: Integration of Heterogeneous Information Sources. Proceedings of 10th Anniversary Meeting of the Information Processing Society of Japan, Tokyo, Japan, 1994, 7-18.
4. Diamond, S.D. The Universal SQL Processor, Internal Johns Hopkins University Applied Physics Laboratory communication. RMI-95-005. 1995.

5. H. Garcia-Molina, Y. Papakonstantinou, D. Quass, A. Rajaraman, Y. Sagiv, J. Ullman, and J. Widom. The TSIMMIS Approach to Mediation: Data Models and Languages. In Proceedings of NGITS (Next Generation Information Technologies and Systems), 1995.
6. V. Kashyap, A. Sheth. Semantic Heterogeneity in Global Information Systems: The Role of Metadata, Context and Ontologies. M. Papzoglou, and G. Schlageter, (Eds.), Academic Press, 1997
7. Z. Lacroix. Retrieving and extracting web data with search views and an xml engine. In International Workshop on Data Integration over the Web in conjunction with the 13th International Conference on Advanced Information Systems Engineering (CAiSE), Interlaken, Switzerland, June 2001.
8. Zoé Lacroix: "Object Views through Search Views of Web data sources", International Conference on Conceptual Modeling (ER99), Paris, France, November 1999 — LNCS 1728, 176-187.
9. Zoé Lacroix: "Querying Annotated Scientific Data Combining Object-Oriented View and Information Retrieval", RIAO 2000, Paris, France, April 2000
10. M. Levene, *The Nested Universal Relation Database Model*. Lecture Notes in Computer Science, vol. 595. Heidelberg, Germany: Springer-Verlag, 1992.
11. A. Y. Levy, A. Rajaraman, and J. J. Ordille. Querying heterogeneous information sources using source descriptions. Proceedings of the 22nd International Conference on Very Large Databases VLDB-96, Bombay, India, September 1996.
12. E. Mena, A. Illarramendi, V. Kashyap, and A. P. Sheth. OBSERVER: An approach for query processing in global information systems based on interoperation across pre-existing ontologies. International Journal on Distributed and Parallel Databases, Vol. 8, No. 2, April 2000, 223-271.
13. G. Mecca, P. Merialdo, P. Atzeni, and V. Crescenzi. The Araneus guide to website development.Technical report, Dipartimento di Informatica e Automazione, Universita' di Roma Tre, March 1999.
14. N. F.Noy, and D. L.Mcguinness, Ontology development 101: a guide to creating your first ontology. Knowledge Systems Laboratory (KSL) of Department of Computer Science at the University of Stanford, Stanford, USA: Technical report, KSL-01-05 (2001).
15. R.Ramakrishnan and J.Gehrke. Database Management Systems (Second Edition). McGraw-Hill Companies, Inc., 2000.
16. A.d.Vries. Content and multimedia database management systems PhD thesis, University of Twente, Enschede, The Netherlands, Dec.1999.
17. R. van Zwol and P.M.G. Apers, The webspace method: On the integration of database technology with information re-trieval, In proceedings of CIKM'00 (Washington, DC.), November 2000.
18. Z.Zhang, LZhou etc. An ontology-based method for modeling and querying the Web data. Technique Report of Tsinghua University Database Group, November 2001.

An Approach to Modelling Legacy Enterprise Systems

Janet Lavery and Cornelia Boldyreff

Department of Computer Science
University of Durham
Science Laboratories, South Road
Durham, DH1 3LE, U.K.
Janet.Lavery@durham.ac.uk
Cornelia.Boldyreff@durham.ac.uk

Abstract. The reclamation and redevelopment of software "brownfield sites" requires a multi-layered understanding of the domain in which the enterprise system lives. A further dimension is added to the interconnectivity of the domain knowledge when the evolution of the system requires the migration of existing services to a web-based system and the creation of new value-added services. Where the enterprise systems are both internal to the organisations and "joined up" into wider inter-organisational networks, there are further challenges to developers. The Institutionally Secure Integrated Data Environment project is addressing the problems and issues surrounding the development and delivery of web based services for "joined up" systems within Higher Education Institutions. In this paper we define the meta-process that has emerged as a way to support incremental implementation of value-added services together with the relationships that exist amongst the generated work products in context with the meta-process.

1 Introduction

The reclamation and redevelopment of software brownfield sites requires a multi-layered understanding of the domain in which the enterprise system lives supported by a modelling approach that provides models of the domain at varying levels of abstraction. The United Kingdom (UK) Government Environment Agency [1] identifies brownfield sites as those which have been "*contaminated by previous industrial use, often associated with traditional processes which are now obsolete, which may present a hazard to the general environment, but for which there is a growing requirement for reclamation and redevelopment*". Software brownfield sites are recognised by their legacy systems comprised of dated software, distributed data, outmoded access procedures, and entrenched business processes.

Higher Education Institutions (HEIs) in the UK are large and complex enterprises systems that are usually comprised of multiple unconnected data repositories, distributed over several sites. Users are often prevented from carrying out work by inappropriate access control mechanisms and the lack of appropriate client software. In an effort to cope with the difficulties caused by this situation numerous ad hoc record systems have been developed at the departmental (both academic and administrative) level within the institutions. The systems are not co-ordinated with

S. Bhalla (Ed.): DNIS 2002, LNCS 2544, pp. 88–102, 2002.
© Springer-Verlag Berlin Heidelberg 2002

each other or with any central services. These systems often replicate work being carried out at in other areas of the institution.

The Institutionally Secure Integrated Data Environment (INSIDE) project is a collaborative project between the Universities of St Andrews and Durham that has been addressing the issues surrounding the development and delivery of web based "joined up" system for institutions. Both these HEIs have a rich legacy of systems predating computerisation quite substantially. The University of St. Andrews was founded in 1411 making it 591 years old whereas the University of Durham is a mere 170 years old. Both institutions are currently facing the challenges created by the need to incrementally migrate existing services to a web-based system and to exploit new technology to provide new value-added services and enterprise systems that are both internal to the organisations and "joined up" into wider inter-institutional networks.

The INSIDE project's remit is to work within the constraints of the existing information base and build value-added services upon them. Any web based value-added services developed will be introduced incrementally. Unlike land brownfield sites, which are often derelict, software brownfield sites are fully operational systems supporting the ongoing institution in its continued existence, even though they may not adequately support the changing needs of their users. HEIs can no longer operated in isolation. Lifelong learning initiatives have persuaded organisations of the need to find the means to enable them to exchange learning objects in a variety of formats that can be found in Managed Learning Environments. These can include student records data as will as learning objects such as bench tests. Currently given the systems employed these problems are common to many HEIs we have sought to identify the issues and solve the problems at a high enough level of abstraction to give sufficiently generic solutions applicable to other HEIs. As part of the work done by INSIDE a generic model of a large and complex process, common to all UK HEIs, has been developed. The process selected for study was the registration of new undergraduate students. The registration process has as its basis a common system for processing student applications through Universities and Colleges Admissions Service (UCAS). Initially institutions derive their student registration records from UCAS data. Thus it is believed that the resulting generic model usefully provides the core domain analysis necessary for requirements gathering in the brownfield site of undergraduate registration systems. More importantly, our experiences have been abstracted in the form of a meta-process to define and describe our work in the area of brownfield site system evolution using UML.

In this paper we define the meta-process that has emerged as a way to support incremental implementation of value-added services in context of brownfield site systems. This definition includes identification of the relationships that exist amongst the generated work products in context with the meta-process. Section 2 provides an overview of the registration process and the associated generic registration model. Section 3 provides the details of the meta-process and the generated work products. Section 4 gives a brief description of a pilot scheme that exploits the domain knowledge and analysis realised in the application of the Meta-Process. Section 5 states the open issues and future work.

2   Overview of the Generic Registration Process Model

2.1   The Registration Process

The process of registering new full-time undergraduate students begins the same for all UK HEIs when the student records for the new academic year entry cohort are distributed from a central "clearinghouse" UCAS [2]. UCAS distributes subsets of student records to the central registration service (admissions department) of the HEIs. Each central registration service then distributes the appropriate student records to academic and non-academic departments involved in the institution's registration process. When in the custody of UCAS, the student records have an identical structure and content base. Once in the custody of the HEIs the student records are manipulated to reconcile their content and structure with the needs of a particular institution. Additional manipulation may also occur to suit the specific needs of the academic and non-academic departments within an institution.

2.2   The Generic Model

Kruchten [3] believes that no single diagram could accurately depict the complexities of a system. We propose that it involves the generation and evolution of several work products, some of which may contain many diagrams, to model a complex enterprise system. The definition of a model most suited to the aim of our generic model can be found in the online Oxford Dictionary [4], which states that a model is a "simplified or idealised description or conception of a particular system, situation, or process that is put forward as a basis for calculations, predictions, or further investigation". We believe that a model of an enterprise system must evolve in conjunction with the evolution of the enterprise system itself.

Developing the current version of the generic model of HEI registration began with analysts at both universities modelling their own institution's registration process. The two models were then compared to identify the commonalities and discrepancies on which the generic model of the process was designed. In its present state, the Generic Registration Model consists of two substantial work products. The first work product is a Rational Rose .mdl file that contains the UML model of the process. A variety of UML tools were considered and Rational Rose 2000™ was selected because it provided the means to develop a coherently partitioned model of the registration process. In addition, Rational Rose was a software engineering support tool in use at both HEIs. Using common support tools facilitates effective interoperability and communication between HEIs. The UML model consists primarily of Use Case or Business Case models, of the registration process. It is divided into two main subsections: the Use Case View that provides the core business model that is used to support domain analysis and requirements gathering; and the Logical View that is used to support those functions that are more strongly coupled to specific institutional or departmental domains such as low level design [5]. It is the Use Case View that currently contains those elements of the model that are generic and potentially reusable by a range of HEIs [2].

The second work product is a domain specific Thesaurus that contains the core generic terms used in the UML model. Each generic term has been allocated a single primary definition, any applicable alternate definitions, and the equivalent common term in use at St. Andrews and Durham. For the purpose of strengthening the usefulness of the Thesaurus and to provide traceability of the terms throughout the development process an object-oriented classification has been applied to each of the generics terms. This approach of associating an object-oriented classification was taken from one found in Protégé 2000; a tool that supports the construction of domain specific ontology [6].

The two formal work products, the UML model and the Thesaurus, are used together to form the Generic Registration Process Model. These two work products are strongly interconnected. For example, within the UML model there is a package, Actors, containing all the model's actors together with the definition of their roles within the HEI and their relationships to each other. The description of each actor given in the Actors package must match the primary definition given in the Thesaurus [7].

The main work products provide the model of the generic registration process, but they were developed to support on-going domain analysis and requirements gathering, and accordingly will be evolved iteratively as domain knowledge increases. They are developed using support tools and are expected to evolve in conjunction with domain knowledge acquisition and subsequent system evolution, as well as providing the base for work products to be developed in the future.

3 Defining the Meta-process

A useful consequence of developing a generic model of the undergraduate registration process using UML has been the emergence of a meta-process model that is applicable to the incremental evolution of enterprise systems while supporting the incremental development of the enterprise model itself. The emergent meta-process reinforces the iterative nature of enterprise domain knowledge capture and modelling, and the evolution of work products in context with the meta-process. The meta-process model, as seen in Figure 1, demonstrates the link between activities performed in the evolution of existing systems to provide value-added services and the work products generated and evolved that comprise the enterprise model. The meta-process that has emerged contains several dependant steps that are predominantly iterative and supportive of the incremental development of value-added services. The exception is Initial Analysis, which is performed only once but provides the foundation for the work products on which the subsequent work products are established.

3.1 Initial Analysis

Initial Analysis is the first pass over an area of the enterprise domain where the informal analysis and capture of the domain knowledge occurs. Where the analysis is to support the development of an inter-organisational enterprise system, the initial analysis must be undertaken at each individual organisation. The emphasis is on the collection of domain knowledge concerning the existing system and the unique subsection of the enterprise under investigation for the potential addition of value-

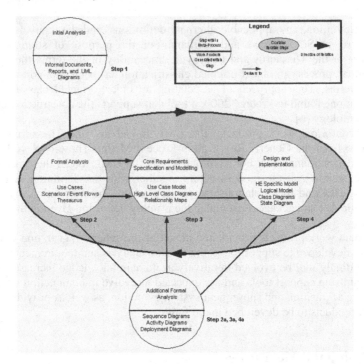

Fig. 1. The Meta Process

added services. Historically subsections of a system were developed independently with their own individual model of the enterprise in which they existed [8]. The emergent meta-process supports the capture of domain knowledge about the subsection of the system under investigation and places in context with the evolving enterprise model. The domain knowledge is gleaned from domain experts during informal interviews, and to a lesser extent from the existing documentation. The knowledge is captured in disjointed conceptual models that are usually disconnected examinations of the data, processes, and behaviour of systems and people and are restricted to particular areas of the enterprise domain [9]. Analysts in the INSIDE project exploited basic block diagrams to model the domain knowledge about the HEIs' registration process. Basic block diagrams consist primarily of analyst-defined rectangles, ovals, and arrows, and require an accompanying textual or verbal narrative to be fully understood. These basic diagrams serve three main purposes: to demonstrate the analyst's increasing domain understanding; to generate discussion amongst domain experts; and to ensure an increasing correctness and completeness in the analyst's understanding of the domain area. The basic block diagrams, with and without textual accompaniment, the records of the informal interviews with domain experts, and any details gleaned from existing domain specific documentation, are developed separately and not interleaved except perhaps in the analyst's narrative. However, as the analyst's knowledge about the domain increases, it is possible to bring cohesion to the conceptual models [9].

As our intention was to create a generic model for use by different HEIs the more formal and generally understood modelling language, the Unified Modelling Language (UML) was used to rework the disjoint conceptual models into a more integrated form. UML is an object-oriented notation in widespread use in the software development industry and is effective for use when a common understanding between software engineers is required [10]. At the Initial Analysis stage the UML models consist mainly of the stakeholder perspective provided by use case diagrams that are used to show the user interaction with the existing system by developing and diagramming user (actor) based scenarios [11]. An unexpected difference in the domain language used by the different institutions to express their concepts and manage the information between the two institutions provided the opportunity to explore possible solutions to common vocabulary problems. For Initial Analysis a simple domain specific dictionary was constructed using generic terms and definitions agreed upon by HEIs. The UML diagrams and the dictionary should be developed in unison with one another i.e. terms used in the UML diagrams should be clearly defined in the dictionary and terminology used in the domain should be clearly defined in the dictionary for when it is needed in a UML diagram.

Initial analysis work products constructed in the first step of the meta-process do not evolve after the start of the second step, Formal Analysis. The knowledge acquired from these work products influences Formal Analysis; however, only the UML diagrams and the dictionary provide the initial input for Formal Analysis. Some, but not all, of the actual UML diagrams, for example, a well-defined use case diagram, may be included in the eventual UML model developed in Formal Analysis. The remaining work products such as the basic block diagrams can effectively be discarded at the start of Formal Analysis.

3.2 Formal Analysis

The remaining sequence of steps in the meta-process are mutually dependant, performed iteratively, with the emphasis on the capture of domain knowledge while evolving an existing enterprise system. The cycle is based on the necessity to expand the domain knowledge while performing incremental development of value-added services to specific areas of existing systems. The focus of Formal Analysis is the capture of domain knowledge that is then exploited in the generation and modelling of the core requirements. These in turn provide the knowledge necessary for the design and implementation of the value-added services. As there has been only one pass over an area of the domain for each organisation prior to the beginning of the iterative cycle the focus of the first few cycles of the meta-process will be in Formal Analysis including the inter-organisational domains of interest. Work products built in formal analysis are developed to support on-going domain analysis and requirements gathering, and accordingly are developed iteratively as domain knowledge increases. They are developed using support tools and are expected to evolve in conjunction with domain knowledge acquisition and subsequent enterprise system evolution.

In Formal Analysis the emphasis is on the generation of use case diagrams, which must be accompanied by detailed scenarios. The scenarios are used as a means of capturing the complexities of the domain that are specific to a use case diagram [12]. Burstard et. al. [11] suggest that there are four perspectives from which to view scenarios: process, situational, choice and use. The process perspective places the focus on events and event triggers. The situation perspective places the focus on "concrete problematic situations". The choice perspective allows for the exploration of a variety of solutions and is for use close to implementation. The use perspective places the focus on the stakeholder view and consequently this is the perspective of scenario used with use cases and most relevant to our modelling approach. Also relevant to our work is Cheesman and Daniels' [13] support of the use of scenarios as Use Case Descriptions with the emphasis on the goal to be achieved by the enactment of the use case. In our work we exploited structured text based scenarios, Event Flows [14] that capture the sequential flow of the ordinary events that occur in within the confines of a use case and allow both the stakeholder view and the goal to be depicted. Event Flows are also used to capture the pre-conditions that must be meet before the use case can be enacted and any of alternative events that are possible within the confines of a use case. As an alternative to textual scenarios it is possible to support use case diagrams with graphically based scenarios. Activity Diagrams provide a sequential listing of events that allows for parallelism and alternatives. They are used with use cases to discover and define behavioural dependencies [15]. Alternatively, sequence diagrams are also effective in showing the behavioural details contained in a use case and are of particular use if concurrency is an issue [15].

Formal Analysis introduces the use and development of the Thesaurus. The initial content for the Thesaurus comes from the dictionary developed during Initial Analysis. A simple dictionary does not sufficiently capture the relationships that exist between the terms used within a specific domain needed for ongoing knowledge capture and evolutionary development. The Thesaurus grows as more domain knowledge is acquired. As the focus of the work in the modelling changes from the more generic Use Case View to the more Institution specific Logical View, the content of the Thesaurus is likely to become increasingly biased to a particular organisational domain. The increased use of domain specific terms will then be reflected in the Use Case models making them less generic. However, where the focus is on an inter-organisation system exchange, model emphasis is in the generic areas of the model and is likely to be of interest to other organisations with similar stakeholders and goals.

3.3   Core Requirements Specification and Modelling

The generation of the Use Case Model illustrating and defining the core business elements of the institution provides the model needed to support specification any requirements for proposed evolution. Initially this will consist primarily of the use cases and scenarios describing the current state of the generic organisation generated in Formal Analysis. Subsequent requirements gathering and elicitation will produce additional use cases generated to explore proposed value-added services, such as web access to legacy data stores. Specifying requirements necessitates a more detailed view of the organisation than the one needed in analysis. As a consequence high-level class diagrams concerning domain elements need to be developed. These class diagrams will model elements close to the domain and are directly traceable to implementation [13, 14]. Once these high-level class diagrams are being generated it is advantageous to map their modelled relationships to the corresponding relationships that exist between actual domain objects. An example of this taken from the Generic Registration Model [7] is in Figure 2.

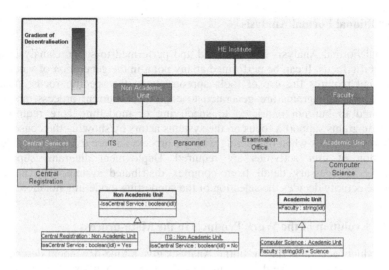

Fig. 2. Relationship Mapping Sample

The Thesaurus generated in Formal Analysis contains the object-oriented classification that is used to support the generation of the high-level classes. However, there is a lack of correlation between the real world objects' relationships and object-oriented relationship implied by the object-oriented classification. For example, the term "faculty" in the UK is "a group of related Academic Units" [7] such as the Faculty of Arts. In the domain a faculty is a core unit comprised of collection of sub-units or academic departments. In the object-oriented classification a faculty is an attribute of the class Academic Unit. One means of depicting relationships is shown in figure 2. The situation were the mappings are developed separately is not ideal. Ideally, the relationships would be obvious in the main model work products. This issue is explored further in Section 4.

3.4   Design and Implementation

The work products developed during the specification of the requirements for value-added services are used as the foundation for work performed in design and implementation. Here the Use Case Model is evolved to include the Logical View where the domain specific use cases with accompanying scenarios, and class diagrams that are less abstract and close to the actual implementation of the value-added services with each organisation [13, 14] are held. As a consequence the Logical View section of the model is less abstract and of less use outside the institutional or individual departmental with the institution. The less abstract domain knowledge is passed into the next iteration of the cycle providing the foundation for evolution to the formal analysis work products. For inter-organisational systems, the design will remain at a higher level of generisity.

3.5   Additional Formal Analysis

Additional Formal Analysis is specialised and performed to support analysis with a more specific focus. It can be performed at any point in the generation of value-added services but requires the use of tools appropriate to the specific focus. As stated before sequence diagrams are generated to explore concurrent process, an activity more suited to but not restricted to specifying or modelling core requirements. Activity diagrams support a focus on the systems actors by showing the consequences of their key activities when interacting within a process and are useful when a detailed examination of user activities are required. Deployment diagrams support the abstracting unnecessary detail from complex distributed system. The motivation behind the activity decides the selection of the supporting modelling notation.

3.6   The Evolution of the Work Products in the Meta-process

Work products generated during Initial Analysis give a time-dependent description of a small area of an enterprise domain, in our case a single complex process within two organisations. The work products are constructed to initially facilitate domain understanding and to provide the initial input into subsequently generated work products. As a consequence, they are not developed to be maintainable beyond the end of initial analysis. Work products built in formal analysis are developed to support on-going domain analysis and requirements gathering, and accordingly are developed iteratively as domain knowledge increases. They are developed using support tools and are expected to evolve in conjunction with domain knowledge acquisition and subsequent system evolution. Work products generated in Formal Analysis provide the foundation for work products generated during Core Requirements Specification and Modelling, these in turn provide the base for the work products generated during Design and Implementation. As new value-added services are implemented, the foundation on which the previously developed work products were based is altered; and, therefore, the consequence of introducing value-added services is to trigger the next iteration of the Formal Analysis work a return to step 2 using as input the existing models. Dependencies between the work products are formed as the enterprise system evolves. The relationship between the work products is shown in Figure 3.

As can be seen in Figure 3, work products can provide the foundation for subsequently generated work products, demonstrated by the use of a unidirectional arrow from base work product to subsequent work product. In addition, Figure 3 illustrates the mutual dependencies between evolving work products, demonstrated by the use of a bi-directional arrow.

4   Analysis of the Student Registration Processes

A common problem with legacy systems is that users are often trying to carry out work using inappropriate access control mechanisms. The analysis of the registration process identified areas supporting the registration process and related processes where access by staff and students to potentially useful student data was hindered by

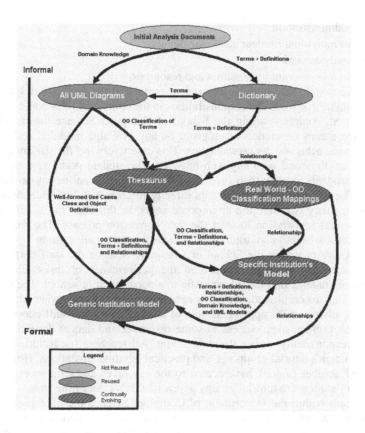

Fig. 3. Work Products Relationships

the inappropriate existing access control mechanisms. As the Internet is in common use by the staff and students at most HEIs it was decided to deploy a web-based front-end access to crucial legacy databases. It was decide to provide user-centric institutional web-based portals as a single point of contact to a range of services specific to the two key user groups, students and staff. A student-oriented view of the data identified the followings student-oriented areas of the domain requiring improvement:

- Specific module enrolment,
- Academic feedback from staff,
- Submission of academic work,
- Tracking of assignment due dates, and
- Students' access to their own records.

Where as a staff-oriented view of the data identified the following staff-oriented areas of the domain requiring improvement:

- Resource planning and allocation of timeslots for tutorial and practicals including communicating the allocated times to the appropriate staff and students,
- Tracking of assessed work's due data and marked by date,

- Module administration,
- Access to individual Student academic details,
- Cohort analysis, and
- Access to role relevant information and resources.

There are two distinct portals, the student portal and the staff portal, based on the institution members' roles and responsibilities in the context of the student registration process. At St. Andrews within the School of Computer Science the student portal provides the means for students to register on any available modules, restricted only by their having achieved the prerequisites. This effectively lets the student enrol from anywhere, anytime and with any web browser. The student portal also provides the means for students to view their own student records and identify any problems with the data. They may not access the data directly to correct it, but once aware of any discrepancies they can take the appropriate steps, in this case the generation of an email to central registration to start the data correction process. The student portal also provides a student's own tutorial and practical lab time allocations.

At St. Andrews within the School of Computer Science the staff portal provides access to data and resources needed in the performance of tasks related to the enrolment of students in a module specific to a department or school. The staff portal will allow staff to enrol students when necessary. For example, when students have had to seek advice on the appropriateness of a module or when staff choose to waive the module's prerequisites. Access to some resources and data is dependent on staff roles and responsibility within the department. All teaching (or lecturing) staff can view the student's tutorial groupings and practical lab time allocations. However, only a restricted number of staff have access to the resources and data necessary for the allocation of students to tutorial groups or practical laboratory time slots.

At Durham within the Department of Computer Science the pilot portals provide students with web-based electronic submission of assigned work and access to their own specific attendance details, assessed work deadline dates and interim marks. The pilot scheme at Durham also provides a staff portal providing web-based electronic submission of student assessed work deadlines and marks. The staff portal also provides staff with the mechanism to review their students' attendance, deadlines, and provisional marks. The evaluation of the appropriateness of the web-based access and the usefulness of the student data accessed are in progress. Preliminary findings indicate that the portals where well used, but a more in-depth review will be performed in the near future.

5 Open Issues and Future Work

The brownfield sites that are the enterprise systems in place in most UK HEIs today contain: legacy systems with their dated software, distributed data, outmoded access procedures, and entrenched business practices are in the processes of being reclaimed and redeveloped to provide the users of these systems with more useful web accessible systems. The INSIDE project has abstracted a meta-process to support the incremental development of the value-added web accessible systems needed by HEIs as well as inter-organisational enterprise systems, such as those required to support lifelong learning. The meta-process reinforces the iterative nature of incremental domain knowledge capture and modelling in conjunction with iterative development of the value-added systems. However, the evolution of large enterprise systems requires a multi-layered understanding of the domain in which the system lives. One proposed foundation for this deep and detailed domain analysis is the construction and use of domain specific ontology.

The use of Ontology supports knowledge acquisition, sharing and reuse by providing a repository for the general and detailed knowledge about specific domains and is used to classify the 'things' or objects of a domain [16]. Within the context of the domain, objects are identified, classified, and defined, as are the relationships between the objects. An ontology contain at its core layer a collection of knowledge that is specific to a particular domain and progressing to an outer layer of knowledge that is more general and useful to a broader range of HEIs. Ontology are complex tools that are intended to support the entire development process of any area of an enterprise. This could make their development very time-consuming [8]. One approach is to grow or evolve the ontology in conjunction with the incremental introduction of value-added services. Initially the Ontology would contain core or generic domain knowledge derived from formal analysis. The ontology may evolve to contain more domain specific knowledge making it useful in the specification of requirements and system design depending on whether an organisation specific or inter-organisational enterprise system is being developed. This approach is depicted in Figure 4 below.

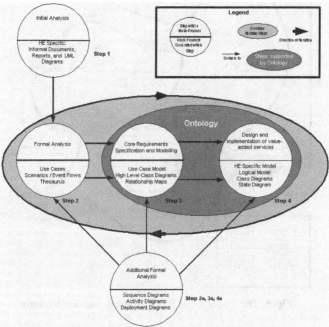

Fig. 4. Evolution of the Ontology in the Meta-Process

The recognition of the ontology within the model arose as a consequence of the addition of an object-oriented classification section to the Thesaurus. The addition of the object-oriented classification has increased the usefulness of the Thesaurus by providing traceability of the terms throughout the development process. But, in practice, the addition of the object-oriented classification area in the Thesaurus revealed the lack of correlation between the real world objects' relationships and object-oriented relationship implied by the object-oriented classification. As a temporary measure, several diagrams depicting the main relationships need to be constructed. An example of the mapping can be seen in Figure 2. It is proposed that an ontology would provide the means to use the object-oriented classification and explicitly define the relationships between the objects. The Thesaurus work product in conjunction with the relationship maps developed to compensate for the Thesaurus's weakness would logically provide the foundation work products upon which the ontology would be constructed. This is concept is illustrated below in Figure 5.

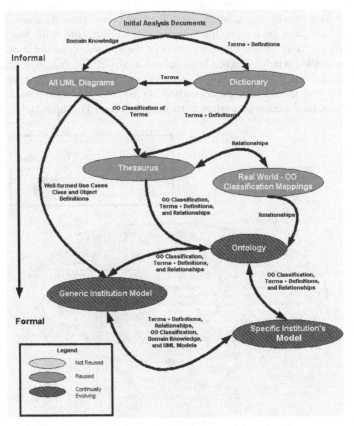

Fig. 5. The Evolution of Work Products with an Ontology

As can be seen in Figure 5 the Thesaurus and the Real World to OO Mappings will be fixed and used as the foundation work products for the ontology, demonstrated by the use of a unidirectional arrow. Thus the ontology work product becomes the target for future evolution. The mutual dependency, demonstrated by the bi-directional arrows, which existed between the Thesaurus and the Generic Model and the Specific

Institution's Model previously seen in Figure 3, are supplanted by the dependency relationship between the Generic Model, Specific Institution's Model and the Ontology, depicted here in Figure 5.

An investigation into the development of an inter-organisational student record exchanged system that would allow student records to be exchanged between HEIs is the next investigation in the INSIDE project. This will extend the Generic Registration Process Model with a more useful Generic Student Information Model. This will require an investigation into data exchange models. Initially this is to take the form of an investigation into the usefulness of the IMS Enterprise [17], which is being continually developed to support interoperability between enterprise systems.

As the meta-process model indicates the domain specific knowledge captured in design and implementation is propagated back to the work products in formal analysis. This is expected to reduce the generic nature of all the work products. For example at present the UML model work product that is part of the Generic Registration Model is divided into two main sections: the Use Case View, containing the core or generic models and the Logical View, containing the institutionally specific models. As domain knowledge is increased and expanded to cover new areas such as student records it is expected that the level of domain specific knowledge reflected in the Logical View will increase and that it will permeate back to the Use Case View making that more domain specific. The challenge for the INSIDE project is to capture and retain the availability of the reusable generic domain knowledge while supporting the capture and use of the domain specific knowledge some of which may only be useable in subsections of the institutions domain.

In this paper, the approach to modelling inter-organisational enterprise systems arose from modelling work carried out by the INSIDE project has been described. In the course of our modelling work a number of work products emerged and various informal and formal modelling techniques have been employed. On reflection, we have distilled our experiences into a meta-process model relating production of work products to various steps in the modelling process. In the course of this modelling work and subsequent reflection our meta-process model has itself evolved to reflect our recognition of the importance of ontology development.

Acknowledgement. The work described in this paper is part of the Institutionally Secure Integrated Data Environment project (INSIDE), which is funded by the JISC Committee for Integrated Environments for Learners (JCIEL) under the Building Managed Learning Environments in Higher Education (7/99) programme. INSIDE is a collaborative project between the Universities of St Andrew and Durham. The work described here has involved contributions from colleagues at both universities. We are especially grateful to our colleagues Brendan Hodgson and Sarah Drummond; and our research partners Colin Allison and Bin Ling (Jordan) at St. Andrews.

References

1. UK Government, Environment Agency, Land Quality, 2002
    http://www.environement-agency.gov.uk/subjects/landquality/
2. Janet Lavery, Cornelia Boldyreff, Bin Ling and Colin Allison "Laying the Foundation for Web Services over Legacy Systems" to be presented at WSE 2002 the 4th International Workshop on Web Site Evolution, 2nd of October 2002.
3. Philippe B. Kruchten, "The 4 + 1 View Model of Architecture", *IEEE Software*, Vol. 12, No. 6, November 1995.
4. OED Online (Oxford English Dictionary), Oxford University Press, 2002.
    http://dictionary. oed.com/
5. Rational Rose Tutorial part of *Rational Rose 2000*, Rose Enterprise Edition, Copyright © 1991-1999, Rational Software Corporation.
6. N. F. Noy, M. Sintek, S. Decker, M. Crubezy, R. W. Fergerson, & M. A. Musen. Creating Semantic Web Contents with Protege-2000. *IEEE Intelligent Systems* 16(2): 60-71, 2001.
7. Janet Lavery, "Report on the Generic Model of the Process of Undergraduate Registration at Higher Education Institutions Version 2.0". An *Institutionally Secure Integrated Data Environment Report*, January 2002 http://www.dcs.st-andrews.ac.uk/inside/report.html
8. Mark S. Fox and Michael Gruninger, "Enterprise Modeling*", AI Magazine*, Fall 1998.
9. Collette Rolland and Naveen Prakash, "From conceptual modelling to requirements engineering", *Annals of Software Engineering,* 10 (2000) pp. 151-176
10. Andrew Watson, "OMG and Open Software Standards" a *Business and Professional Lecture*, the University of Durham 2001/02.
11. D.W. Bustard, Z. He, F.G. Wilkie, "Linking soft systems and use-case modelling through scenarios". In *Interacting with Computers*, Vol. 13, pages 97-110, 2000.
12. J.M. Carroll, "Five reasons for scenario-based design". In *Interacting with Computers*, Vol. 13, pages 43-60, 2000.
13. Cheesman, John, and John Daniels, UML Components A Simple Process for Specifying Component-Based Software, Addison-Wesley, New Jersey, USA, 2001.
14. Quatrani, T., Visual Modeling with Rational Rose 2000 and UML, Addison-Wesley, New Jersey, USA, 2000.
15. Fowler, Martin, with Kendall Scott, UML distilled : a brief guide to the standard object modeling language, 2nd edition, Addison-Wesley, New Jersey, USA, 2000.
16. B. Chandrasekaran, John R. Josephson and V. Richard Benjamins, What are Ontologies, and Why Do We Need Them? In *IEEE Intelligent Systems*, Vol. 14, No.1, January/February 1999.
17. Geoff Collier and Wayne Veres, "IMS Enterprise Information Model Version 1.01", IMS Global Learning Consortium, Inc., December 21, 1999.

Explicit Representation of Constrained Schema Mappings for Mediated Data Integration

C. Altenschmidt and J. Biskup

Fachbereich Informatik, Universität Dortmund, D–44221 Dortmund
{altensch|biskup}@ls6.cs.uni-dortmund.de

Abstract. In an environment of heterogeneous data sources it may be necessary to integrate these in order to provide a single global view to the data. Nowadays this problem is solved by mediators, which are tolerant not only to heterogeneity of the sources, but also of their availability and of structural changes. For some mediation problems it is reasonable to assume the existence of a fixed structured target schema as the global view. In these cases, mismatches of target concepts and source concepts can occur, which make it impossible for a mediator to interpret the data correctly and completely at the same time. We will show how to enforce correct interpretations by imposing constraints on the mappings between the target schema and the source schemas. The strength of such constraints can be decreased in a flexible and controlled way, for the sake of exploiting more sources, and at the cost of potentially loosing assurance in correctness. Additionally, we treat interpretation completeness of sources. A careful specification of data structures and algorithms allows for using mappings of this kind in a generic mediation system. The data structures represent mappings explicitly by linking structural descriptions of source data to the target schema expressed in an object oriented data model.

1 Introduction

When looking for information in a computer network you can access a wide variety of sources today. There are databases and web sites of various kinds, and probably many of them provide some of the information you are looking for.

Even though the sheer number of data sources makes it likely that the desired information can be found somewhere, there are some difficulties in finding the information:

- You have to locate the relevant data sources.
- You must get familiar with the provided data formats and access protocols.
- In general, the information you are looking for will be distributed across several sources, so you must relate the partial information of the single sources.

For some fifteen years now this problem is dealt with by data integration systems. A data integration system adapts to a variety of data sources, by its ability to

S. Bhalla (Ed.): DNIS 2002, LNCS 2544, pp. 103–132, 2002.
© Springer-Verlag Berlin Heidelberg 2002

communicate with these sources and to relate the information these sources provide. At the same time the system has got a uniform data format and a uniform access protocol for interaction with users.

Thus, you only need to know about the data format and the access protocol of the data integration system, but you gain access to all information of the underlying sources.

1.1   Our Approach to Data Integration

One of the problems arising from the integration of several data sources is the heterogeneity of their conceptual descriptions. Electronic information systems provide a formally specified schema, or they demand a formal self-description from the data – in this case referred to as "semi-structured" by many authors –, in order to enforce a conceptual basis for interaction with the user. We will refer to any structural description of data, no matter whether it is schematically specified or semi-structured, as a *type*. In general, two different information systems, no matter whether they are data sources or data integration systems, describe the same data by different terms, resulting in different types. When integrating these sources, we need to find the relationships between these types. This enables the translation of queries and the transformation of the resulting data to the appropriate terms.

Unfortunately, the relationships between types are not obvious. Firstly, type specifications might be ambiguous, i.e. the real world concept being represented by a type might be unclear. Possible reasons are the use of homonyms, abbreviations, misspellings, or imprecise descriptions. A lot of work has been done to cope with this kind of heterogeneity, so we will not examine that in this paper. But secondly, the two real world concepts being represented by two types might match exactly, i.e. both types represent the same concept, or these concepts might match only partially. If we use partial matches in addition to perfect matches for data integration, we can employ more data sources, but we lose precision of query results to some extent. Imagine you are looking for cats, but the integration system only knows a data source describing pets. A cat is a pet, so the integration system might exploit the more general concept also. But then, if you query the integration system about cats, you will get information about dogs also – and you may not even notice.

In order to solve this problem, we have built a data integration system using explicit type mappings. These type mappings model the above mentioned relationships between types by first deriving additional properties of the types, and then mapping the derivations. Thereby we have examined constraints we can put on these type mappings and on the derivations, thus getting a varying "degree of correctness".

The most strict constraints allow for perfect matches only. This enforces interpretation correctness, i.e. you will never get feigned information that the data sources do not actually provide. But in the cats and pets example above, the source knowing about pets would not be taken into account if you pose a query about cats. There are more relaxed constraints, which allow for more complex relationships to be expressed in the type mappings. Therefore, more data sources can be employed, and due to the explicit representation of the type mappings, the integration process, while being performed automatically, can be made comprehensible to the user.

More specifically, our work aims at analysing and solving the problem of specifying and employing relationships between types for the purpose of data integration. Our achievements are roughly visualised in Fig. 1.

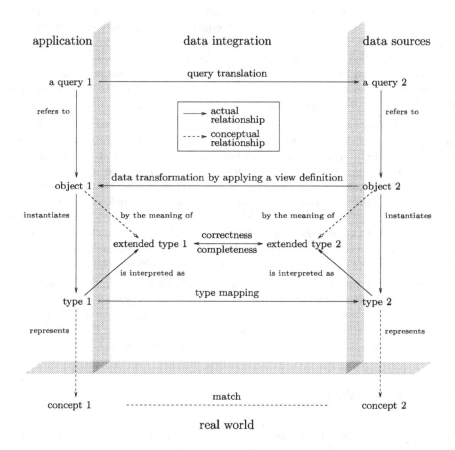

Fig. 1. Layers of the integration process

We distinguish three layers:

– An *application* poses queries referring to objects of some type.
– A *data integration system* translates queries to the context of some data sources, and transforms the resulting data to the application context by using

a view definition derived from a type mapping. For controlling correctness and completeness of the type mappings, types are enhanced into appropriate extended types when the type mappings are established.

- *Data sources* evaluate queries referring to some objects of some type.

A type in both the application context and the source context is a representation of a concept of the *real world*. Two of these concepts may match completely or partially.

As announced above, throughout the paper we suppose non-ambiguous type specifications, and we concentrate on dealing with relationships between types. We postulate a fictitious integration administrator who declares both the extensions for types and the type mappings, whether using automatic tools where available or guided by human insight. The quality of the administrator's declarations is assessed by the extent of satisfying a constraint. Satisfaction of such a constraint implies certain correctness assertions concerning automatically generated view definitions, query translations and data transformations.

Our achievements sketched so far stem from two lines of investigations. In our earlier theoretical work [4], we emphasised the goal of fully automating a well-comprehensible integration process. Thereby, we could deal only with restricted cases of the integration task. In our practical work [7,8,3], we are favouring to provide most flexible expressiveness for assisting an integration administrator. Thereby, we have lost full automation and run at the risk of getting rarely predictable integration behaviour. Now, in the present paper, we present our insight on how to balance automation and comprehensibility on the one hand and expressiveness on the other hand. Our insight is still preliminary and exemplary, allowing many options for meaningful variations and deeper studies.

The rest of this paper elaborates selected details of Fig. 1 and its explanation sketch so far. After looking at the work done by other groups in Chap. 2 we present our idea of types in Chap. 3, and how we map them in Chap. 4. In addition, we present a data integration system called MMM in Chap. 5. Finally, we conclude on our ideas and give some hints for future work.

2   Related Work

The most important early approach towards data integration was to build federated databases [23]. These federations were mostly static, and the data models of the integrated sources had to be quite similar. Modern integration systems follow the mediation paradigm presented by Wiederhold [26]. Examples for mediators are TSIMMIS [13], HERMES [2], SIMS [5], DISCO [24], Garlic [22], Carnot [11], and our approach, called MMM [3,4,7,8]. These systems span a wide variety of implemented features and application contexts.

One important property of mediation systems is whether or not they provide a fixed schema to the applications. The TSIMMIS approach and its successor Med-Maker [20] avoid schemas by using a semi-structured data model called OEM

[21]. This allows for maximum flexibility, thus being well suited for answering spontaneous queries of human users. On the other hand, it sacrifices computational efficiency when used by applications using a fixed set of queries. Some systems, e.g. HERMES or Garlic, allow for flexible adaption of the schema as further sources are integrated. But many other systems, e.g. SIMS or DISCO, have a fixed application schema like conventional databases, and so has MMM. A fixed application schema can be especially designed for a particular application, by that minimising conceptual mismatches between the application and the data integration system.

Most of these approaches use views of various kinds for translating queries and for transforming the result data. This is quite flexible and makes the integration process efficient. For instance, Papakonstantinou et al. use logic oriented views over OEM expressions in MedMaker [20], and the theory of translation schemes applied to database design uses a view for each relation in the target schema (cf. [17]). In contrast, we only specify type mappings, i.e. relationships on the level of structural descriptions, and then we derive the necessary view definitions. This is still efficient, but it allows for controlling the "distance" of mapped types, and it increases transparency to the user.

The properties of our type mappings are determined by extended types, i.e. types enhanced by additional properties derived from the structure of the types by rules. Specifying these rules is equivalent to adding ontological knowledge, as it is done in several approaches. For example, Biskup and Embley [6] include knowledge about class extensions in their target schema, and the Carnot project [11] uses parts of the global ontology Cyc [14] as a target schema, and exploits the ontological knowledge in Cyc for integrating source schemas.

Some work has been done on comparing the expressive power of data integration systems. The authors often refer to three classes of systems:

- Global As View (GAV) systems, presented by Adali and others in 1996 [1],
- Local As View (LAV) systems, presented by Levy and others in the same year [15],
- GLAV, a combination of GAV and LAV, first presented by Friedman, Levy and others in 1999 [12,9].

Ullman pragmatically compared GAV and LAV [25], showing that LAV systems are easier to maintain, but in GAV query processing is easier. Cali and others examined the expressive power of all three classes [9], showing that LAV and GAV are incomparable in general, but both LAV and GLAV systems can be transformed into GAV systems with additional constraints. In chapter 4.4 we will sketch that the expressive power of our approach ranges from GAV to a class, which is conjectured to be in the spirit of GLAV.

Our implementation of MMM might remind of DISCO [24] and Garlic [22]. Both DISCO and Garlic exploit the proposal of the Object Data Management Group (ODMG) [10] for defining schemas and posing queries, and so does MMM. But in contrast to DISCO, MMM represents source schemas explicitly in the data integration component. Furthermore, MMM type mappings are specified for each source separately using a language we called TYML (see Chap. 5.2), which relates single target attributes to source attributes. DISCO extends the Object Data Language of the ODMG by specifications of view definitions over the schemas of external data source wrappers.

The Garlic architecture basically consists of a query processor and a wrapper for each source. In Garlic, the application schema is a union of the external schemas of all wrappers. The architecture of MMM is very similar to the Garlic architecture, but MMM maps the external schemas of the wrappers to a predefined application schema.

There are several problems, which are important in the context of data integration, but beyond the scope of this paper. Much work has been done on the problem of finding relationships between data sources (semi-)automatically. Some approaches try this by analysing the source data, or its schema, syntactically, e.g. the extensible TranScm system described by Milo and Zohar [18], which can, among other things, resolve structural mismatches and naming differences. Others try a semantic analysis, e.g. Biskup and Embley [6], using data samples and some user interaction. Madhavan et al. have done a broad survey of schema matching techniques, and they presented a system using many of these [16]. A related problem is how to match data objects in different sources which correspond to the same real world entity. Another problem is how to deal with inconsistencies between sources. Sometimes consensus methods are used to solve this problem, see [19] for an example.

3   Types and Their Informational Content

We want to define a class of mappings of types similar to the one presented in an earlier paper [4]. We first generalise the definition of types presented in that paper. As before, we assume that we can describe each data item by a tree. In most cases, we wish to use the inner nodes for describing the structure, and the leaves for describing the domain of some content data. There are labels on the nodes which are used to provide a textual description of the desired interpretation of a node as its basic property. For inner nodes, these descriptions are names of appropriate type constructors. Leaves are labelled with domain names like *integer*, *real*, or *string*. Later on, these domain names are interpreted by the respective domains. Labels on the edges identify a relationship between nodes in the context of some ontology. This comprises the relationship between a collection constructor and an element type, and the relationships between a tuple constructor and its attributes, in which case the labels should be treated like attribute names.

Definition 3.1 (type[1]). Formally, let **T** be the smallest set that contains all elements τ which are defined as *types* as follows. τ is a triple $\langle (V, E), label_V, label_E \rangle$, where (V, E) defines a finite, rooted, unordered tree with

---
[1] Surely, other variants of this notion could be useful. Hence, the following definition is intended to be a representative example.

nodes V and edges E, $label_V : V \to \mathcal{L}_V$ associates labels to the nodes of the tree, and $label_E : E \to \mathcal{L}_E$ associates labels to the edges of the tree. The labelling of nodes and edges must fulfil additional constraints, which also define the sets of labels $\mathcal{L}_V$ and $\mathcal{L}_E$:

1. Inner nodes may be labelled with the type constructors *tuple_of*, *set_of*, *list_of*, and *dictionary_of*.
2. Leaves may be labelled with a domain name, or with a type name for representing references[2]. Examples for domain names are *integer*, *real*, or *string*, but there may be others.
3. If a node is labelled *tuple_of*, then the outgoing edges are uniquely labelled with attribute names.
4. If a node is labelled *set_of*, then it has got exactly one child, which is a leaf. The respective edge might be labelled with the empty string ϵ.
5. If a node is labelled *list_of* or *dictionary_of*, then it has got exactly two children, which are leaves. The label of one of these children must be interpreted by a domain suitable for the usual list operations or dictionary operations. The respective edge must be labelled *index* if a list is indicated, or *key* if a dictionary is indicated. The edge to the other child must be labelled *element*.

If further structuring of a collection element is required, this can be accomplished by labelling the respective leaf with a type name, indicating a reference to a (structured) type.

Fig. 2 shows a graphical representation of an example for a type representing a person. The person has a name, a place, some phone numbers, and a birthday. The place is further structured, telling us about the city and the ZIP code of the city. The labels at the nodes tell us how to interpret the data. For example, *phone* should be interpreted as a set of strings, while *birthday* is a single date.

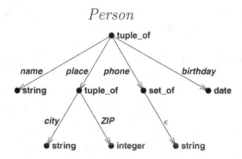

Fig. 2. A type representing a person

---

[2] In this paper, we do not deal with all the subtle problems of recursively or even mutually referencing types and their corresponding objects. Instead we tacitly assume that either such problems do not actually occur or have been solved appropriately.

Definition 3.2 (Object). Instances of types are called *objects*. An object of type τ is identified by a value o_{id} taken from the set Id_τ of all object identifying values for type τ. The actual definition of Id_τ does not matter for now.

The set of objects is completely characterised by functions yielding the types and two values of the objects. The typing function $type : Id \to \mathbf{T}$, with $Id = \bigcup_\tau Id_\tau$ being the set of object identifiers for all types, maps object identifiers to types. Object values are composed of atomic values taken from a suitable set called **Val**. **Val** is defined with respect to the usual interpretations of the above mentioned domain names at the leaves of the type tree, i.e. there is a partial function $dom : \mathcal{L}_V \to \mathcal{P}(\mathbf{Val})$. For instance, if *integer*, *real*, and *string* are possible leaf labels, then $dom(integer) := \mathbb{N}$, $dom(real) := \mathbb{R}$, and $dom(string) := \Sigma *$ over an appropriate alphabet Σ are subsets of **Val**. We also allow for references by labelling leaves with type names, and by defining for each type symbol τ that $dom(\tau) := Id_\tau$ and Id_τ is a subset of **Val**. The valuation function *value* is a partial function on pairs of object identifiers and nodes that valuates a given object identifier o_{id} on *valuated nodes* $V_\tau^e \subset V_\tau$ of the tree of $\tau = type(o_{id})$. More formally, the restriction of *value* on Id_τ, $value_\tau : Id_\tau \times V \to \mathbf{Val} \cup \mathcal{P}(\mathbf{Val}) \cup \mathbf{Val}^{\mathbf{Val}}$ is defined as follows, with $v, w, v_{element}, v_{aux}$ being nodes of $type(o_{id})$:

1. If v is a leaf under a node labelled *tuple_of*, then
   $value_\tau(o_{id}, v) \in dom(label_V(v))$.
2. If v is a leaf under a node w labelled *set_of*, then
   $value_\tau(o_{id}, w) \subset dom(label_V(v))$.
3. If $v_{element}, v_{aux}$ are leaves under a node w labelled *list_of* or *dictionary_of*, with $label_E(w, v_{aux}) \in \{index, key\}$ and $label_E(w, v_{element}) = element$, then $value_\tau(o_{id}, w) \in dom(label_V(v_{element}))^{dom(label_V(v_{aux}))}$, denoting the set of all partial functions from $dom(label_V(v_{aux}))$ to $dom(label_V(v_{element}))$, i.e. all suitably typed indexes or dictionaries.

There is a concept of type substructures we need for comparing types. We are interested in the largest class of substructures of a type which are types themselves. We call members of this class fragments.

Definition 3.3 (fragment). A type $\tau_s := \langle (V_s, E_s), label_{V_s}, label_{E_s} \rangle$, is a fragment of the type $\tau := \langle (V, E), label_V, label_E \rangle$, iff (V_s, E_s) is a finite, rooted, unordered tree with $V_s \subseteq V$ and $E_s \subseteq E$, and $label_{V_s}$ and $label_{E_s}$ have their domains restricted to V_s and E_s, respectively, but work like $label_V$ and $label_E$ otherwise.

In general, the tree of a fragment is a pruned subtree of the tree of the containing type. At each node of this subtree some, but not all, branches may be pruned. Note that the root of the tree of a fragment is not necessarily the root of the containing tree, but each path of the fragment from an inner node to a leaf is also a path in the containing tree ending in a leaf there, too. Figure 3 depicts some examples for fragments. You can see a type *Detailed Person* representing a more complex concept of a person in the upper left, and three fragments in the right and at the bottom. The fragment at the upper right has got the same root as the type *Detailed Person*, but it has got most of the leaves pruned. The fragment in the lower right is cut out of the centre of the original type, representing only the address part of the type *Detailed Person* and additionally pruning some of the leaves. The fragment at the lower left represents the complete street part of a person's address.

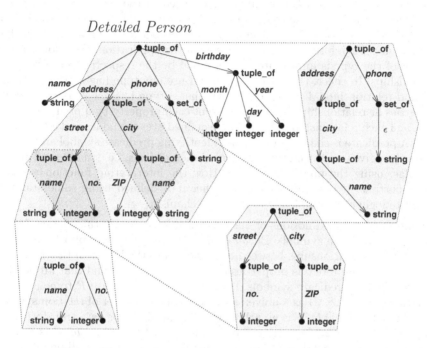

Fig. 3. The type *Detailed Person* and three fragments of it.

3.1   What's in a Type?

When examining types we should keep in mind that we want to establish a definition of a type mapping to be used by data integration technologies. As mentioned before data integration transforms data provided by one or more data sources to a representation being useful for a user or an application. Therefore, when talking about a type mapping, we will call the type being used by an application the *target type*, and the type of the respective source data the *source type*, no matter in which direction we define the mapping.

Intuitively, a (syntactical) mapping of types is correct iff the target type contains a subset of the information of the associated source type. Now what is the informational content of a type? We need a formal model of information itself, making pieces of information comparable to each other. Clearly, the constitutional parts of a type, as syntactically specified in Def. 3.1, and the standardised rules for forming instantiating objects, following Def. 3.2, provide information. However, beyond this "standard information" supposed to be given for commonly granted in the following, the nodes, edges, and labels constituting a type can be further interpreted in some way to yield additional, more specific information. So we should take into account an application as the interpreting instance.

A specific application will not only be interested in the structure of a type as such, but in particular information derived from the structure. The application uses specific properties of that type, and it uses properties and relationships of its components. Therefore, seen from the view of the application, the informational content of the type is immediately determined by the respective properties and relationships. In effect, the application could use any type having these properties and relationships. For expressing whether a type has one of the respective properties or relationships, we can represent each property by a predicate of the type, and each relationship by a predicate defined over the nodes and edges of the type. A predicate is characterised by an identifying predicate symbol and a function which, given an actual type, returns the set of facts, i.e. true ground atomic formulae, using the predicate symbol. How the interpreting function works is not important. It does not matter whether it is defined using some standard predicate logic or a completely different mechanism.

Exploiting established notions of mathematical logic, we postulate a set P containing all predicate symbols. Because the labels on the edges of a type can be interpreted as relationships between two nodes, and the labels on the nodes of a type can be interpreted as properties of the nodes, we demand that all possible label values are predicate symbols, i.e. $\mathcal{L}_V \cup \mathcal{L}_E \subset P$. We use P to construct a signature $S = (\mathcal{R}, \mathcal{F}, \mathcal{C})$ as a universe of discourse, with a set of relation symbols $\mathcal{R} := \{\text{node}, \text{edge}\} \dot\cup P$. $\mathcal{F}$ is an arbitrary set of symbols for data transformation functions including at least a symbol for the identity function id. $\mathcal{C}$ is a set of constant symbols, including at least all possible node identifiers, all possible type identifiers, and the atomic values in **Val**. For each predicate, symbolised by p, there is an (Herbrand) *interpreting function* $f_p : \mathbf{T} \to Facts(S)$ with $Facts(S)$ being the set of ground atomic formulae of S. Specifying interpretations by subsets of $Facts(S)$, i.e. on the semantical level by Herbrand interpretations in the sense of mathematical logic, is both highly flexible and expressive. For some purposes however, e.g. specifying integrity constraints for databases, specifications on the syntactical level could turn out to be more convenient. The interpreting functions are supposed to be defined independent of any application. Because there are infinitely many predicate symbols, and letting the problems related to ambiguities apart as before, we can assume that the interpreting functions express some kind of common knowledge global to all possible applications.

As stated before, each application is interested in particular information, and thus in a set of predicates. Therefore, we assume that there is a set of predicate symbols P_a associated with an application a. This set of predicate symbols is the only specific aspect of a we will use, so for our purpose P_a suffices to characterise the application completely. From now on we will identify a by P_a. The *informational content* $IC(\tau, P_a)$ of a type τ for the application P_a is the union of all pertinent predicate interpretations, i.e. $IC(\tau, P_a) := \bigcup_{p \in P_a} f_p(\tau)$.

The informational content comprises all properties and relationships of τ which the application could potentially use during its execution.

3.2   Using Predicate Logic as an Example

In the remainder of this text we will use predicate logic as an example for defining interpreting functions. Therefore, we choose an alternative representation for a given type $\tau := \langle (V, E), label_V, label_E \rangle$ by defining a finite set of S-formulae ST_τ. For each node $v \in V$ with $label_V(v) = l$, the following facts are in ST_τ:

$$\mathbf{node}(v, \tau) \text{ and } l(v, \tau)$$

For each edge $(v, w) \in E$ with $label_E(v, w) = l$, the following facts are in ST_τ:

$$\mathbf{edge}(v, w, \tau) \text{ and } l(v, w, \tau)$$

ST_τ reflects the syntactical structure of τ by the relation symbols $\mathbf{node}$ and $\mathbf{edge}$, and gives, at least partially, an (Herbrand) interpretation of the predicate symbols identified by the labels associated with τ.

A *semantic predicate* p is derived from ST_τ by a set of S-formulae I_p. Given ST_τ and I_p, we can define the interpreting function f_p as the result of an evaluation function $eval_X$ for logic programs using an arbitrary evaluation mechanism X being applied to a set of S-formulae containing ST_τ and I_p, i.e. $f_p(\tau) := eval_X(ST_\tau \cup I_p)$. In principle, we can plug in any evaluation function we like for $eval_X$, e.g. prolog evaluation $eval_{\text{PROLOG}}$, datalog evaluation $eval_{\text{DATALOG}}$, or stratified datalog evaluation $eval_{\text{sDATALOG}}$. We assume all type specifications to be complete in the local context, so we can do the evaluation under a closed world assumption here. Note that this assumption of a closed world with respect to a single type does not prevent us from assuming a more open world with respect to a mapping of two types.

We use the same logic oriented framework to describe our object model. For representing objects we further extend the set of all relation symbols $\mathcal{R}$ by the symbols $\mathbf{type}$ and $\mathbf{value}$, and by all type identifiers. Without loss of generality we assume that this union is disjoint. In a data integration environment with sources using independent domains for object identifiers, we must be able to identify an object by its value. In consequence, we assume that for each type τ there is a partial function $key_\tau : \mathcal{P}(V_\tau \times \mathbf{Val}) \to Id_\tau$ assigning an object identifier to a type and its full valuation, such that $key_\tau(\{(v, value_\tau(o_{id}, v)) | v \in V_\tau^e\}) = o_{id}$ for each o_{id} with $type(o_{id}) = \tau$. Actual definitions of key_τ must satisfy the usual constraints, i.e. the values must be in the domain associated with the respective leaf, and this domain must consist of scalar values. Accordingly, we represent an object identified by o_{id} with $type(o_{id}) = \tau$ by a set of facts, specifying the type of the object and the value of each valuated node v_i of τ with $value_\tau(o_{id}, v_i) = x_i$:

$\textbf{type}(o_{id}, \tau)$

$\textbf{value}(o_{id}, v_i, x_i)$ if x_i is scalar

$\textbf{value}(o_{id}, v_i, y_j)$ for all $y_j \in x_i$, if x_i is the set $\{y_1, \ldots, y_m\}$

$\textbf{value}(o_{id}, v_i, y_j, z_j)$ for all y_j such that $f(y_j) = z_j$, if x_i is the function f
with $f(y_1) = z_1, \ldots, f(y_m) = z_m$

Many data sources store objects as tuples, ignoring any structure. We can simulate this by alternatively representing an object o_{id} as a set of facts, having relation symbol τ and containing all values as terms, enumerated in an arbitrary, but fixed, order. Let $x_1, \ldots, x_n$ be the scalar values of o_{id}, $Y_1, \ldots, Y_m$ be the sets of o_{id}, and $f_1, \ldots, f_l$ be the functions of o_{id}. Then we obtain the set of facts by combining the scalar elements with the Cartesian product of all sets and of the function graphs:

$$\tau(x_1, \ldots, x_n, y_{j_1}, \ldots, y_{j_m}, d_{j_1}, r_{j_1}, \ldots, d_{j_l}, r_{j_l}) \text{ for all } y_{j_k} \in Y_k,\ f_k(d_{j_k}) = r_{j_k}$$

This plain representation is unique under the assumption on identification by values. Moreover, an unambiguous enumeration algorithm for the values can be defined using the lexicographic order of path expressions build from the respective edge labels. The plain representation of an object can be easily converted to the above defined structured representation by a set of logical implications:

$$\textbf{type}(key_\tau(\{(v_1, X_1), \ldots, (v_n, X_n)\}), \tau)$$
$$\Longleftarrow \tau(X_1, \ldots, X_n, X_{n+1}, \ldots, X_{n+m}, D_1, R_1, \ldots, D_l, R_l);$$

for each position j for a scalar value or the element of a set

$$\textbf{value}(key_\tau(\{(v_1, X_1), \ldots, (v_n, X_n)\}), v_j, X_j)$$
$$\Longleftarrow \tau(X_1, \ldots, X_n, X_{n+1}, \ldots, X_{n+m}, D_1, R_1, \ldots, D_l, R_l);$$

and for each position j for a function

$$\textbf{value}(key_\tau(\{(v_1, X_1), \ldots, (v_n, X_n)\}), v_{n+m+j}, D_j, R_j)$$
$$\Longleftarrow \tau(X_1, \ldots, X_n, X_{n+1}, \ldots, X_{n+m}, D_1, R_1, \ldots, D_l, R_l).$$

3.3   Some Useful Predicates for Types

In an earlier paper [4] we introduced a class of constrained type mappings called *embeddings*. In that paper, types are defined similar to the types in this paper, but without labels at the edges, and with a partial order for the labels on the leaves, i.e. domain names, and another partial order for the labels at the inner nodes, i.e. for the type constructor names. Roughly speaking, an embedding is defined as a mapping of nodes of a target type to nodes of a source type, satisfying the following constraints:

1. The mapping *discriminates leaves*, i.e., the images of two different leaves of the target type must not be connected in the source type.
2. The mapping *strictly preserves connections*, i.e., if two nodes are connected in the target type, then their images must be connected by a non-empty path in the source type.
3. For each node v of the target type, the label of v and the label of its corresponding node in the source type must be compatible with the pertinent partial orders on node labels. In particular, in case of leaf nodes the domain of the source node label must be coercible into the domain of the target node label, according to the given partial order on domain names. And for inner nodes, a more subtle condition is suggested, according to the given partial order on constructor names.

In this chapter we will examine some predicates we can exploit for simulating these constraints as a (rather abstract) example. We choose to define the respective interpreting functions by the terms of predicate logic using the signature S, including the extensions to the set of relation symbols $\mathcal{R}$ done in the previous section. There are five predicates called path, no-connection, leaf-discrimination, coercible, and domain-of. A frequently used relationship on the nodes is the transitive closure of the tree of a type, giving us all paths in the tree. We can define the predicate path as datalog evaluation applied on the logic oriented type representation and a set of two horn clauses:

$$I_{\text{path}} := \{ \text{ path}(v, w, t) \Longleftarrow \text{edge}(v, w, t)$$
$$\text{path}(v, u, t) \Longleftarrow \text{edge}(v, w, t) \wedge \text{path}(w, u, t) \ \}$$
$$f_{\text{path}}(\tau) := eval_{\text{DATALOG}}(ST_\tau \cup I_{\text{path}})$$

For ensuring discrimination of leaves we must check that two leaves are different in the target type and that the images of these leaves are not connected in the source type. The predicate different-leaves defines the first relation. We need negation here, so we use stratified datalog for defining it:

$$I_{\text{different-leaves}} := \{ \text{ inner-node}(v, t) \Longleftarrow \text{edge}(v, w, t)$$
$$\text{different-leaves}(v, w, t) \Longleftarrow \text{node}(v, t) \wedge \text{node}(w, t) \wedge$$
$$v \neq w \wedge$$
$$\neg\text{inner-node}(v, t) \wedge$$
$$\neg\text{inner-node}(w, t) \ \}$$

$$f_{\text{different-leaves}}(\tau) := eval_{\text{sDATALOG}}(ST_\tau \cup I_{\text{different-leaves}})$$

The second relation is defined by the predicate no-connection:

$$I_{\text{no-connection}} := I_{\text{path}} \cup$$
$$\{ \text{ no-connection}(v, w, t) \Longleftarrow \text{node}(v, t) \wedge \text{node}(w, t) \wedge$$
$$v \neq w \wedge$$
$$\neg\text{path}(v, w, t) \wedge \neg\text{path}(w, v, t) \}$$

$$f_{\text{no-connection}}(\tau) := eval_{\text{sDATALOG}}(ST_\tau \cup I_{\text{no-connection}})$$

For checking whether the type of a leaf is coercible into some other type, we need to determine its domain. Given that $\{integer, real, string\} \subseteq \mathcal{L}_V$ and $\{integer, real, string\} \subseteq \mathcal{C}$, we can make the interpretation of a leaf label as a domain name explicit by a predicate `domain-of`:

$$I_{\text{domain-of}} := \{ \text{ domain-of}(v, integer, t) \impliedby \text{integer}(v, t)$$
$$\text{domain-of}(v, real, t) \impliedby \text{real}(v, t)$$
$$\text{domain-of}(v, string, t) \impliedby \text{string}(v, t) \quad \}$$

$$f_{\text{domain-of}}(\tau) := eval_{\text{DATALOG}}(ST_\tau \cup I_{\text{domain-of}})$$

Now we can define the predicate `coercible`. We use an auxiliary predicate `type-coercible` here, which specifies whether one domain can be coerced into another. We use two rules for ensuring reflexivity and transitivity of the coercion relation. The definition of `coercible` uses `type-coercible` and `domain-of` to determine whether a node has a domain being coercible into another domain.

$$I_{\text{coercible}} := I_{\text{domain-of}} \cup$$
$$\{ \text{ type-coercible}(integer, real)$$
$$\text{type-coercible}(real, string)$$
$$\text{type-coercible}(string, string)$$
$$\text{type-coercible}(x, x) \impliedby \text{type-coercible}(x, y)$$
$$\text{type-coercible}(x, z) \impliedby \text{type-coercible}(x, y) \wedge$$
$$\text{type-coercible}(y, z)$$
$$\text{coercible}(v, x, t) \impliedby \text{domain-of}(v, x, t)$$
$$\text{coercible}(v, y, t) \impliedby \text{domain-of}(v, x, t) \wedge$$
$$\text{type-coercible}(x, y) \quad \}$$

$$f_{\text{coercible}}(\tau) := eval_{\text{DATALOG}}(ST_\tau \cup I_{\text{coercible}})$$

We will use the set $\{$`edge`, `different-leaves`, `domain-of`$\}$ at the end of chapter 4 for adapting our definition of embeddings from the earlier paper, so we call it EDD for short.

3.4   Extended Types

As stated above the informational content of a type varies with the application it is used in. In order to represent the information of a type in the context of an application, we extend our types by a set of predicates. These extended types can be used as source types and target types for a type mapping later.

Definition 3.4 (extended type). Let τ be a type, $\tau = \langle (V, E), label_V, label_E \rangle$, and some facts $R \subset Facts(S)$. We construct a corresponding extended type τ_e with additional properties and relationships: $\tau_e = \langle (V, E, R), label_V, label_E \rangle$.

In the context of an application, we can transform a type into an appropriate extended type by a function *extend* taking a type τ and an application P_a and yielding an extended type[3]. If $\tau = \langle (V, E), label_V, label_E \rangle$, then $extend(\tau, P_a) := \langle (V, E, IC(\tau, P_a)), label_V, label_E \rangle$.

Fig. 4 illustrates an example for an extended type in the context of an application interested in non-empty paths of the type tree. The type is *Person* again, extended by the predicate **path** described in the beginning of Chap. 3.3. Note that not all predicates can be represented graphically by an arrow. Predicates of arity 0 are global properties independent of any type. Predicates of arity 1 are local properties of the type or a node. Predicates having an arity greater than two can be interpreted as n-ary relationships.

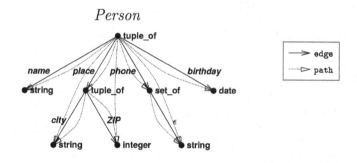

Fig. 4. The *Person* type extended by the relationship **path**

4   Correct and Complete Interpretations

As mentioned before our task is to establish links between representations of partially matching real world concepts. We achieve this on the schema level by mapping types, as well as on the instance level by transforming objects. Before we define our notion of type mappings, we first provide some means for transforming values. We postulate the existence of a set of globally defined *data transformation functions*, denoted by the set of sorted function symbols $\mathcal{F}$ from our signature S. As sorts for arguments and results we allow domain names, as used for labelling leaves of type trees, as well as generalised domain names to be used for inner nodes. These generalised domain names are defined as follows. If x and y are suitable domain names, then $set\_of\langle x \rangle$, $list\_of\langle x, y \rangle$, and $dictionary\_of\langle x, y \rangle$ are generalised domain names not being in $\mathcal{L}_V$ for valuated inner nodes. We also extend our partial function dom accordingly, where, as before, B^A denotes the set of all partial functions from A

---

[3] More abstractly, the extension can be interpreted as just a precondition imposed on the type by an application. Under this view, our approach aims at exploiting a particular form of preconditions for the purpose of data integration.

to B: $dom(set\_of\langle x\rangle) := \mathcal{P}(dom(x))$, $dom(list\_of\langle x,y\rangle) := dom(y)^{dom(x)}$, and $dom(dictionary\_of\langle x,y\rangle) := dom(y)^{dom(x)}$.

Additionally, we use the label *tuple_of* for inner nodes that are not valuated as generalised domain name. For the sake of succinctness, we do not explicitly specify the definition of $dom(tuple\_of)$, roughly meaning the class of all appropriately constructible types. Henceforth speaking about domain names is often meant to include generalised domain names, too.

We can express the application of a data transformation function on the values of an object by a sorted data transformation term, which uses constant symbols and node symbols as syntactical arguments for the data transformation function.

Definition 4.1 (Data transformation term with result sort). Let $\tau = \langle (V,E), label_V, label_E\rangle$ be a type.

1. For each node $v \in V$, v is a data transformation term the result sort of which is defined as follows:

    $label_V(v)$ if v is a leaf.

    $set\_of\langle label_V(w)\rangle$

            if $label_V(v) = set\_of$ and w is the child of v.

    $list\_of\langle label_V(w_{index}), label_V(w_{element})\rangle$

            if $label_V(v) = list\_of$, and w_{index} and $w_{element}$ are the children of v.

    $dictionary\_of\langle label_V(w_{key}), label_V(w_{element})\rangle$

            if $label_V(v) = dictionary\_of$, and w_{key} and $w_{element}$ are the children of v.

    $tuple\_of$ if $label_V(v) = tuple\_of$.

2. For each constant symbol $c \in \mathbf{Val} \subset \mathcal{C}$, c is a data transformation term the result sort of which is any domain name d with $c \in dom(d)$.

3. If $t_1, \ldots, t_n$ are data transformation terms with result sorts $d_1, \ldots, d_n$ all being leaf labels or collection domain names, and dt is an n-ary function symbol from $\mathcal{F}$ with argument sorts $d_1, \ldots, d_n$ and result sort r, then $dt(t_1, \ldots, t_n)$ is a data transformation term with result sort r.

The set of all data transformation terms over τ is called $\mathbf{DT}(\tau)$. We will call data transformation terms consisting of a leaf only *trivial data transformation terms*, and all data transformation terms containing at least one function symbol *non-trivial data transformation terms*.

Intuitively, a non-trivial data transformation term with result sort r and using node symbols $v_1, \ldots, v_n$ of a tree for type τ represents a function, which can be used for taking its non-constant arguments from the nodes $v_1, \ldots, v_n$ of an object of type τ. As before, we are not specific about inner nodes labelled *tuple_of*.

Now we are ready to define a class of type mappings. We map target types on source types, because we wish to use these mappings for query translation.

Definition 4.2 (type mapping). Let $\tau_e = \langle (V_\tau, E_\tau, R_\tau), label_{V_\tau}, label_{E_\tau}\rangle$ and $\sigma_e = \langle (V_\sigma, E_\sigma, R_\sigma), label_{V_\sigma}, label_{E_\sigma}\rangle$ be extended types. A *type mapping* $i : V_\tau \rightarrow$

$\mathbf{DT}(\sigma)$ maps each node of τ_e labelled *tuple_of* to a trivial data transformation term $w \in \mathbf{DT}(\sigma)$, and each valuated node of τ_e to a non-trivial data transformation term $dt \in \mathbf{DT}(\sigma)$. In either case, i must satisfy the constraint that the node v being mapped has a sort – as defined in Def. 4.1.1 – being the same as the result sort of $i(v)$.

The type mapping i induces three further mappings:

1. a mapping of nodes returning sets of nodes of σ, $i_V : V_\tau \to \mathcal{P}(V_\sigma)$, with
   $i_V(v) := \{w | w \in V_\sigma$ occurs in $i(v)\}$,
2. a mapping of edges returning pairs of nodes of σ (which are not necessarily edges in E_σ), $i_E : E_\tau \to \mathcal{P}(V_\sigma \times V_\sigma)$, with $i_E(v_1, v_2) := i_V(v_1) \times i_V(v_2)$,
3. a mapping of additional properties and relationships returning facts concerning σ, $i_R : R_\tau \to \mathcal{P}(Facts(S))$, with
   $$i_R(p(v_1, \ldots, v_n, \ldots)) = \{p(w_1, \ldots, w_n, \ldots) | w_j \in i_V(v_j)\}$$
   for each fact in R_τ where $v_1, \ldots, v_n$ are all nodes occurring in that fact.

Note that a non-trivial data transformation term can be the identity function applied on a node symbol, thus indicating a pure data access. Later on, only values on the valuated nodes are actually transformed. The mapping of other inner nodes is important for ensuring correctness only.

In general, we do not need to map the labels. However, if a mapping of labels is important, we can do the job by including an additional predicate in P_a for each label value.

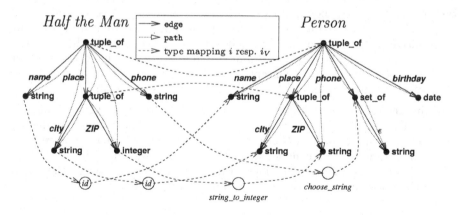

Fig. 5. A type mapping

See Fig. 5 for an example. The type *Person* from the previous examples serves as the source type here. The target type represents a somewhat reduced concept of a person, called *Half the Man*, which is similar to *Person*, but lacks some of the attributes. The ZIP attribute of the place is mapped via the coercion function *string_to_integer* : $\Sigma * \to \mathbb{N}$, and the attribute *phone* is mapped to the function *choose_string* : $\mathcal{P}(\Sigma*) \to \Sigma*$. The other leaves are mapped using the identity function.

Fig. 6 shows an example using a more complex data transformation term. You can see the birthday parts of our type *Person* and of our type *Detailed Person*. The birthday attribute of *Person*, which is an atomic date, is mapped to the date components of the birthday attribute of *Detailed Person* via a data transformation function *tuple_to_date* : $\mathbb{N} \times \mathbb{N} \times \mathbb{N} \to$ **Date**, with **Date** being the set of all atomic dates.

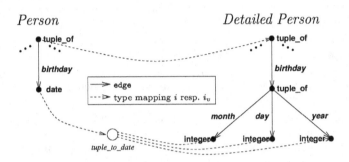

Fig. 6. A part of a type mapping with a more complex data transformation term

Now we can relate the informational content of the source type and of the target type by analysing the behaviour of the induced mappings of edges and tuples. Intuitively, the basic requirement on a type mapping is to ensure correct interpretation of types, meaning that only types corresponding to the same real world concept should be mapped. But as stated above, a data integration system should also be able to relate concepts matching only partially, thus striving for integrating as much meaningful data from the sources as possible.

Relaxing the requirement – from aiming at perfect matches only to allowing also partial matches – we loose assurance of correct interpretations, but we possibly gain access to more sources. Hence, there is a tradeoff between "interpretation correctness" and "source-completeness". Accordingly, we will define several notions of correctness of type mappings with a decreasing assurance on the degree of matching between the represented real world concepts.

4.1 Interpretation Correctness of Type Mappings

First we introduce structure preservation as a very restrictive notion of interpretation correctness, allowing to map a type to another one representing a concept perfectly covering the concept represented by the first type. By a structure preserving type mapping, a target type may only be mapped on a fragment of the source type isomorphic to the target type, not allowing for any information to be dropped, added, or modified.

Definition 4.3 (structure preservation). A type mapping i from an extended type $\tau_e = \langle(V_\tau, E_\tau, IC(\tau, P_a)), label_{V_\tau}, label_{E_\tau}\rangle$ to another extended type $\sigma_e = \langle(V_\sigma, E_\sigma, R_\sigma), label_{V_\sigma}, label_{E_\sigma}\rangle$ in the context of an application P_a is structure preserving, iff it satisfies the constraint from Def. 4.2 that

1. the node v being mapped has a sort – as defined in Def. 4.1.1 – being the same as the result sort of $i(v)$,

and additionally the following constraints:

2. For each valuated node v, there is a valuated node $w \in V_\sigma$ and $i(v) = id(w)$.
3. i, interpreted as a mapping of nodes, is one-to-one.
4. All resulting edges of the induced mapping i_E are in E_σ.
5. All resulting facts of the induced mapping i_R are in R_σ.
6. $label_{E_\tau}(v, w) = label_{E_\sigma}(i(v), i(w))$ for all edges $(v, w) \in E_\tau$.

Structure preservation is widely independent of the application. In fact, only the fifth constraint on the inclusion of the informational content $IC(\tau, P_a)$ refers to the application. Thus, usually we can expect high assurance on a perfect match between the related concepts.

A more flexible notion of interpretation correctness allows to make interpretation correctness strongly dependent on the application. This notion does not care about structural relationships, and it abandons the constraint of being one-to-one. But, under the discretion of the application, the notion still demands the strict preservation of explicitly stated application semantics by maintaining the fifth constraint concerning the inclusion of informational contents.

Thereby, from the point of view of an application only, the pertinent real world concepts might still match reasonably well, while there is no general assurance any more. Accordingly, in general this notion will allow to exploit more sources.

Definition 4.4 (P_a-correctness of a type mapping). A type mapping i from an extended type $\tau_e = \langle(V_\tau, E_\tau, IC(\tau, P_a)), label_{V_\tau}, label_{E_\tau}\rangle$ to an extended type $\sigma_e = \langle(V_\sigma, E_\sigma, R_\sigma), label_{V_\sigma}, label_{E_\sigma}\rangle$ is P_a-correct, iff all resulting facts of the induced mapping i_R are in R_σ.

The example in Fig. 5 is {path}-correct. But it is not structure preserving, because it violates the second constraint by mapping two of the nodes of the target type to data transformation terms containing the functions $string\_to\_integer$ and $choose\_string$, respectively.

Note that we can use P_a-correctness to simulate structure preservation (except for the constraint on the data transformation terms) by "copying" the structural relationships node and edge into semantic predicates, declaring the edge labels as interesting for the application, and including a predicate called different-node for imposing the one-to-one constraint on the mapping:

$$I_{\texttt{node-of}} := \{\ \texttt{node-of}(v, t) \Longleftarrow \texttt{node}(v, t)\ \}$$

$$f_{\texttt{node-of}}(\tau) := eval_{\text{DATALOG}}(ST_\tau \cup I_{\texttt{node-of}})$$

$$I_{\text{edge-of}} := \{ \text{ edge-of}(v, w, t) \impliedby \text{ edge}(v, w, t) \}$$

$$f_{\text{edge-of}}(\tau) := \text{ eval}_{\text{DATALOG}}(ST_\tau \cup I_{\text{edge-of}})$$

$$I_{\text{different-node}} := \{ \text{ different-node}(v, w, t) \impliedby \text{ node}(v, t) \land \text{node}(w, t) \land$$
$$v \neq w \quad \}$$

$$f_{\text{different-node}}(\tau) := \text{ eval}_{\text{sDATALOG}}(ST_\tau \cup I_{\text{different-node}})$$

Obviously, $(\{\text{node-of}, \text{edge-of}, \text{different-node}\} \cup \mathcal{L}_E)$-correctness and structure preservation are equivalent. But in general, P_a-correct type mappings are not necessarily structure preserving. In fact, we can map each type on another if the first type contains a subset of the information of the second type.

Finally, even if an application is willing to restrict itself to correct interpretation of its explicitly stated interests, it might happen that a source would not allow to specify type mappings that satisfy the constraint of P_a-correctness, although there a relationships being obvious to a human. In this situation, the integration administrator can assist by finding meaningful connections between target semantics and source semantics. In order to enable this administration task, we introduce an even more flexible notion of interpretation correctness that allows for substitution of predicates. Then, in general, the application relies on the decisions of the administrator, and thus both the assurance on matches and the actual degree of matches between the represented concepts might decrease.

Definition 4.5 ($P_a|s$-correctness of a type mapping). Assume that $\tau_e = \langle(V_\tau, E_\tau, IC(\tau, P_a)), label_{V_\tau}, label_{E_\tau}\rangle$ and $\sigma_e = \langle(V_\sigma, E_\sigma, R_\sigma), label_{V_\sigma}, label_{E_\sigma}\rangle$ are extended types. Let $s : P \to P_a$ be a function indicating a substitution of predicates having the same arity. Let $R_{s,\sigma} = \{s(p)(\boldsymbol{x})|p(\boldsymbol{x}) \in R_\sigma\}$ be the set of facts in the source type under the substitution s. A type mapping i from τ_e to $\langle(V_\sigma, E_\sigma, R_{s,\sigma}), label_{V_\sigma}, label_{E_\sigma}\rangle$ is $P_a|s$-correct, iff all resulting facts of the induced mapping i_R are in $R_{s,\sigma}$.

We assume that a predicate substitution function substitutes most of the predicates by themselves, so we will describe the function by the non-trivial substitutions only. Let s_{pnc} be a predicate substitution function with

$$s_{pnc}(\text{path}) := \text{edge}$$
$$s_{pnc}(\text{no-connection}) := \text{different-leaves}$$
$$s_{pnc}(\text{coercible}) := \text{domain-of}$$

We call $EDD|s_{pnc}$-correct type mappings *embeddings*. See section 3.3 for the definition of EDD. This definition of embeddings simulates the definition in our earlier paper [4], if we use the same edge labels. Fig. 7 illustrates an example for an embedding. For the sake of readability we focused on the substitution of no-connection by leave-distinction. Note that each connection of kind different-leaves is mapped to a connection of kind no-connection, and each edge of the tree of the target type has a corresponding path in the source type.

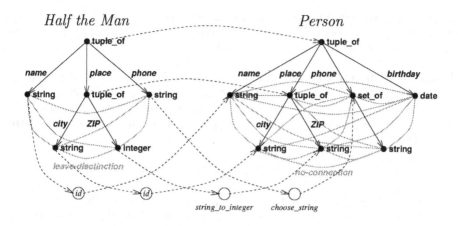

Fig. 7. An example for an embedding

Note that $P_a|id$-correctness is equivalent to P_a-correctness, if id is the identity function over predicates.

You can easily imagine more flexible definitions of interpretation correctness, by replacing the substitution function used in the definition of $P_a|s$-correctness by suitable functions doing more complex transformations.

4.2 Interpretation Completeness of Type Mappings

The more flexible notions of interpretation correctness are intended to deal with the tradeoff between "fully correct interpretations" and "exploiting all available sources". The latter demand is directed to some kind of completeness, i.e. to take the best advantage of all connected sources. In this section we consider a somewhat different, though also related, notion which we call *interpretation completeness*. Here we consider each single source type, and we ask whether its semantics are covered by the collection of all previously declared type mappings to it.

As a starting point, let us assume that an actual data integration system has a target schema consisting of many target types, several source schemas consisting of many source types, and many type mappings. In particular, there will be many type mappings between several target types and a single source type. An intuitive concept of interpretation completeness of a data integration system demands that, in the context of an application, all information contained in a source type must also be contained in the target schema. The information contained in that source type will be distributed throughout the target schema in general, in the end because we also treat partial matches of the real world concepts represented by the types. In consequence, it is not sensible to define a notion of interpretation completeness of a single type mapping, but of the set of type mappings having the same source type.

Analogous to structure preservation we define a most strict notion of interpretation completeness, demanding that each structural or semantical element of the source type is reflected by the target schema:

Definition 4.6 (structural completeness). A set $\{i_1, \ldots, i_n\}$ of type mappings from the extended types $\tau_{1_e} = \langle (V_{\tau_1}, E_{\tau_1}, R_{a,\tau_1}), label_{V_{\tau_1}}, label_{E_{\tau_1}} \rangle, \ldots,$ $\tau_{n_e} = \langle (V_{\tau_n}, E_{\tau_n}, R_{a,\tau_n}), label_{V_{\tau_n}}, label_{E_{\tau_n}} \rangle,$ respectively, to the extended type $\sigma_e = \langle (V_\sigma, E_\sigma, R_{a,\sigma}), label_{V_\sigma}, label_{E_\sigma} \rangle$ is structural complete, iff it satisfies the following constraints:

1. For each i_k and each valuated node v, there is a valuated node $w \in V_\sigma$ and $i_k(v) = id(w)$.
2. The union of all i_k, interpreted as mappings of nodes, is onto.
3. All edges in E_σ are in the union of the sets of resulting edges of the induced mappings i_{k_E}.
4. All facts in R_σ are in the union of the sets of resulting facts of the induced mappings i_{k_R}.
5. $label_{E_\tau}(v, w) = label_{E_\sigma}(i_k(v), i_k(w))$ for all i_k and all edges $(v, w) \in E_\tau$.

As a more flexible notion, we introduce P_a-completeness the definition of which is analogous to the definition of P_a-correctness:

Definition 4.7 (P_a-completeness). A set of n type mappings $\{i_1, \ldots, i_n\}$ from the extended types $\tau_{1_e} = \langle (V_{\tau_1}, E_{\tau_1}, R_{a,\tau_1}), label_{V_{\tau_1}}, label_{E_{\tau_1}} \rangle, \ldots, \tau_{n_e} = \langle (V_{\tau_n}, E_{\tau_n}, R_{a,\tau_n}), label_{V_{\tau_n}}, label_{E_{\tau_n}} \rangle,$ respectively, to the extended type $\sigma_e = \langle (V_\sigma, E_\sigma, R_{a,\sigma}), label_{V_\sigma}, label_{E_\sigma} \rangle$ is P_a-complete, iff $R_{a,\sigma}$ is a subset of the set of resulting facts of all induced mappings i_{k_R}.

For both notions of interpretation completeness and the corresponding notion of interpretation correctness, respectively, if a type mapping is both correct and, being the only element of a set, complete, then there is sufficient assurance that the represented concepts reasonably match. Then, in the case of strong structural relationships, the assurance is widely independent of the application, whereas in the flexible application-dependent case, the assurance only applies locally to the point of view of the application under consideration. Or speaking otherwise, in the strong case, the integration administrator can consider the situation as evidence that the mapping relates types representing concepts having the same structure and the same interpretation, whereas in the flexible case the concepts might still match well regarding the interpretation, although there representations may differ.

4.3   Partial Type Mappings

In many cases it is not possible to map each of the nodes of the target type to an appropriate source type node, because the target type models a broader part of the real world than the source type. In these cases, we want to specify *partial type mappings*, which may map nodes also to a special value called *undefined*.

In consequence, we include *undefined* into our set of values **Val** and into our set of constant symbols $\mathcal{C}$. The defined part of the target type, i.e. the nodes not being mapped to *undefined* and the edges connecting these nodes, must be a fragment of the target type. With the latter restriction the above defined notions of interpretation correctness and interpretation completeness can be applied to partial mappings by examining the mappings of such fragments to the source type.

Note that we can map larger parts of the target type to the source type by defining several mappings, each being defined over a fragment of the target type. See Fig. 8 for an example. There are two type mappings, called i and j, which map different parts of the type *Person* to the type *Company*. The mappings of nodes to *undefined* are not explicitly shown. Instead, these nodes do not have an outgoing arc of the respective type mapping.

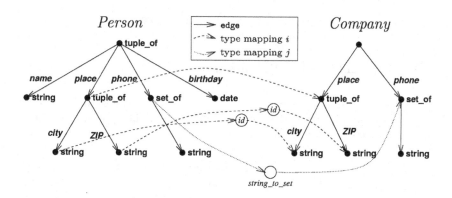

Fig. 8. Two partial type mappings

Partial type mappings allow for arbitrarily mapping nodes to *undefined*. But we should still demand that partial type mappings are "as complete as possible", i.e., if a node could be mapped, then it must be mapped.

4.4   Integrating Data

A type mapping i from a type $\tau_e \langle (V_\tau, E_\tau, IC(\tau, P_a)), label_{V_\tau}, label_{E_\tau} \rangle$ to a type $\sigma_e = \langle (V_\sigma, E_\sigma, R_\sigma), label_{V_\sigma}, label_{E_\sigma} \rangle$ induces a view definition which can be applied on the instances of these types. The view uses an evaluation function $eval_{\text{dtt}}$ of data transformation terms t on a source object identifier o_{src}. $eval_{\text{dtt}}$ is defined as follows:

1. if t is a valuated node in V_σ, then $\qquad eval_{\text{dtt}}(o_{\text{src}}, t) := value_\sigma(o_{\text{src}}, t)$
2. if $t \in \mathcal{C}$, then $\qquad\qquad\qquad\qquad eval_{\text{dtt}}(o_{\text{src}}, t) := t$
3. if $t = f(t_1, \ldots, t_n)$, then
$$eval_{\text{dtt}}(o_{\text{src}}, t) := F(eval_{\text{dtt}}(o_{\text{src}}, t_1), \ldots, eval_{\text{dtt}}(o_{\text{src}}, t_n)),$$
where f denotes the function F

$eval_{\text{dtt}}$ is not defined for trivial data transformation terms being an inner node labelled $tuple\_of$.

Given a set of identifiers of source objects, each having source type σ, we can iterate over this set:

1. for each object identifier o_{src}, we exploit the valuated leaves in order to determine a corresponding object identifier of target type τ by means of key_τ, and
2. for the resulting object identifier o_{tgt}, we set its type τ and valuate it.

More formally, using the evaluated data transformation terms, we define

$$o_{\text{tgt}} := key_\tau(\{(v_j, eval_{\text{dtt}}(o_{\text{src}}, i(v_j)))|v_j \text{ is a valuated leaf in } V_\tau\}),$$
$$type(o_{\text{tgt}}) := \tau,$$
$$value_\tau(o_{\text{tgt}}, v) := eval_{\text{dtt}}(o_{\text{src}}, i(v)) \text{ for all valuated nodes } v \in V_\tau.$$

4.5   Logic Oriented View Definitions

The induced view mapping can be easily expressed with the means of our logic, if there is no mapping to collections or functions in the source type. Let the mapping i be defined as follows:

$i(v_j) := dtf_j(w_{j_1}, \ldots, w_{j_{n_j}})$ for all valuated nodes $v_j \in V_\tau$,
with $w_{j_1}, \ldots, w_{j_{n_j}}$ being valuated nodes in V_σ,
and $dtf_j(w_{j_1}, \ldots, w_{j_{n_j}})$ being a representation of the data transformation term emphasising the dependency on a set of node values; for the sake of simplicity, in the following we identify such terms with the denoted functions.

The logic oriented view definition results from substituting all occurrences of nodes in the data transformation terms by variables bound to the respective values of the structured representation of the source type. For a source type having m valuated leaves $w_1, \ldots, w_m$, we define the view as follows:

$$\textbf{type}(key_\tau(\{(v_j, dtf_j(X_{j_1}, \ldots, X_{j_{n_j}}))|v_j \text{ is a valuated leaf in } V_\tau\}), \tau)$$
$$\Longleftarrow \textbf{value}(O, w_1, X_1) \wedge \cdots \wedge \textbf{value}(O, w_m, X_m)$$

For each valuated leaf v_k of the target type:

$$\textbf{value}(key_\tau(\{(v_j, dtf_j(X_{j_1}, \ldots, X_{j_{n_j}}))|v_j \text{ is a valuated leaf in } V_\tau\}),$$
$$v_k, \ dtf_k(X_{j_1}, \ldots, X_{j_{n_k}}))$$
$$\Longleftarrow \textbf{value}(O, w_1, X_1) \wedge \cdots \wedge \textbf{value}(O, w_m, X_m)$$

For each inner node v_k labelled *set_of* of the target type:

$\{$ value$(key_\tau(\{(v_j, dtf_j(X_{j_1}, \ldots, X_{j_{n_j}}))|v_j$ is a valuated leaf in $V_\tau\}), v_k, Y)|$
$\quad Y \in dtf_k(X_{j_1}, \ldots, X_{j_{n_k}})$
$\qquad$ with the X_i bound by value$(O, w_1, X_1) \wedge \cdots \wedge$ value(O, w_m, X_m) $\}$

And for each inner node v_k labelled *list_of* or *dictionary_of* of the target type:

$\{$ value$(key_\tau(\{(v_j, dtf_j(X_{j_1}, \ldots, X_{j_{n_j}}))|v_j$ is a valuated leaf in $V_\tau\}), v_k, Y, Z)|$
$\quad dtf_k(X_{j_1}, \ldots, X_{j_{n_k}}) = f$ and $f(Y) = Z$
$\qquad$ with the X_i bound by value$(O, w_1, X_1) \wedge \cdots \wedge$ value(O, w_m, X_m) $\}$

4.6   Comparison with Other Approaches

In other works three classes of data integration systems are distinguished: Global As View (GAV) systems [1], Local As View (LAV) systems [15], and GLAV systems [12]. Roughly speaking, GAV systems are built from view definitions as conjunctive queries, having the general form

$$r(\boldsymbol{X}) \Longleftarrow v_1(\boldsymbol{X}, \boldsymbol{Z}_1) \wedge \cdots \wedge v_n(\boldsymbol{X}, \boldsymbol{Z}_n)$$

where r is a target item and $v_1, \ldots, v_n$ are source items.

In contrast, LAV systems constrain individual source items to a query on target items. GLAV systems in some sense combine both features, constraining a query on source items to a query on target items.

For comparing our approach to the ones described above, we translate our view definition to a representation using the plain representation of objects, as far as possible. For instance, for a target type having m valuated nodes, and a source type having l valuated nodes all of which are scalar, the plain view is defined as follows:

$$\tau(dtf_1(W_{k_1}, \ldots, W_{k_{n_1}}), \ldots, dtf_m(W_{k_1}, \ldots, W_{k_{n_m}})) \Longleftarrow \sigma(W_1, \ldots, W_l)$$

Then, if we only examine a single non-partial type mapping, our induced view definition has the form of a GAV expression. However, if the type mapping is only partial, we would get

$$\tau(dtf_1(W_{k_1}, \ldots, W_{k_{n_1}}), \ldots, dtf_{m-j}(W_{k_1}, \ldots, W_{k_{n_{m-j}}}),$$
$$undefined, \ldots, undefined) \qquad\qquad \Longleftarrow \sigma(W_1, \ldots, W_l)$$

Furthermore, in a data integration system with many such type mappings for one target type, we choose to combine the induced view definitions by a not purely conjunctive combination:

$$\tau(\boldsymbol{X}, \boldsymbol{Y}) \quad \Longleftarrow \sigma_{1.1}(\boldsymbol{X}_{1.1}, \boldsymbol{Z}_{1.1}) \wedge \cdots \wedge \sigma_{1.m_1}(\boldsymbol{X}_{1.m_1}, \boldsymbol{Z}_{1.m_1}) \quad \vee \ldots \vee$$
$$\sigma_{n.1}(\boldsymbol{X}_{n.1}, \boldsymbol{Z}_{n.1}) \wedge \cdots \wedge \sigma_{n.m_n}(\boldsymbol{X}_{n.m_n}, \boldsymbol{Z}_{n.m_n})$$

with $\boldsymbol{X} = \bigcup_{i,j} \boldsymbol{X}_{i.j}$, and $\boldsymbol{Y} = (undefined, \ldots, undefined)$.

Each X_i must contain a key serving as the object identifier. This is no standard datalog anymore, but it can still be efficiently evaluated. The idea is, roughly spoken, to evaluate each conjunction by each, plugging the resulting data into the result tuple identified by the key. This differs substantially from datalog evaluation of a set of horn clauses, because the latter would result in extra tuples for each rule, while our mechanism minimises the number of undefined values in the resulting tuples. If we further allow for extending the view definitions by conditions extracted from a query, then the expressive power of these combined view definitions appears to be in the spirit of GLAV, though a precise comparison would require much more formal investigations.

5   The Generic Mediation System MMM

We implemented a software called MMM capable of integrating data using types and type mappings of the above presented kind. It comprises data structures for representing types and objects of the target schema as well as types and objects of the source schemas, and data structures for representing type mappings. MMM stores type definitions and type mapping definitions in an object database. This object database (by the time being it is an O_2 system) is made ODMG compliant by an abstraction layer put in between. Queries can be specified using OQL, the Object Query Language of ODMG.

When a query is posed to an MMM instance, MMM uses the type mappings to decompose the query into several subqueries each of which can be processed by a single source. The decomposition process is roughly outlined as follows:

1. Identify all attributes used in the query.
2. Find all type mappings that map these attributes to something else but *undefined*.
3. For each mapping, construct a subquery for retrieving all objects of the respective source type.
4. If the query contains additional conditions, which can be mapped to the source, add these conditions to the respective subquery.

The subqueries are passed to the sources, and the resulting objects, each conforming to the source schema, are materialised in the database system of the MMM. Afterwards, we apply the appropriate induced view definitions on the materialised source objects, thus constructing a set of target objects. Finally, we evaluate the original query over the target objects. We call this process *two-pass-approach* [8], because the query evaluation is divided into two phases, one for retrieving data from the sources and one for transforming the data to the output format specified in the query.

5.1   The Data Structures

The type representations of MMM conform to Def. 3.1, but the node labels are restricted to the type system proposed by the ODMG [10]. The ODMG type system comprises

- atomic literal types like long, float, or string,
- collection literal types for sets, lists, and dictionaries (there are bags and arrays, too, but we do not handle them yet),
- structured literal types like date or time and the generic type constructor struct,
- classes, i.e. object types for atomic objects, and object types for the above mentioned kinds of collection literals and time-related structured literals, and
- references to object types.

We represent an MMM type by an ODMG class. At the leaves, we only allow ODMG atomic literal types, and references to other classes. ODMG structured literal types like date or time are modelled by tuples having the appropriate attributes. *tuple_of* corresponds to ODMG structs, *set_of* corresponds to ODMG sets, *list_of* corresponds to ODMG lists, and *dictionary_of* corresponds to ODMG dictionaries. We store the MMM types using their ODMG representation in the schema of the object database system.

The ODMG type system includes collections with structured elements. In our MMM type system, we simulate such collections by using appropriate reference types as element types, as mentioned in Chap. 3.

The rough idea of the data structures representing type mapping is a set of pairs. Each element of the set maps a node of the target type to one or more nodes of the source type, and additionally contains the specification of a data transformation function suitable for transforming source data to target data. This way, all type mappings can be represented, including structure preserving, P_a-correct, and $P_a|s$-correct type mappings.

Instances of MMM types, i.e. objects, are stored as database objects. In effect, the database system can be used for query evaluation and transformation of the materialised data.

5.2   The Specification Languages

The target schema as well as the source schemas are specified using ODL, the Object Description Language of the ODMG. The ODMG model allows for modularising schemas by two concepts called module and repository, both serving as containers for schema elements. We exploit repository for keeping the target schema and the source schemas in different name spaces.

Type mappings are specified using a language called TYML. Each TYML type mapping contains the specification of a source type and a target type, and a set of TYML expressions. The target type and the source type are specified using the respective ODMG class names, along with the names of the repositories in which the classes are defined. A TYML expression associates an attribute of the target type with an OQL expression over attributes of the source type. After importing the TYML specification into an MMM instance, the OQL expression is used as a data transformation term in the first phase of query evaluation.

There are tools for translating ODL specifications and TYML specifications to the internal data structures of MMM.

6   Conclusion and Future Work

We outlined a data integration system enabling a controlled degree of interpretation correctness. Our implementation, MMM, allows for representing type mappings for all levels of interpretation correctness. Furthermore, it can integrate actual source data according to these type mappings, thus translating the level of interpretation correctness to the data integration process.

While outlining our achievements, we postulated several assumptions and introduced input parameters for the integration process. In order to complement the summary and Fig. 1, given in the introduction, it might be worthwhile to gather the main assumptions and inputs:

- The inputs are provided by an integration manager.
- Type specifications non-ambiguously represent real world concepts.
- Types contain some standardised information w.r.t. domain names, collection constructors etc. and instantiating objects.
- Any application is characterised by a set of predicates which specify additional more specific information for types.
- The interpreting functions for predicates are global common knowledge.
- Within a logic oriented framework, these functions can be determined by appropriate rules and plugged-in evaluation mechanisms.
- For converting source data into target data, there are globally defined data transformation functions.
- The integration administrator declares application specific type mappings based on the standardised information content and the specific information content of types and and the data transformation functions.
- The integration administrator analyses the quality of type mappings based on his choice of constraints.

Clearly, the results of the whole integration process strongly depend on the degree of concretely meeting the abstract assumptions and actually providing inputs that are appropriate in the concrete application case.

Today, the MMM prototype still lacks a mechanism for enforcing certain degrees of interpretation correctness. Neither the data integration system nor the tools interpreting the specifications actually check for interpretation correctness. This can lead to unpredictable behaviour of the integration system. In particular, compliance to coercion rules is not enforced, i.e. a leaf having a domain a can be mapped to a leaf having a domain b, with a being not coercible to type b. In these cases, the respective view definitions must use functions converting values of type b to values of type a.

Furthermore, type mappings must be specified manually, although there are approaches for finding type mappings automatically with a high confidence level.

The integration of MMM with one or more of these approaches is desirable. Last but not least, MMM must be tested for scalability with respect to the size of the data sets, the number of data sources, and the complexity of schema definitions.

References

[1] S. Adali, K. Candan, Y. Papakonstantinou, and V. Subrahmanian. Query caching and optimization in distributed mediator systems. In H. V. Jagadish and I. S. Mumick, editors, *Proceedings of the 1996 ACM SIGMOD International Conference on Management of Data*, pages 137–148, Montreal, Canada, 1996.

[2] S. Adali and R. Emery. A uniform framework for integrating knowledge in heterogeneous knowledge systems. In Yu and Chen [27], pages 513–520.

[3] C. Altenschmidt, J. Biskup, U. Flegel, and Y. Karabulut. Secure mediation: Requirements, design, and architecture. *Journal of Computer Security*, 2002. to appear.

[4] C. Altenschmidt, J. Biskup, J. Freitag, and B. Sprick. Weakly constraining multimedia types based on a type embedding ordering. In *Proceedings of the 4th International Workshop on Multimedia Information Systems*, volume 1508 of *Lecture Notes in Computer Science*, pages 121–129, Istanbul, Turkey, Sept. 1998. Springer-Verlag.

[5] Y. Arens, C. Y. Chee, C.-N. Hsu, and C. A. Knoblock. Retrieving and integrating data from multiple information sources. *International Journal of Intelligent and Cooperative Information Systems*, 2(2):127–158, 1993.

[6] J. Biskup and D. W. Embley. Extracting information from heterogeneous information sources using ontologically specified target views. *Information Systems*, 2002. to appear.

[7] J. Biskup, J. Freitag, Y. Karabulut, and B. Sprick. A mediator for multimedia systems. In *Proceedings of the 3rd International Workshop on Multimedia Information Systems*, pages 145–153, Como, Italia, Sept. 1997.

[8] J. Biskup, J. Freitag, Y. Karabulut, and B. Sprick. Query evaluation in an object-oriented multimedia mediator. In *Proceedings of the 4th International Conference on Object-Oriented Information Systems*, pages 31–43, Brisbane, Australia, Nov. 1997.

[9] A. Calì, D. Calvanese, G. De Giacomo, and M. Lenzerini. On the expressive power of data integration systems. In *Proceedings of the 21st International Conference on Conceptual Modeling – ER 2002*, 2002. to appear.

[10] R. G. G. Cattell and D. Barry, editors. *The Object Data Standard: ODMG 3.0*. Morgan Kaufmann, San Francisco, 2000.

[11] C. Collet, M. N. Huhns, and W.-M. Shen. Resource integration using a large knowledge base in carnot. *IEEE Computer*, 24(12):55–62, 1991.

[12] M. Friedman, A. Y. Levy, and T. D. Millstein. Navigational plans for data integration. In *Proceedings of the Sixteenth National Conference on Artificial Intelligence*, pages 67–73. AAAI Press / The MIT Press, 1999.

[13] H. Garcia-Molina, J. Hammer, K. Ireland, Y. Papakonstantinou, J. Ullman, and J. Widom. Integrating and Accessing Heterogeneous Information Sources in TSIMMIS. In *Proceedings of the AAAI Symposium on Information Gathering*, pages 61–64, Stanford, California, Mar. 1995.

[14] D. B. Lenat. CYC: A Large-Scale Investment in Knowledge Infrastructure. *ACM Transactions on Information Systems*, 38(11):32–38, Nov. 1995.

[15] A. Y. Levy, A. Rajaraman, and J. J. Ordille. Query-answering algorithms for information agents. In *Proceedings of the Thirteenth National Conference on Artificial Intelligence, AAAI 96*, pages 40–47. AAAI Press / The MIT Press, 1996.

[16] J. Madhavan, P. A. Bernstein, and E. Rahm. Generic schema matching with cupid. In P. M. G. Apers, P. Atzeni, S. Ceri, S. Paraboschi, K. Ramamohanarao, and R. T. Snodgrass, editors, *Proceedings of the 27th International Conference on Very Large Data Bases*, pages 49–58. Morgan Kaufmann, Sept. 2001.

[17] J. Makowsky and E. Ravve. Translation schemes and the fundamental problem of database design. In *Proceedings of the 15th International Conference on Conceptual Modeling – ER'96*, volume 1157 of *Lecture Notes in Computer Science*, pages 5–26. Springer, 1996.

[18] T. Milo and S. Zohar. Using schema matching to simplify heterogeneous data translation. In A. Gupta, O. Shmueli, and J. Widom, editors, *Proceedings of the 24th International Conference on Very Large Data Bases*, pages 122–133. Morgan Kaufmann, Aug. 1998.

[19] N. T. Nguyen. Using consensus methods for solving conflicts of data in distributed systems. In *Proceedings of the 27th Conference on Current Trends in Theory and Practice of Informatics (SOFSEM 2000)*, volume 1963 of *Lecture Notes in Computer Science*. Springer, 2000.

[20] Y. Papakonstantinou, H. Garcia-Molina, and J. Ullman. MedMaker: A mediation system based on declarative specifications. In S. Y. W. Su, editor, *Proceedings of the 12th International Conference on Data Eng.*, pages 132–141. IEEE Computer Society, 1996.

[21] Y. Papakonstantinou, H. Garcia-Molina, and J. Widom. Object exchange across heterogeneous information sources. In Yu and Chen [27], pages 251–260.

[22] M. T. Roth and P. Schwarz. Don't Scrap It, Wrap It! An Architecture for Legacy Data Sources. In M. Jarke, M. J. Carey, K. R. Dittrich, F. H. Lochovsky, P. Loucopoulos, and M. A. Jeusfeld, editors, *Proceedings of the 23rd International Conference on Very Large Data Bases*, pages 266–275, Athens, Greece, Aug. 1997. Morgan Kaufmann.

[23] A. P. Sheth and J. A. Larson. Federated database systems for managing distributed, heterogeneous, and autonomous databases. *ACM Computing Surveys*, 22(3):183–236, Sept. 1990.

[24] A. Tomasic, L. Raschid, and P. Valduriez. Scaling Heterogeneous Databases and the Design of DISCO. In *Proceedings of the 16th International Conference on Distributed Computing Systems*, pages 449–457, May 1996.

[25] J. D. Ullman. Information integration using logical views. *Theoretical Computer Science*, 239(2):189–210, May 2000.

[26] G. Wiederhold. Mediators in the architecture of future information systems. *IEEE Computer*, 25(3):38–49, 1992.

[27] P. S. Yu and A. L. P. Chen, editors. *Proceedings of the 11th International Conference on Data Eng.*, Taipei, Taiwan, Mar. 1995. IEEE Computer Society.

Xeena for Schema: Creating XML Data with an Interactive Editor

Mark Sifer[1], Yardena Peres[2], and Yoelle Maarek[2]

[1] School of IT, University of Sydney, NSW, 2006, Australia
`sifer@it.usyd.edu.au`
[2] Knowledge Management Group, IBM Research Lab in Haifa
Matam, 31905, Israel
`{yardena, yoelle}@il.ibm.com`

Abstract. With the advent of the web there has been a great demand for data interchange between existing applications using internet infrastructure and also between newer web services applications. The W3C XML standard is becoming the internet data interchange format. Such XML data is typically produced by applications. However during application development and maintenance there remains a significant need for manual creation, editing and browsing of XML data by application and system developers. XML editors can fill this need. This paper presents an interactive XML editor design. We show how an interface that uses a tight coupling between grammar and content views facilitates the rapid creation of data centric documents. Our design is realised in the Xeena for Schema tool which we demonstrate. Xeena for Schema supports the latest version of XML, XML Schema, which offers better support for data oriented applications.

1 Introduction

With the advent of the web there has been increasing demand for data interchange between existing applications using internet infrastructure and also between newer web services applications. The W3C XML [4] recommendation is becoming the internet data interchange format. Such XML data will typically be produced by applications. However during application development and maintenance there remains a significant need for manual creation, editing and browsing of XML data by application and system developers. XML editors can fill this need.

XML or rather the eXtensible Markup Language defines a standard way to markup data and documents as text files. These files (or data streams) which are referred to as documents may be restricted to comply with a grammar – a Document Type Definition (DTD) or an XML Schema [12], but this is not compulsory. Tags are used to denote the start and end of elements which are nested, forming a tree of elements. A mid level element may denote a whole purchase order record while a leaf element may capture a numeric cost. Data interchange between applications, in addition to a com-

S. Bhalla (Ed.): DNIS 2002, LNCS 2544, pp. 133–146, 2002.

mon data format, requires a data exchange protocol such as the Simple Object Access Protocol (SOAP) [9].

XML was originally developed as a simplified version of the Standard Generalized Markup Language (SGML) [7] for the web. SGML is primarily used for maintaining large technical document collections. SGML grammars are defined with DTDs which include complex features that were not included when XML DTDs were defined. However, a general limitation of DTDs is their poor support for data typing. Recently XML Schema has been defined to add much richer data and structure typing which better supports data oriented applications and data exchange.

Apart from data interchange to support web services XML has many other uses. Specific applications of XML include MathML (Mathematics Markup language), X3D (XML 3D) and XHTML (XML HTML). These applications define how data intended for display in a web browser should be marked up, where display rules are defined in separate style sheets. Because of the increasing availability of XML software libraries, XML is also being used as a data storage format for persistent data when the overhead of a database is not needed. Such applications of XML can also require a generic XML editor for the creation and editing of XML data and documents.

Because XML documents are human readable text files, a standard text editor can be used as a generic XML editor. For users that are already familiar with XML syntax, using a text editor can the easiest way of creating or modifying small XML documents. Otherwise a dedicated XML editor may be easier to use. In this paper we present our design for an interactive XML editor design for documents which conform to an XML Schema. The benefits of our editor are: (i) users do not need to know XML syntax, (ii) they do not need to remember the schema grammar and (iii) through the use of interactive templates users can rapidly build and alter XML documents. Our editor achieves these benefits through the use of novel coordinated grammar and instance views of a document.

In the second section an example XML document fragment and schema are introduced. Requirements for an editor are established in section three. Our interface is demonstrated in sections four and five, then defined in section six. Validation is covered in section seven. Then finally, related work is described and conclusions given.

2 Example

In this section we introduce the example data and schema that will be used throughout this paper, a small addressbook document. An example scenario is the regular temporary transfer of staff between different subsidiaries of a large company. Because the subsidiaries have different personnel systems, they exchange XML data over the companies intranet to prepare for the transfers. During integration of these systems many sample XML documents were needed, some of which were created manually. Our example is one of these samples:

```
<?xml version="1.0" encoding="UTF-8"?>
<addressbook xmlns:xsi=http://www.w3.org/2001/XMLSchema-instance>
<person first-name="Robert" family-name="Brown" middle- initial=
  "L." employee-number="A7000">
  <contact-info>
   <email address="robb@iro.ibm.com" />
   <home-phone number="03-3987873" />
  </contact-info>
  <address state="NY" city="New York" street="118 St." number=
   "344" />
  <job-info is-manager="true"  job-description="Group Leader"  em-
   ployee-type="Full-Time" />
  <manager employee-number="A0000" />
 </person>
  ...
</addressbook>
```

The document contains an addressbook which includes multiple person records, one of which is shown. A person record includes name, contact, address, job info and manager information. Names are stored in attributes while contact, address, job info and manager info are stored in sub elements. A contact-info element may contain one or more home or work phone numbers or email addresses. This structure is captured by the following addressbook grammar presented as an XML schema:

```
<?xml version="1.0" encoding="UTF-8"?>
<xsd:schema xmlns:xsd="http://www.w3.org/2001/XMLSchema">
  <xsd:element name="addressbook" type="Addressbook"/>
  <xsd:complexType name="Addressbook">
   <xsd:sequence>
    <xsd:element minOccurs="0" maxOccurs="unbounded"
      name="person" type="Person"/>
   </xsd:sequence>
  </xsd:complexType>
  <xsd:complexType name="Person">
   <xsd:sequence>
    <xsd:element name="contact-info" type="Contact-info"/>
    <xsd:element name="address" type="Address"/>
    <xsd:element name="job-info" type="Job-info"/>
    <xsd:element name="manager" type="Manager"/>
    <xsd:element minOccurs="0" name="misc-info" type="Misc-info"/>
   </xsd:sequence>
   <xsd:attribute use="required" name="first-name"/>
    ...
  </xsd:complexType>
  <xsd:complexType name="Contact-info">
   <xsd:choice maxOccurs="unbounded" minOccurs="0">
    <xsd:element name="home-phone" type="Home-phone"/>
    <xsd:element name="mobile-phone" type="Mobile-phone"/>
    <xsd:element name="email" type="Email"/>
   </xsd:choice>
  </xsd:complexType>
  <xsd:complexType name="Home-phone">
   <xsd:attribute use="required" name="number"/>
  </xsd:complexType>
   ...
</xsd:schema>
```

Note the schema is also an XML document. If one person is involved in creating both schema and conforming data, and they are small it may be practical to use a text editor to create them. However when the schema is bigger and several people are involved, a dedicated XML editor can make creation of such documents much easier.

Some definitions are needed. A document is well-formed when it follows XML tag syntax and element nesting. If a well-formed document also follows all the rules specified in a grammar (whether its a DTD or schema) it is valid. A document is structurally valid when it is well-formed and follows all the structure (element typing) rules in a grammar, but perhaps does not follow some data type rules. When documents are manually created they will often be in an invalid state. If a document is structurally valid except for some missing choice elements (alternatives in the grammar) it is partially valid. If a document is partially valid except for some missing compulsory elements then it is weakly valid. A weakly valid document is said to *conform to the grammar*, as there are no parent-child element pairs which violate any parent-child rules in the grammar.

3   Requirements for an XML (Schema Instance) Editor

Requirements for an XML editor can be very broad. Editors can be used in a wide variety of roles, such as: assisting with the conversion of text documents into XML, data entry for a database system, ad-hoc creation and editing of specialised applications such as XHTM and the creation and editing of data for data interchange systems. Another dimension is whether the documents to be edited will conform to a specified grammar and if so what kind of grammar. Choices include DTDs (Document Type Definitions), XML Schema, Relax, Schematron and others. The first two are W3C recommendations, while the latter are private proposals which have been widely disseminated. When grammar conformance is required, other dimensions include: the likely size and complexity of the grammar, how familiar users are with the grammar and what level of conformance to the grammar the input documents will have.

Our interface design targets the editing of documents that have an XML Schema grammar and are weakly valid. We wanted to support a spectrum of grammars, from small ones for novice users to large and complex ones for experienced users. In particular, we wanted the interface to make the maximum use of the grammar information, so that a user can create and edit documents with a minimum number of choices and steps, where editing steps that can be inferred are done automatically. Users should be provided with an editing context, so that editing operations proceed by making choices from alternatives that are always visible rather than expecting a user to remember parts of a grammar. This will suit both specialised applications and data interchange, where conformance to a grammar can be expected.

For data interchange, XML Schema or Relax are the best grammar candidates because of their strong support for data typing. Our interface design does not support the conversion of arbitrary text documents into XML, because even if there is a grammar, it cannot be used to accurately guide edit operations. Further such text documents will typically contain sections that are not be well formed.

Once editor requirements are defined, there are still a variety of interface styles that can be used. Content focused and structured focused are two styles. The former typically uses a free form text view of the document supplemented with tag highlighting and perhaps a coordinated tree (structure) overview. The latter typically uses a tree view of the document supplemented with a coordinated views of element content such as attributes and character content.

We choose to use the latter style, and extend it with a coordinated grammar view to provide better support to users that are less familiar with XML syntax and grammars. With our interface user do not need to see markup tags or read an XML schema grammar, rather they are guided by a coordinated tree view of the grammar.

4   Browsing with Coordinated Grammar and Document Views

A key feature of our design for interactive XML editing is the use of a coordinated grammar and instance views of an XML document. Figure one shows a screenshot of our editor browsing addressbook data. Tree representations of the addressbook schema (grammar view) and instance (document view) are shown in the left and right panels respectively. Editing operations are done via the toolbar on the frame's top.

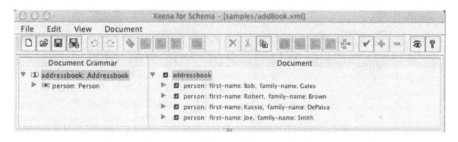

Fig. 1. Our editor interface showing grammar and instance views of addressbook data

Figure one shows the startup screen (minus an attribute table at the bottom of the frame) where the root document element „addressbook" is selected. Only one level of children is shown in both document and grammar views. The (1) and (*) icons in the grammar view indicates one addressbook element is required while an arbitrary number of person elements are required. A user browses a document by selecting elements (by clicking it's title) and by expanding or contracting the element subtrees in the document view. Figure two shows the result of selecting the first person element in the document view.

Figure two shows a changed grammar view. Selecting a person element in the document view changed the grammar view automatically, so that the person node and its children are visible. If the user selects a node in the grammar view there is a similar effect on the document view. For example, if the contact-info node in the grammar view is selected, the document view will change to show the corresponding sub-element in the first person element, as shown in figure three. However, note that if another person element subtree (such as for Kassie) were open prior to selecting the contact-info grammar node, it would remain open after the grammar node selection. Selections in the grammar view open additional document subtrees, allowing multiple top-level document nodes to remain open.

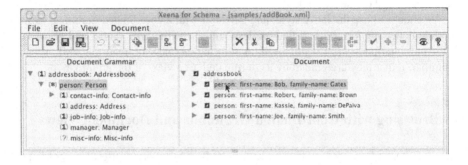

Fig. 2. Selecting the person element in the document view changes the grammar view

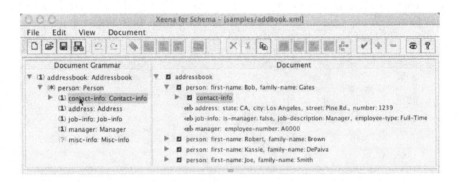

Fig. 3. Selecting the contact-info grammar node changes the document view

Moving the grammar cursor from person to contact-info has moved the document cursor to the contact-info element within the first person element, which has been made visible by unfolding the document tree. The transitions from figure one to two and from two to three show there is a tight coupling between the grammar and document views. Changing the cursor in one view, changes the other view so the corresponding cursor is visible and selected. The purpose of this tight coupling is to support editing operations.

5   Editing with Coordinated Grammar and Document Views

The main task of an XML editor is to support the creation and editing of XML documents. This is done through editing operations such as adding, moving, changing and deleting elements. When an XML document conforms to a grammar, elements can not be added anywhere. Particular elements can only appear in certain contexts. The grammar defines for each element type what these contexts are. Our interface uses a grammar view panel to provide users with a continuous grammar context for the selected document cursor element. Some examples will make this clearer.

As noted in section four, the grammar view and document share a coordinated cursor which is shown as the selected grammar node and document element in each view. Highlighting is also used to indicate which grammar nodes have been instantiated in the document. For example in figure three, the selected contact-info node and three of its siblings have coloured (dark) icons, while the fourth sibling misc-info has a ghosted icon. Glancing across at the document view reveals the selected contact-info element has only three sibling elements. There is no misc-info element.

The difference in icon colour in the grammar view highlights the misc-info info element could be added into the document at the current document cursor position by selecting the misc-info grammar node then clicking the add element button on the upper toolbar. A misc-info element would then be added in the correct position in the document view. The coordinated grammar view has highlighted via icon colouring what additions can be made to the current document position, so that when a grammar node is chosen, new elements can be created in the correct position automatically.

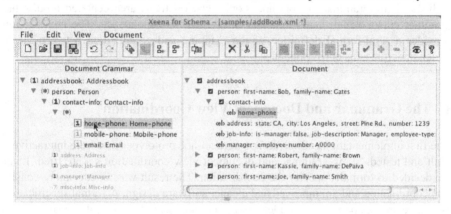

Fig. 4. The result of adding a home-phone element by clicking in the grammar view

Another example of editing is shown in figure four. The contact-info grammar node was expanded so its child nodes home-phone, mobile-phone and email were visible, followed by SHIFT-selecting the home-phone grammar node. Alternatively, the user could have selected the home-phone grammar node then clicked the add element button on the toolbar. This creates a home-phone element in the document nested in the correct position within the contact-info element. If there were any intermediate types between the home-phone grammar node and its ancestor contact-info, instances of these would also have been created in the document. If home-phone had any compulsory children they also would have been created by this edit operation. In general, if the grammar requires an element to exist in the document after an edit operation, it is added automatically. This ensures our editor always maintains a document as a partially valid document.

While new documents can be rapidly built by just deciding which elements to add and filling in their attribute and content data, other edit operation such as moving elements (with their data and nested elements) and changing elements types are also needed. Our interface supports moving elements via cut, copy and paste operations, while changing element types is supported via the grammar view. To change a home-phone element to a mobile-phone element in figure four a user selects the mobile-phone grammar node then click the change element button on the toolbar. This operation uses a heuristic to preserve home-phone attributes, data and sub-elements as best as possible. If element content may be lost during the change operation the user is warned.

Note in figure four some grammar node icons and titles such as address and job-info are smaller and ghosted. This is done to cope with larger grammars. Recall as the document cursor changes, the grammar view also changes to show the corresponding grammar node, its children, its ancestors. Because of the tree presentation, all grammar node cursor ancestor siblings are also shown which helps maintain a consistent context, but when the number of these grammar nodes is large, visual correspondence with the document view can be lost. Shrinking those grammar nodes which are the siblings of the grammar cursors ancestors creates a focus area centered around the grammar cursor which helps maintain this visual correspondence. The next section provides a semi-formal definition of the mapping and coordination between views which underpins this correspondence.

6   The Grammar and Document View Coordination

The first implementations of our design were ad-hoc prototypes that were interactively built and tested. Many grammar and document view coordination's were tried. Later we decided to formally specify the coordination. The result was a better more consistent coordination and an improved and cleaner software design. A formal specification is precise but compact, so its an ideal way to communicate the basis of a design, which we do here. The view coordination is defined by a mapping between the grammar tree and document tree. The mapping sets up corresponding grammar nodes for each document element.

Figure five shows the coordination mapping after the contact-info element within the second person element (Robert) was selected. Like the example shown in figure three, only the optional misc-info element does not exist. Recall the grammar nodes that participate in the mapping (all the nodes in figure five except misc-info) are displayed with coloured icons. But most document nodes such as the person elements for Bob, Kassie and Joe do not participate in the mapping. Only the selected document element, the person Robert's contact-info and its contextual elements participate; an elements context includes its ancestors, siblings and siblings descendants. In particular, when there is a grammar node like person (which can occur multiple times in a document) it only appears in the grammar view once, the document element which

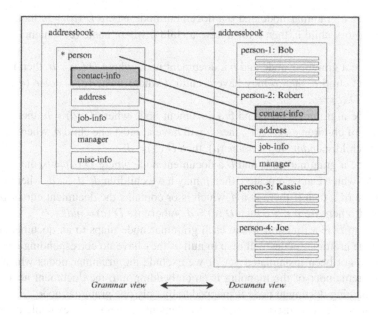

Fig. 5. The grammar and document view mapping when element person-2 is selected

this node maps to is determined by the current selected document element. Changing the selected document element hence changes the grammar view. The mapping between views has several roles:

i. to determine the position of the grammar cursor when the document cursor is moved.
ii. to determine the visible grammar tree, that is, which subtrees are expanded or collapsed when the document cursor is moved.
iii. to determine the size and shading of grammar node icons and titles when the document cursor is moved.
iv. to determine the position of the document cursor when the grammar cursor is moved.

6.1 Grammar Mapping Definition

We can now define the grammar mapping. Recall it is the mapping between the document and grammar cursors that determines the overall mapping between all nodes and elements. We require the document to be partially valid. Let us call this mapping from nodes in the grammar view to nodes in the document view, for a given document cursor node position p, D then:

i. Let a be a grammar node and b a document node, then $D(a) = b$ implies *name* $(a) =$ *name* (b)
ii. Let a be the root of the grammar tree and b the root of the document tree, then $D(a) = b$.

iii. Let a be a grammar node and b a document node where $D(a) = b$, then if a has a compulsory child c, then b must have a child d where name (c) = name (d), then D $(c) = d$.

iv. Let a be a grammar node and b a document node where $D(a) = b$, then if a has an optional child c, then b may have a child d where $name(c) = name(d)$, then if d exists, $D(c) = d$.

v. Let a be a grammar node and b a document node where $D(a) = b$, then if a has a choice of children $c_1, c_2 \ldots c_n$, then b will have at most one child d, where if c_i is one of the children $name(c_i) = name(d)$, then $D(c_i) = d$.

vi. Let a be a grammar node and b a document node where $D(a) = b$, then if a has a child c which can be repeated, then b may have children $d_1, d_2 \ldots d_n$ where $name(b)$ = $name(d_i)$, then if there is a d_i which is or contains the document cursor p then D $(c) = d_i$ otherwise if $n > 0$ then $D(c) = d_1$, otherwise $D(c) = null$.

The map D is a function where each grammar node maps to an document node or null. Some grammar nodes will map to null as they have no corresponding instance, as they have not been instantiated yet. If we exclude the grammar nodes which map to null, the remainder of the mapping is an embedding into the document nodes, that is each remaining document node is mapped to by only one grammar node.

The *name* function used in (i) gives the element tag name, for example the name of the root grammar node is „addressbook“ as is the root document element. If the grammar was expressed as a DTD this would not cause any confusion. But once the grammar is expressed as a W3C Schema, both element tag names and types are used. In our grammar view we have shown element tag names with their schema types.

If a grammar contained only sequences of compulsory elements, there would be a unique mapping between the grammar and document views which was document cursor independent. In practice a grammar will contain choices and repeatable elements. Where the grammar defines a choice there will be at most one instance element in the document to be mapped to, and where the grammar defined a repeatable element there may be many instance elements in the document that could be mapped to, but only one of which will be mapped to. Rules (v) and (vi) addressed these latter two cases.

For example consider the grammar node addressbook whose child element person which may be repeated. Because the second person element contains the document cursor, rule (vi) requires the second person element to be in the mapping D. If the document cursor were set to the document root element, addressbook, the grammar person node would be mapped to the first person element in the document instead.

6.2 Coordinating Views with the Grammar Mapping

The mapping from grammar view nodes to document view nodes applies to the whole grammar view tree, not just the portions of this tree which happens to be visible. Arbitrary grammar subtrees can be expanded revealing the mapping from the contained nodes which is shown through icon shading, indicating the existence of corresponding document elements. Moving the grammar cursor causes the document cursor to move to the location defined by the grammar mapping.

When a user moves the document cursor the mapping D changes (as it is defined by the document cursor position p). The grammar view changes in the following ways, for a new position of p:

i. set the grammar cursor to node n, where $D(n) = p$, the definitions ensure such an n exists

ii. all ancestors of the grammar cursor node are expanded and all other grammar nodes are shown collapsed, except the grammar cursor which is also expanded if it has children.

iii. grammar nodes which map to a document node (not to a null value) are shown with a coloured icon, otherwise a grayed icon is used. Siblings of the grammar cursor's ancestors are shown with a small icon and small title while the grammar cursor, its direct ancestors and children nodes are shown with full size icons and titles.

When the user moves the grammar cursor n, the mapping D is used to locate the new document cursor:

i. if $D(n) != null$, then the new cursor is $D(n)$.

ii. if $D(n) = null$, then the new cursor is $D(a)$ where a is the lowest ancestor of n, such that $D(a) != null$.

When a user moves the grammar cursor, only the document view changes. The document cursor position is updated, while the visible document tree changes so that the new document cursor is visible. With earlier prototypes, the grammar view focus area was also changed to match the document focus area. However, this meant the grammar node that had just been selected would suddenly move, which we found very disorientating so we removed this.

7 Validation

The paper so far, has concentrated on presenting our grammar and document view design, illustrated with screenshots from our XML editor, Xeena for Schema. This section describes how our editor supports validation.

Xeena for Schema is a Java application that uses the Apache project Xerces parser as its underlying XML parser. Xeena expects documents it loads for editing will be weakly valid. Within Xeena, all editing operations preserve at least weak validity. For documents created entirely within Xeena, the editing operations preserve partial validity. An XML document does not just contain a nested tree of elements, there are also attributes and other atomic data associated with elements which must conform to type definitions in the document's schema for the document to be valid. The Xerces parser is used for this overall validity check which highlights invalid elements in red, and shows element error messages in a separate message panel when selected.

Internally all operations and data structures operate on a simple BNF grammar. When Xeena for Schema starts it converts the document schema it is given, expanding all macro's (groups), unnesting all anonymous types and unfolding all subtypes into a simple flat BNF grammar. This is done by a single conversion class. This suggests that other grammars such as Relax (which follows the data type part of the W3C schema definition) could easily be supported, provided the underlying parser also supported it.

8 Related Work

Many syntax directed program editors have been developed. Editors such as SUPPORT [15] and Pan [2] supported both structural and content editing. Structural editing proceeds top-down as nodes are elaborated according to grammar rules, while content editing is bottom-up; users directly edit text fragments which are parsed and integrated into the rest of the document.

Grif [5] and Rita [3] are editors for document preparation systems. They use document grammars to provide context sensitive type information to guide editing. They use coordinated content and structure views. The structure view shows the element tree structure. Rita also uses an additional panel which shows the alternatives of a selected element when the grammar contains a choice. Arbitrary cut and paste of element subtrees can require type transformation [1]. This has been added to Grif [8].

Xeena [11], the previous version of our tool provides a content sensitive template for adding types. However the template presents types as an ordered list (by type name) which makes choosing a type and seeing the relationships between them difficult. XML Spy [13] presents a document with a nested tree view. Like the original Xeena it uses a separate panel to show which elements that can be added at the current document position. This interface works well for form based data entry. However changing a document's element structure is difficult without the multi-level grammar view that our editor provides.

Large grammars can result in large and deep grammar trees. Navigating such deep hierarchical trees appears to be difficult for users [14]. TreeViewer [10] uses font, shade, size and animated transitions to help navigate such trees. Many interfaces for information visualisation which use multiple views of data coordinated with synchronised cursors have been built [6].

9 Conclusion

The manual creation of XML files (documents) can be a daunting prospect for users. If conformance to a XML Schema grammar is also required, it can be even more daunting. As XML is becoming the data interchange standard between web applications, many application developers will have to specify and create XML files. We presented an editor design targeted at such users, implemented as the Xeena for Schema tool.

We presented a novel design, based on the use of coordinated grammar and document views where the grammar view acts as an interactive template which shows what documents changes are possible in any given context, and provides a multi-level document overview. Example use and semi-formal definitions of our design were given. With our interface, users are able to create and edit XML documents by making choices from presented alternatives, and are able to later revisit and change those choices. Users do not need to remember the grammar .

The major tradeoff of our design is the requirement that input documents are weakly valid, that is, they follow their grammar element structure rules but may be incomplete. However document grammars are not static, they will change, particularly during initial development phases. Documents created with an old grammar may no longer conform to the new grammar. Conversion could be done via style sheets. But when the difference between the old and new grammar is small, and there are only a few documents to change, manual change would be better. We have identified extensions of our design which would support this, though their implementation remains future work.

Acknowledgements. Mark Sifer was with the IBM Research Lab in Haifa, Israel when this work was done. We wish to thank Roni Raab for her help in programming parts of Xeena for Schema, and the rest of the Knowledge Management group for their feedback.

References

1. Akpotsui E., Quint V. and Cecile Roisin.: Type modeling for document transformation in structured editing systems. Mathematical and Computer Modeling, Vol 25(4), Feb 1997, 1-19.
2. Balance, R.A., Graham S.L. and Van De Vanter M.L.: The Pan language-based editing system. Proceedings of the Fourth ACM SIGSOFT Symposium on Software Development Environments, 1990.
3. Cowan D.D., Mackie E.W., Pianosi G.M. and Smit G. V.: Rita – an editor and user interface for manipulating structured documents. Electronic Publishing, John Wiley, Vol 4(3), Sept. 1991, 125-150.
4. Extensible Markup Language (XML) 1.0 (Second Edition), W3C Recommendation, 6 October 2000, http://www.w3.org/TR/2000/REC-xml-20001006.
5. Furuta R., Quint V. and Andre   J.: Interactively editing structured documents. Electronic Publishing, John Wiley, Vol 1(1), April 1988, 19-44.
6. North, C. and Shneiderman, B.: A taxonomy of multiple window coordinations. Technical Report dCS-TR-3854. University of Maryland, College Park, Dept of Computer Science, 1997.
7. Overview of SGML Resources. http://www.w3.org/Markup/SGML.
8. Roisin C., Claves P. and Akpotsui E.: Implementing the cut-and-paste operation in a structured editing system. Mathematical and Computer Modeling, Vol 26(1), July 1997, 85-96.
9. SOAP Version 1.2 Part 0: Primer, W3C Working Draft 26 June 2002, http://www.w3.org/TR/2002/WD_soap12_part0-20020626.
10. Wittenbug, K. and Sigman, E.: Visual Focusing and Transition Techniques, Proceedings of the IEEE Symposium on Visual Languages, (1997) 20-27.
11. Xeena at Alphaworks. http://www.alphaworks.ibm.com/tech/xeena.

12. XML Schema Part-0: Primer, W3C Recommendation, 2 May 2001,
    http://www.w3.org /TR/2001/REC-xmlschema-0-20010502.
13. XML Spy. http://www.xmlspy.com/manual.
14. Zaphiris P., Shneiderman B. and Norman K. L.: Expandable indexes versus sequential menus
    for searching hierarchies on the world wide web, (1999) 99-15,
    http://www.cs.umd.edu/hcil/pubs/tech-reports.shtml.
15. Zelkowits, M.: A small contribution to editing with a syntax directed editor. Proceedings of
    the ACM SIGSOFT/SIGPLAN Software Engineering Symposium on Practical Software De-
    velopment Environments. 1984.

Coding and Presentation of Multimedia for Data Broadcasting with Broadcasting Markup Language

Hun Lee[1], Gun Ho Hong[2], Ha Yoon Song[2], and Sang Yong Han[1]

[1] School of Computer Science and Engineering Seoul National University
56-1 Sinlim, Kwanak Seoul, Korea 151-742
{artilla, syhan}@pplab.snu.ac.kr
[2] College of Information and Computer Engineering Hongik University
72-1 Sangsu, Mapo Seoul, Korea
{ghhong, song}@cs.hongik.ac.kr

Abstract. Data broadcasting is an emerging technology which provides numerous services that exceeds services provided by the traditional TV broadcasting. ARIB STD-B24 is one of such standards for Data Broadcasting and it has defined a new markup language for multimedia coding and presentation called BML. Other standards such as ATSC DASE, OCAP, and DVB MHP incorporate traditional HTML or XHTML technologies. The contents presented by these standards can be processed by the existing HTML browser and the browser can be implemented on an embedded system without serious modification. BML, however, has extended features for Data Broadcasting and requires a new browser and middleware especially designed for BML. This paper describes the design and implementation of the BML browser on an embedded system for Satellite Data Broadcasting. We provide the architecture, algorithm and problems and solution for implementing the BML browser in detail. Our objectives are not only to provide how the standard technologies can be extended and integrated seamlessly for an embedded browser of a BML, but also, to offer a useful template for other researches.

1 Introduction

Data Broadcasting provides interactive multimedia-based contents, such as VOD (Video on Demand), e-commerce, commodity information, tele-education and so on, to the audience by exploiting the underlying digital transmission technology. Several standards have been established to realize Data Broadcasting[1]: ATSC (Advanced Television Systems Committee) DASE (Digital TV Application Software Environment) [2] and OCAP (OpenCable Application Platform) [3] of USA, DVB (Digital Video Broadcasting Project) MHP (Multimedia Home Platform) [4] of EU, and ARIB STD-B24 [5] of Japan. These standards specify the encoding/decoding methods of information, the middleware architecture and the content presentation scheme.

S. Bhalla (Ed.): DNIS 2002, LNCS 2544, pp. 147–160, 2002.
© Springer-Verlag Berlin Heidelberg 2002

Diverse information provided by Data Broadcasting are encoded in the content presentation technology and transmitted to the receiving station such as set-top-box (STB), then, the browser on the receiver displays the contents on the screen. To make the various data broadcasting services available, the browser that conforms to the specification of content presentation technology should be implemented on the receiver side which is usually in a form of an embedded system to compromise intelligence and activeness.

DASE, OCAP, and MHP adopted HTML (Hyper Text Markup Language) [6] or XHTML (eXtensible Hyper Text Markup Language) [7] as content presentation technology. General Web browsers can process the contents encoded in HTML or XHTML and they can be ported to the embedded systems with a little effort of modification. ARIB STD-B24, however, defined Broadcasting Markup Language (BML) which is a extended markup language for multimedia based on XML (eXtensible Markup Language) [8]. Because BML has numerous special functionalities prepared for broadcasting services, existing HTML or XHTML browser cannot process the contents encoded in BML. An advanced browser especially designed for BML should be implemented to be able to handle the BML standard.

This paper describes the design and implementation of a BML browser which can process BML documents on the embedded system for Satellite Data Broadcasting. We discuss the architecture, algorithm, and problems and solutions for implementing the BML browser. The remainder of the paper is organized as follows. Section 2 surveys the BML specification especially with the extended parts from the standard W3C technologies. In section 3, the design and implementation of a BML browser and the overall process to integrate the extended standards will be discussed. Finally, section 4 presents future works and conclusions.

2   Related Works

In this section, we will summarize and compare various multimedia data coding schemes and metadata structures of various standards for data broadcasting. The common objectives of the Data Broadcasting standards such as MHP, ATSC-DASE, OCAP and BML, are coding, managing and presentation of multimedia information. However, the mechanism and metadata structure that organize and describe the multimedia data are defined differently for each standard.

The MHP which was standardized by DVB (Digital Video Broadcasting) consortium adopted Java Virtual Machine as its primary execution engine. To accommodate broadcasting specific features, APIs for user interface and class libraries have extended and integrated into the standard virtual machine. Based on these extensions, Java applications can be downloaded and can present interactive multimedia contents. To support HTML based contents, a user agent (browser) is implemented on the virtual machine, and HTML based applications of the multimedia contents encoded by HTML are executed by the agent. Because of this feature, most of the multimedia information and metadata representation of multimedia data are managed by virtual machine based applications. OCAP is based on MHP middleware specification, thus OCAP shares these characteristics in common.

In ATSC-DASE specification, the underlying middleware is consists of two distinct parts: Declarative Application Environment and Procedural Application Environment. Procedural Application Environment is similar to MHP middleware in many ways. Both MHP and Procedural Application Environment have Java-based virtual machines which have extended class libraries and API sets, data model and metadata structure for multimedia data. However, Declarative Application Environment has different features from HTML application of MHP. Declarative Application Environment is a separated part of the underlying middleware and executes on top of native operation system. Although Declarative Application Environment has similar features with the BML, the metadata structure, XDML (eXtensible DTV Markup Language), defines different coding schemes.

BML defines the metadata structure and coding schemes using a new markup language that is based on XHTML and extended for data broadcasting. And multimedia data and information are modeled, decoded and presented by a BML browser application that executes on top of native operation environment. Compared to the MHP, BML treats multimedia information as structured data, and the procedural aspects of the data are presented by ECMA scripts and handled by ECMA script engine of the BML browser.

To summarize, virtual machine based middleware architecture that includes MHP, OCAP and Procedural Application Environment of ATSC-DASE treats multimedia data coding and metadata information in an application-centric way. On the other hand, BML and Declarative Application Environment of ATSC-DASE treat the multimedia information as structured data. (Figure 1)

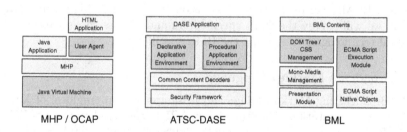

Fig. 1. Middleware Standards for data broadcating

It is difficult to implementing a BML browser especially on embedded system. There is no outstanding commercial BML browser and little information is available for implementing it. Unlike HTML or XHTML, BML is a new markup language that has many special features for multimedia and Data Broadcasting. The BML browser should decode and present multimedia data of BML and handle procedural aspects of the data. Because of the limited computing environment of embedded system, the BML browser should be implemented to be compact and efficient.

The BML browser in this paper has two major characteristics; modularity and portability. First, BML is based on XHTML which is designed to be modularized for extending the functionality easily. In addition, the BML specification (ARIB B-24) is still under evolution. It would be possible to modify the existing modules of BML, to extend new element and attributes for multimedia and to add new services for broadcasting. Therefore, browsers for BML have to be designed to accommodate the modifications and extensions in the future. The BML browser in this research is designed according to the modularization of the BML and has the flexible architecture for future modifications and extensions. With little effort, the BML browser can be modified, and be extended with new elements and attributes for multimedia, and new services for data broadcasting from its modularity. Second, we considered the portability of the BML browser in order to possibly minimize the cost of the porting of the BML browser to other embedded systems. As embedded systems have heterogeneous hardware/software interfaces, many parts of the BML browser implementation are dependent on the specific embedded system architecture. To resolve the dependency and improve portability, we applied layered architecture to the BML browser. The BML browser has the hardware independent interface layers for lower middleware components and upper application level components. Therefore, little modification of the codes will be required when the BML browser is ported to the other STB.

3   XML Based Multimedia Coding Scheme

BML is a newly defined markup language for multimedia coding and presentation, and it is based on the current Internet standards such as XHTML, DOM, CSS, and ECMA Script, and their extensions for broadcasting services. In this section, we will survey the BML specification and discuss the extensions of the standard technologies to support the BML specification.

3.1   Broadcast Markup Language

BML (Broadcasting Markup Language) is an application language of XML defined for the presentation of multimedia by ARIB. It is based on parts of XHTML 1.0 [7], DOM (Document Object Model) [9], CSS (Cascading Style Sheets) Level 1 [10], and CSS Level 2 [11] of W3C (World Wide Web Consortium). As a script language, ECMA Script is adopted with extension of functions for broadcasting services. In addition, it is required XSL (eXtensible Stylesheet Language) [12] and XSLT (XSL Transformations) [13] to be understood in order to process BML and to construct BML browser since BML requires preprocessing by XSLT.

BML extends XHTML as a markup language for Data Broadcasting by the modularization of XHTML [14]. Most of the elements and attributes of BML are conformed to the strict document type of XHTML 1.0. In addition, BML has the extended modules shown as table 1.

Table 1. Extended modules of BML

Extended modules	Description
Bevent element	events to be processed in the document
Beitem element	mapping between events and their ECMA Script handlers
remain attribute of *object* element	sharing objects between documents
attributes related to *stream* of *object* element	control of status, position, speed, looping, and volume of objects
orient attribute	orientation of character composition
Listtable element	definition of attributes of menu display
litem element	selected menu item
effect attribute of *anchor* element	specifications of special effect such as slide-out, wipe, or roll performed during s creen transition
invisible attribute of *body* element	hiding of the whole document

3.2 Document Object Model

DOM (Document Object Model) is a set of APIs (Application Program Interfaces) for a valid HTML document or a well-formed XML document. Through the DOM APIs, the contents and elements of a BML document can be added, modified, and deleted. The DOM APIs used in BML conform DOM Level 1 [9] of W3C. DOM interfaces of BML consist of Core DOM interfaces, HTML DOM interfaces and Extended DOM interfaces. Core DOM interfaces and HTML DOM interfaces are used without modification as defined in DOM Level 1. Extended DOM interfaces of BML are divided into CSS DOM interface, Event DOM interface, and BML Extended DOM interface. CSS DOM interface and Event DOM interface are shown in table 2. However, updated DOM 2 standards includes style and event properties extended by BML specification in a similar way [15][16].

BML Extended DOM interface is the extended DOM interfaces for elements and attributes defined by BML, and consists of BML Document DOM Interface and BML Element DOM Interface. BML Document DOM Interface is a set of operations for the whole document. BML Element DOM Interface is a set of extended interfaces for elements, attributes, and CSS properties of BML. DOM interfaces for the most of BML elements which are based on XHTML 1.0, are inherited from HTML DOM interfaces in DOM Level 1.

Table 2. Additional DOM interfaces for CSS and Event

DOM interface	Description
BMLCSS2Properties	interface for CSS properties of BML elements
BMLEvent	interface for context information of BML events
BMLIntrinsicEvent	interface for key events of remote control
BMLBevent	interface for events of broadcasting events

Figure 2[1] is the diagram of BML DOM Interface hierarchy. In addition, there are three sets of extended interfaces. First, apart from HTML DOM interfaces which do not have operations for CSS properties, extended DOM interfaces for CSS properties are supplied such as style, normalStyle, focusStyle, and activeStyle. Second, there is another extension of DOM interfaces for attributes which are newly added to elements for Data Broadcasting. Finally, DOM interfaces for newly defined elements are added.

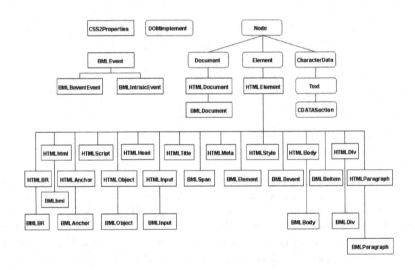

Fig. 2. Structure of BML DOM Interface

3.3 Cascading Style Sheet

BML employs CSS (Cascading Style Sheets) to define the styles of documents. BML uses tv media type for devices like a television set that has color display capability and limited scroll functions [5]. Most of CSS properties used in BML

---

[1] ARIB STD-B24 p279 Figure 5-9 Inheritance of DOM Interface

are based on CSS Level 2 [11] and new properties for Data Broadcasting are added or extended as shown in table 3.

Table 3. Additions and extensions of CSS properties in BML

Name of properties	Description
border-color-index	specifies the colors of the four box borders
border-top-color-index	
border-right-color-index	specifies the top, bottom, left,
border-bottom-color-index	and right border color of a box
border-left-color-index	
clut	specifies the resource of color map data
color-index	specifies the foreground color of an element
background-color-index	specifies the background color of an element
outline-color-index	specifies the frame color
resolution	specifies the resolution of the text graphic plane
display-aspect-ratio	specifies the aspect ratio of the text graphic plane
grayscale-color-index	specifies grayscale colors
nav-index	specifies an index for the element on which the focus is set
nav-up	specifies the value of the nav-index property
nav-down	which the focus is set to when the up, down,
nav-right	right, or left arrow key is pushed
nav-left	
used-key-list	specifies the type of remote control keys to be accepted by the BML browser

3.4 ECMA Script Language

The syntax and semantics, and embedded objects of ECMA (European Computer Manufactures Association) Script of BML conform to ECMA-262 [17]. But, there are the following exceptions in implementation [5].

1. Employment of EUC-JP for character encoding
2. Integer representation in (smaller than) 64 bits
3. Removal of implementation of floating pointer number

As an extension of APIs, Broadcasting Extended Object Group and Browser Pseudo Objects are added. Broadcasting Extended Object Group is for handling table data as shown in table 4. Browser Pseudo Object is a built-in object in ECMA Script engine used for BML browser. It supports functions specific to broadcasting services that are not part of standard ECMA Script. Functions of Browser Pseudo Object are shown in table 5.

Table 4. Extended object group for Data Broadcasting

Name	Description
CVSTable	object for two-dimensional table data and a sub-table, data consists of character strings, and line and column delimiting characters
BinaryTable	same as CVSTable, but data is represented in binary

Table 5. Functions of Browser pseudo objects

Extended functions	Description
EPG functions	functions for controlling EPG
event group index functions	functions for handling events in embedded system
series reservation functions	reservation functions for the series specified by the series descriptor (only for ARIB STD-B10 version 1.3)
Subtitle presentation control functions	functions for controlling the display state of subtitles and language selection
persistent memory functions	functions for storing subscriber information in a persistent storage device
interactive channel functions	communication functions for interaction
operational control functions	functions for controlling the operation of embedded system
receiver sound control	functions for controlling the sound of embedded system
timer functions	functions for controlling timer of embedded system
external character functions	functions for loading and unloading external character data
other functions	utility functions such as random, date
Ureg pseudo object properties	stores the properties of Browser pseudo object

3.5 The System Architecture of Set-Top-Box for Satellite Data Broadcasting

The general hardware architecture of STB for Satellite Data Broadcasting is depicted in figure 3[2]. The operation sequence proceeds: RF (Radio Frequency) receives the satellite signals and Tuner gets Transport Stream through demodulator. Then, with this signal, MPEG (Moving Picture Experts Group) stream is generated. Voices, pictures, or data reproduced from MPEG stream by the decoder are displayed on the screen or generates events, which make embedded system perform specified operations. Contents of Data Broadcasting are also separated from MPEG stream and displayed through an embedded browser.

---

[2] ARIB STD-B24 p24 Figure 2. Construction example of the receiver with class B and representation function level A

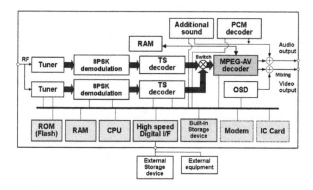

Fig. 3. The architecture of STB as a Satellite Receiver

4 The Design and Implementation of a BML Browser

In this section, we describe the design and implementation of a BML browser including the functionalities aforementioned. First, the whole architecture and the method of implementing the BML browser are discussed. Then, the procedure of processing a BML document including parsing, DOM tree generation, CSS processing, rendering and display, and ECMA script and event handling will be presented.

4.1 The Architecture of a BML Browser

The general architecture of the BML browser is depicted in figure 4. The BML browser is implemented in C and C++. The BML browser is composed of major components such as BMLDocument, ECMAScriptEngine, and RenderingEngine. BMLDocument is a data structure for the BML document that is being processed. BMLParser is a parser which generates elements and constructs the DOM tree. BMLElement is a data structure for representing DOM interfaces. The inheritance of DOM interfaces is implemented by the inheritance of C++ classes and a DOM tree is represented by a linked list. CSSStyleSheet is a data structure for a style sheet of a BML document. CSSManager manages several style sheets in a document and sets style values for elements generated by BMLParser. RenderingEngine calculates rendering values for displaying elements on the screen after the style of elements are set. RenderObject is the data structure for storing values required to render elements based on CSS values. ECMAScriptEngine executes the scripts to which BMLParser sends. When an event occurs by a user, the browser transfers the event to EventListener. Event is the data structure for representing the event attributes of a BML document. EventListener registers the event which is generated when elements or attributes related to the event are parsed. If a user generates an event, EventListender calls the associated function.

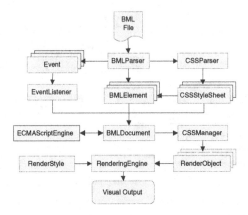

Fig. 4. The architecture of a BML Browser

4.2 Processing a BML Document

After a BML document is received through satellite channel, the browser processes the document, and displays it on the screen of the device (usually an HDTV) connected to the STB. Processing a BML document includes several steps in a sequence: parsing, DOM tree generation, CSS processing, rendering, ECMA script processing, and event handling. In this section, we describe each step with examples.

Parsing a BML document and Generating a DOM Tree. The first step for processing a BML document is parsing. BMLParser generates BML elements according to the tag names. If the generated element is a style element, BMLParser calls the CSSParser. CSSParser sets the style sheet of the document while parsing the CSS rules in the style element. After generating an element, the attributes of the element are parsed. When a style attribute is presented, values of the style attribute are added to the CSS rule of that element. If the attribute is related to an event such as 'onclick', to bind the event and ECMA script function (event handler), EventListener is generated by ECMAScriptEngine and registered to the element that has the attribute. After finishing the attribute parsing, the element is appended to the DOM tree.

Cascading Style Sheet Processing. The CSSParser creates a style sheet and stores it in the data structure of CSSStyleSheet if a style element is generated by BMLParser or a style sheet is linked by a link element. When BMLParser parses an element, it examines whether a style attribute exists in the element, and if there is, CSSManager updates CSSStyleSheet for the element with that style. BMLParser asks CSSManger for a style of the generated element to set the style of it. Then CSSManager searches CSSStyleSheets for the style of the element and apply the result style found in CSSStyleSheet to the element according to the rules of applying CSS.

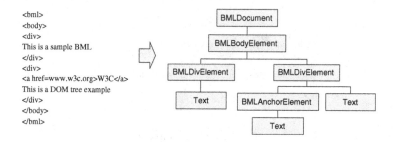

```
<bml>
<body>
<div>
This is a sample BML
</div>
<div>
<a href=www.w3c.org>W3C</a>
This is a DOM tree example
</div>
</body>
</bml>
```

Fig. 5. An example of DOM tree generation

An example of CSS in BML is shown in figure 6. In this example, the extended features of CSS of BML are presented. When the value of the color property is specified, usually the index of color lookup table is used. For this purpose, clut (color look up table) property specifies the URI (Uniform Resource Identifier) of the color look up table which has the RGB values. Properties such as background-color-index use the index of that table to specify its value. The resolution and display ratio of the content is specified by resolution and display-aspect-ratio property, respectively. When these properties are encountered during the parsing phase, CSSParser should set up the screen resolution and ratio according to the values of these properties.

To control the movement of focus on the screen, the CSS has extended properties like navIndex, navUp, navDown, navLeft, navRight, and usedKeyList. As in figure 7, we can arrange the order and direction of focus movement using extended CSS properties. When a user presses arrow-keys on the remote controller, the browser moves the focus according to the value of these properties. The element which loses focus and the element which gets focus should be displayed according to their status. The change of focus status can invoke associated event handler in ECMA script as described in section 3.2.4

```
<bml>
. . .
<body style="clut:url(0024); resolution:960x540; display-aspect-ratio:16v9">
<div style="background-color-index:30"/>
<p style="background-color-index:168">BML CSS Example </p>
. . .
</body>
</bml>
```

Fig. 6. CSS Example 1

```
<body>
  <div id= iv1" style= ">
    <object id= ?sytle=  nav-index:1;nav-up:2;nav-down:3" />
    <object id= ?sytle=  nav-index:2;nav-up:1;nav-down:2" />
    <object id= ?sytle=  nav-index:3;nav-up:4;nav-down:1" />
    <object id= ?sytle=  nav-index:4;nav-up:3;nav-down:4" />
  </div>
</body>
```

Fig. 7. CSS Example 2

Rendering and Display. After CSS processing is finished, RenderingEngine calculates the values required to display elements on the screen using the CSS values of RenderStyle. As a result, a rendering tree including objects derived from RenderObject is constructed (Figure 7.b). Then, RenderEngine traverses the tree in preorder sequence to display elements on the screen. If the z-indexing (as defined by ARIB, however it stands for depth ordering of objects on the screen) is required among the displayed elements, the rendering tree is constructed so that the z-indexing is automatically set up while the tree is being generated (Figure 7.c).

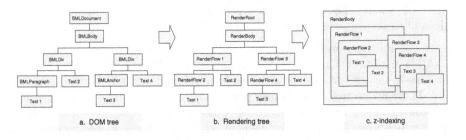

Fig. 8. An example of the rendering tree construction and vertical ordering

If there are changes in CSS values after displaying the BML document, RenderEngine traverses the rendering tree again, recalculates the value of RenderElement and updates the screen.

ECMA Script Engine and Event Handling. While the BML document is being displayed, the browser can receive remote control inputs from the user. Providing a user input, the node in the DOM tree to which the event is targeted will be located. The DOM node calls registered EventListener and EventListener calls the ECMA Script function which is mapped to the event. The executed function can generate another event, and it is passed to the DOM node again. The ECMA Script function which handles the event performs operations on the element in the DOM tree and change CSS values of the element. RenderingEngine recalculates the rendering values and updates the screen according to the changed CSS values. Figure 9 describes the over all procedure of event handling.

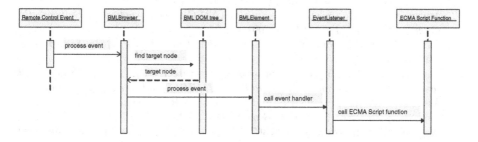

Fig. 9. The procedure of event handling

5   Conclusions

In this paper, we introduced BML, an XML based multimedia coding scheme which is defined in ARIB STD-B24, and described the design and implementation of a BML browser on a STB in a form of an embedded system for Satellite Broadcasting.

Though the BML browser was implemented according to the specification, it needs a few improvements. First, as ARIB STD-B24 is a continuously progressing specification, the BML browser should reflect the changes in time. Second, more efficient algorithms should be devised for the equipment with low computing power which is usual in embedded system environment. For example, tree traversal operation is required frequently for CSS processing and rendering of a BML document. In order to accelerate CSS processing and rendering, a tree traversal algorithm that is designed to operate fast under inadequate computing resources should be contrived. Finally, portability issues require more consideration. We used the layered design architecture to implement the BML browser so that it is independent to the hardware of STB. However, the layer between the BML browser and target platform cannot be verified to be universally applicable without immense interoperability test. It is possible to develop another layer to increase the portability between BML browser and hardware devices as a form of API set, so called a middleware for the middlewares.

Data Broadcasting needs consistent study because it is highly value-added industrial and academic topic. It is the study on content presentation technology that is the very core of Data Broadcasting. Our experience on the BML browser may help other researchers and developers to understand and implement the content presentation technology of Data Broadcasting and make it easy to implement browsers of other standards or even make it possible to develop a versatile system which can adopt several standards concurrently with lower cost and small effort.

References

1. Myung Hyun. Trend of information and communication industry. Technical report, Electronics and Telecommunications Research Institute, 2001.
2. Advanced Television Systems Committee (ATSC). *DTV Application Software Environment LEVEL 1 (DASE-1)*, 2001.
3. Cable Television Laboratories, Inc. *OpenCable Application Platform Specification*, 2.0 edition, 2002.
4. European Telecommunications Standards Institute(ETSI). *Digital Video Broadcasting (DVB); Multimedia Home Platform (MHP) Specification*, 1.1 edition, 2001.
5. Association of Radio Industries and Businesses(ARIB). *Data Coding and Transmission Specification for Digital Broadcasting (ARIB STD-B24)*, 1.2 edition, 2000.
6. World Wide Web Consortium (W3C). *HTML 4.01 Specification*, first edition, 1999.
7. World Wide Web Consortium (W3C). *XHTML 1.0 The Extensible HyperText Markup Language*, second edition, 2000.
8. World Wide Web Consortium (W3C). *Extensible Markup Language (XML) 1.0*, second edition, 2000.
9. World Wide Web Consortium (W3C). *Document Object Model (DOM) Level 1 Specification*, first edition, 1998.
10. World Wide Web Consortium (W3C). *Cascading Style Sheets, level 1*, second edition, 1999.
11. World Wide Web Consortium (W3C). *Cascading Style Sheets, level 2 Specification*, first edition, 1998.
12. World Wide Web Consortium (W3C). *Extensible Stylesheet Language (XSL) Version 1.0*, 2001.
13. World Wide Web Consortium (W3C). *XSL Transformations (XSLT) Version 1.0*, 1999.
14. World Wide Web Consortium (W3C). *Modularization of XHTML*, 2001.
15. World Wide Web Consortium (W3C). *Document Object Model (DOM) Level 2 Style Specification*, 2000.
16. World Wide Web Consortium (W3C). *Document Object Model (DOM) Level 2 Events Specification*, 2000.
17. European Computer Manufacturer Association (ECMA). *ECMAScript Language Specification (Standard ECMA-262)*, third edition, 1999.

A Proposal for a Distributed XML Healthcare Record

Francesco Barbera[1], Fernando Ferri[2], Fabrizio L. Ricci[3], and Pier Angelo Sottile[1]

[1]GESI s.r.l., Via Rodi 32, 00195 Rome, Italy.
{barbera,pas}@gesi.it
[2]IRPPS – CNR, Via Nizza 128, 00198 Rome, Italy.
{f.ferri}@irp.rm.cnr.it
[3]Ist. Scienze Neurologiche (Sez. Catania) - CNR, Via R. Margherita, 6, 95123 Catania, Italy.
{ricci}@isrds.rm.cnr.it

Abstract. The management of clinical data is a complex task. Patient related information reported in patient folders is a set of heterogeneous and structured data accessed by different users having different goals (in local or geographical networks). XML language provides a mechanism for describing, manipulating, and visualising structured data in web-based applications. XML ensures that the structured data is managed in a uniform and transparent manner independently from the applications and their providers guaranteeing some interoperability. Extracting data from the healthcare record and structuring them according to XML makes the data available through browsers. The MIC/MIE model (Medical Information Category / Medical Information Elements) [1], which allows the definition and management of healthcare records and used in CADMIO, a HISA [5] based project, is described in this paper, using XML for allowing the data to be visualised through web browsers.

1 Introduction

The integration and evolution of existing systems, together with the development of new systems, represents one of the most urgent priorities of healthcare information systems to allow the whole organisation to meet the increasing clinical, organisational, and managerial needs, both at local level and with respect to co-operative working across organisational and national boundaries.

This paper discusses a Healthcare Record System, namely Cadmio. The information and functional framework for Cadmio is based on the DHE®[1] middleware [6]. The DHE provides a set of common healthcare-specific services that can be used to manage the complete information heritage of a healthcare organisation. Due to the architectural aspects of such framework, the Cadmio system is automatically integrated with the functional and information basis common to the whole (territorial) organisation. On top of such framework new applications can also be rapidly developed or integrated with the rest of the system. Such architecture has been already demonstrated in practice and is conformant to what has been formalised through the proposed European Standard, defined by the CEN/TC251 ENV 12967-1

---

[1] The DHE (DISTRIBUTED HEALTHCARE ENVIRONMENT), is a product registered by GESI - Gestione Sistemi per l'Informatica srl, that provides an open infrastructure, capable of federating (integrating) multi-vendor, heterogeneous applications which interact through a set of common healthcare-specific components

S. Bhalla (Ed.): DNIS 2002, LNCS 2544, pp. 161–172, 2002.
© Springer-Verlag Berlin Heidelberg 2002

'Architecture for Healthcare Information Systems' [5]. By providing a uniform and integrated heritage of all organisational, clinical and managerial data, the architecture also allows the natural establishment of a 'holistic' healthcare information system [7]. Such comprehensive environment not only ensures a consistent support to the operational activities of all sectors of the healthcare organisation, but also allows the managerial monitoring of costs, activities and performances as well as the establishment of the healthcare records.

Cadmio is based on the MIC/MIE model [1], which allows a physician to define the Local Entity Dictionary (LED); i.e. the local entities, commonly identified by the physicians of a ward to describe the patient's state, constituting the patient folder and their logical organisation. The awareness of the existence of a natural hierarchical organisation among the entities, which expresses the various medical concepts, is at the basis of the definition of the MIC/MIE model. In order to define an entity belonging to the LED, it is essential to identify the context in which the entity is used, the properties which describe it, and finally the management of its properties. The purpose of constructing the LED is not only to provide a simple classification of the entities that have to be managed, but also to provide a tool to describe their logical organisation.

The management of the healthcare record represents one of the major requirements in the overall process, but it is also necessary to ensure that the record and any other healthcare data is integrated within the context of an overall healthcare information system. Treating the healthcare record in isolation, as a stand-alone, alien component of the overall system, would give rise to the same technological and operational problems, which have bedevilled migrating the previous generations of healthcare information systems.

Further requirements, tied to the exchange of clinical information between different healthcare organisations, need to be considered. The concepts of "continuity of care" and/or "shared care" imply sharing clinical data relating to the patient's state between different actors that can be achieved only through Internet via XML.

The definition of the healthcare records in XML (eXtensible Markup Language) allows the accessing of the data through web-based browsers. It allows publishing the healthcare data to remote users like general practitioners or specialists, according to the appropriate authorisation and security rights that allow reading and/or updating the information.

Other research activities have been carried out in the frame of XML applied to healthcare. Among these we can mention a Japanese Ministry of Health and Welfare's research project for electronic medical records started since 1995, creating a Medical Markup Language (MML) [2]. MML is an SGML DTD for medical record information with a hierarchical description of clinical information. Other activities have been carried out in the frame of the SynEx EU project [3][4].

2   The Healthcare Record in the HISA Middleware-Based Architecture

According to existing literature, the healthcare record is an aggregation of information which *'may contain anything'* relating to the patient. Each user must be free to include in the healthcare record of one patient the various types of information available, according to the specific needs and depending on reasons based on the clinical speciality, the health conditions of the patient, the organisational needs, etc. For this reason, it is difficult, if not almost impossible to reach agreement on the precise definition of a healthcare record architecture that can lead to record systems that could be implemented. This problem is addressed by Cadmio and described in this paper. HISA [5] also addresses the issue of the Healthcare Record (HCR), fundamental in any healthcare community, through a homogeneous view, capable of integrating the various needs and ensuring the consistency of the whole information heritage of the organisation. In fact, it must first of all be considered that in most cases the information being included in the healthcare record is not generated 'per-se', but is the result of some activities being carried out with respect to the patient. Moreover, the same information, which might be present in the healthcare record, represents fundamental data used to support a number of other processes in the organisation .

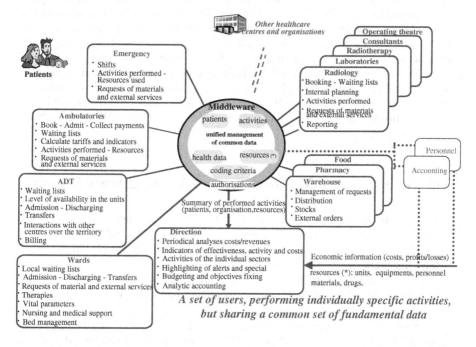

Fig. 1. Categories of Users/Functional units having common access to fundamental data.

For example, the same information regarding a request for a radiology examination (being part of the HCR of the patient) might also be necessary for planning purposes in the radiology department, for accounting reasons in the administrative department, and from the clinical point of view to the physicians/technicians actually performing the examination. This means that the way the data is made available needs to take into account the wide range of users of the data in addition to the principal clinical users of the HCR.

It can be argued that managing the healthcare record as a completely separate entity in the information system would therefore be a strategic error, unavoidably leading to technical problems and even to organisational conflicts. On the other side, it can be considered that the same information-centred perspective discussed for the whole organisation (see Figure 1), is also valid as concerns the healthcare record information. Also in this case, in fact, we have a number of different users, individually responsible for certain activities, but all of them needing to share a set of common data, fundamental for doing their daily work, as shown in the Figure 1.

The question that then arises is what constraints need to be put in place to provide those elements of the common data that various users require without making every piece of data available to everyone: some control in addition to 'authorisation' needs to be in place. And the need to be able to construct meaningful aggregations of data to users and categories of users is dependent on the application of rules defined by the users and accepted by the organisation. For the HCR as a special aggregation of fundamental data EU research projects like *SynEx* have proposed a solution [4].

Through such an approach, the HCR can be considered as an aggregation of (parts of) the information available in the information system, being clustered according to different views, criteria and perspectives according to the specific needs and characteristics of the individual users (integrated of course with specific, locally defined healthcare data managed directly by the clinician). As a consequence, each user will be free to define the most suitable HCR (and to select the HCR application better suiting their needs). Multiple HCRs may co-exist in the (local or territorial) organisation, nevertheless ensuring the integrity of all data as well as the possibility of other applications using them for other purposes. But each of these HCRs will adhere to some constraints.

3 The Methodological Approach for an XML Healthcare Record

The used methodological approach refers to the XML specifications by W3C (World Wide Web Consortium) Version 1.0. In particular, the main rules followed are:

❑ the information related to each "medical object" is reported following the restrictions defined for the "Namespace XML".
❑ The formats date, hour and date+hour follow the ISO 8601 specifications.
❑ The set of used characters follows the specifications of the W3C; then, all non-printable characters are coded on the base of the referred standard.
❑ The available data types are conformant to "Content-Type" described by the standard MIME *(RFC 2045, 2046, 2047).* Moreover, other contents defined in MERIT-9 (MEdical Image Text Information eXchange) can also be considered [2].
❑ The hypermedia data are not embedded directly into an XML document but they are linked through DHE references.

In order to maintain a flexible information description, it is possible to standardise only part of the exchanged information. This assumption can cause a possible loss of certainty of an exact matching of the exchanged information; however it presents the advantage of allowing a description of the information and services according to specific necessities of the different organisational structures of the hospital.

3.1 Information Management

The schema displayed in figure 2, presents the methodology used to represent the content of the DHE by means of an XML schema. The left part of the figure 2 shows how clinical data (entities) are organised in a medical folder. The right part of the figure 2 shows how clinical data can be translated in an XML representation.

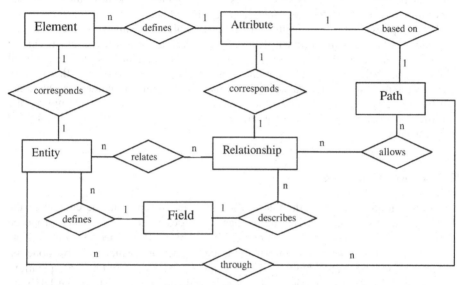

Fig. 2. The methodology used in order to represent the content of the DHE by means of an XML schema.

The relations designed to represent the logical organisation of these entities are the classic ones of generalisation (IS_A) and aggregation (PART_OF). Entities (in the left part of the figure) are organised by levels of abstraction, which relate each one to more general entities, which specify increasingly general properties and application-oriented contexts. Moreover, each entity may be broken down into more elementary entities and, vice versa, various entities may be aggregated in more complex entities. It is possible to associate different properties and characteristics to these aggregations depending on whether they are the consequence of the temporal, spatial or semantic composition of information.

The most complex issue is "constraining" a system, structured according to the entity-relationship model, into a hierarchic model, such as an XML document. The choice of which information to represent has been the focus to resolve this problem.

The CADMIO project envisages the release of a healthcare record that can be consulted and modifiable by a remote user; the nature of the information to transmit is intrinsically tied to the identity of the patient. The patient data represents thus the starting point for representing the healthcare record.

Now that we have identified the root of the XML tree we can proceed refining gradually the information contained in the document. In this way, the information content is partitioned in concentric portions, each constrained by the data present in the father element.

In our case, once identified the patient identity, it is possible to identify his or her hospital contacts. For each of these it is possible to collect the list of activities carried out during the stay and also the list of clinical data (results, vital parameters, etc.) also collected. Following this criterion, for each path in the XML sub-tree, a choice is made that selects more detailed information.

The resulting XML document should be considered as describing the contents of all related DHE concepts –expressed as XML elements/modules- and "filtered" according to constraints deriving from each father module.

This implies that the "HealthCare Data module" contained in the "Contact Module" contains just the clinical data collected during that precise contact. On the other hand, the same "Healthcare Data Module" in the "Patient Module" contains all clinical data belonging to the patient's history. In order to reduce the loss of information due the hierarchical structure of the XML document, numerous functional attributes have been identified, the presence of which doesn't complete the information content of the element, but allows to keep track of the relationships between concepts.

3.2 Services Management

In the paragraph 3.1, the methodology used in order to represent the content of the DHE by means of an XML schema has been described. The format proposed describes only the characteristics of clinical information. If it is necessary to activate services useful for managing information, the operations which can be done on clinical information also have to be considered. In this section the operations necessary to request information, add, modify or delete clinical data in the DHE are considered. The information exchange protocol, which has been proposed, operates through suitable Processing Instructions defined in the XML document. For each instruction an operation to be implemented is specified. When the XML document processor reads incoming files, it recognizes the instructions required by the client and executes the correspondent operation. The commands defined for exchanging information are presented in table 1:

Table 1. Commands for exchanging information

Processing instruction	Description
DheQuery	Request of a Query on the DHE
DheAppend	Request of inserting information in the DHE
DheDelete	Request of deleting information from the DHE
DheModify	Request of modifying information in the DHE
DheResult	Response with transaction result

4 The XML Patient Record

Depending on his/her own particular specialisation, a physician might want this part of the patient folder to be organised differently (for example, with greater or less detail given to the entities which may be part of case history or anamnesis) in such a way as to highlight the aspects which interest him most. And these concepts might of course be extended naturally to each and every other part of the patient folder.

The aim of enabling the physician to define the set of entities which he/she wishes to fit into the patient folder together with definition of how they must be organised was achieved by defining a hierarchy of classes. Such a hierarchy has to match the entity hierarchy represented in the patient folder. The properties of the classes are described by attributes. In table 2 the main tables of the DHE used for structuring the XML document are shown.

Table 2. Main tables of the DHE used for structuring the XML document

Name	Description
Table: Patient (dhePA:PatientModule)	It holds all personal information about patient.
Table: Contact (dheTT:ContactModule)	It holds information concerning each contact with healthcare organisations.
Table: Act (dheAA:ActModule)	An act corresponds to a request/execution of a clinical exam within a contact.
Table: ClinicalDatum (dheHD:HealthdataModule)	Clinical Datum is the result or more results obtained from the execution of an exam.

In figure 3 the XML structure of the document representing patient's healthcare record (or a part of it) is shown.

The XML document is divided into four main sections according to the functionalities that the exchanging protocol has to execute.

Header. This section holds general information concerning the information exchanged between Client and Server. The data in the headerdata allow to identify:
-   The identification code concerning client/server 'conversation' (*dheProcessId, dheAddress)*
-   The coordinates of information applicant (*dheAdressee).*
-   The coordinates of the information provider (*dheSender*

This section provides all information required to execute the Login operation on a DHE Server. The calling agent's authentication allows identifying the access right to visualize information and the existence of possible personalized records.

Further information concerning the coding process of exchange formats can be stored in this section.

Action. This section stores the possible operations foreseen in the exchange protocol between the Client and Server.

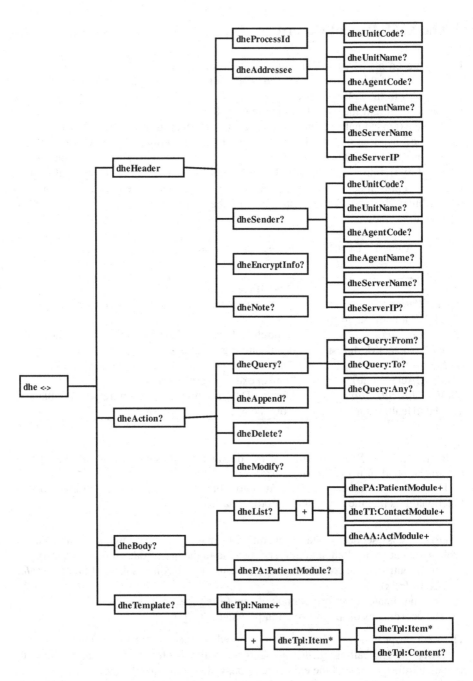

Fig. 3. The XML structure of the document representing patient's healthcare record

The aim of planning an XML healthcare record is gathering in one file all the information concerning a given patient and making this format readable and/or interpretable by a suitable viewer (http Browser, WAP mobile, etc.).

The information provider (e.g. http SERVER + ASP and/or VBCLASS) manages the continuity of dialogue between client and server and the applicant's identity is recognized according to parameters that are in the document's header.

During dialogue accessing, modifying and cancelling the information recorded in the DHE (e.g.: X-rays, Reports, and other multimedia objects) is possible.

A set of standard services are foreseen to allow a correct consultation of the healthcare record (e.g.: the request of in-patients list to select a single patient).

At the beginning of the document, between the tags **<dhe>** and **<dheHeader>,** all the processing instructions can be found.

When the processor of the DHE's XML document receives the *dheQuery, dheAppend, dheDelete and dheModify* comand, it has to respond with a message in which it specifies the request's result *(dheResult).*

Some commands need a set of parameters which are too extended/structured to fit within the *processing instruction*. In this case, the necessary parameters are kept in a suitable *dheAction* section of the XML document.

Body. Healthcare record contents are in this section. The "Information values" of the XML document have been divided into 11 different data types (text, real number, entire number, date, time, date and time, choice, records' key, identifier code and blob) according to the characteristics of their information contents. Such characteristics depend on the field in which the same information is recoded within the DHE. To each data type corresponds an XML element that expresses, besides the fields' contents, the complexity of the relationships among the different database's entities.

Blobs are used to manage extended data such as sounds, images, word files. All "types of clinical datum" managed by the hospital have to be referred to in the XML document to have a complete description. If no value is specified for a "type of datum", the correspondent XML element contains null.

This sector is structured in order to:

find patient's clinical/personal/data,

identify the coding and the hierarchical structure concerning the clinical data of the hospital involved

In each healthcare record is foreseen a "standard view" that hold all types of clinical data adopted by healthcare structure (previous item b), and a set of "personalized views" built by user through the builder of healthcare records.

The "personalized views" are subsets of the "standard view", also structured according to a different hierarchical order.

Template. The different "personalized views" built by user through the BUILDER OF HEALTHCARE RECORDS are found in this section. These views are recorded as "Templates" directly in the DHE and can change according to the different target of the XML document (e.g. HTML, WML, etc.).

The template's function is describing how to present graphically a "healthcare record". In the Template the page layout is described; instead of the value of patient's "clinical data" some "descriptive fields" are found. Such fields are referred to data of the document BODY section.

Even if some clinical data depends on the single healthcare structures, values held in the BODY are coherent with suchfields" held in the TEMPLATE, because both are managed by the same database.

5 An Example

The format of an "information request" XML document is composed by a processing instruction that specifies the command to be executed and, where necessary, by the correspondent element in the *dheAction* section in which there are parameters to elaborate the request.

For instance, to obtain the list of patients born between 12/11/1970 and 5/7/1971, the XML document to be sent is the following:

```
<dhe>
  <?dheQuery type="List" ?>
  <dheHeader>
        .
        .
  </dheHeader>
  <dheAction>
    <dheQuery dheTable:Name="A_PATIENT" dheTable:Prefix="PA_">
      <dheQuery:From>
        <dhePA:PatientModule dheTable:Name="A_PATIENT" dheTable:Prefix="PA_">
          <dheBase:PersonIdentity>
            <dheBase:dateBirth>
              <dheField:Data dheField:Name="PA_BIRTH"
                          dheField:DateValue="1970/11/12">12NOV 1970</dheField:Data>
            </dheBase:dateBirth>
          <dheBase:PersonIdentity>
        <dhePA:PatientModule>
      </dheQuery:From>
      <dheQuery:To>
        <dhePA:PatientModule dheTable:Name="A_PATIENT" dheTable:Prefix="PA_">
          <dheBase:PersonIdentity>
            <dheBase:dateBirth>
              <dheField:Data dheField:Name="PA_BIRTH"
                          dheField:DateValue="1971/07/05">5 LUG 1971</dheField:Data>
            </dheBase:dateBirth>
          <dheBase:PersonIdentity>
        <dhePA:PatientModule>
      </dheQuery:To>
    </dheQuery>
  </dheAction>
</dhe>
```

5.1 The DHE Reply

The XML document server's reply holds the *dheResult* processing instruction, in which the DHE error code concerning the elaboration and a textual description of it is specified. If there are no errors, the *dheBody* section holds the module/s required.

If the instruction modifies data such as *dheAppend*, *dheModify* or *dheDelete*, the *dheBody* section is empty.

```
<dhe>
  <?dheResult command="dheQuery" dheErr=0 dheDescrErr="..........." ?>
  <dheHeader>
        .
        .
  </dheHeader>
  <dheBody>
    <dheList>
      <dhePA:PatientModule dheRecord:Icode="07888765">
        <dheBase:PersonIdentity> . . . . </dheBase:PersonIdentity>
        <dhePA:HealtcareName> . . . . </dhePA:HealtcareName>
        <dhePA:Notes> . . . . </dhePA:Notes>
      </dhePA:PatientModule>
      <dhePA:PatientModule dheRecord:Icode="04657643"> . . . . </dhePA:PatientModule>
      <dhePA:PatientModule dheRecord:Icode="04765348"> . . . . </dhePA:PatientModule>
      <dhePA:PatientModule dheRecord:Icode="05632924"> . . . . </dhePA:PatientModule>
      <dhePA:PatientModule dheRecord:Icode="06721342"> . . . . </dhePA:PatientModule>
      <dhePA:PatientModule dheRecord:Icode="08231466"> . . . . </dhePA:PatientModule>
                .
                .
    </dheList>
  </dheBody>
</dhe>
```

6 Conclusions

This paper describes how to extract data from the Cadmio HISA-based healthcare record and structure them according to XML making the data available through browsers. Depending on his or her own particular specialisation, a physician might want part of the patient's folder to be organised differently (for example, with greater or less detail given to the entities which may be part of case history or anamnesis) in such a way as to highlight the aspects, which interest most. And these concepts might of course be extended naturally to each and every other part of the patient folder.

The aim of enabling the physician to define the set of entities, which he wishes to fit into the patient folder together with definition of how they must be organised, has been achieved by defining a hierarchy of classes. Such a hierarchy has to match the entity hierarchy represented in the patient folder.

References

[1] Ferri-F, Pisanelli-D-M, Ricci-F-L, Consorti-F, Piermattei-A. - Toward a general model for the description of multimedia clinical data. Methods Of Information In Medicine {Methods-Inf-Med} 1998 Sep, VOL: 37 (3), P: 278-84, ISSN: 0026-1270.

[2] M. Kimura, K. Ohe, H. Yoshihara, Y. Ando, F. Kawamata, T. Hishiki, et.al.: MERIT-9; a patient information exchange guideline using MML, HL7, and DICOM. International Journal of Medical Infotmatics, 59-68,51(1),1998

[3] Jung, B., Andersen, E. P., Grimson, J., SynExML as a vehicle for the exchange of Electronic Patient Records - A status report from the SynEx project, presented at XML Europe 2000, Paris, France, June 2000.

[4] http://www.gesi.it/synex/

[5] CEN ENV 12967-1 "Healthcare Information System Architecture"

[6] The DHE Middleware documentation, published by Swedish Institute for Health Services Development (SPRI), Hornsgatan 20 Stockholm

[7] Pier Angelo Sottile, Fabrizio Massimo Ferrara, William Grimson, Dipak Kalra, Jean-Raoul Scherrer The holistic healthcare information system. A middleware-based solution for supporting operational, managerial and healthcare record needs, presented at TEHRE '99.

Some Experiences on Large Scale Web Mining

Masaru Kitsuregawa, Iko Pramudiono, Yusuke Ohura*, and Masashi Toyoda

Institute of Industrial Science, The University of Tokyo
4-6-1 Komaba, Meguro-ku, Tokyo 153-8505, Japan
{kitsure,iko,ohura,toyoda}@tkl.iis.u-tokyo.ac.jp

Abstract. Web mining is now a popular term of techniques to analize the data from World Wide Web(WWW). Here we will report some of our experiences in large scale web mining. The first is the development of user query recommendation system based on web usage mining of a commercial web directory service, and the second one is cyber community mining from Japan domain web structure.

1 Introduction

The challenge to discover valuable knowledge from the chaotic WWW has driven the development of various web mining techniques. In general web mining can be classified into web structure mining and web usage mining. Here we introduce some experiences on large scale web mining of both categories.

First we report the application of web usage mining to help user query with category expansion [4]. Many websites are overwhelmed by the accumulation of the access logs only, and could not afford to extract valuable knowledge from the data but simple statistics. We perform mining on web access logs of i-Townpage, a commercial directory service. The total size of the logs accumulated in one year is about 500 GB.

Then we will also report the application of link analysis to extract web communities. A web community is a collection of web pages created by individuals or any kind of associations that have a common interest on a specific topic[2, 1]. We proposed a technique to create a web community chart, that connects related web communities[5].

The scale of exponentially growing WWW has posed new challenges to the research community. We will discuss some problems we face on large scale web mining in order to make usable applications of web mining.

Section 2 explains the development of category recommendation system based on web log mining. Section 3 describes our approach to mine web communities from millions of hyperlinks gathered in Japan domain and to generate web community chart. Section 4 concludes the paper.

---

* Currently at NTT Docomo

S. Bhalla (Ed.): DNIS 2002, LNCS 2544, pp. 173–178, 2002.
© Springer-Verlag Berlin Heidelberg 2002

2   Recommendation Based on Log Mining

Here we report results of log data mining and query expansion experiments of i-Townpage[4]. There are not so many reports for complete process of producing end-user assistant application through Web log mining [3,6].

2.1   i-Townpage

i-Townpage is an online directory service of phone numbers in Japan. It started the online service at 1995, with URL http://itp.ne.jp/. It consists 11 million listings under 2000 categories. Currently i-Townpage records about 40 million page views monthly. The visitors of i-Townpage can specify the location and some other search conditions such as business category or any free keywords and get the list of companies or shops that matched, as well as their phone number and address. Visitors can input the location by browsing the address hierarchy or from the nearest station or landmark.

If users of i-Townpage wish to search from categories, they can input the keywords directly to the form or pick a category in an alphabetical list or from a category hierarchy. For example, a category "Hotels" is found by selecting "Leisure Industries" from the top level, and then "Accommodations" from the second level.

2.2   Web Usage Mining

We analyzed 450 million lines of iTOWNPAGE log data and created session clusters from 24 million lines of selected log data. We found 27.2 % of search sessions with category as their variable input are multiple category sessions; that includes more than two different categories in sequence. 75.2 % of them used non sibling categories which do not share the parent in the category hierarchy iTOWNPAGE provides. This points out that there can be a gap in category structures between users and the designer of the service provider, or some users have multiple purposes at the same time. The second issue is that 25 % of search sessions finished search without any listings in category-and-address searches,

We use the well known K-means algorithm to cluster those search sessions. However since we can not predict the number of clusters in advance, we improve the algorithm so that it can dynamically decide the number of clusters to be generated. Instead of setting the initial number of clusters K, we define a similarity threshold.

Some clustering results that contain "Hotels" are shown in Table 1. The clusters are shown with the total number of sessions(members), the categories chosen during those user sessions and the number of sessions for each member category.

From the results, we can infer that the search session with the same input such as "Hotels" are performed on various demands and contexts. Some users indeed look for place to stay, while some others look for wedding halls, rent-a-car or meeting rooms.

Table 1. Example of clustering results

#	Cluster Size (# of Members)	Category	# of Input
1	15318	Hotel	15318
		Business Hotel	13654
2	3293	Spa Inn	3293
		Spa	1153
		Hotel	1145
		Hot Spring Supply	549
4	1805	Assembly Hall	1805
		Rental Meeting Room	719
		Hotel	331
		Auditorium and Assembly Hall	211
6	1258	Wedding Hall	1258
		Hotel	609
		Assembly Hall	303
7	1158	Rent-a-car	1158
		Hotel	120

2.3   Query Expansion

We propose a two-step query expansion; recommending categories from user requests clusters. The first step is to recommend the sibling categories classified close in the yellow page's category hierarchy, and the second step is to recommend non-sibling categories. We name the first one "Intra-Category Recommendation", the second one "Inter-Category Recommendation".

Intra-Category Recommendation. Recommending sibling categories from the clusters that have high frequency for the requested category (the ratio of requested category's frequency to the size of the cluster)

  Ex) When "Hotel" is requested, sibling categories in clusters 1, 2 in Table 1, "Business Hotel", and "Spa Inn", are recommended

Inter-Category Recommendation. Recommending non-sibling categories from the top members of the clusters that have high frequency for the requested category. Only clusters that have more size (number of members) than the specified similarity threshold (TH_{inter}) employed.

  Ex) When "Hotel" is requested, non-sibling categories on the top members of the clusters 4, 6, 7 in Table 1, such as "Assembly Hall", Wedding Hall", "Rent-a-car", are recommended.

Search example is illustrated in Figure 1. The left frame displays the expanded categories from our method and the right one is for the query answers from iTOWNPAGE. In the left frame, Intra-Category Recommendation results are displayed on the upper part while results from Inter-Category Recommendation are displayed on the lower part.

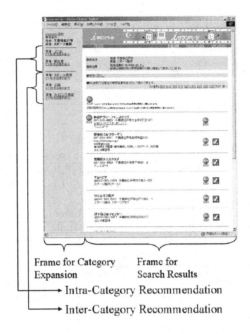

Fig. 1. Result page of query expansion system

3   Cyber Community Mining

Link analysis has been used to reveal the structure of the web, and to rank search results. Recently some researches also point out its potential to extract web communities, interconnected web pages whose content with similar interest[2,1]. Our approach goes further to visualize those web communities in the form of a navigatable chart.

3.1   Hyperlinks Archive

Our data set for experiments is an archive of Japanese web pages. The archive includes about 17 million pages in the 'jp' domain, or ones in other domains but written in Japanese characters. We collected these pages from July to September 1999 by running web crawler that collects web pages from given seed pages.

From the archive, we built a connectivity database that can search outgoing and incoming links of a given page. Our database indexed about 120 million hyperlinks between about 30 million pages (17 million pages of pages in the archive, and 13 million pages pointed to by pages in the 2000 year archive).

3.2   Web Community Mining

Our algorithm mine web communities from a given seed set[5]. The main idea is applying a related page algorithm (RPA) to each seed, then investigate how each seed derives other seeds as related pages. RPA first builds a subgraph of the Web around the seed, and extracts authorities and hubs in the graph using HITS[2]. Then authorities are returned as related pages.

We define that a community is a set of pages strongly connected by the symmetric relationships, and that two communities are related when a member of one community derives a member of an another community.

3.3   Web Community Chart

We depict one of the connected components that includes 29 nodes on multiple categories in Figure 2. In total, this component can be regarded as a community of companies related to computer hardware. However, further observation of this component reveals that it includes three communities. There are computer vendors (NEC, TOSHIBA, SONY, etc.) on the top-left, companies of computer devices (Adaptec, Intel, Logitec, etc.) on the top-right, and companies of digital

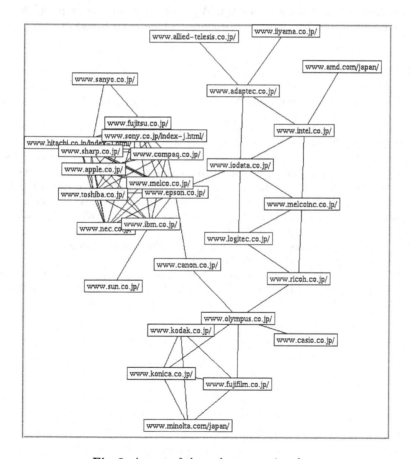

Fig. 2. A part of the web community chart

still camera (OLYMPUS, Minolta, etc.) at the bottom. In this case, we can partition the component into these three communities, by cutting the edge between any two communities.

We are able to find our related cyber communities by exploring the community chart. Since the most current information will be up on the web first, we are able to find out effective relationship among the community in a timely fashion, which could be useful for various applications.

4   Conclusion

We have reported some applications based on web mining of large scale real data. Vast amount of data is analyzed to create a chart of web communities or give visitors of a web site recommendation based on their query.

There are many techniques have been developed for web mining. However serious applications of web mining need powerful platform since they need to analyze growing large amount of data. We are planning to develop scalable parallel platform as well as parallel algorithms to handle such task.

References

1. J. Dean, M.R. Henzinger "Finding related pages in the World Wide Web" In *Proc of the 8th WWW Conf.*, 1999
2. J.M. Kleinberg "Authoritative Sources in a Hyperlinked Environment" In *Proc. of the ACM-SIAM Symposium on Discrete Algorithms*, 1998
3. B. Mobasher, H. Dai, T. Luo and M. Nakagawa "Effective Personalization Based on Association Rule Discovery from Web Usage Data" In *Proc. of ACM Workshop on Web Information and Data Management (WIDM) 2001*, pp. 103-112, 2001.
4. Y. Ohura, K. Takahashi, I. Pramudiono, and M. Kitsuregawa "Experiments on Query Expansion for Internet Yellow Page Services Using Web Log Mining" In *Proc. of VLDB 2002*, pp.1008-1018, 2002.
5. M. Toyoda, M. Kitsuregawa "Finding related pages in the World Wide Web" In *Proc. of Hypertext 2001*, pp. 103-112, 2001.
6. T.W. Yan, M. Jacobsen, H. Garcia-Molina and U. Dayal "From User Access Patterns to Dynamic Hypertext Linking" In *Proc. of 5th WWW*, pp. 1007-1014, 1996.

An Approach for Distance Learning via Internet and Its Evaluation

Tomoyuki Sowa and Kotaro Hirano

Kobe Design University, 8-1-1, Gakuen-Nishi-Machi, Nishi-ku,
Kobe-shi, 6512196 Hyogo, Japan
{hirano, sowa-t}@kobe-dri.gr.jp
http://www.kobe-du.ac.jp

Abstract. This paper presents the quality evaluation of distance learning system where an instructor controls the classroom at a distance. First the structure of the system is outlined and the data management for distance learning system is discussed. Then, the approach for quality evaluation via Internet is proposed. Finally, the experimental results using DSL are presented with the discussion for future direction.

1 Introduction

With the recent progress of Internet broadband access, the application area of Internet has been rapidly expanding, from a simple use of e-mail or Web browsing to more complicated system. Especially, the Internet telephone and the streaming video distribution are highly expected now as the new type of communication tools.

The environment of broadband provides us not only the high-speed information transmission, but also enables mutual communication environment among users at a lower cost. Although, until now, the preparation of a radio or TV programs requires a lot of staffs, a special knowledge on it, and huge amount of investment, it can be now easily produced and distributed from ordinary homes. Moreover, it has influenced on the communications style, because people have been able to exchange easily their own information each other. Previously it was not easy for those who are in a distance to communicate, using their voice or real time video. The environment of broadband access has made this possible.

The recent trend of information environment begins to have a big influence on the education style. Certainly, it is very effective for education and communication that one teacher instructs many students in one big classroom. The education system via Internet has different form of communication from the conventional education system [1]. At present, students can communicate with people being in a different country and talk with a specialist via distance learning system.

The present paper discusses about the teaching materials necessary for a distance learning via Internet and how to perform the effective education, by collecting the fundamental data on it. Then we will find out basic important points about distance learning system via Internet.

S. Bhalla (Ed.): DNIS 2002, LNCS 2544, pp. 179–187, 2002.

2 Structure of Distance Learning System for Evaluation

There are various styles of distance learning system. We assume the learning system that an instructor and students are located separately. For example, in English education, students in Japan communicate and learn English with an instructor staying in the country of English native.

2.1 Basic Functions of Distance Learning

At the conversation of education status, the basic function to establish the communication includes voice of an instructor and students, atmosphere including images of an instructor or students, and characters of textbooks, notebooks, and white board.

At a distance learning environment, an instructor needs to instruct students using various types of teaching materials for the establishment of communications between an instructor and students. And he has to manage the synchronous rich contents, such as video, still image, text, and audio [2] ~ [4]. The basic functions of establishing communication in a distance learning are same as the conventional face-to-face instruction. The education via the Internet requires suitable CODEC that conveys a mixture of information efficiently to the remote terminal.

From the above discussion, the basic functions for a distance learning include the followings.
(1) Sounds and images are used in various way, in order to share the scene at both location.
(2) A visual presentation tool can be used.
(3) Communication between computers can be performed smoothly.
(4) The technology, which enables compound communication, is supported.

2.2 Details Descriptions of Basic Functions

(1) Sounds and images
Sounds include voice of an instructor or students, and others that consist of atmosphere. In a distance learning, it is desirable that their conversation must be carried out naturally as much as possible. Especially, in the lesson on English pronunciation, it is not enough for students only to hear, but also it is required to listen the tone with the high quality.

Quality of images is also important to understand the atmosphere of both sides. Gesture of an instructor, including the motion of his eyes or mouth, must be transferred to students, and an instructor must check reactions from students. Several functions such as zoom, panning and tilt are helpful for instructor.

(2) A visual presentation tool
As various type of visual presentation tools such as whiteboard, or OHP are installed in a conventional classroom, similar tools have to be installed in a distance leaning system. The presentation with Power-Point made by Microsoft is highly welcomed.

(3) Communication among computers

A personal computer (PC) is one of the most powerful tools for an instructor and students, in a distance learning system via Internet. In a distance learning, occasionally PC is used as a whiteboard, canvas, and sometimes notebooks. An instructor can communicate with students, by sharing PC's screen each other.

(4) The ability of compound communication

The coding/decoding system (CODEC) plays the most important role in a distance learning system, in order to transmit sounds and video images efficiently. It is also desirable that CODEC can operate on a variety of the communication routes, such as xDSL, CATV, wireless, for Internet access.

2.3 Sample System for Evaluation

The system used in the experiment is shown in Fig.1, which consists of (1) Personal computer, (2) Video or RGB monitor, (3) Speaker and microphone, (4) TV camera or VTR, (5) CODEC, (6) Internet access.

(1) Personal computer (PC)

All members both an instructor and students will use PC. As shown in Fig. 2 (a), they share applications each other and perform bi-directional communication for exercises, such as drawing and text composition. PC can be used effectively as shown in Fig.2 (b), when an instructor evaluates students interactively

(2) Video or RGB monitor

Video monitors are installed at both sides, which are used to project the appearance of both sides. Additionally, a high resolution RGB monitor with 1024*768 pixels is installed at student side, which supports clear display when an instructor give a presentation by using PC.

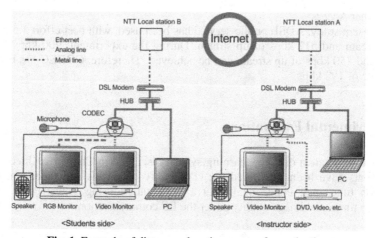

Fig. 1. Example of distance education system for evaluation

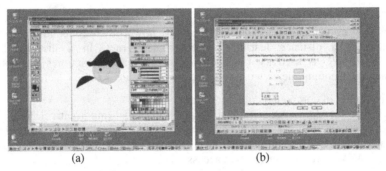

(a)   (b)

Fig. 2. Example of interactive learning contents

(3) Speaker and microphone
Echo-cancelled speaker and microphone are used for establishing voice communication between an instructor and students.

(4) TV camera or VTR
A television camera is used in order to project the atmosphere at both sites.
TV camera built in CODEC is used in this experiment. Moreover, an instructor can use VHS video tape recorder, when he teaches using the video materials.

(5) CODEC
CODEC made by Polycom Inc. is used in the present experiment. The CODEC "ViewStation" has been developed as a TV conference system for a small number of people, using ISDN (H.320) or LAN (H. 323). The transmission rate will vary according to the environment of a network: 128 kbps via ISDN and max rates 768 kbps via LAN.
    ViewStation has input/output terminals of RGB, video and audio, and can transmit the video images of 15 fps under the transmission rate of 56-320 kbs. It has also the function that Power-Point data can be converted into JPEG files and it can be manipulated from remote terminals.

(6) Internet Access
In the present study, ADSL public service has been used, with best effort 1.5 Mbps of down stream and 512 kbps of up stream. During the experiment, 900 kbps of down stream and 450 kbps of up stream can be achieved. Therefore, CODEC has been used at the rate of 192 kbps.

3 Experimental Evaluations

In order to evaluate a distance learning system discussed in Chapter 2, three types of experiments have been performed on; (1) Quality of sounds and video images, (2) Operation times and image quality at a presentation using Power-Point, and (3) Operation times and image quality under the PC communication.

3.1 Quality of Sound and Video Images

Figure 3 shows sound and video rates, video jitter, and packet loss for sound and video data, during the data transmission between an instructor and students. Maximum data rate 192 kbps of CODEC guarantees the bandwidth of 64 kbps for sound and 128 kbps for video. Normally video rate is stable varying from 126 to 127 bits, but in some case video rate decreases to 100 kbps.

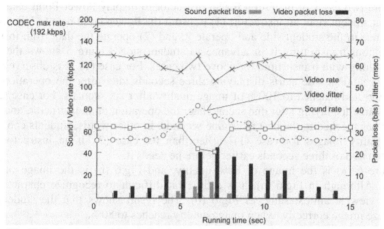

Fig. 3. Packet loss and jitter of sound and video data, observed at network load

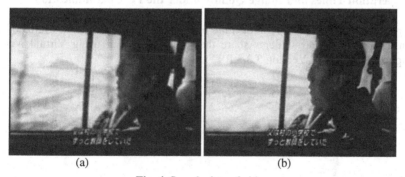

(a)   (b)

Fig. 4. Sample data of video

A sample scene with normal video rate is shown in Fig.4. Figure 4 (a) shows the appearance of a screen when data rate of video becomes lower. Comparing with Fig.4 (b), the image in Fig.4 (a) is not clear and some of characters are difficult to recognize. In our experiment, one change of video rate from 110 to 128 kbps happened irregularly within several minutes. One rate down has observed for one or two seconds.

For this reason, characters like the title which changes within one or two seconds may not appear on a screen, which has not been recognized by students. Because the packet loss of 10 ~ 20 was observed per one second during the lower data rate, the authors observe that characters were not displayed on a student's screen.

About sounds, although we observed some packet loss, the delay of conversation or loss of communication by failure in hearing was never happened. However, since echoes occurred in the case of simultaneous conversation, they needed to talk by turns.

3.2 Operation Time and Image Quality Using Power-Point

There are two cases of operation for an instructor to display Power-Point data on the screen at student side: an instructor: (1) transmit the Power-Point data to ViewStation in advance to the student side and operate it, and (2) operate the data from instructor side without transmitting it in advance to student side. Figure 5 shows the image quality along with transit time for above two cases. For case (1), it is observed that a screen at student side starts displaying three seconds later after the operation of an instructor, and reached to 100% of image quality after six seconds. For case (2), the image starts displaying after one second later the operation of an instructor, and image quality has reached to the best after nine seconds. In other words, students can view a good quality images for case (1) earlier than for case (2), if an instructor starts operation two or three seconds earlier before he needs it.

Figure 6 (a) is the image of 80% quality, and Fig.6 (b) is the image of 100% quality. Although in Fig.6 (a), it is a little bit difficult to recognize characters, the overall view is almost same as Fig.6 (b). The result shows that the students can recognize image correctly, when image quality reaches to 80%.

3.3 Operation Times and Image Quality under the PC Communication

The relation between the operation time and image quality has been evaluated here when an instructor and students share their PC each other, using Virtual Network Computing "WinVNC Version 3.3.3 R9"[1].

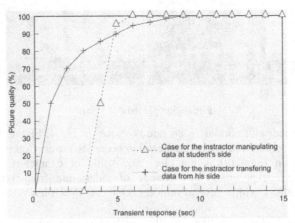

Fig. 5. Transmission delay of JPEG Power Point data between an instructor side and student side

---

[1] University of Cambridge and AT & T Laboratories Cambridge (2001).

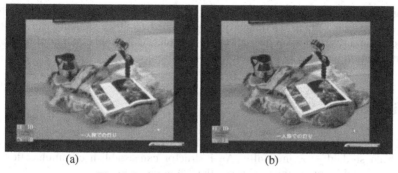

Fig. 6. Sample data of Power-Point display

Figure 7 shows the relation between image quality and the transient time. From this result, it is understood that a student started to operate his PC from four seconds later after an instructor had begun to operate his PC. At that time, the image quality was 80%. The image quality at both sides has reached to 100% by ten seconds later after the operation at opposite sides.

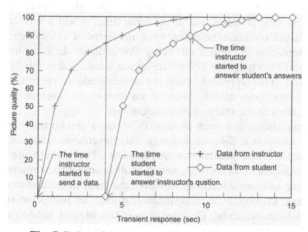

Fig. 7. Delay of data transmission for both directions

Fig. 8. Sample data of Power Point display

Figures 8 (a) and (b) show the image qualities at student side when they shared their own screen. When the image quality reached to 80%, students can recognize characters and respond to an instructor. As a result, the authors could confirm that PC communication has a delay for about four seconds.

4 Discussions

In this paper, the basic elements of a study system required for a distance learning have been studied experimentally. An instructor can establish communication with students smoothly, by taking case about the following points,

When an instructor uses video contents, he has to keep in his mind packet loss of several seconds. Students cannot recognize the images whose screen change in several seconds. By taking packet loss or irregular frame rate into account, it is desirable to prepare teaching materials, which keep unchanged within three second or more.

Concerning sounds, the present distance learning system has no particular problem and can be used without paying special attention. Although echo may cause a little bit problems when several people speak at the same time, it will not be serious problem to disturb the smooth communication between an instructor and students.

When a presentation is carried out using Power-Point data, an instructor should transmit the data to student side before the lesson starts, and control it from his side during the lesson. This approach does not make students recognize the delay of presentation by data transmission. Then an instructor can continue his presentation, without any attention to the image at the student side.

A system that shares a screen among PCs has a possibility of deepening the communication more in a distance learning. At present, the communication among PCs at an instructor and students is not smooth. The authors are expecting the research and development on software which enables smooth communication.

We predict that a distance learning will have the great future due to the wide use of broadband access. Of course, at a distance learning, an instructor is sitting at the remote location from students. This distance is the biggest barrier when they will establish communication. Even if image or communication technology may have a great progress, the distance learning will not have a perfect reality compared with the conventional face-to-face education. Therefore, we have to make strong effort to collect know-how on the study method and the development of contents suitable for distance learning [5].

In this paper, the authors have studied the fundamental element of a distance learning system. As the next step of our study, the authors will introduce this system into actual schools, and will collect more quality data.

References

1. H. A. Latchman, Ch. Salzman, Denis Gillet, and Hicham Bouzekri, "Information technology enhanced learning in distance and conventional education," IEEE Trans. Education, vol.42, November 1999.

2. T. Watanabe, I. Kamiya, T. Ito, I. Yoda: A study on the design and manufacture approach of synchronous rich content (in Japanese). The 64th annual conference of Information Processing Society of Japan, 1.4R-01, pp.4-197–198, March 13, 2002.K.
3. Nishio, M. Muraoka, T. Watanabe, I. Yoda, "A study on web-based multimedia testing system (in Japanese)," The 2002 annual conference of Institute of Electronics, Information and Communication Engineers, Information and System Society, p.207, March 28, 2002.
4. T. Ito, M. Muraoka, K. Nishio, I. Yoda, "The method of authoring for a web-based multimedia training system (in Japanese) ," The 2002 annual conference of Institute of Electronics, Information and Communication Engineers, Information and System Society, p.208, March 28, 2002.
5. Sergio Cesare Brofferio, "A university distance lesson system: Experiments, services, and future developments," IEEE Trans. Education, vol.41, February 1998.

A Graph Based Approach to Extract a Neighborhood Customer Community for Collaborative Filtering

P. Krishna Reddy[1], Masaru Kitsuregawa[2], P. Sreekanth[1], and S. Srinivasa Rao[1]

[1] International Institute of Information Technology,
Gachibowli, Hyderabad-500019, India.
pkreddy@iiit.net
[2] Institute of Industrial Science, The University of Tokyo
4-6-1, Komaba, Meguro-ku, Tokyo, Japan.
kitsure@tkl.iis.u-tokyo.ac.jp

Abstract. In E-commerce sites, recommendation systems are used to recommend products to their customers. Collaborative filtering (CF) is widely employed approach to recommend products. In the literature, researchers are making efforts to improve the scalability and online performance of CF. In this paper we propose a graph based approach to improve the performance of CF. We abstract a neighborhood community of a given customer through dense bipartite graph (DBG). Given a data set of customer preferences, a group of neighborhood customers for a given customer is extracted by extracting corresponding DBG. The experimental results on the MovieLens data set show that the recommendation made with the proposed approach matches closely with the recommendation of CF. The proposed approach possesses a potential to adopt to frequent changes in the product preference data set.

Keywords: Electronic commerce, Recommender systems, Mass-customization, Interface, Customer loyalty, Cross-sell, Up-sell

1 Introduction

With the advent of Web, it is possible to sell products electronically. The largest E-commerce sites offer millions of products for sale. Choosing among so many options is challenging for customers. Recommender systems have emerged to solve this problem. A recommender system for an e-commerce site receives information from a customer about which products he/she is interested in, and recommends products that are likely to fit his/her needs. Today, recommender systems are deployed on hundreds of sites, serving millions of customers.

Collaborative filtering (CF) is a widely employed algorithm in recommendation systems. CF works by building a database of preferences for products by customers. It recommends products to the customer, based on the ratings of other customers who have similar product preferences. It is widely used in recommender systems such as Amazon.com (www.amazon.com) and CDNow.com

S. Bhalla (Ed.): DNIS 2002, LNCS 2544, pp. 188–200, 2002.
© Springer-Verlag Berlin Heidelberg 2002

(www.cdnow.com). Currently, research efforts are going on to improve the scalability of CF without reducing the quality of recommendation.

In the literature, there are graph based approaches to extract community knowledge from a large data set of web pages. In this paper, we propose an alternative approach to improve the performance of CF by extending the ideas from Web structure mining. In [1] and [2], an approach is proposed to extract community structures from a large set of web pages by abstracting the community structure as a set of web pages that form a dense bipartite graph (DBG). In this paper we extend the DBG approach to improve the performance of CF. Given a data set of customer preferences, we find a small group of neighborhood customers of a given customer using the proposed DBG extraction approach. Next, products are recommended by employing CF among that extracted small group of customers. The experiment results on the MovieLens data set [3] show that the recommendation made by the proposed approach closely matches with the results of other variants of CF.

When a large number of customers buy products during the peak period, the preference data set is updated whenever a customer buys a new product. We believe that the proposed approach suits well for dynamically changing data sets to recommend products online, because, it suffices to extract DBG for a given customer.

The rest of the paper is organized as follows. In the next section we discuss the related work. In section 3, we explain CF. In section 4, we present the proposed approach. In section 5, we report the experimental results. The last section consists of summary and future work.

2   Related Work

We briefly discuss the research works related to recommendation systems and Web mining.

Recommendation systems:

In [4], a CF-based system is developed based on the customer opinions of people from a close-knit community, such as an office work group. Ringo [5] and Video Recommender [6] are e-mail and web-based systems that generate recommendations on music and movies respectively. The GroupLens research system [7] provides a pseudonymous CF solution for Usenet news and movies. A special issue of Communications of ACM [8] presents a number of recommendation systems. In [9], Schafer et al., present detailed taxonomy and examples of recommendation systems used in E-commerce and show how they can provide one-to-one personalization and at the same time capture customer loyalty. In [10], it has been shown that the scalability of CF-based algorithms can be improved by applying dimensionality reduction techniques on large data sets.

In the literature there have been efforts to overcome the weaknesses of CF using clustering methods [11] [12] [13]. The clustering methods identify groups of users based on similar preferences. After completion of the clustering process, the customer preferences about the products are computed using CF through the results of evaluation of the same products by the neighbors within the cluster.

In [14], a graph based approach, called horting, has been proposed in which nodes are users and edges indicate the similarity between two users. Products are recommended by walking through graph to nearby nodes and combining the preferences of the nearby users. This approach exploits the transitive relationship between the users and thus differs from the nearest neighbor algorithm.

Differing from the earlier approaches which are based on customer-customer similarities, in [15], an approach is proposed by computing item-item similarities to address the scalability problem. Item-based techniques first analyze the user-item matrix to identify relationships between different items, and then use these relationships to indirectly compute recommendations for users in an online manner.

Community detection:

World Wide Web (or simply a Web) can be viewed as a graph by considering web pages as nodes and links as edges. There are research efforts to extract community knowledge from the Web by identifying dense regions of the Web graph. We briefly discuss some of these approaches.

Given a set of web pages on a certain topic, Kleinberg [16] proposed Hyper-link-Induced Topic Search (HITS) algorithm to extract authoritative web pages by using link information only. In [17], communities have been analyzed which are found based on the topic supplied by the user by analyzing the link topology using the HITS algorithm [16]. Ravi Kumar et al. [18] proposed an approach to find the potential community cores by abstracting a core of the community as a group of pages that form a complete bipartite graph (CBG). After extracting a community signature, the real community can be extracted using HITS. A CBG abstraction extracts a small set of potential pages that have common links. In [1] and [2] an approach is proposed by abstracting a community structure as a DBG over a set of Web pages. As compared to CBG structures, it has been shown that the DBG abstraction extracts fairly big community structures.

In [19], given a set of the crawled pages on some topic, the problem of detecting a community is abstracted to maximum flow /minimum cut framework, whereas the source is composed of known members and the sink consists of well-known non-members. Given the set of pages on some topic, a community is defined as a set of Web pages that link (in either direction) to more pages in the community than to the pages of outside community. In [20], the Companion algorithm is proposed to find the related pages of the given page presented by specializing the HITS algorithm. By exploiting the weight of the links and the order of the links in a page, the Companion algorithm first builds a subgraph of the Web near the given web page and extracts the related pages using HITS. In [21], the companion algorithm is extended to find the related communities by exploiting the derivation relationships between the pages.

In this paper, we extended community extraction approach based on DBG to find the neighborhood community of customers for a given customer to improve the performance of CF.

3 Collaborative Filtering

We briefly explain CF [10]. The input to the CF algorithm is the details of purchase transactions of n customers on m products. It is usually represented as $n \times m$ customer-product matrix R such that, r_{ij} is one if the i'th customer has purchased the j'th product, and zero, otherwise. CF based recommendation approach consists of following steps: finding similarity between each pair of customers, selection of a neighborhood community for the given customer, and recommending products for a given customer.

1. **Similarity:**
   We denote customers with c_1, c_2... and products with p_1, p_2,..... Similarity between each pair of customers can be computed using either the correlation or the cosine measure.
   - Correlation
     Similarity between two customers c_i and c_j is measured by computing *Pearson* correlation coefficient $corr_{c_i\ c_j}$, which is given by

     $$corr_{c_i\ c_j} = \frac{\sum_{s \in k}(r_{c_i,s} - \bar{r_{c_i}})(r_{c_j,s} - \bar{r_{c_j}})}{\sqrt{\sum_{s \in k}(r_{c_i,s} - \bar{r_{c_i}})^2 \sum_{s \in k}(r_{c_j,s} - \bar{r_{c_j}})^2}}$$

     In this equation, $\bar{r_{c_i}}$ and $\bar{r_{c_j}}$ are the averages of customer c_i's ratings and customer c_j's ratings, respectively. The variable k denotes the set of common products rated by both c_i and c_j. For a product s, the values $r_{c_i,s}$ and $r_{c_j,s}$ indicate the ratings of customers c_i and c_j, respectively.
   - Cosine
     Each customer is considered as a vector in the m dimensional product-space. The similarity between the two customers, c_i and c_j, is measured by computing the cosine of the angle between the two vectors, which is given by

     $$\cos(\boldsymbol{c_i}, \boldsymbol{c_j}) = \frac{\boldsymbol{c_i} \cdot \boldsymbol{c_j}}{\|\boldsymbol{c_i}\|_2 * \|\boldsymbol{c_j}\|_2}$$

     where, . denotes the dot-product of the two vectors.

2. **Neighborhood community calculation:**
   Neighborhood community of a given customer can be calculated using one of the following methods.
   - Center-based:
     In this method, a neighborhood of fixed size is calculated for an active customer, by selecting a fixed number of nearest customers.
   - Aggregate neighborhood:
     This scheme forms a neighborhood of fixed size in an iterative manner. Initially it picks up a closed neighbor of a given customer. Then, the centroid is computed. Next, the neighbors close to the centroid is picked up. This process is repeated until the algorithm picks up a fixed number of neighborhood customers.

3. **Recommendation:**

In this step, a fixed number of products are recommended to the active customer based on the product preferences of neighborhood customers. The following methods are available to perform the task.

- Most-frequent item recommendation (MFIR):

  In this method, for each product (rated by neighborhood customers) we calculate the frequency of the neighborhood customers who preferred that product. The top N products that have high frequency values and not yet preferred by the customer are finally recommended.

- Association rule-based recommendation:

  In this method, association rule mining [23] algorithm is used to recommend products. Let us denote a collection of m products $\{p_1, p_2, \ldots, p_m\}$ by P. A transaction $T \subseteq P$ is a set of products that are purchased together by a customer. An association rule between two sets of products X and Y, such that $X, Y \in P$ and $X \cap Y = \phi$, states that the presence of products of set X in transaction T indicates a strong likelihood that products from set Y are also present in T.

  Using association rule mining algorithm, top N products are recommended based on the association rules generated on a fixed size of neighborhood customers [10].

4   Dense Bipartite Graph Based Neighborhood Selection

In [1] and [2], an approach is proposed to extract community structures from the Web by abstracting a community structure as a set of web pages that form a dense bipartite graph. In this paper we have extended the DBG-based community extraction approach to find the neighborhood of a given customer for CF.

In this section, we first explain DBG and explain how the community structure in the Web can be abstracted with DBG. Next we explain how DBG can be used to abstract a neighborhood community of a given customer for CF. Then, we explain the community extraction algorithm using DBG.

4.1   Dense Bipartite Graph and Web Communities

Here, we give the definition of a bipartite graph.

Definition 1. Bipartite graph (BG) *A bipartite graph BG(C,P) is a graph whose node-set can be partitioned into two non-empty sets C and P. Every directed edge of the BG joins a node in C to a node in P.*

Web pages are denoted by P_i, P_j, ...; where i, j, ... are integers. We refer a page and its URL interchangeably. If there is a hyperlink (or simply a link) from a page P_i to a page P_j, we say P_i is a parent of P_j and P_j is a child of P_i; Also we say P_i has an out-link to P_j and P_j has an in-link from P_i. For P_i, parent(P_i) is a set of all its parent pages and child(P_i) is a set of all its children pages.

Note that a BG is dense if many possible edges between C and P exist. In this paper, for a BG, the term link density criteria is used to specify the minimum number of out-links (in-links) each member in C (P) establishes with the members of P (C). In a BG, link-density criteria between the sets C and P is not specified. Here, we define a dense bipartite graph by specifying the link-density criteria in a BG as follows.

Definition 2. Dense bipartite graph (DBG) *Let p and q be the nonzero integer variables. A DBG(C, P, p, q) is a BG(C, P), where each node of C establishes an edge with at least p ($1 \leq p \leq |P|$) nodes of P, and at least q ($1 \leq q \leq |C|$) nodes of C establish an edge with each node of P.*

(Note that the notion of density of a graph is nonstandard. Goldberg [22] proposed that density of the graph is a ratio of the number of edges to the number of vertices, and proposed an algorithm to extract a density graph by combining network flow techniques with binary search. However, our interest is to capture the link-density between the two groups in a BG.)

Here, we define a complete bipartite graph that contains all the possible edges between C and P.

Definition 3. Complete bipartite graph (CBG) *A CBG(C,P, p, q) is a DBG(C,P, p, q), where $p = |P|$ and $q = |C|$.*

It can be observed that in DBG(C,P, p, q), both p and q specify the link-density criteria whereas the same specify both the number of nodes in P and C, and the link-density criteria in CBG(C, P, p, q). The difference between a CBG(C, P, p, q) and a DBG(C, P, p, q) can be observed from Figure 1.

Note that not all DBGs are of interest in the context of communities. Now we give the community definition by fixing the threshold values for both p and q in a DBG.

Definition 4. Web Community. *Let both P and C be the sets of web pages. Also, let p_t and q_t be the integer values that represent the threshold values. The set C contains the members of the community if there exists a dense bipartite graph DBG(C, P, p, q), where $p \geq p_t$ and $q \geq q_t$.*

It can be observed that we have defined the community by keeping the number of nodes in both C and P unspecified. We specify only linkage denseness with both p and q for a given data set. The values of p_t and q_t are fixed with a feedback after examining the potential correspondence with the real community patterns. These values are fixed such that by extracting such patterns we should establish a close relationship among the members of C.

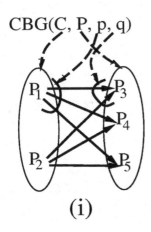
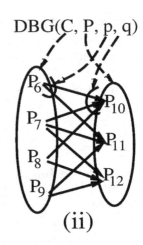

Fig. 1. Bipartite graphs: (i) CBG(C, P, p, q) (ii) DBG(C, P, p, q). In these graphs, the members of both C and P are web pages.

4.2   Abstraction of Neighborhood Communities with DBG

In the preceding section we explained how DBG can be extended to abstract a web community. In CF, the products are being recommended to the customer based on the product preferences of the neighborhood customers. Here we explain how DBG can be used to abstract the neighborhood customer community.

Note that, the customer data set contains the details of customers and product preferences. In case of customer data set, the notation C in DBG(C,P,p,q) indicates the set of customers and P indicates the set of product identifiers. Also note that the notation c_i indicates the i'th customer and p_j represents the j'th product. Also, in the customer dataset, an edge (or link) from customer c_i to p_j indicates the fact that c_i prefers the product p_j. The notion of child and parent is extended accordingly. That is, if a customer c_i prefers a product p_j, c_i is a parent of p_j or p_j is a child of c_i.

The set parent(p_j) is a set of customers who rated the particular product p_j, and child(c_i) is a set of products which have been rated by customer c_i. Here we define the customer community by extending the the definition of web community.

Definition 5. Customer community. *Let C be the set of customers and P be the set of products. Also, let p_t and q_t be the integer values that represent the threshold values. The set C contains the community of closely knit customers if there exists a dense bipartite graph DBG(C, P, p, q), where $p \geq p_t$ and $q \geq q_t$.*

Figure 2 depicts a sample CBG and DBG in the customer data set.

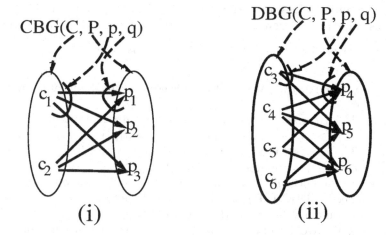

Fig. 2. Bipartite graphs for the customer data set: (i) CBG(C, P, p, q) (ii) DBG(C, P, p, q). In this figure C is a set of customers and P is a set of products.

4.3   Extraction of DBG from the Customer Data Set

The input is a customer data set: the details of customers and products. And the output is the DBG. The process consists of two phases. In the first phase, for a given customer c_i, we first gather the related customers. In the next phase we extract DBG by computing the appropriate p_t and q_t values through iterative techniques.

1. **Gathering phase**
   The variable *threshold* is an integer variable. The variable *rel_cust_set* denotes a set of customers. Given the customer (c_i) the following routine finds a set of related customers, *rel_cust_set*.

   a) Input: *data_set* (a set of customers); Output: *rel_cust_set*.
   b) *threshold*=1; *rel_cust_set* = { c_i };
   c) For all $c_j \in$ *data_set* such that $child(c_i) \cap child(c_j) \geq$ *threshold*, *rel_cust_set* = $c_j \cup$ *rel_cust_set*.

2. **Extracting a DBG**
   We extract a DBG(C, P, p_t, q_t) from *rel_cust_set*. Let the variable *edge_set* be the set of elements $< c_i, p_j >$ where c_i is a parent (source) of child p_j (destination). The *edge_set* is set to ϕ. Both p and q are integer variables.

   2.1 *edge_set* = ϕ. For each $c_i \in$ *rel_cust_set*, the edge $< c_i, p_j >$ is inserted in *edge_set* if $p_j \in child(c_i)$. (In the following steps, notations $child(c_i)$ indicates the set of products, p_j, such that $< c_i, p_j > \in$ *edge_set*, and $parent(p_j)$ indicates the set of nodes, c_i, such that $< c_i, p_j > \in$ *edge_set*.)

2.2 The initial values for p and q, say p_{avg} and q_{avg}, respectively are fixed as follows. Let there be m $= \mid \{c_i \mid < c_i, p_j >\in edge\_set\} \mid$, and and n$= \mid \{p_j \mid < c_i, p_j >\in edge\_set\} \mid$. Then, $p_{avg} = \lceil \frac{\sum_{i=1}^{m} |child(c_i)|}{m} \rceil$ and $q_{avg} = \lceil \frac{\sum_{j=1}^{n} |parent(p_j)|}{n} \rceil$.

2.3 p$=p_{avg}$ and q$=q_{avg}$. While $edge\_set$ is not converged, repeat the following steps:

    2.3.1 The $edge\_set$ is sorted based on the destination. Each edge, $< c_i, p_j >\in edge\_set$, is removed if $\mid parent(p_j) \mid < q$.

    2.3.2 The $edge\_set$ is sorted based on the source. Each edge, $< c_i, p_j >\in edge\_set$, is removed if $\mid child(p_i) \mid < p$.

2.4 Note that both p_{avg} and q_{avg} may not be optimum values to extract an effective DBG(C,P,p_t,q_t). Here, we followed a simple method to find the optimum values of both p_t and q_t, say p_{opt} and q_{opt}, respectively. The objective is to find a DBG that maximizes F1 metric. For this, we iteratively extract the DBG(C,P,p_t,q_t) at different values of p_t and q_t, by following above routine (2.3) and computing the F1 metric. First, we fix q at q_{avg} and determine the new value of p, say p_{new}, through binary search method by maximizing the F1 metric. Next, we fix p at p_{avg} and determine the new value of q, say q_{new}, by binary search method. Then, with both p_{new} and q_{new}, we determine the p_t and q_t, scaling (up or down by 10 %) both p_{new} and q_{new} by maximizing the F1 metric of the DBG.

Calculating the F1 metric for DBG(C,P,p,q). Given the test and training data sets, the F1 metric for DBG(C,P,p_t,q_t) is computed by evaluating the variables: $size\_of\_topNset$ and $size\_of\_hitset$ (see section 5.1). Here, the value of $size\_of\_topNset$ is equal $\mid P \mid$ and the value of $size\_of\_hitset$ is equal to the number of elements common to P and the set of products present in the test data set for the active customer.

The set C in DBG(C, P, p_t, q_t) represents a set of neighborhood community for the customer c_i.

5 Experimental Evaluation

We first explain about the data set and metrics employed. Next, we briefly discuss the approaches evaluated. Subsequently, we explain the experimental results.

5.1 Data Set and Metrics

We have conducted experiments on MovieLens data set [3]. The dataset contains totally 100,000 ratings, where 943 customers have rated 1682 movies. This data has been divided into training data (80 %) and test data (20 %). The training data is used to recommend products and the test data is used to evaluate the recommendation.

We use the following metrics to evaluate the approaches: precision, recall and F1 metric. Let the variable $topNset$ is the total number of products that are being recommended to the customer and the variable $test\_set$ be the set of products that are present in test data of the active customer. Also, the variable $size\_of\_topNset$ indicates the total number of products that are recommended to the customer and variable $size\_of\_hitset$ indicates the total number of common products that appear both in $topNset$ and $test\_set$.

- **Precision:**
  It is defined as the ratio of $size\_of\_hitset$ to the total number of movies recommended.
  $$precision = \frac{size\_of\_hitset}{size\_of\_topNset}$$

- **Recall:**
  It is defined as the ratio of $size\_of\_hitset$ to the total number of movies that we found in test data for active customer.

  $$recall = \frac{size\_of\_hitset}{size\_of\_testset}$$

- **F1 metric :**
  Note that the above two measures are conflicting in nature. Because as we increase N, $recall$ increases but at the same time $precision$ decreases. So, both measures are combined into a single measure which is called F1 metric.

  $$F1 = \frac{2 * recall * precision}{recall + precision}$$

5.2 Approaches

We have evaluated the following approaches. In these approaches after extraction of neighborhood customer set for a given customer we recommend products using the MFIR method.

- **Collaborative filtering (CF) :** For the given customer, all the customers in the training data set are belong to neighborhood customer set.
- **K-Neighborhood collaborative filtering (KNCF) :** In this method, we first calculate the similarity between the active customer and all other customers present in the neighborhood community using cosine similarity criteria. Here, the neighborhood of fixed size K is extracted using the center-based neighborhood community selection method.
- **DBG :** This is the proposed approach. Here, we first extract DBG for the given customer. The set C in DBG(C,P,p,q) is considered as a neighborhood community for the active customer.
- **DBG-KNCF:** In this method, we follow KNCF after extracting the DBG.

5.3   Experimental Results

The MovieLens data set is divided into five parts. Each part has training data and test data. We have selected one group of data set for evaluating above approaches. We have selected 10 customers randomly from one group and calculated the average values of precision, recall and F1 metric. For KNCF, we fixed the value[1] of K as 100.

Figure 3 shows the experimental results. In the DBG and DBG-KNCF approaches, the average values of C, P, p and q in DBG(C,P,p,q) for 10 customers are as follows: C=171, P=169, p=90, q=48. Figure 3 shows the values of precision, recall and F1 metric for CF, KNCF, DBG, and DBG-KNCF. The figure also shows the average number of good movies recommended to the active customer out of 10 recommended movies (the size of $size\_of\_topN\,set$) and the corresponding percentage values. The results show that the recommendation of proposed approach matches closely with the recommendation of the other variants of CF. So, we can conclude that that the proposed approach successfully extracts the neighborhood community of customers for a given customer by extraction corresponding DBG.

Approach	Precision	Recall	F1 Metric	Avg. # of good movies	% of good movies
CF	0.59000	0.09001	0.15342	6	60
KNCF	0.78636	0.12985	0.21949	8.2	82
DBG	0.72272	0.11469	0.19429	7.3	73
DBG-KNCF	0.75757	0.12542	0.21065	7.8	78

Fig. 3. Comparison of various approaches.

6   Summary and Conclusion

In this paper we have proposed a graph based approach to extract a neighborhood community of a given customer. Given a data set of customer preferences, a group of neighborhood customers for a given customer is extracted by extracting corresponding dense bipartite graph. The experimental results on MovieLens data set show that the proposed approach successfully extracts a neighborhood community for the given customer. The results also indicate that the recommendation with the proposed approach matches closely with the recommendation of CF.

We believe that the proposed approach suits well for dynamically changing data sets to recommend products online. Because, it suffices to extract DBG

---

[1] In [10], it has been reported that, the maximum F1 metric can be obtained by selecting K between 80 to 120.

for a given customer, if customers change the preferences or a new group of customers is included in the data set.

As a part of future work, we will investigate for the efficient methods to determine the optimal values of p and q to extract $DBG(C,P,p,q)$. We are planning to investigate the scalability issue by comparing the performance of proposed approach with other clustering based CF approaches by conducting experiments on the large data sets. We are also planning to investigate how the proposed approach provides online performance by adopting frequent changes in the data set by conducting experiments by considering the dynamic data sets.

Acknowledgments. The authors are thankful to the anonymous referees for their useful comments.

References

1. P.Krishna Reddy and Masaru Kitsuregawa, An approach to relate the web communities through bipartite graphs, in proc. of the Second International Conference on Web Information Systems Engineering (WISE2001),IEEE Computer Society (2001)
2. P.Krishna Reddy and Masaru Kitsuregawa, An approach to build a cyber-community hierarchy, Workshop on Web Analytics, April 13, 2002, Arlington, Virginia, USA
3. Index of /Research/GroupLens/data, "http://www.cs.umn.edu/Research /GroupLens/data/", May 2002
4. Goldberg, D., Nichols, D., Oki, B., Terry, D.: Using collaborative filtering to weave an information tapestry. Communications of the Association of Computing Machinery (1992) 35(12):61-70
5. Shardanand, U., Maes, P.: Social information filtering: Algorithms for automating " word of mouth ". In Proceedings of Conference on Human Factors in Computing Systems (CHI'95), Denver CO (1995) 210-217
6. Hill, W., Stead, L., Rosenstein, M., Furnas, G.: Recommending and Evaluating Choices in a Virtual Community of Use. In Proceedings of CHI, ACM Press (1995) 194-201
7. Konstan, J., Miller, B., Maltz, D., Herlocker, J., Gordon, L., Riedl, J.: GroupLens: Applying Collaborative Filtering to Usenet News. Communications of ACM (1997) 40(3):77-87
8. Resnick, P., Varian, H.R.: Recommender Systems. Special issue of Communications of ACM, (1997) 40(3)
9. Ben Schafer, J., Joseph Konstan, John Riedl: Recommender Systems in E-commerce. In proceedings of ACM E-Commerce conference, (1999)
10. Badrul Sarvar, George Karypis, Joseph Konstan, and John Riedl :Analysis of recommendation algorithms for e-commerce, ACM Conference on Electronic Commerce (EC'00), October , Minneapolis, Minnesota, USA (2000)17-20
11. John S.Breese, David Heckerman, and Carl Kadie: Empirical Analysis of Predictive Algorithms for Collaborative filtering. Proceedings of the Conference on Uncertainity in Artificial Intelligence, (1998) 43-52

12. Connor, M.O., Herlocker, J.: Clustering items for collaborative filtering. In the proceedings of the AAAI Workshop on Recommendation Systems, (1999)
13. Ungar, L.H., Forster, D.P.: Clustering methods for collaborative filtering. In the proceedings of the AAAI workshop on recommendation systems, (1998)
14. Aggarwal, C.C., Wolf, J.L., Wu, K., Yu, P.S.: Horting Hatches an Egg: A New Graph-theoretic approach to Collaborative Filtering. In Proceedings of the ACM SIGKDD Conference (1999) 201-212
15. Sarwar, B., Karypis, G., Konstan, J., Riedl, J.: Item-based collaborative filtering recommendation algorithms. In the proceedings of 10th World Wide Web Conference, May 1-5, (2000)
16. Kleinberg, J., Authoritative sources in a hyperlinked environment, in proceedings of ACM-SIAM Symposium on Discrete Algorithms (1998)
17. D.Gibson, J.Kleinberg, P.Raghavan. Inferring web communities from link topology, in proc. of ACM Conference on hypertext and hyper-media, 1998, pp. 225-234
18. Ravi Kumar, S., Prabhakar Raghavan, Sridhar Rajagopalan, Andrew Tomkins: Trawling the Web for Emerging Cyber-Communities. WWW8 Computer Networks 31(11-16):1481-1493 (1999)
19. G.W.Flake, Steve Lawrence, C.Lee Giles, Efficient identification of web communities, in proc. of 6th ACM SIGKDD, August 2000, pp.150-160
20. Jeffrey Dean, and Monica R.Henzinger, Finding related pages in the world wide web. in proc. of 8th WWW conference, (1999)
21. Masashi Toyoda and Masaru Kitsuregawa, Creating a Web community chart for navigating related communities, in proc. of 12th ACM Conference on Hypertext and Hypermedia, August 2001, pp. 103–112.
22. Goldberg, A.: Finding a maximum density subgraph, University of California, Berkeley, Technical report, CSD,(1984)84-171
23. Agrawal, R., Srikant, R.: Fast algorithms for mining association rules.In proceedings of VLDB (1994).

An Interactive Programming Environment for Enhancing Learning Performance

Mungunsukh Jambalsuren[1] and Zixue Cheng[2]

[1] Graduate School of Computer Science and Engineering,
[2] School of Computer Science and Engineering,
The University of Aizu
Aizu-Wakamatsu, Fukushima 965-8580, Japan
{d8041202, z-cheng}@u-aizu.ac.jp

Abstract. Constructivist and social learning environments have attracted considerable research effort in recent years. However, our experience in teaching programming languages has shown that it is an unavoidable difficulty for a programming environment to have a method that enables the system to determine how students think and plan to program. Students often feel perceiving programming subjects as requiring significantly more work than other general courses. Although, novice programmers have their own mental plan to programming, technically they do not have a systematic plan to write a program. In this paper, we investigated novice programmers' learning performance during programming in a VLB[1] programming environment. The system we designed enables students to reach their goal without high cognitive loads and with minimum efforts. The system builds a knowledge tree using a source program written by students and then maintains changes of the source code using a special technique in order to gain students' learning performance. This also helps the system to minimize error messages of the source code, and increases quality of their explanations.

1 Introduction

Constructivist and social learning environments have attracted considerable research efforts in recent years [1] [2]. However, our experience in teaching programming languages has shown that it is an unavoidable difficulty for a programming environment to have a method that enables the system to determine how students think and plan to program. Programming is difficult, since programmers are required to understand complex programming rules, concepts, and basics of algorithm design and to have general problem solving skills for particular subjects simultaneously [3][5]. Certainly, they are also challenged to develop logical thinking skills to be able to translate a problem description into appropriate logic structures and coding statements. Therefore, novice programmers often

---

[1] Visual Legacy Basic is an imperative programming language designed for beginners to learn programming.

S. Bhalla (Ed.): DNIS 2002, LNCS 2544, pp. 201–212, 2002.

feel perceiving programming subjects as requiring significantly more work than other general courses [4][6]. Programming is a translation operation from a mental plan for reaching particular objectives by following special rules that are very similar to native language rules or syntax. In the programming language courses, students always make mistakes because of misunderstanding or forgetting of the complex programming rules, or hardware specific operations. Even the mistakes that students made were straightforward to solve, they are always confused with the mistakes and would like to ask someone else. One of the significant reasons why students are confused with the mistakes is obviously dependent on what they are given by compilers.

We also consider some essential programming language concepts. There are several ways to write programs that are not directly to be followed the programming rules, depending on particular problems and originality of programming languages. Consequently, compilers may give no mistakes during the compiling, that will cause programs to be crashed during the execution. Not only crash a program, but also such kind of mistakes may cause mismanaged memory (e.g. dangling pointers, memory garbage, etc.), miscalculation of floating-point numbers, etc. Certainly, some of the programming languages provide special functionality to control such kinds of mistakes, and notify error messages earlier at compile time (usually referred as strongly typing languages). Although programming languages notify errors correctly, the most of programming languages skip maintenance issues of programming during development of a program. Thus, students are required to have more efforts for learning programming.

Recently, many research trends emphasize on supporting students by analyzing their learning performances during programming. However, most of them emphasize on correction of the students' goal, but not parts of the goal. We investigated in case to gain students' learning performance during programming continuously, and provide students with relevant documents, advice and hints that can help students to solve particular problems, and to understand current situations.

2   Related Work

According to Recker et al., cognitive skill acquisition can be divided into two tiers [7]. Knowledge, Comprehension and Application belong to basic levels of cognitive skills based on Blooms [8] taxonomy. The second tier is higher-level skills of Analysis, Synthesis and Design. Over the past three decades, several research efforts designed for novice programmers to learn programming focus mainly on the first tier. It is important to acquire basic knowledge of programming such as remembering keywords, syntax, concepts and jargons for novices [15].

Many approaches of analyzing a program structure [9][8] have attracted considerable research efforts in this field. These trends emphasize on the construction of the method of comparing students' program with the existing patterns in order to evaluate students' performance. Some of the approaches emphasize on signaling to highlight important information of a program code, based on the result of comparison of the programs. Many environments have been developed which highlight keywords of the language automatically, even it is not the most important information for students. [10]. Whether highlighting keywords is important to someone, or not, the environments should also highlight semantically important information. Highlighed information must be correct, since misleading signals become a cause of misunderstanding.

Techniques for determining the semantic differences between two programs are suggested by many researchers [12] in order to evaluate the performance of students' programming. However, it is difficult to compare two programs without any limitations. Usually researchers assume limits for comparing programs((eg, programming paradigms, a short programs, etc).

Jonhson and Soloway [14] suggest some essential approaches to understand students program. They attempt to create a specification for a source code and detect lexical, syntactic and semantic errors from the source code. Similar approaches are also suggested by Murray (1988) and Rich & Wills (1990).

3   Programming Difficulties

Novice programmers have difficulties learning how to program for a lots of reasons. One reason appears in the messages given by compilers. Students need to get good error messages to control their work. Once they fall behind in his/her understanding of the work, they may lost their attention and they will continue to fall further behind [16]. The study of errors in programming has shifted from an emphasis on syntactic errors to an emphasis on semantic and conceptual errors, particularly for beginners. In the last decade, most of the compilers could give only two kinds of error messages (Compile-time and Runtime) to programmers. Recently, compilers (languages that have a Graphic User Interface) give three kinds of error messages (Design-time, Compile-time, and Runtime). Although programmers need to get runtime errors, compilers should reduce runtime errors and then recognize them earlier in the compile time or in the design time. In this system, we assume that compilers must detect errors not in the compile time, but in the design time in order to improve quality of program development life cycle and support students immediate feedback.

For compiling a source code, almost all compilers (without considering programming paradigms such as Imperative, Procedural, Event-based, Object Oriented, etc) have the same method to translate source code into their own internal representations. In other words, compilers compile a source code in TOP-DOWN and LEFT-TO-RIGHT way. The problem for compiling in this way is that learners may be given many errors that are not relevant to the real situations.

For example:

1. Make a parse to be having a mistake, in fact, one of the previous parses has a mistake, or makes a parse that would have no mistakes, because of unrecognized or misjudged of previous parses.
2. Compilers may notice more than one error messages, because of misdiagnosing parses, which can be skipped.
3. For the block operation, compilers give an error message at the end of the block, while the block has an error at the beginning part of the block.

Depending on compilers' compiling methods, programmers might be given misreports same as above. Although compilers give error messages, they are also weak in providing explanations about fixing errors.

The program development life cycle follows a simple rule of writing a code and compiling, checking errors and compiling the code again and so on. Some of the programmers think it is normal; they suppose that they do not lose any time with this consecution. In fact, it takes at least two times more than possible way. Depending on errors, for example, if a program has just a simple error, compilers have to compile the same code twice or more and have to connect all related libraries. Compilers cannot keep unchanged parts for further use. They compile everthing in each time. Especially, JAVA is not suitable for slow computers. We do not need to consider it for a big systematic program, since there are many advanced technologies for programming (eg, Object Oriented Programming) and for developing a large system (eg, COM[2], EJB[3] etc.) We should consider above problem only for a small case for the beginners rather than experts and masters.

Compilers also consider scope problems higher level than other simple statements, which usually become the main cause of oversight of error messages. For example, in order to reduce the compiling time, compilers should never consider an assignment that is in the outside of the global scope.

4   Performance during Learning Programming

We investigate two types of data items as performance during learning programming. Data events during typing of a source code and error messages given by compilers are discussed in this sections.

4.1   Data Events during Typing

We assume a source code as the main "knowledge" that consists of particular sub sections called statements (See Figure 1). A statement itself can be divided into several parses. All parses are divided into small objects (same as a parse, but the

---

[2] The Component Object Model (COM) is a software architecture that allows applications to be built from binary software components.

[3] The Enterprise JavaBeans (EJB) is a transaction server development technology. It both enables transaction processing and control transactions across multi-platform enterprise systems and database servers.

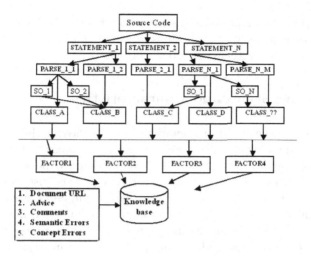

Fig. 1. Extracting a source code for observing data events.

smallest meaningful part of a statement. e.g, assignment, logic operation, etc). Each of them can be classified to several classes (by their meaning) and each of which has special data events that can be countable by the system during programming.

Some essential data events which are used to recognize and detect students' characteristics are explained in the next section (See Table 1). In data observation, each independent operator, keyword and function are considered as units (predefined class) that have several own properties and methods in order to calculate and count data events.

4.2 Type of the Error Messages

Type of error messages given by compilers can be divided in various ways depending on paradigms. The imperative languages do not have such many types of error messages comparing with the OOP (Object Oriented Programming) languages and the Procedural Oriented Programming Languages. In the imperative programming languages we can consider at least following three error messages:

1. Syntax Error
2. Logic errors
3. Pragmatic errors or Idiomatic errors

In the OOP languages, we can include the consistence error. The system should distinguish the consistence errors from the logic errors. In some of the languages (especially in OOP), students can declare a function twice or more, and we call them overloaded functions. They are different with each other by their parameters. In such case, suppose a student writes overloaded functions without difference, then such kinds of errors are definitely neither syntax errors nor logic errors. Or we can say that such kinds of errors can be either of them. In this research work, we call them consistence errors.

5   Learning Styles and Characteristics

Some of the psychological characteristics are defined in the proposed system based on the data events. The observer agent is responsible for creating create the psychological characteristics of students to simplify the analysis and the diagnosis parts of a source code. Learners will be supported just after their learning behaviors are detect by the system. The system supports learners through its environment (e.g, web browsers, a color editor, an animated characters, etc). We create and analyze following learning styles and characteristics in order to evaluate learning performance. The learning styles and characteristics are extracted from the observed data events. In other words, the observed data events are explained as human factors, that we can support learners easily using them.

Table 1. Observed Data Events

Events	Description
MV	**Minimum writing time of an unit.** Observer agents collect learners typing speed of an unit and calculate minimum typing speed of every unit. This data event is calculated throughout all tasks.
AV	**Average writing time of an unit.** Observer agents collect learners typing speed of an unit and calculate average typing speed of every unit. This data event is calculated throughout all tasks.
NM	**Number of typing mistakes of an unit.** After reserved word is recognized as an unit, number of mistakes will be counted.
NR	**Number of reminders.** After compiling or execution, number of reminders for units will be counted, if the units have mistakes.
NF	**Fixed times after a reminder.** After a reminder, this data event will be counted if learner fixes mistakes of the unit.
NB	**Fixed times before reminder.** Before compiling or execution, this data event will be counted, if the units have no mistakes.
ND	**Deleted times before reminder.** Before giving a reminder, this data event will be counted if learner deletes the units.
NA	**Deleted times after reminder.** After a reminder, this data event will be counted if learner deletes the units.
NW	**Deleted times without any mistakes.** Learner may delete units while the units do not have any mistakes. This data event will be counted in such situation.
NS	**Used times in successful tasks.** This data event will be counted when its task is successful.

Remembering degree and forgetting degree. How much students read and experienced in the current work and how much they could remember in the present time will be counted in this property. To define remembering degree properly is a big deal to provide students with suitable support. The problem is that agents may support students, while they know the situations. The research work is not to support better than what learners think but make possibilities to understand the current situation broadly.

Understanding degree. This property is considered when a student solves given tasks with fewer mistakes in a shorter time comparing with other students' performance.

Knowledge degree. This property is considered depending on the students previous experience; experience of successful tasks, reading related contents etc.

Motivation degree. We consider well-known motivational model called ARCS[4] According to Dr. Keller, a student has attention if the student takes less time in writing a task comparing with all other students' average performance on the same task. A student has relevance if his/her performance became better than the previous tasks' performance, and a student has confidence if his/her NA, ND and NW (See Table 1) data events became less than previous performance. Finally, we assume a student has satisfaction if his/her working time is less than the previous performance on the task, and executes the task much. ARCS model is addressed sequentially by its order. For example, it is impossible for a student to have confidence without attention, or without relevance, there are no confidence or satisfaction. Without relevance and attention, nobody able to be satisfied by their work. It is helpful to address students' motivation properly.

Interest degree. Students may have an interest on the work, if they still keep working on it the task by changing parts of the source code after finishing their work on the present task. Even students take less time on coding and more time on executing and/or updating programming code can be considered that the students may be interested in the work.

6   Design of the Learning Environment

The system has three sub systems: A student-side interface, An authoring interface and a server-side implementation that supports web documents and knowledge base (See Figure 2). The student-side consists of a syntax editor, web browsers and the agents. Only the analyzer agent appears in the server-side. The web server is located in the same server with the analyzer agent and renders relevant services to learn the programming language. The reason to locate the analyzer agent and the web server on the same machine is simply explained as a further development. The integration of web server and the analyzer agents

---

[4] Initials of four major categories of motivational strategies: *Attention, Relevance, Confidence, and Satisfaction*

is for reducing network traffic of dynamic contents, since managing dynamic web contents on the fly are not the best way in all cases, even it is considered the best way for supporting students individually.

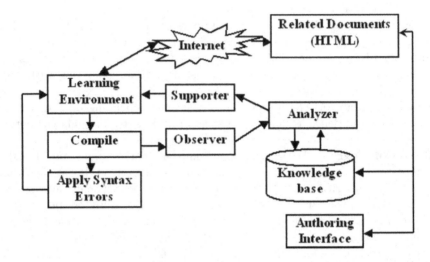

Fig. 2. System architecture

The authoring interface is responsible to check misconstructions of the knowledge base and improve some of them, including the web contents.

The agents are supposed to be reactive agents without considering animated human-like agents. By the all mean, observer and analyzer agents are active agents in order to accomplish their roles in the system, so are supporter agents. The knowledge embedded in the system has to be represented in a formal way. There are various contributions by AI approaches to accomplish it, for example, rule based, case-based, model-based and so on. The system has case-based knowledge representation scheme.

6.1   Compiling a Source Code

We propose a new technique to compile a source code (See Figure 4). The old system receives special signals from the user interface, and then it first asks a source code from an editor and checks if the source code has errors. Then notifies error messages to the user through the editor or others tools (See Figure 3). If there are no errors in the source code, it creates internal representation files of the source code. For instance, class file for Java. Although the proposed system is required to compile whole source code, it partially receives only changed lines from the Syntax editor and converts them into internal codes. In this case, the compiler does not need to compile whole source code again after a small error. Changes of the source code are registered to the objects (considered in the previous section) for creating data events from the typing.

7   User Interface and Implementation Issues

The Learning Environment is implemented in Windows platform as a stand-alone application that consists of the VLB compiler and web browsers. The system consists of six kinds of browsers (Contents map, Table of Index, Lecture notes, Slides, Examples and Tasks browsers). Each of which has special role for supporting learners with different kinds of way. The core of the system is called Task part, which is illustrated in Screen 5. The Task part consists of five sub sections called Syntax editor, Task browser, Variable table, Result window and Converted source code window.

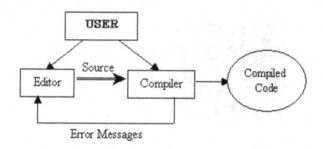

Fig. 3. Old System : Life cycle of compiling a source code

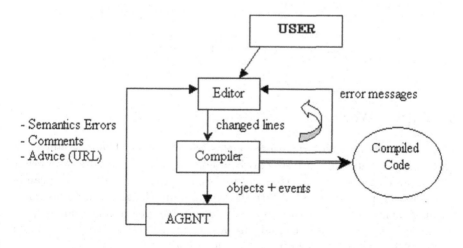

Fig. 4. New System: Life cycle of compiling a source Code

The animated agent OZZAR[5] is employed as an Interface agent of the system. Hints, suggestion, error messages and agents impression are dangled to the animated characters role.

The syntax editor is another tool for supporting learner with extremely pleasant programming environment. The current syntax editor is suitable to the VLB programming and its special functionality. Although the VLB is just an imperative language, it possesses many advantages for the novices (eg, Implementation of "Look into Machine" [8][4] and Translation into native like language, etc.).

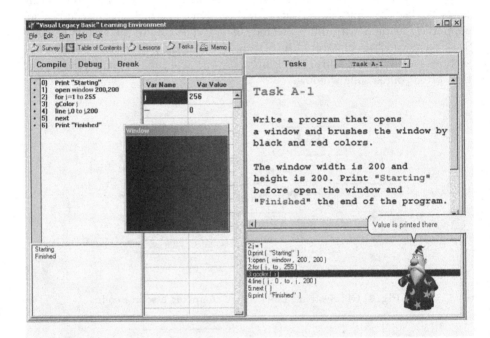

Fig. 5. Screen capture : The main window

8   Future Work

There are many possible expansions on this research work. The most appealing expansion is to intensify analyses part based on experimental results. As a result, system can diagnose students characteristics more than present level and can be better assistant for students to learn the programming language in the distance-learning environment. Moreover, not only imperative programming language for the novices, we supposed to extend this project to object oriented programming language (for learning JAVA) in distance learning.

---

[5] Name of the animated character for the Microsoft Agent

We realize such kind of extension will give us more interesting results than the present work, because of needs of OOP programming, popularity of JAVA language and motivation to learn JAVA, etc.

9 Conclusions

The research work is focused on supporting students to learn programming languages in distance learning environment. In this system, we are trying to solve several different issues that can be tied to students to learn programming languages in distance learning system. For the compatibility of the system we design visualization model for the system integrating with web browsers, which can reflect relevant documents, tasks, problems and advice.

Then finally, we build agents that are employed as an essential role in the system and can understand students' behaviors by diagnosing students' problems such as programming and motivational problems. Remembering the keyword and understanding simple concepts are some of the examples of the programming problems. The psychological factors, such as attention, interest and confidence are considered as motivational problems.

References

1. Xu, S., Chee, Y.S.: "Transformation-based Diagnosis of Student Programming Errors," Proceedings of ICCE98, pp.405-414, 1998.
2. Bredo, E.: "Reconstructing educational psychology: situated cognition and Deweyian pragmatism," Educational Psychologist, 29(1), pp.23-25, 1994
3. Zdancewic, S., Grossman, D. and Morrisett. G. : "Principals in Programming Language: A Syntactic Proof Technique," ACM SIGPLAN Notices, 34(9), pp.197-207, Sept. 1999.
4. Garner, S.: "The Flexible learning of Software Development: A Review of some of the Approaches and Suggestions for the Future," Proceedings of ICCE99, pp.429-435, 1999.
5. Lisack, S.K. : "Helping Students Succeed in a First Programming Course: A Way to Correct Background Deficiencies," International Association for Computer Information Systems Conference, Mexico, Oct, 1998.
6. Green, R. : "Learning Programming through JavaScript," Computers in Education Conference, Australia, 1998.
7. Recker, M.M. and Peter, P.: "Student Strategies for Learning Programming from a Computational Environment," Proceedings of the International Conference on Intelligent Tutoring Systems, pp.382-394, German, 1992.
8. Tomek, I, Muldner, T. : "PMS a program to make learning Pascal easier," Computers and Education 4(9), pp.205-212, 1985.
9. Buhr, P.A. : "A Case for Teaching Multi-exit Loops to Beginning Programmers," SIGPLAN Notices, 20(11), pp.14-22, 1985.
10. Baecker, R., Mantei, M., and Orbeton, P. : "Design Principles for the Enhanced Presentation of Computer source Text," Proceedings on Human factors in computing systems, United States, 1986.

11. Gellenbeck, E.M., Cook, C.R. : "An Investigation of Procedure and Variable Names as Beacons during Program Comprehension," Empirical Studies of Programmers: Fourth Workshop, Ablex Publ. Co., pp.65-81, 1991.
12. Orbeton, P. : "Identifying the Semantic and Textual Differences between Two Versions of a Program," Proceedings of the ACM SIGPLAN 90 Conference on Programming Design and Implementation, 1990.
13. Buiu, C., and Aguirre, G. : "Learning Interface for Collaborative Problem Solving," Proceedings of ICCE99, pp.301-304, Japan, 1999.
14. Johnson, W, L., Soloway, E. : "Knowledge-based program understanding," IEEE Transactions on Software Engineering, SE-11, pp.11-19, Mar, 1985.
15. Thiry, M., Ling, C.K. : "Effects of Learning Styles on Undergraduates Attitudes, navigational Patterns, and Use of navigational Tools in HyperMedia-Based Learning," The Electronic Journal on Information Systems in Developing Countries, EJISDC, Aug, 2001.
16. Blaise, W.L., Robert, A. : "A Novice Programmer's Support Environment," Proceedings of the SIGCSE/SIGCUE Conference on Integrating Technology into Computer Science Education, Spain, Jun, 1996.

Business Operation Intelligence

Fabio Casati, Umeshwar Dayal, and Ming-Chien Shan

Hewlett-Packard
1501 Page Mill Road, MS 1142
Palo Alto, CA, 94304, USA
casati,dayal,shan@hpl.hp.com

Abstract. In the last decade we have witnessed an increased trend towards automating all the interactions that a company has with its customers, suppliers, and employees. This trend is continuing even in the economic downturn, since automation not only allows for faster processing, but can also reduce costs and errors due to the diminished need for human involvement. Once a robust e-business infrastructure has been developed and deployed, companies quickly turn their attention to the problem of *assessing* and *managing* the quality of their e-business operations. This paper presents the concepts and architecture of a system that supports users in managing their infrastructure from a both a business (qualitative) and IT (quantitative) perspective. The platform also provides for the "intelligent" analysis of e-business operations as well as for making predictions over the quality of ongoing and future operations.

1 Introduction and Motivations

To increase revenue, improve efficiency, and reduce costs, companies deploy and integrate different kinds of software systems and applications that can automate and manage the execution of mission-critical business processes, within and across organizations. The resulting software architectures are typically complex, and include a variety of technologies and tools. Fig. 1 shows a quite common infrastructure that supports both the execution of internal business processes and the management of B2B and B2C interactions. This architecture may include several components, such as:

- A *Web server*, to accept and serve static HTTP requests and redirect dynamic ones.
- An *Application Server* (AS), to provide efficient access to applications and to support the reliable, personalized, multi-device service delivery. In addition, they also provides XML document management capabilities [1].
- A *Workflow Management System* (WfMS), to automate the execution of business processes within and across organizations. WfMSs also allows simple forms of business process monitoring and analysis [6].
- An *integration* platform (typically a message broker), that hides the heterogeneity of the back-end applications and provide a homogeneous model and protocol to access heterogeneous applications. Vendors currently provide tools that can perform both internal (EAI) and external (B2B) integration [1].
- *Back-end applications*, that support specific, vertical functionalities, such as procurement, inventory management, or financials.

S. Bhalla (Ed.): DNIS 2002, LNCS 2544, pp. 213–224, 2002.

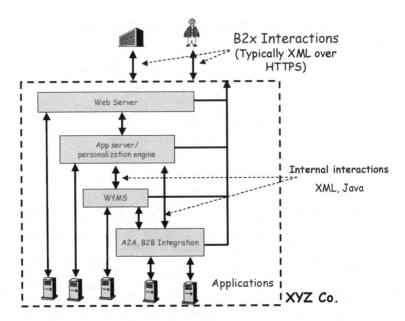

Fig. 1. A typical software system that support the execution of internal processes and external interaction

Until now, the focus of both e-business software vendors and as well as of customers in need of an e-business solution has been on the development and deployment of infrastructures that provide the functionalities required for performing internal and external interactions with adequate reliability and performance. As more and more companies succeed in this effort and conduct more and more business over the web, the problem quickly shifts from *enabling* business operations to *managing* them. In particular, customers are faced with the need of quickly identifying problems affecting their operations, of assessing the impact of such problems in terms of quality of their business operations, and of understanding the root cause of the problems. As the complexity of the system grows, it becomes harder and harder to perform these tasks manually. However, identifying and resolving problems only covers one aspect of e-business operation management. Indeed, in an ideal scenario, the entire e-business infrastructure should be self-managing, by automatically reacting to problems by executing corrective actions [7]. An additional aspect of management that is appearing more and more in the priority list of our customers further involves *predicting* the quality and the nature of their e-business operations and *optimizing* their executions to maximize business-level metrics. As an example, consider the nowadays "traditional" supply chain automation scenario. The concerns of business managers is that operations run smoothly, that there are no delays, and that customers demands are met in a timely manner and with minimal costs. When supply chain operations are cooperatively managed by many different systems, and when a company performs hundreds of transactions per day, it can be hard to merely figure out whether operations are running efficiently and up to the customers' expectations, let alone the problem of understating what is the source of the problem and how to solve it.

To address these needs, at Hewlett-Packard Labs we have developed an architecture and a set of applications that enable the analysis, monitoring, and optimization of e-business systems. The work involves the definition and implementation of measurement models and tools, as well as the development of Business Intelligence (BI) solution that covers the entire e-business suite, combining and aggregating raw operational data from each component, as shown in Fig. 2. Data mining techniques have been traditionally applied to Customer Relationship Management (CRM), in order to better define and target marketing strategies and to personalize service delivery. In our work, we explore how to apply such techniques to analyze internal operations and external interactions, in order to understand issues regarding internal business processes, the operational behaviors of partners and customers, to improve the quality and efficiency of the business systems, and consequently to gain competitive advantage. We refer to this research and applicative area as *Business Operation Intelligence* (BOI), since it applies BI techniques to the execution of business operations.

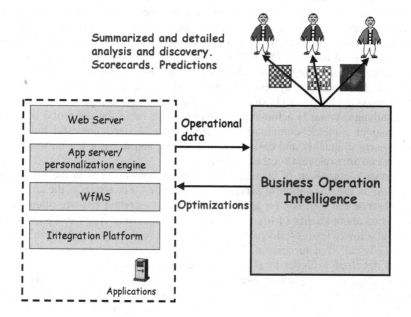

Fig. 2. Business Intelligence techniques can be applied to the entire software infrastructure

In this paper, we first present the goals, requirements, and concepts behind a BOI solution. Then, we provide an overview of the BOI model and architecture. Note that the purpose of this paper is not that of providing a detailed description of the platform. Rather, we will outline its main characteristics, and refer the reader to other papers and technical reports for the details of the different specific aspects of the platform.

2   Goals of an *E-business System Intelligence* Solution

This section presents the goals and requirements of a BOI solution, obtained after interviewing customers in different sectors of the industry. From a general perspective, the purpose of BOI lies in the ability to perform the analysis, prediction, and optimization of the operations of business systems.

The main goal of "intelligent" business system **analysis** is to assess and understand operation execution *quality*, identify problems and inefficiencies, understand the causes, and propose improvements. For example, the analysis may reveal that the fulfillment of certain customer orders (e.g., those involving microchips) are often delayed, and that the cause is that the purchasing department for microchips is understaffed with respect to other departments. The analysis may also highlight that requests involving certain employees, customers, or suppliers consume more resources and generate smaller profit margins.

The solution should support the analysis of both *internal* and *external* operational quality. Internal quality is as perceived by the e-business operators, such as e-business portals or e-service providers, in terms of operating costs. External quality is that perceived by the user of the e-business application or service, for instance in terms of time, cost, ease of use, etc. The BOI approach should be agnostic with respect to the notion of quality, meaning that we should not make assumptions on what constitutes a "good" or "bad" business system execution. Indeed, the notion of quality will differ from business application to business application, and from company to company. The main challenges towards achieving this requirement lie in the definition of a metric model and of a metric computation engine that is fast and powerful but that also enables users to quickly and easily define, analyze, and monitor the business metrics that they consider relevant for their business.

A further requirement of business operation analysis consists in the identification of *patterns* in the invocation of services and processes. For instance, the analysis tool could observe that requests for apartment rentals in a certain city are often followed by inquiries about quality of life in that city (e.g., cost of living, weather, crime rate, etc) or, at a lower level of abstraction, it may observe that some java bean's methods are typically called in succession. The results of such analysis can be used to identify ways of developing higher-level services and applications that pre-package several operations, thereby simplifying user interaction. Pattern analysis can be also used to understand partners' and customers' behavior, and in particular to understand (or discover) *their* business process logic (flow). Similar techniques are applied in the automatic auctions field, but here we extend them to cover generic B2B interactions. This approach will become more and more applicable in the future, as human interventions are reduced and business logic becomes more and more automated, thereby following pre-specified, fixed, procedures. Understanding a partners' business logic is very helpful in understanding how to serve them better or more efficiently.

Business operation **prediction** aims at developing models that can be applied to predict partners' behavior, service execution quality, workload on human, software, and hardware resources, and more. For example, BOI can derive models that help predict the occurrence of exceptions, or that calculate the risk of failing to meet a Service Level Agreement (SLA).

In particular, predictive models can be tailored so that they can make predictions as early as possible in the execution of a business operation, and then refine those predictions as the execution proceeds. For instance, the models will give an indication of the probability of expiration of a process-level deadline at process instantiation time, and then continuously refine the prediction.

Business operation **optimization** has the goal of improving the design and execution of business processes, software and hardware configurations, and the use of (human or automated) resources. For instance, the BOI platform can suggest the increase of the thread pool size if the number of Java threads or objects available to deliver a certain service is detected as the bottleneck.

Optimizations can be static or dynamic. Static optimizations are related to changes in the definition of business processes, system and software configurations, and resource allocation. Dynamic optimizations instead involve on-the-fly changes applied to react to an exception or to allow a quality improvement in a particular situation. For instance, an interesting dynamic optimization application is that of *exception prevention* [4]. Once the occurrence of an exception in a service or process execution is predicted, BOI can dynamically modify the execution of the process instance at risk (e.g., take a different path in the workflow) in order to avoid the exception. Dynamic optimization is not limited to prevention of undesired situations, but can be used as a way to improve normal operations. For example, dynamic optimization algorithms could be executed to prioritize the work in order to increase the throughput [5]. Another example is the automated selection of suppliers to process a given purchase order, based on customers' requirements and on the predictable quality of service that suppliers can deliver.

3   Divide and Conquer vs. Joint Analysis

Achieving even a subset of these goals would certainly provide huge benefits to many companies. The other side of the medal is that the design and development of a BOI solution is a quite complex undertaking. However, the problem can be addressed with a *divide and conquer* approach, by first separately addressing each class of business system components (e.g., WfMSs or application servers) and by then developing a complete BI solution that integrates all the individual components. For instance, a *Business Process Intelligence* (BPI) solution could focus on analysis, prediction, and optimization of business processes [4]. Similarly, an Application Server Intelligence (ASI) solution could focus on supporting and automating decision making for ASs. These problems can be further reduced into simpler, more confined and targeted problems (e.g., predicting exceptions in a business process, or determining the optimal web service configuration), as shown in Fig. 3.

Besides being a viable approach towards achieving the overall goal of developing a BOI platform, providing BI solutions for each component of a business system in itself can provide huge benefits and offer a wide range of functionalities for managing that component, including those described in the examples above. Indeed, we have performed detailed investigations in the areas of Business Process Intelligence and Web Service Intelligence, developing platforms that are being used to manage business processes and web services [4,11].

Despite the many benefits, component-specific solutions are limited to the information and the perspective provided by the system component. Instead, the *joint* analysis of several middleware components can provide higher-level, more

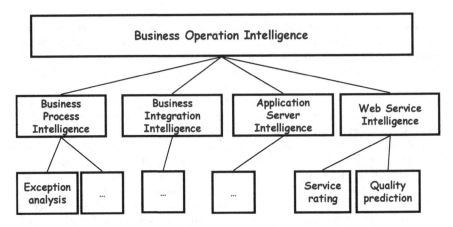

Fig. 3. BOI includes many Business Intelligence sub-problems

informative results and allows for more effective, end-to-end optimizations. The benefits of applying BI techniques to the entire e-business software infrastructure go beyond what is achievable by separately analyzing the individual systems. In fact, the execution of many business functions involves the use of many different components. Therefore, in order to analyze and optimize such functions, we must be able to access data from all such components. As an example, consider the processing of a RosettaNet [8] Request for Quote (RFQ) message. A typical situation, is the following: the RosettaNet XML message is first received by the web server (or by a SOAP server) and passed (through a servlet) to a Java bean, running on top of an application server. The bean checks the type of message received, extracts data items of interest from the XML message, and invokes a workflow that processes the request. During its execution, the workflow accesses several internal and external applications (such as the suppliers' product database) through the integration middleware. Eventually, the workflow terminates by generating quote information. Another Java application packages the information into a RosettaNet compliant XML document and returns the document to the requestor.

To assess the quality of the overall RFQ processing, a BI solution would need to analyze the execution of all the system components involved, and be able to follow the processing steps from component to component, so that it is possible to spot problems (e.g., bottlenecks and points of failures) and suggest solutions for improving RFQs processing quality.

4 BOI Architecture

This section presents the overall approach and architecture of the BOI tool suite. In our architecture, we assume that either the individual components of the BOI platform have facilities for logging data to a file or a relational database, or that instrumentation has been put in place for this purpose, as described in [9].

Once logged, data are periodically collected by an ETL application and inserted into a staging data warehouse (a temporary warehouse where data are loaded and processed before being transferred to the actual warehouse). The ETL performs "traditional" activities, analogous to what other ETL tools do, such as data cleaning and data transformation to the format required by the data warehouse. Data in the staging warehouse is then processed by the correlation engine, that inserts correlation information, to denote records that logically belong to the same business transaction. For example, consider again the RosettaNet-based interaction described earlier in the paper. As exemplified above, such interaction will span across several systems and cause log entries to be generated by several different components in the BOI stack. Therefore, to enable a more effective analysis, we need to be able to "label" records with additional information denoting that they belong to the same business transaction.

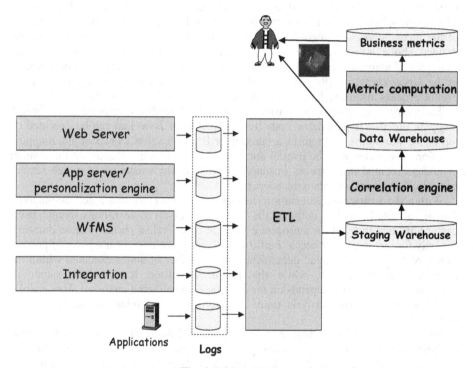

Fig. 4. BOI architecture

We will describe the technique that we adopt for performing correlation later in the paper, when we present the notion of business-level metrics. Indeed, we will see that the same mechanism for providing users with abstracted, business level information can be used for defining and performing the correlation. Once correlation information has been computed, then the data is loaded into the warehouse.

The warehouse is designed to support high-performance OLAP and multidimensional analysis of execution data coming from heterogeneous sources. Hence, the warehouse is a very useful component in itself, providing a wide range of reporting functionalities that are still missing in commercial e-business platforms, and even in more traditional middleware platforms. However, BOI aims at enabling a higher-level, business view of the collected information. While the warehouse can provide information about number of execution or average duration of each execution, users are likely to need information at higher abstraction levels. For example, they may be interested in analyzing the cost or the quality of a business transaction, where *cost* or *quality* are user-defined criteria, whose computation depends on the specific business domain and on the nature of the business transactions.

To enable and simplify the business-level analysis of low-level execution data collected by system logs, BOI provides users with a metric and metric computation framework. This framework allows users to define *business metrics*, i.e., measurable properties that can be associated to data elements stored in the warehouse. The *cost* for a business transaction is an example of a business metric. Metrics are characterized by a *definition* and an *implementation* part. The metric definition includes the metric *name* and a *data type*, that can be *Numeric*, *Boolean*, or *Enumeration* (taxonomy*)*. For enumerations, the definition also includes a description of the metric classes (categories) that are part of the taxonomy. The *quality* metric defined above is an example of a taxonomical metric, while *cost* or *profit* are examples of numeric metrics. Finally, the metric definition includes the specification of the *target entity*, i.e., the type of elements to which the metric is applied to (e.g., events, process instances, business transactions, web service operations).

The metric implementation consists of a set of references to *mapping functions*. A mapping function is parametric code (typically SQL or Java) that can be executed on top of the warehouse and returns a numeric or Boolean value. For example, mapping functions could compute the overall duration of a business transaction, or the number of nodes executed in a process instance, or whether the execution of a web service operation has been faster than the average.

Within the metric implementation, it is possible to specify that a certain mapping function should be used to compute the metric for a given *context*. For example, users can specify that the cost for a process execution is dependent on the process duration, but only for instances of process "Fulfill order", while the cost for instances of process "approve proposal" is instead dependent on the number of nodes executed within the process instance. Hence, while the metric definition remains the same, its implementation actually depends on the specific element being analyzed. This enables users to get, at metric analysis time, a uniform view of otherwise heterogeneous properties.

Once metrics and mappings have been defined, the *metric computation* engine executes the mapping functions and determines the metric data, also stored in a relational database. Such data can then be analyzed through either commercial reporting tools or through a built-in console provided within by the BOI solution. A detailed discussion of the metric framework is outside the scope of this paper. We refer the reader to [11] for details.

We can now look back at the problem of data correlation, described earlier. The metric framework basically tells the BOI system how the different data elements (e.g., process instances) should be stamped with a qualitative or quantitative measure. This suggests that the very same metric framework used for mapping low level data into business metrics can also be used for "labeling" execution data with correlation identifiers, that define whether two or more data records logically belong to the same business transaction. It is up to the users to define what correlation means, and what are the characteristics of the records that imply a correlation. They can do so by defining special "correlation" metrics, and by using mappings to define how the correlation should be determined. For example, for a RosettaNet transaction the correlation can be determined by looking at User IDs, product IDs, or other information embedded in the data records. BOI will take care of executing the mappings and therefore of generating the correlation identifiers.

5 Adding Intelligence

The BOI metric framework, along with the data warehouse, can provide analysts with information about the business metric they consider relevant for their business domain. While this is a very important aspect of the solution, it also naturally leads users to desire more advanced functionalities. In particular, besides metric analysis, business users typically demands for more "intelligent" information processing that can provide:
- Identifications of the causes of high and low quality executions.
- Prediction of process and service execution quality, and in general prediction of user-defined business metrics specified through the metric framework.
- Identification of patterns in the invocation of business transactions, to restructure and compose service interfaces into value-added services and simplify user interaction.

To provide these and other form of intelligent data analysis, BOI is equipped with a business intelligence engine that operates on top of both the warehouse and the metric data, and identifies explanations for the value of business metrics, prediction of the future value of such metrics, as well as service invocation patterns (see Fig. 5). The engine includes simple algorithms that perform basic analytics. In addition, it can also prepare data so that it can be consumed by a commercial data mining tool, such as Oracle Darwin or SAS.

The approach towards generating analysis and prediction models out of metric data consists in building classifiers, often in the form of a decision tree. Classification applications take as input a labeled training data set, in which each row (tuple) describes an object (e.g., a *customer* in a customer management application) and the *class* to which this object belongs (e.g., "profitable", "neutral", or "unprofitable" customer). The classifier then produces a set of *classification rules*, i.e., mappings from a condition on the objects' attributes to a class, with the meaning that objects whose attributes satisfy the condition belong to the specified class. Therefore, classification rules identify the characteristics of the objects in each class, in terms of values of the objects' attributes.

The metric analysis problem can be mapped to a classification problem, where measured elements (process instances, operations, events, etc) are the *objects,* and the different metric values (e.g., *good* or *bad*) are the classes. We are interested in finding classification rules that identify which are the characteristics of the elements belonging to each of these classes. Once these characteristics have been identified, the user can have a much better understanding of the causes of the metric values, and can then try to address such causes.

A similar approach can be taken to perform predictions. To understand how classification can be used for predictions, consider the problem of trying to predict the *quality* of a web service conversation (see [3,8] for a discussion on web services conversations). A conversation between a client and a service provider can go through several stages. The BOI engine can process past execution data and build a separate classifier for each conversation stage, correlating service execution data available at that stage with the quality metric.

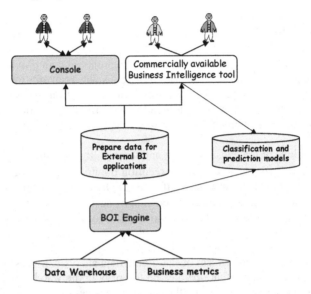

Fig. 5. The BOI Engine prepares data for BI applications and generate classification and prediction models

At run time, BOI can examine live execution data, determine in which stage the conversation whose quality is to be predicted is, and apply the classifier to determine the (predicted) quality, along with a confidence level. We successfully applied this technique in several domains, and specifically in the context of workflow management [4].

6 Management

The above sections have presented methods and techniques for gathering information about the quality of e-business operations. We now briefly discuss how BOI can interact with the system in order to take corrective actions and, in general, to manage system operations in reaction to the computed values of business metrics. Note that, while this is an important aspect of a BOI solution, it is highly system-specific, since the kinds of reactions that can be performed depend on the specific system that BOI manages. Still, some aspects of system management can be factorized into a generic solution. More specifically, system management in BOI is defined through simple *policies*, comprising a *condition* and an *action*. The condition is a Boolean expression over the value of metric data. The action can be one of the following (see Fig. 6):

- Send a message to a JMS compliant bus
- Send an event to a business process

- Invoke a Java application
- Trigger BOI optimization algorithms
- Send an email or SMS to a user

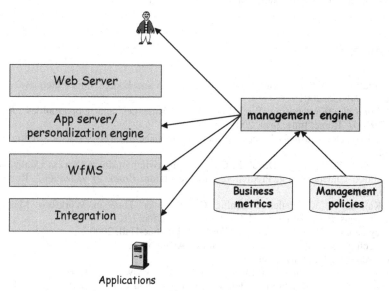

Applications

Fig. 6. Management component of the BOI solution

A sample policy, defining that once the completion of a process instance I is predicted to be late more than 3 hours, an event should be notified to the process instance. How the event is handled depends on the business logic implemented by the process. The management engine only takes care of notifying the process.

```
IF  predicted_completion_delay(I)> 03:00:00
THEN send_event(I,large_delay_predicted)
```

Conditions of policies are continuously monitored by BOI. As soon as the condition becomes true, the action is performed by invoking the proper system. The configuration of which action correspond to which system occurs at deployment time.

7 Concluding Remarks

This paper has presented goals, concepts, and architecture of a *business operation intelligence* solution. In particular, we have described which are the basic components that such a solution should include, and we have described how they are combined into an overall architecture that can achieve the desired goals.

We have implemented most of what has been described in this paper. The aspects that are still missing, and that populate our future research agenda, include the generalization of the analysis and prediction algorithms so that they can be applied to any context and to any business metric, without requiring any data mining knowledge by the (business) user who defines the metrics. To achieve this goal, we are currently working towards generalizing the initial, case-specific and system-specific solution that we have developed, to progressively factorize all the "generic" portions, so that they can be applied to any metric and to any context.

References

1. D. Linthicum. B2B Application Integration: e-Business-Enable Your Enterprise. Addison-Wesley Pub Co. 2001
2. A. Bonifati. Warehousing Workflow Data: Challenges and Opportunities. *Procs. of VLDB2001*. Rome, Italy. Sept. 2001.
3. F. Curbera, et al. Business Process Execution Language for Web Services, Version 1.0. July 2002.
4. D. Grigori, F. Casati, U. Dayal, M.C. Shan. Improving Business Process Quality through Exception Understanding, Prediction, and Prevention. *Procs. of VLDB2001*. Rome, Italy. Sept. 2001.
5. E. Kafeza, K. Karlapalem: Gaining Control over Time in Workflow Management Applications. Procs. of DEXA 2000. Sept 200. London, UK.
6. F. Leymann, D. Roller: *Production Workflow*. Prentice-Hall, 2000.
7. Research program in Autonomic Computing. Available at www.research.ibm.com/autonomic
8. The RosettaNet consortium. Information available at www.rosettanet.org
9. Akhil Sahai, Vijay Machiraju, Mehmet Sayal, Aad van Moorsel, Fabio Casati, Li Jie Jin. Automated SLA Monitoring for Web Services. *Procs. of the International Workshop on Distributed Systems: Operations & Management*. Montreal, Canada. Oct 2002.
10. Arindam Banerji et al. Web Services Conversation Language (WSCL) 1.0. W3C Note 14 March 2002.
11. F. Casati, U. Dayal, M. Shan. Semantic Management of Web Services. Submitted for publication and available upon request.

Peer-to-Peer File Sharing with Integrated Attribute Descriptions in XML and an Embedded Database Engine

Shuichi Takizawa[1] and Qun Jin[2]

[1] Department of Computer Systems,
Graduate School of Computer Science and Engineering,
The University of Aizu,
Aizu-Wakamatsu City, 965-8580 Japan
m5061221@u-aizu.ac.jp
[2] Information Systems Laboratory,
School of Computer Science and Engineering,
The University of Aizu,
Aizu-Wakamatsu City, 965-8580 Japan
jinqun@u-aizu.ac.jp

Abstract. As a new distributed computing paradigm, peer-to-peer (P2P) networks and systems have attracted more and more attentions in recent years. This study aims at proposing and constructing a new information resource sharing system based on the P2P paradigm. In this paper, we focus on solving and improving the hit rate and search speed problems that exist in Gnutella, one of the most popular P2P file sharing systems. We discuss how to introduce XML to describe the attributes and properties of each shared file and integrate an embedded database engine to increase the search speed. Preliminary experiment results have demonstrated that the approach proposed in this study is efficient and useful.

1   Introduction

In recent years, peer-to-peer (P2P) [3,15,6,12,13,2,10,7,8] networks and application systems have attracted more and more attentions, due to the popularity of file sharing systems such as Napster and Gnutella [12,13,19]. As a new distributed computing paradigm, peer-to-peer is highly expected to be a proper utilization model for the next generation Internet.

P2P is a system that many computers connect each other and share information resources, such as a file or computation capability. It provides a way for people to connect each other for a common purpose, and allows people to search for the information they want, and exchange information directly with many unspecified individuals directly and share a variety of resources easily across the networks.

Among many P2P application systems, Gnutella is the most famous and popular one that provides a very large-scale network for file sharing over the Internet [12,13]. However, its search efficiency is rather poor. In the level of searching

S. Bhalla (Ed.): DNIS 2002, LNCS 2544, pp. 225–238, 2002.

algorithms, too many queries are produced and forwarded, which resulting in flooding the P2P network with queries and heavy traffic on the network. Some techniques have been proposed to improve search efficiency in [20,5]. On the other hand, in the interface level, users can search a file only by the file name and its extension, so that it is not so easy for users to locate and search a file. As a result, it takes a significant amount of time and effort to find out an exact file that the user is looking for.

This study focuses on solving the above problems and drawbacks in the interface level, and aims at constructing a new information resource sharing system by applying P2P and XML technologies. In this paper, we introduce an integrated attribute description file for each file that has been shared through the P2P mechanism. The attribute description file is produced in XML (Extensible Markup Language) [11,14] data format, which is well-known as a universal, flexible and portable data format, and good at representing data for a structured document interchange on the Internet. When a peer accepts a search request, it searches and checks the XML contents of the attribute description file. In this way, the hit rate of a search can be increased.

On the other hand, it is considered that the search speed is decreased as the number of shared files is increased. To solve this problem, we propose to integrate a database engine in the P2P file sharing system. We design and develop a prototype systems based on a Gnutella clone software system called Furi that is implemented in Java.

The rest of this paper is organized as follows. Section 2 gives a brief introduction on peer-to-peer computing and Gnutella protocol, network, and client software. Section 3 overviews the architecture of the improved file sharing system that introduces XML to describe each shared file and is integrated with an embedded database engine as well to increase the search speed. Section 4 discusses the performance of the system based on the preliminary experiment results. Finally, Section 5 addresses concluding remarks and future works.

2   Peer-to-Peer Computer Networking Paradigm and Features

2.1   Models for Computer Networking

Up to now, the client/server model, as shown in Figure 1(a), is the mainstream of the network application systems. In a client/server system, any processing executed between clients is always performed through the server, resulting in a concentrated load on the server.

P2P model could solve this problem. P2P shown in Figure 1(b) is a system that many computers connect each other without a central server and share resources, such as a file or computation capability. A computer in P2P networks is called a *peer* or *servent* (<u>ser</u>ver and cli<u>ent</u>) [10], since it works as both a server and a client. By using P2P, users can exchange information directly with many unspecified individuals directly and share a variety of resources easily across the networks.

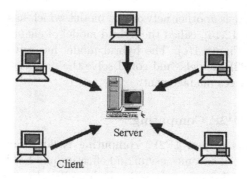

(a) The Client/Server Model

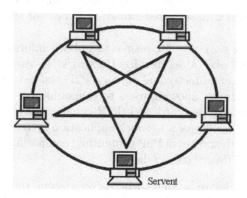

(b) The Peer-to-Peer Model

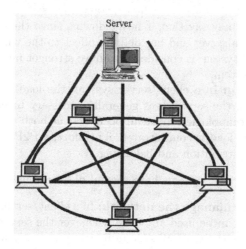

(c) The Hybrid Model of Client/Server and Peer-to-Peer

Fig. 1. Networking models.

In addition, there is another networking model, which has been proposed and applied in Napster [12,13], called the hybrid model of client/server and peer-to-peer, as shown in Figure 1(c). The hybrid model has advantages of both the client/server and P2P models, and could solve the problem of difficulty in P2P networks and resources management.

2.2 Features of P2P Computing

The concept of peer-to-peer (P2P) computing is not brand-new [12,13,2,10]. However, P2P network becomes useful and effective and has been widely applied in many network application systems, as the broadband networks rapidly spread and the performance of personal computers greatly improves in the recent years. As is well known, P2P computer networking is popularized by Napster and Gnutella [12,13], which have raised broad awareness of the potential peer-to-peer applications.

P2P provides an easy way for people to publish information and share resources and services over a decentralized network, by exchanging information between two computers directly and equally. P2P makes it easy to create some sort of online community, allowing users to communicate, interact, or share directly with other users. Designed well, P2P could greatly improve availability, productivity and reliability of a network application system.

There are some advantages of P2P computing, comparing with the traditional client/server model, described as follow:

- **Strong fault tolerance:** In a client/server system, the whole system works dependent on the server. If the server downs, the whole system stops. In addition, any troubles with the peripheral devices and networks of the server also lead to system down. On the contrary, in a system based on the pure P2P model, we may say that it never downs, since there is not a machine that works like a server and has definite affect to the whole system. In this context, a P2P system is considered to have stronger fault tolerance than a client/server system.
- **Load balancing:** In a client/server system, the load of any processing is concentrated on the server. It is generally necessary to have load balanced using various technologies. Since all peers acts as both server and client in a P2P system, no load is concentrated. Therefore, a P2P system has also the merit of load distribution and balancing.

On the other hand, P2P systems have several disadvantages:

- **High traffic to manage the network:** In a client/server system, it usually works well and can be used any time whenever the server is working. However, since a servent in a P2P system may operate only when it is required, and stop for some reasons of its owner, the working status of the system and network always varies according to the operating status of servents. Consequentially, it is necessary to check and monitor all servents that are under operation, which results in extra traffic to manage the P2P network.

 – **Difficulty in managing the network and contents:** In a system based on pure P2P model, there is not any central administrator who has the responsibility to keep the network stable, and there is no mechanism that can control and recover the system when a communication obstacle or network bottleneck occurs. As a matter of fact, the P2P system will be out of control in these cases, since the whole system is generally dependent on each servent's autonomy. A hybrid P2P system based on the hybrid model of client/server and P2P could partly solve this problem in managing the network related to a server as in a client/server system. The networks between servents are still not manageable. The same problem exists also for the contents management.

2.3   Gnutella: Protocol, Network, and Client Software

Before discussing the system proposed and developed in this study, we give a brief introduction of Gnutella and its related technology. Originally, Gnutella was the name of a prototype client developed and released in early 2000. It is now a generic term with meanings of Gnutella protocol and the deployed Internet network called Gnutella Net [10].

Gnutella protocol is relatively simple, and is firmly anchored in the established HTTP protocol for the Internet [4,9,10]. It defines five descriptors: Ping, Pong, Query, QueryHit, and Push [4], to implement the P2P network functionality. Each descriptor message is in turn defined by a message header that includes five fields: Descriptor ID, Payload Descriptor, TTL (Time to Live), Hops (the number of times the descriptor has been forwarded), and Payload Length [4].

Gnutella Net is a file sharing and exchange network that supports arbitrary file types. It builds a distributed network without a central server based on the P2P networking model. It is a kind of system for a peer to mutually share and exchange a file in the local storage to other peers. The basic function of the Gnutella Net is getting across to the whole Gnutella Net by forwarding the message sent from a peer to other peers, and enabling the peer who has sent the request to receive the result. For example, a peer generates a message of Search Query, and transmits it to the peer group to which the peer connects directly. A peer receiving the message forwards it in turn to other peer groups, and so on. The message reaches to the whole Gnutella Net as shown in Figure 2(a). When a file specified in the message is discovered in one or more peers, the "Found" message will be sent and forwarded back to the peer who requested, following the course of the previous message forwarding conversely, as shown in Figure 2(b).

If a file is found, a peer can get the file by transmitting it from the remote to the local. For data transmission in Gnutella, a subset of HTTP protocol is used. That is, each Gnutella client is equipped with the functionality as an HTTP server, and data transmission is performed from a peer to another by using this function.

There are a large variety of Gnutella clients (we call them Gnutella clones) that support the basic Gnutella protocol, but may have some extensions. Generally, these clients can communicate with each other. In this study, we implement a prototype based on Furi, a clone of Gnutella. Furi has been selected, since it

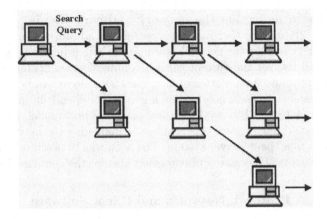

(a) Searching and forwarding a search query

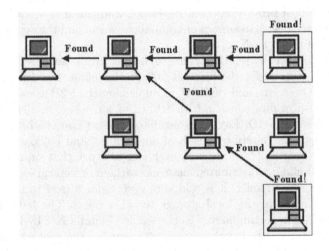

(b) Search results are found

Fig. 2. Searching mechanism of Gnutella.

has been implemented in Java language, and works on any platforms that support Java, such as MS-Windows, Macintosh, Linux, and Solaris. Furi has some functions such as the IRC chat, automatic connection, specifying of files to be downloaded and uploaded, and unrestricted number of simultaneous search.

3   Design of the Enhanced Peer-to-Peer File Sharing System

3.1   System Architecture

As discussed in the previous section, Gnutella and its clones are the file sharing system based on the pure P2P model. They are popular and useful for file sharing and exchanging. But their search function is very limited. Users can search a file only by the file name and its extension [12,13,19]. Therefore, it is not easy for users to locate and search a file. In order to solve this problem, we propose and develop a new mechanism for enhanced P2P file sharing with advanced searching functions.

We firstly introduce an additional attribute description file for each file that has been shared in the P2P networks. The attribute description file is produced in XML [11,14] data format. Figure 3 shows the architecture of this enhanced P2P file sharing system, which has been based on Furi, a Gnutella client implemented in Java. When a peer accepts a search request, it searches and checks the XML contents of the attribute description file. In this way, the hit rate of a search can be increased.

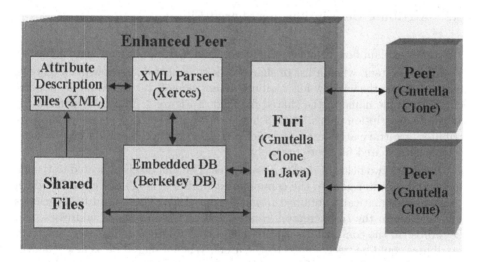

Fig. 3. System architecture of the enhanced P2P file sharing system.

On the other hand, it could be expected that the search speed is decreased as the number of shared files is increased. To solve this problem, we integrate an embedded database engine in the P2P file sharing system.

232   S. Takizawa and Q. Jin

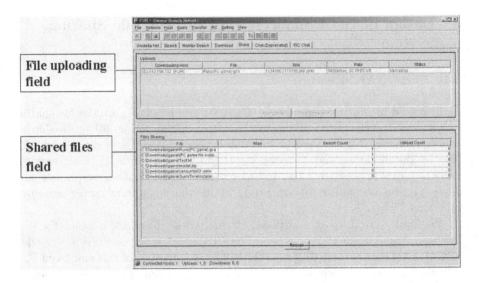

File uploading field

Shared files field

Fig. 4. A snapshot for the enhanced P2P file sharing client.

3.2   Attribute Descriptions for Shared Files

We firstly explain how to create the attribute description file for shared files.

In this system, when a list of shared files is displayed, as shown in Figure 4, users can open the window for attribute description of any shared file by double-clicking the file name in the shared file field of Figure 4. Then, the window for attribute description opens. A snapshot is shown in Figure 5, where common attributes, arbitrary attributes, and their detailed descriptions could be produced to specify a shared file more precisely.

There are two fields of common attributes. The first one is allocated to the file name and its extension (in the common description field (1) of Figure 5), which could be automatically obtained from the shared file. The second field includes information on the title, creator, created date, URL and e-mail addresses, and keywords (in the common description field (2) of Figure 5). Moreover, arbitrary attributes could be freely added by the users. When a shared file is newly added, other fields except the field of the file name and its extension are blank. They should be described by its owner in a later convenient time.

The attribute description file for each shared file is then created and saved in XML, which is then converted and transferred to the database (we have used the Berkeley DB [16,17] for the prototype) through an XML parser (here Xerces [1] has been used). When an attribute description file is newly created or modified, the corresponding information in the database is updated as well.

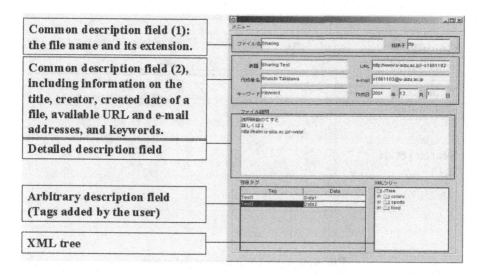

| Common description field (1): the file name and its extension. |
| Common description field (2), including information on the title, creator, created date of a file, available URL and e-mail addresses, and keywords. |
| Detailed description field |
| Arbitrary description field (Tags added by the user) |
| XML tree |

Fig. 5. A snapshot for the attribute description of a shared file.

3.3   Enhanced Search Function

In addition to the usual search by the file name and its extension in Gnutella and its clones, search function in our system has been enhanced with the attribute description file and embedded database engine.

When a search request is given, it searches from the database first. All of these attributes described in the previous section could be used when users conduct an enhanced search for a shared file. Figure 6 shows a snapshot of the enhanced search window, which have three fields: Gnutella search, enhanced search, and display of search result.

Moreover, since the enhanced search also follows the usual Gnutella protocol [4,9], the enhanced peer can connect to any clients of Gnutella clones.

4   Experimental Results for Searching Performance Evaluation

In this study, in order to conduct an efficient and high speed search, as the database engine, Berkeley DB has been integrated into the P2P file sharing and searching system. To evaluate the searching performance, we compare the searching time of the system without a database engine with that the database engine is integrated. The following experiment environment was used.

- OS : MS-Windows 2000
- CPU : Pentium III - 1GHz
- Memory: SDRAM 384 MB
- HD : 20 GB

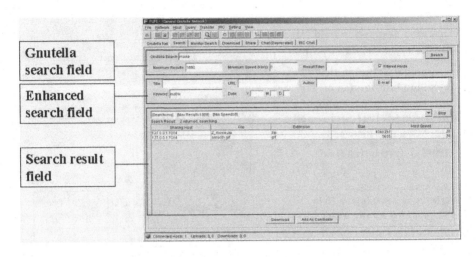

Fig. 6. A snapshot for enhanced search.

We measured the search time for ten times, when the number of shared files is 10, 100, and 1,000 respectively, and calculated the average search time each. In despite of the database engine integrated or not, the caching is performed for the first time search. Therefore, the search time becomes shorter in the second time search and henceforth. We show the result of first time search and that of second time search and henceforth separately.

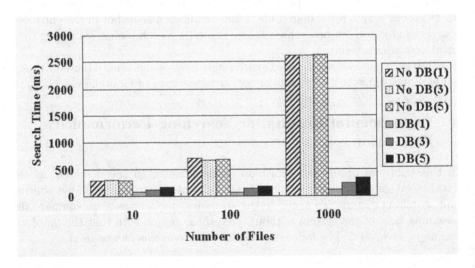

Fig. 7. Comparison of search time without a DB and with a DB for the first time search.

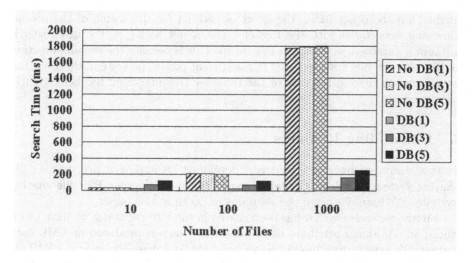

Fig. 8. Comparison of search time without a DB and with a DB for the second time search and henceforth.

The results are shown in Figures 7 and 8. The numbers 1, 3, and 5 within the parentheses in the figures represent the number of keywords to search. From the graphs shown in Figures 7 and 8, we can see that the search time of the usual search without the Berkeley DB increases greatly in proportion to the number of shared files, while the search time increases slightly when the system is integrated with a database engine. On the other hand, the search time also increases in proportion to the number of the search keywords in the case that the DB engine is integrated. On the contrary, the search time almost does not change as the number of the search keywords increases in the system without the Berkeley DB.

These two graphs show the same trends for both the first time search and the second time search and henceforth, though the values are smaller in the second time search and henceforth. We thought the reasons are that in the case of the usual search without the database engine, processing time to perform all the search of the attribute description files that are represented in XML has to be taken. On the other hand, when searching with a database engine, since the database has all the information and elements for each attribute description file, the search is conducted from the database according to the number of keywords in the search query. Therefore, it is thought that search time is shorter, but increases in proportion to the number of the search keywords.

Next, we compare the search time of the first time search with that of the second time search and henceforth. The results are shown in Figures 9 and 10, where "(No) DB(*)-2" means the search of second time and henceforth (here, * = 1, 3, 5, representing the number of search keywords). From Figure 9, we could see that the caching takes effect for the usual search without a database engine. On the other hand, the effect of caching for the search of the second time and henceforth with the Berkeley DB is not as big as the usual search without a database, as shown in Fugure 10. This is because the caching function of Berkeley DB has not been used in the current prototype system. However, the overall search time in the case of the Berkeley DB integrated has been greatly shortened.

5   Concluding Remarks

In this study, we have proposed and developed an improved peer-to-peer file sharing system based on Gnutella, one of the most popular P2P file sharing systems. We have discussed the solutions in detail in this paper.

Firstly, for each file that has been shared in the P2P networks, we have introduced an additional attribute description file, which is produced in XML data format. We have further integrated an embedded database engine in the P2P file sharing system. Our system could solve the hit rate and search speed problems that exist in Gnutella and improve the search efficiency as well. Preliminary experiment results have demonstrated that the approach proposed in this study is efficient and useful. By using this system, it is easier for users to share and exchange information resources across the networks effectively and efficiently.

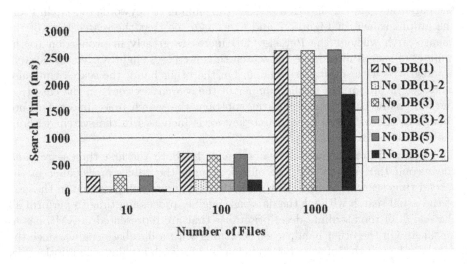

Fig. 9. Comparison of the search time of the first time and the second time and henceforth for the system without a DB.

Our prototype system has been constructed in Java Programming Language (JDK 1.3.1) [18], based on Furi, a Gnutella clone, under the Integrated Development Environment (IDE): Forte for Java 2.0 Internet Edition, in the MS-

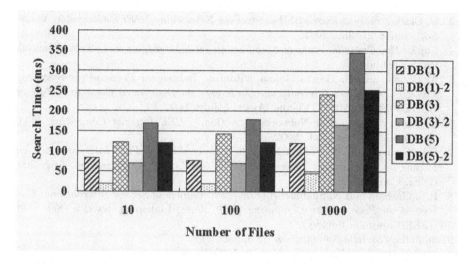

Fig. 10. Comparison of the search time of the first time and the second time and henceforth for the system with a DB.

Windows 2000 Operating System. Xerces 1.4.4 [1] has been used as the XML Parser, and Berkeley DB 4.0.14 [17] has been integrated as the database engine.

The system is still under the way to be developed and improved. There are several problems left unsolved, such as the preview of an attribute description file before downloading, utilization and optimization of the caching function of the embedded Berkeley DB, and so on. In addition, more experiments should be conducted on how many percent the hit rate is increased with the improved system.

Other improvements including the security and the P2P network management, forming support of online community for file sharing and exchanging shall be done as well in our future works.

Acknowledgment. This work has been partly supported by 2000-2002 Japanese Ministry of Education Grant-in-Aid for Scientific Research Contract No. 12558012, 2001 University of Aizu Research Grants Nos. R-9-2, P-9 and G-28, and 2002 University of Aizu Research Grants Nos. R-9-1 and G-25. The authors wish to express their gratitude.

References

1. Apache Software Foundation, *Xerces API Document*, http://xml.apache.org/xerces-j/api.html.
2. D. Barkai, *Peer-to-Peer Computing: Technologies for Sharing and Collaborating on the Net*, Intel Press, 2001.

3. D. Clark, "Face-to-Face with Peer-to-Peer Networking," *IEEE Computer*, Vol.34, No.1, pp.18–21, Jan. 2001.
4. Clip2, *The Gnutella Protocol Specification v0.4*, http://www.clip2.com/Gnutella Protocol04.pdf.
5. A. Crespo and H. Garcia-Molina, "Routing Indices for Peer-to-Peer Systems," *Proceedings of 22nd International Conference on Distributed Computing Systems (ICDCS'02)*, pp. 23–32, Vienna, Austria, July 2002.
6. L. Gong, "Peer-to-Peer Networks in Action," *IEEE Internet Computing*, Vol.6, No.1, pp.37–39, Jan./Feb. 2002.
7. R.L. Graham and N. Shahmehri (Eds.), *Proceedings of First International Conference on Peer-to-Peer Computing (P2P 2001)*, Linköping, Sweden, Aug. 2001 (IEEE Computer Society).
8. R.L. Graham and N. Shahmehri (Eds.), *Proceedings of Second International Conference on Peer-to-Peer Computing (P2P 2002)*, Linköping, Sweden, Sep. 2002 (IEEE Computer Society).
9. Jnutella, *Gnutella Specification* (in Japanese), http://www.jnutella.org/ jnudev/spec1000819.shtml.
10. B. Leuf, *Peer-to-Peer: Collaboration and Sharing over the Internet*, Addison-Wesley, 2002.
11. B. McLaughlin, *Java and XML*, O'Reilly, 2000.
12. M. Miller, *Discovering P2P*, SYBEX, 2001.
13. A. Oram (Ed.), *Peer-to-Peer: Harnessing the Benefits of Disruptive Technologies*, O'Reilly, 2001.
14. E.T. Ray, *Learning XML*, O'Reilly, 2001.
15. M.P. Singh, "Peering at Peer-to-Peer Computing," *IEEE Internet Computing*, Vol.5, No.1, pp.4–5, Jan./Feb. 2001.
16. Sleepycat Software Inc., *Berkeley DB*, New Riders, 2001.
17. Sleepycat Software Inc., *Online Berkeley DB Documentation*, http:// www.sleepycat.com/docs/index.html.
18. Sun Microsystems, Inc., *Java 2 SDK Documentation (Standard Edition)*, http://java.sun.com/docs/.
19. S. Yamasaki, "P2P Network Systems," *Journal of Japanese Society for Artificial Intelligence*, Vol.16, No.6, pp. 834–840, Nov. 2001 (in Japanese).
20. B. Yang and H. Garcia-Molina, "Improving Search in Peer-to-Peer Networks," *Proceedings of 22nd International Conference on Distributed Computing Systems (ICDCS'02*, pp. 5–14, Vieenna, Austria, July 2002.

In Search of Torrents: Automatic Detection of Logical Sets Flows in Network Traffic

Koide Kazuhide[1], Glenn Mansfield Keeni[2], and Shiratori Norio[1]

[1] Research Institute of Electrical Communication/Graduate School of Information
Sciences, Tohoku Univ.
Katahira 2-1-1, Aoba-ku, Sendai-shi, Miyagi, Japan
{koide,norio}@shiratori.riec.tohoku.ac.jp
[2] Cyber Solutions Inc.
ICR bld 3F, Minamiyoshinari 6-6-3, Aoba-ku, Sendai-shi, Miyagi, Japan
glenn@cysol.co.jp

Abstract. For network monitoring, management and operations it is
important to understand the nature of the network traffic flowing at a
point in the network. *Torrent*, the set of all flows on a network link and
s-torrents, logical sets of flows of network traffic are very useful in this
context. However detecting and measuring *torrent* and the constituent
s-torrents automatically is a challenge. In this work we describe a novel
method to detect and measure *torrents*. We show the usefulness of the
method in obtaining a more effective and deeper insight into the network's behavior and utilization.

1 Introduction

For network monitoring, management and operations it is important to understand the nature of the network traffic flowing at a point in the network. Aggregation is the key to understanding network traffic in this context. One example is
the statistical data obtained by monitoring network devices. It provides a good
insight into the performance of these devices but does not provide any further
clue about the network traffic. As another example, polling a network interface
may show that there is a surge in network traffic seen by that interface. But,
it does not provide any idea about which user, host, subnetwork, network or
organization is generating that traffic.

Passive network monitoring techniques[11] access individual packets seen at
the point of observation, examine the contents and provide results based on
analysis of the contents. This method is very powerful and it does not have any
influence on the observed link and traffic. Yet, a drawback of this method is
that it needs to be configured to supply "interesting information". Without any
configuration the user is left with un-aggregated data where the level of detail
is that of the individual packets. Several specialized frameworks have been built
using the passive monitoring techniques.

The definition, property and methodology of flows have been researched in
detail[7][9]. A flow is an arbitrary grouping of IP-datagrams satisfying various

temporal and spatial conditions. There will be various levels of granularity in the definition of a flow. The *flow* attributes may be a 5-tuple (protocol, source address, destination address, source port, destination port), a pair of network addresses or, a pair of sets of network addresses. Datagrams with a common sets of attributes, are aggregated into a flow.

The set of all flows on a network link is defined as a *torrent* in [10]. It is common practice to use 'rule-sets' to define address attributes of the flows of interest. The general traffic aggregation model of traffic flows vastly reduces captured traffic data without sacrificing much of the information content.

But the static nature of the rule-sets and the requirement that the rule-sets must be pre-defined is a major problem. A traffic observer has to have prior knowledge about the traffic and the important flows he wants to monitor. It is possible to have rules for major traffic flows. But that will mean that flows for which there are no matching rule-sets, are ignored even if they are important from the management or operational point of view.

Any method that does not use pre-defined rule-sets will be required to monitor all the flows by maintaining individual counters with all possible combination of values for the flow attributes. This will be very computation intensive, and the output will be unwieldy. Collection of trace files for later offline analysis is not a good option considering security and privacy issues as well as the storage requirements that would be required in today's massive bandwidth networks. Moreover, if all the flows were computed, that would be a veritable data swamp. In general one is not interested in all the individual flows seen at some point in a network.

A *torrent* is the set of flows seen at by a probe at the point of observation. While observing a local *torrent*, one may be interested in a subset of flows in the *torrent* that is a subset of another *torrent* observed at some other point in the network. This subset of flows represents the flows that have transited the AS and/or network at which the remote *torrent* is observed. We term such logical subsets of flows *torrent*, *s-torrents*.

Detecting and measuring *torrents* automatically is a challenge. In this paper we propose an alternate algorithm which adapts to the traffic. It uses the hierarchical nature of the IP address space to develop data structures which are convenient for hierarchical aggregation. The hierarchical aggregation is constrained to adapt to the non-uniformity of the real-world IP address space. The algorithm captures the traffic trends in real time. We propose an algorithm for more suitable real-time traffic monitoring and trend analysis. We describe, a novel method to detect and measure *torrents*. We show the usefulness of the method in obtaining a more effective and deeper insight into the behavior and utilization of network traffic.

2   Modeling of IP Address Space for Aggregation

IP address space has a hierarchical structure. Based on this structure, it seems possible to carry out traffic aggregation in a hierarchical and adaptive fashion

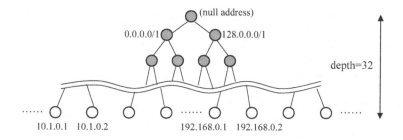

Fig. 1. Hierarchical Structure of IP address space

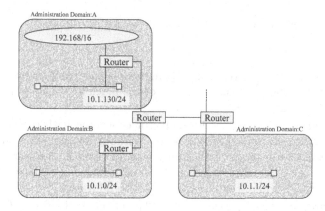

Fig. 2. Example: IP addresses are not assigned to organizations perfectly hierarchically

to detect the significant flows in a *torrent*. The hierarchical IP address space can be modeled as a binary tree where each node has a 32-bit label. All nodes at depth d $(0 < d < 32)$ have two offspring with labels formed by setting the d-th bit of the parents label to 0 and 1 respectively.

Data/statistics about monitored packets correspond to leaf nodes based on IP address, and information aggregation will be realized by the node aggregation from child to parent.

On the other hand, Fig. 2 is the example of network configuration in real world. There are cases that some organizations' network are not assigned IP address block completely hierarchically. We model those configurations in the binary tree.

The IP address space consists of several *CBlocks* where a *CBlock* represents a CIDR block of addresses. A *CBlock* is described by an IP-address and a prefix length. It characterizes a logical group of contiguous IP addresses. The grouping may be recursive, that is, a *CBlock* will be a member of a larger *CBlock*.

ABlock represents a group of *CBlocks*. It characterizes a logical group of *CBlocks* belonging to an administrative domain. The *CBlocks* in an *ABlock* are not necessarily contiguous.

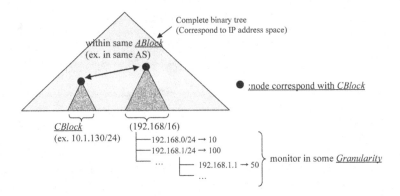

Fig. 3. Our Model: CBlock, ABlock and Granularity

In the binary tree representing IP address space, each node represents a *CBlock* such that the label is the address of the block and the depth of the node represents the prefix length.

The *Granularity* of the flow is the factor concerned with the volume of the traffic (or related statistics) at the node. Without any aggregation the traffic volume is available in terms of the leaf nodes, or (source, destination) host addresses. This level of detail is generally undesirable, particularly at a transit point in a network where there may be 2^{32} host addresses.

The desired level of aggregation will depend on the kind of information an observer seeks. For example, if the *CBlock* representing an organization's IP address space is 130.34.0.0/16 and, if one is interested in the traffic of the organization as a whole, this *CBlock* will be the focus of the aggregation. On the other hand if a person wants to know the activity of a host, the desired level of *Granularity* will be the same as that offered by a leaf node in the tree. Yet another user wanting to analyze the network activity of a department in the organization, would need to have a *Granularity* at the level of subnetwork of the department e.g. 130.34.202.0/24.

The aggregation logic is as follows

> *if*
>> - *the traffic corresponding to a node is not of the desired level of Granularity and,*
>> - *node belongs to the same ABlock as the parent*
>
> *then*
>> *aggregate the traffic into that of the parent node*

The above concepts are explained in Fig. 3. These concepts are used to control the IP-address based traffic aggregation algorithm.

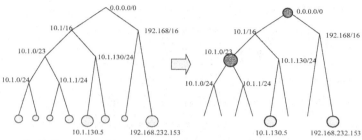

Traffic Summarizing Image(a size of circle means the traffic amount of each flow)

Fig. 4. Aguri's aggregation concept

3   Related Works

Flow-based traffic monitoring[9] scheme is one of the widely used examples of traffic aggregation. Several flow-based traffic-monitoring systems are presently in use[1][8]. These systems offer powerful features for monitoring traffic using metrics of flow.

While defining a flow, it is important to decide the flow's timeout. An adaptive timeout strategy is presented in [2].

The above approaches are very powerful but they require the existence of a skilled network manager who will know and be able to analyze network statistics and has a good command over the tools for defining meaningful rule-sets for the flows of interest. These systems are widely used when the metrics that need to be monitored are known a priori, such as, in the case of accounting or billing.

Research about grouping IP addresses into prefixes is being carried out in the area of Content Delivery Networks. In [3], the BGP routing table is used to obtain IP address groups(*clusters*). A client is assigned a *cluster*. A cluster is assigned a content server. In their method, clusters are same to *CBlocks* in our model but don't contain the concept of *Granularity* because their objective is to distribute accesses, not to measure traffic.

In Aguri[6] traffic aggregation based on the binary address tree is carried out. But in Aguri the aggregation is unconstrained. See Fig. 4. If the traffic volume in a *CBlock* is not of sufficient *Granularity* the traffic is aggregated into that of the parent *CBlock* irrespective of whether the parent and the child belong to the same *ABlock*. As a result, Aguri's output, contains some meaningless aggregates. For example, Aguri may generate (Fig. 5) an aggregated traffic for an address-prefix like 128.0.0.0/1. This does not map onto any logical communication entity.

In this paper, we propose an aggregation algorithm based on our model of the IP address space. We compare the results with those of Aguri to show the advantages of our IP address space model over the prevalent uniform IP address space model.

```
%!AGURI-1.0

[src address] 2931476 (100.00%)
0.0.0.0/0          14948 (0.51%/99.83%)
      10.1.0.0/16      39032 (1.33%/9.13%)
            10.1.0.1         37188 (1.27%)
            10.1.0.105       38556 (1.32%)
            10.1.11.4        152782 (5.21%)
            10.134.0.1       195585 (6.67%)
            61.114.30.15     99370 (3.39%)
            61.121.245.150   31006 (1.06%)
            66.163.171.128   49800 (1.70%)
      128.0.0.0/1      29778 (1.02%/77.38%)
            130.34.0.0/16    36108 (1.23%/61.21%)
                  130.34.202.0/27    40702 (1.39%/55.24%)
                  130.34.202.1     1257806 (42.91%)
                  130.34.202.14    320758 (10.94%)
                  130.34.202.47    138847 (4.74%)
                  202.211.224.50   111573 (3.81%)
      208.0.0.0/4      38713 (1.32%/11.35%)
            210.139.253.5    229350 (7.82%)
            211.13.168.106   64678 (2.21%)
```

Fig. 5. Example of Aguri's output

4   Our Proposed Algorithm

4.1   The Unconstrained Aggregation Algorithm

First we describe the algorithm in which the aggregation is unconstrained by the
ABlock membership attributes of the parent and child *CBlocks*. This algorithm is
straightforward to implement as it does not require any information other than
the address itself. *ABlock* information is not required. The algorithm is described
below.

The unconstrained address tree algorithm

type

    packet=(IPAddress);
    treenode=**record**
        addressprefix=integer;
        counter=integer;
        depth=integer;{depth in binary-tree}
        seqno=integer;{sequence number of node starting with 0 at the leftmost}
    end;{'tn.addressprefix' denotes the addressprefix of treenode tn}
    decided-time=real;
    threshold=real;

var

    d,i,D,I:integer;
    p:packet;
    n_i^d:treenode(n.depth=d, n.seqno=i)$(0 \leq d \leq 31, 0 \leq i \leq 2^d - 1)$;
    tree:$\{n_0^{31} \ldots n_{2^{32}-1}^{31}, n_0^{30} \ldots n_0^0\}$;
    tn:treenode;
    S:decided-time;
    t:threshold;

```
begin
        S:=(defined); t:=(defined);
        while p:=(caputured packet) do
        begin
                if n_i^d.addressprefix == p.IPAddress then
                increment n_i^d.counter;
                if S time exceeded from start then
                begin
                        foreach tn in tree do
                        begin
                                if tn.counter < t then
                                begin
                                        D=tn.depth-1; I=tn.seqno/2;
                                        add tn.counter to n_I^D.counter;{merge to its parent}
                                        remove tn from tree;
                                end
                        end
                        foreach tn in tree do
                        output tn.addressprefix and tn.counter;
                        reset tree and all treenode;
                end
        end
end
```

In the above algorithm, all leaf nodes(related to IP address) and intermediate nodes(related to network prefix) are treated equally. The threshold is same at every node and they will be aggregated in the same way. It assumes that neighboring IP Addresses or network prefixes sharing the same prefix belong to the same *CBlock* and are aggregatable. That assumption is likely to be true when the prefix length is sufficiently long, for example longer than 24bit. But in cases where the prefix length is short, it is not always correct because a big cluster(with a short network prefix) always contains some *CBlocks* which belong to different administrative control and cannot be logically aggregated. When the nodes whose prefixes are equal to network prefixes of subnetworks that exist in real world as independent entities, care must be taken in aggregating these nodes. If there is little relation between these subnetworks, there is no reason to aggregate them.

4.2   The Constrained Aggregation Algorithm

The unconstrained algorithm carries on the aggregation beyond the *CBlocks*, freely, as and when the occasion arises. In the constrained part the aggregation is constrained. Aggregation takes place if the parent and child belong to the same *CBlock*. The pertinent parts of the Algorithm are shown below.

The constrained address tree algorithm

```
type
        treenode=record
                addressprefix=integer;
                counter=integer;
                depth=integer;depth in binary-tree
                seqno=integer;
                cblock=boolean;
                        {If this node's addressprefix is equal to CBlock, cblock:=true}
        end;
var
        CACHE={};
begin
        S:=(defined); t:=(defined);
        while p:=(caputured packet) do
        begin
                if n_i^d.addressprefix == p.IPAddress then
                increment n_i^d.counter;
                if S time exceeded from start then
                begin
                        foreach tn in tree do
                        begin
                                if tn.counter < t then
                                begin
                                        if tn.cblock == true then
                                        copy tn to CACHE;
                                        else
                                        D=tn.depth-1; I=tn.seqno/2;
                                        add tn.counter to n_I^D.counter;
                                        end
                                        remove tn from tree;
                                end
                        end
                        foreach tn in (tree and CACHE) do
                        output tn.addressprefix and tn.counter;
                        reset tree and all treenode;
                end
        end
end
```

In this algorithm, a *CBlock's ABlock* membership information is used to constrain the aggregation process.

According to the above refinement, as shown in Fig. 6, if a node's address prefix is smaller than that of its parent's and the node's address itself is not a *CBlock*, it will be aggregated. If the node's address is a *CBlock*, its traffic will not be aggregated any further. In other words, the aggregation ceases at *CBlock*. If constrained aggregation is employed there will no longer be meaningless aggregates like 128.0.0.0/1.

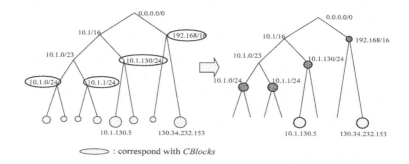

: correspond with *CBlocks*

Fig. 6. Our constrained aggregation algorithm image

```
route:        130.34.0.0/16
descr:        Tohoku University
              Katahira, Aoba-ku
              Sendai-shi, Miyagi 980, JAPAN
origin:       AS2503
member-of:    RS-COMM_NSFNET
remarks:      *#*
mnt-by:       MAINT-AS2503
changed:      jm@sinet.ad.jp 19960329
source:       SINET
```

Fig. 7. Example: IRR database

4.3   Implementation

One challenge in implementing the unconstrained algorithm is, to determine the *CBlocks*. It is important to realize this without requiring the skills of a well informed network administrator. One solution is to use an external knowledge database. It is quite possible to find out information about a (sub)network's, organization, and their relation from IP Addresses. For instance, using DNS, we can collect information about the hierarchical structure of organizations to which the IP Addresses belong. This information will be used to define some kind of relation. For example country or organization for IP Addresses and subnet prefixes.

In this work, we used the network prefix of IP Addresses to constrain the act of address aggregation algorithm. To get the information on network prefixes, we used the IRR(Internet Routing Registry)[4][12] database. Originally, IRR was established for advertising AS(Autonomous System)-level routing information. We can get information of route prefix of each AS, that is, the network prefixes that belong to each AS. Fig. 7 is an example of IRR database entry.

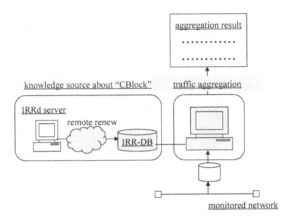

Fig. 8. Experiment Environment

5   Experiments and Results

We carried out experiments of aggregating traffic data with the unconstrained and constrained algorithms and, compared the results.

5.1   Experiment

We used the traffic data monitored and collected by mawi-WG in WIDE-project [5], at the transit point of the research backbone network. We used the data collected from 14:00 at Mar 11 2002 which contains 3,000,000 packets. We aggregated the traffic data at 1 minute intervals. We examined the outbound traffic and carried out aggregation based on destination IP Addresses using the same threshold value for the constrained and unconstrained algorithms. Fig. 8 is the experiments environment.

5.2   Results

The sample output for the unconstrained mode is shown in Fig. 9 and the results from the constrained algorithm are shown in Fig. 10.

In Fig. 10, prefixes with leading hyphens correspond to *CBlocks*. These nodes can be mapped to ASes. There are fewer meaningless aggregated prefixes, such as 0.0.0.0/0 or 128.0.0.0/1 in the results from the constrained aggregation algorithm. On the other hand, the results from the unconstrained algorithm (Fig. 9) contains many prefixes that can't be mapped onto ASes. These nodes have network prefixes that do not correspond to logical network entities.

Now we return to our primary objective of detecting and measuring *torrent* and *s-torrents*. Here, these outputs summarize traffic by IP addresses and have a *torrent* form. In the constrained aggregation algorithm resultant *s-torrents* are easily defined based on *CBlock* and *ABlock* membership. For example, the *s-torrents* mapped onto "RoadRunner(AS11426)" each belong to a *CBlock* which

```
[src address] 44664002 (100.00%)
%LRU hits: 74.68% (60730/81316)
  0.0.0.0/2      1775757 (3.98%/4.43%)      (AS NOT FOUND!)
 32.0.0.0/3       203337 (0.46%/0.46%)      (AS NOT FOUND!)
    64.0.0.0/12      2072574 (4.64%/4.84%)      (AS NOT FOUND!)
       64.4.***.***    88616 (0.20%)         ASN-HOTMAIL (AS12076)
  65.0.0.0/10       53198 (0.12%/0.12%)      (AS NOT FOUND!)
       66.26.***.***  1100518 (2.46%)       RoadRunner (AS11426)
128.0.0.0/1       991872 (2.22%/78.36%)     (AS NOT FOUND!)
192.0.0.0/3      1466354 (3.28%/76.14%)     (AS NOT FOUND!)
200.0.0.0/5      1435046 (3.21%/20.65%)     (AS NOT FOUND!)
202.0.0.0/8        61756 (0.14%/1.66%)      (AS NOT FOUND!)
      202.249.***.*** 679798 (1.52%)        AI3-NET (AS4717)
204.0.0.0/6      1932153 (4.33%/15.78%)     (AS NOT FOUND!)
      205.188.***.*** 110742 (0.25%)        ATDN (AS1668)
  207.0.0.0/9      2621629 (5.87%/11.21%)    (AS NOT FOUND!)
      207.46.***.***  2383894 (5.34%)       ASN-MS-SJC (AS8073)
208.0.0.0/6       121708 (0.27%/33.01%)     (AS NOT FOUND!)
209.0.0.0/8      1715684 (3.84%/3.84%)      (AS NOT FOUND!)
210.0.0.0/8      2551128 (5.71%/5.71%)      (AS NOT FOUND!)
211.128.0.0/10     93108 (0.21%/19.14%)     (AS NOT FOUND!)
      211.155.***.*** 6755360 (15.12%)      CHINANET-BJ-AS (AS4808)
      211.161.***.*** 1701438 (3.81%)       DXTNET (AS17964)
216.0.0.0/8      3532302 (7.91%/8.28%)      (AS NOT FOUND!)
  216.128.0.0/9      165104 (0.37%/0.37%)    (AS NOT FOUND!)
218.0.0.0/8       110696 (0.25%/6.48%)      (AS NOT FOUND!)
      218.124.***.*** 2784612 (6.23%)       GIGAINFRA (AS17676)
:::::
```

Fig. 9. Example : Outputs from the unconstrained algorithm(Aguri's output) with AS information(partial list)

```
[src address] 44664002 (100.00%)
%LRU hits: 74.83% (60852/81316)
  0.0.0.0/2       253220 (0.57%/0.57%)         (AS NOT FOUND!)
----12.0.0.0/8   2232          ATT-INTERNET4 (AS7018)
-------------12.27.44.128/26  186          (AS16584)
----13.0.0.0/8   887           SBCIS-5673-ASN (AS5673)
----15.0.0.0/8   487           HP-INTERNET-AS (AS71)
---------15.211.128.0/20  222          AS151 (AS151)
-------15.224.0.0/13   164          HP-INTERNET-AS (AS71)
----16.0.0.0/8   2093          (AS33)
--------17.72.0.0/16   147          (AS714)
----------20.139.0.0/22  200          CSC-IGN-AUNZ-AP (AS17916)
-------24.0.0.0/14   145          ATHOME-1-ASN (AS6172)
---------24.26.96.0/19 186          RoadRunner (AS10994)
---------24.26.192.0/19  424          RoadRunner (AS11427)
---------24.27.0.0/18   156          RoadRunner (AS11427)
---------24.29.96.0/19 624          RoadRunner (AS12271)
---------24.31.192.0/19  85          ATDN (AS1668)
---------24.31.224.0/19  204          RoadRunner (AS11955)
-------24.42.0.0/15   3594          ROGERS-CABLE-AS (AS812)
-------------24.48.33.0/24  78          (AS1325)
---------24.58.0.0/18   372          RoadRunner (AS11351)
---------24.58.128.0/18 180          RoadRunner (AS13343)
---------24.64.32.0/19 696          ASN-SHAWFIBER (AS6327)
---------24.64.64.0/19 28316          ASN-SHAWFIBER (AS6327)
---------24.64.160.0/19  1254          ASN-SHAWFIBER (AS6327)
---------24.64.192.0/19 98          ASN-SHAWFIBER (AS6327)
---------24.66.0.0/19   7413          ASN-SHAWFIBER (AS6327)
---------24.67.192.0/19  20376          ASN-SHAWFIBER (AS6327)
:::::
```

Fig. 10. Example : Outputs from the constrained algorithm(our method's output) with AS information(partial list)

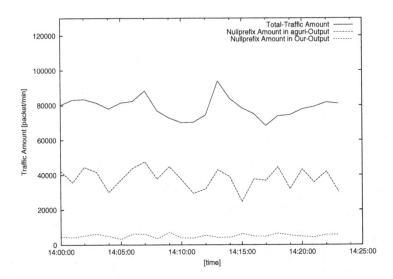

Fig. 11. Comparison of the uncovered('null-prefix') data in Aguri and Our Method

Table 1. Qualitative Evaluation

	NeTraMet	Aguri	Our Method
CBlock	aware (pre-defined)	ignore	aware
Granularity	static	dynamic	dynamic
ABlock	aware (pre-defined)	ignore	available

is a member of the *ABlock(AS11426)*. On the other hand, the unconstrained aggregation algorithm results in several "AS NOT FOUND!" entries. These cannot be mapped to any logical network entity (do not correspond to *s-torrents*). The prefixes of these entries are termed 'null-prefixes' in the rest of this paper. Fig. 11 shows the amount of traffic aggregated into 'null-prefix' per minute in the two modes of aggregation.

In the unconstrained mode, almost half of the traffic got aggregated into 'null-prefixes' whereas in the constrained aggregation method the amount of traffic that accumulated in the 'null-prefix' was much less.

However, the number of traffic profiles (prefixes) increased in the constrained aggregation algorithm. This result is expected. The degree of aggregation and the adequacy of the results are a trade-off. Of course in our proposal aggregation may be continued further till an "interesting" entry is arrived at.

5.3   Qualitative Evaluation

Table 1 is a qualitative evaluation of our model and the algorithm based on the model. The output of the proposed algorithm has the benefits of being *CBlock*-aware and dynamically adjusting the *Granularity*. The outputs are more easily analyzed in the context of the relation(*ABlock*) between *CBlocks*. The output is useful for both long and short term traffic monitoring and analysis because it catches the dynamics of traffic changes as the network configuration changes.

6   Conclusion

In this paper, we have proposed to model the IP address space as a binary tree where the nodes in the tree have a property that decides the aggregatability of the sibling traffic. The binary tree based network traffic aggregation algorithm based on this model effectively constrains the aggregation process preventing meaningless aggregations. This detects *s-torrents*, logical sets of flows in traffic, automatically and leads to a more accurate picture of the traffic on the wire. There is a trade-off in the quality and the quantity of aggregation achieved. But the benefits of the quality far outweighs the loss in quantity. The results provide a deeper insight into the long term and short-term traffic trends. In effect the proposed algorithm offers a novel way of dynamically discovering "interesting" flows of traffic. This will have a potential impact on technology that will lead to better managed and more secure networks.

References

1. CoralReef website,
   http://www.caida.org/tools/measurement/coralreef/
2. B.Ryu, D.Cheney, and H-W.Braun, "Internet Flow Characterization - Adaptive Timeout and Statistical Modeling," PAM2001 workshop paper.
3. B.Krishnamurthy, and J.Wang, "On network-aware clustering of web clients," In Proceedings of ACM SIGCOMM '00, August 2000.
4. D.D.Clark, "Policy routing in Internet protocols," RFC1102, IETF, 1989.
5. K.Cho, K.Mitsuya, and A.Kato, "Traffic data repository at the WIDE project," In USENIX 2000 Annual Technical Conference: FREENIX Track, page 263-270, June 2000.
6. K.Cho, R.Kaizaki, and A.Kato, "Aguri:An Aggregation-based Traffic Profiler," In Proceedings of QofIS2001 (published by Springer-Verlag in the LCNS series). September 2001.
7. K.C.Claffy, H-W.Braun, and G.C.Polyzos, "A parameterizable methodology for Internet traffic flow profiling," IEEE Journal of Selected Areas in Communications, 13(8):1481-1494,1995.
8. N.Brownlee, "Using NeTraMet for Production Traffic Measurement," Intelligent Management Conference(IM2001), May 2001.
9. N.Brownlee, C.Mills, and G.Ruth, "Traffic flow measurement: Architecture," RFC 2722, IETF, October 1999.
10. N.Brownlee, and M.Murray, "Streams,Flows and Torrents," In PAM 2001.

11. S.Waldbusser, "Remote Network Monitoring Management Information Base," RFC 1271, IETF, November 1991.
12. T.Bates, E.Gerich, L.Joncheray, J-M.Jouanigot, D.Karrenberg, M.Terpstra, and J.Yu, "Representation of IP Routing Policies in a Routing Registry(ripe-81++)," RFC 1786, IETF, 1995.

Dynamic Location Management with Caching in Hierarchical Databases for Mobile Networks

Chang Woo Pyo[1], Jie Li[2], Hisao Kameda[2], and Xiaohua Jia[3]

[1] Doctoral Program Systems & Information Engineering, University of Tsukuba,
Tsukuba Science City, Ibaraki 305-8573, Japan
cwpyo@osdp.is.tsukuba.ac.jp
[2] Institute of Information Science & Electronics, University of Tsukuba,
Tsukuba Science City, Ibaraki 305-8573, Japan
{lijie, kameda}@is.tsukuba.ac.jp
[3] Department of Computer Science, City University of Hong Kong,
83 Tat Chee Ave., Kowloon, Hong Kong
jia@cs.cityu.edu.hk

Abstract. In location management which is one of the key issues in mobile networks, the mobile user location update and the incoming calls behavior significantly affect the network performance. To reduce the signaling load and delay, this paper purposes dynamic location management with caching in hierarchical databases for personal communication networks. The performance analysis of dynamic location management has the complicated problems, since the local update area, namely the *paging area*, is dynamically changed by the mobile users mobility patterns. We propose an analytical model to analyze the mobility patterns with complexity in practical HLR/VLR architectures. By using the analytical model, we provide formulas for the performance analysis and the overall cost minimization of the proposed scheme. And also, the effect of the caching method on dynamic location management and the performance comparison among the proposed scheme, the existing static scheme, and the dynamic scheme without caching are studied.

1 Introduction

One of the key issues in mobile networks is to economically and quickly transfer any form of information between any desired locations at any time for mobile subscribers. How to perform location management so that mobile terminals (MTs) can move freely in the wireless network is one of the important problems in PCS networks [2,5,6,7,8,9]. For correctly delivering calls, the PCS network needs to maintain the current location of the MTs. To maintain the MT's location, two level hierarchical databases [5] such that two types of the location database, the Home Location Register (HLR) and the Visitor Location Register (VLR), are commonly used in all interesting PCS networks such as IS-41 [3] and GSM [4].

There are two basic operations in location management: *location update* and *call delivery*. To facilitate the tracking of a moving MT, PCS network is partitioned into many Location Areas (LAs). Each LA includes tens or hundreds of

S. Bhalla (Ed.): DNIS 2002, LNCS 2544, pp. 253–267, 2002.
© Springer-Verlag Berlin Heidelberg 2002

cells. In existing PCS networks, the size of an LA is fixed. This means that the location update is performed whenever an MT crosses the LA boundaries. When an MT reports its up-to-date location information dynamically to the system, the location entries of the MT are updated both the HLR and the VLR. The call delivery is the process of determining the serving VLR and the cell location of the called MT.

Under static location management [2] using a prior determined LA, an MT located near the boundary of the LA may excessively perform the location updates, as it moves back and forth between two LAs. And also, since the signaling messages concentrate on the centralized HLR, the volume of signaling and database access traffic may increase beyond the capacity of the network as the number of MTs keeps increasing.

To deal with the problems of the current static location management scheme, we purpose *dynamic location management with caching* in two level hierarchical databases architecture. Our dynamic location update focuses on dynamically changing the size of a local update area, called a paging area (PA), in an LA according to MT mobility patterns and the interval between incoming calls. And the caching scheme also improves the system performance when some MTs are called several times from the same MSC in a short time interval. Another important contribution of our paper is establishing an analytical model for studying the performance of dynamic location management with caching under the practical HLR/VLR architectures. To evaluate the performance of the proposed location management scheme, it is necessary to carefully consider the movement between both PAs and LAs under HLR/VLR architectures since the size of the PA is changed while the size of the LA is fixed. This makes the analysis much more difficult. We establish a novel analytical model in spite of the complexity of modeling.

The proposed analytical model enables us to derive the location update cost and the call delivery cost with dependent in the system parameters, including the mobility and incoming call arrival patterns of each MT in detail. Our model provides the formulas to solve the minimizing problem of the overall cost that is a trade-off between the location update cost and the call delivery cost. By using the model, we present the performance evaluation and comparison of the proposed scheme and the existing location management schemes using various parameters. This studies show clearly how much the performance improvement can be achieved by the dynamic location management scheme with caching comparing to the existing location management schemes. And also, The caching method for call delivery using the cached information of a particular MT may affect the size of a PA and the performance of dynamic location management in contrast with static location management. Thus, we study the effect of the caching scheme on the size of a PA and on the performance of the dynamic location management scheme.

The rest of this paper is organized as follows. In Section 2, we describe the system for our proposed dynamic movement-based location management with caching. The cost evaluation for location update and call delivery is shown in Section 3. We determine the optimal size of a paging area, and study the performance of our location management in Section 4 and 5. Section 6 concludes our paper.

2   System Description

The existing PCS networks, IS-41 and GSM, use two types of location databases (HLR and VLR) organized in two level data hierarchy. The location databases manage the current location of mobile terminals (MTs) in a service area. The location management functions are achieved by the exchange of signaling messages through a signaling network. *Signal System 7* (SS7) [11] is the protocol used for signaling exchange. The SS7 signaling network connects the HLR, the several VLRs and MSCs. It represents an interface between the MTs (via base stations) and the backbone network. To reduce the frequent signal exchanging, the PCS network supports the group of cells, Location Area (LA). In general, all base stations belonging to the same LA are connected to the same MSC.

2.1   Dynamic Movement-Based Location Update

In static location update, PCS networks currently require that an MT performs a location update whenever the MT enters a new Location Area (LA). Otherwise, in the dynamic movement-based location update scheme, a location update for an MT is occurred when the number of cell boundary crossings since the MT last location update is occurred equals the pre-defined threshold.

To support the dynamic updates, the system allows the sub-areas in an LA called *Paging Areas* (PAs). We consider PCS networks with a *hexagonal cell configuration* for the purpose of demonstration. For the hexagonal cell configuration, cells are hexagonal shaped and each cell has six neighbors. Assume that the *center cell* to be the cell where the last location update occurred. The innermost ring (i.e., ring 0) consists of only the center cell. Ring 0 is surrounded by ring 1, which in turn is surrounded by ring 2, and so on. The number of cells in ring i, denoted by $g(i)$, is given by

$$g(0) = 1, \quad g(i) = 6i, \quad i = 1, 2, 3, \ldots.$$

Note that the covering area within a distance $d - 1$ from the center cell may cover more than one LA. The number of cells in a PA, denoted by $PA(d)$, is upper bounded by $\sum_{j=0}^{d-1} g(j)$. We note that if the number of cells in an LA is much larger than $\sum_{j=0}^{d-1} g(j)$, the upper bound is a good approximation to $PA(d)$. We use the upper bound as an approximation to $PA(d)$,

$$PA(d) = \sum_{i=0}^{d-1} g(i) = 1 + 3d(d - 1). \tag{1}$$

In general, the size of a PA is less than or equal to its LA. In addition, the size of the PA is dynamically determined according to the relation between the MT

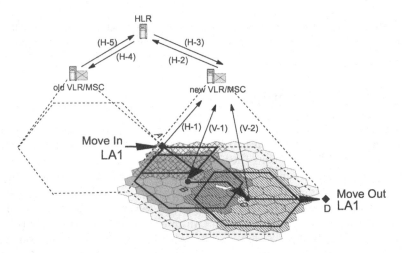

Fig. 1. Dynamic location update in the two-level hierarchical databases

mobility and call arrival patterns. As an MT has a high mobility, the size of the PA may be bigger. In contrast of dynamic location update, a PA and an LA have an identical size for a system using static location update.

HLR Location Update and VLR Location Update: In the dynamic based scheme, the location management databases, HLR and VLR, register an MT's location as a function of the number of PA or/and LA boundaries crossing. To simplify the description and analysis of dynamic location update, we define *HLR location update* and *VLR location update*.

Consider the MT freely travels in the wireless network shown in Fig.1. For example, the MT moves in an A cell and freely travels and passes on B cell and C cell in the LA. And then, the MT moves out the LA at D cell. Assume that d is the pre-defined threshold, called the *movement threshold*, as 4 cells. If an MT *moves in/moves out of* an LA at A cell and D cell, the HLR updates the current serving VLR location of the MT. And the current serving VLR also updates the current residing cell location of the MT. The previous old VLR cancels the location information of the MT that is not useful any more. That we call the *HLR location update*. The procedures of signaling for the HLR location update are the following steps $((H-1) \rightarrow (H-2) \rightarrow (H-3) \rightarrow (H-4) \rightarrow (H-5))$ shown in Fig.1. There are the same procedures of the static location update.

In the other case, when an MT crosses 4 cell boundaries in the same LA at B and C cell, then not the HLR but the VLR only updates the new cell location of the MT with the procedures $(V-1)$ at B cell and $(V-2)$ at C cell. That we call the *VLR location update*. Note that the VLR location update is an extra procedure compared to the static location update. However, the VLR location update is not complicated and does not affect the system performance

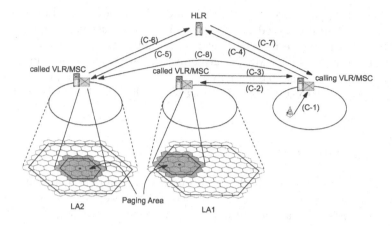

Fig. 2. Call delivery with caching in the two-level hierarchical databases

significantly since the processing time for the VLR location update is short compared with its the HLR location update.

2.2 Call Delivery with Caching under the Dynamic Location Update

Two major steps involved in call delivery are to determine the serving VLR of the called MT (i.e., *call setup*) and to locate the current cell of the called MT (i.e., *paging*). When an MT initiates a call in existing PCS networks, IS-41, the system performs the call setup between a calling MSC and a called MSC shown in Fig.2. The base station forwards the call to the MSC serving the MT and a HLR with procedures $(C-1)$ and $(C-4)$. The HLR sends a location request message to the MSC serving the called MT with $(C-5)$, and then the called MSC sends a Temporary Location Directory Number (TLDN) to the HLR with $(C-6)$. The HLR forwards the TLDN to the calling MSC with $(C-7)$. The calling MSC sets up the call connection to the called MSC using this TLDN with $(C-8)$. The called MSC sends a polling message to all base stations in an LA.

In the call delivery with caching [6], the MSC maintains the cached entries (i.e., MT's ID, updated VLR's ID, etc.,) for the MTs residing a local network. Each time when a call is attempted, the cached information is checked first at a calling. The calling MSC can see the VLR location for the called MT by the cached entries. If the location information for the called MT is already cached and is still served in a same LA since the MT's last location is updated (i.e., cache hit), then the call is directly connected to the called MSC without looking up the called MT's location entry at the HLR with $(C-2)$. In this case, the call delivery time may be significantly reduced by cached information. Otherwise, if the called MT has already moved to another LA before a call at the calling MSC attempts to the MT, the cached data is not valid at all (i.e., cache miss), then the extra signal procedures, $(C - 2)$ and $(C - 3)$, are needed and that call follows the call setup procedures of the call delivery without caching. In this case, the call setup time may be longer than that of the call delivery without caching. Finally, the called MSC pages only the coverage cells within a Paging Area (PA). This dynamic paging may reduce the delay of polling time to locate the MT in contrast to static based paging where the size of a PA is equal to its LA.

3   Analytical Model

The factors attributing to the location update cost and the call delivery cost greatly depend on network topologies, the radio power of base stations and mobile terminals, the capacity of databases, and so on. For the purpose of cost analysis, we consider the costs of location update and call delivery between two call arrivals.

3.1   Dynamic Location Update Cost

In HLR/VLR architecture, dynamic location updates are involved in two kinds of location updates shown in previous section 2: HLR location updates and VLR location updates. Let HU be the expected cost for performing a HLR location update, and VU be the expected cost for performing a VLR location update which account for the wireless and wireline bandwidth utilization and the computational requirements in order to process each location update. Thus, the expected overall location updates cost between two calls, denoted by $C_{DU}(d)$, is expressed by

$$C_{DU}(d) = n_{HLR} * HU + n_{VLR} * VU, \tag{2}$$

where d is the pre-defined movement threshold and n_{HLR} and n_{VLR} are the average number of HLR/VLR location updates between two call arrivals, respectively. Note that the number of VLR location updates, n_{VLR}, depends on the size of a PA, $PA(d)$. We derive n_{HLR} and n_{VLR} as follows.

The average number of HLR location updates. The average number of HLR location updates between two call arrivals should be calculated carefully. Consider the timing diagram that an MT moves around K LA boundaries between consecutive two calls shown in Fig.3. Then, n_{HLR} is expressed by

$$n_{HLR} = \sum_{K=1}^{\infty} K\alpha(K), \tag{3}$$

where $\alpha(K)$ be the probability that there are K LA boundaries crossing between two call arrivals. To derive $\alpha(K)$, we assume that the residence time t_{M_i} of an MT p in an LA_i $(0 \le i \le K)$ is an exponentially distributed variable with mean

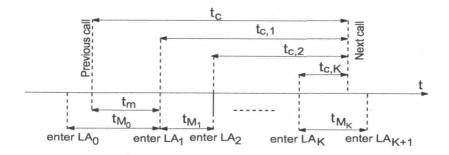

Fig. 3. Timing diagram for $\alpha(K)$

$\frac{1}{\lambda_m}$ and the call arrival to the MT p is a Poisson process with rate λ_c. Let t_c be the call inter-arrival time between the previous call and the next call to the MT p. Without loss of generality, we suppose that the MT p resides in an LA LA_0, when the previous call arrived. After the call, p visits another K LAs, and resides in the ith LA for a period t_{M_i} $(0 \le i \le K)$. Let t_m be the interval between the arrival of the previous call and the time when p moves out of LA_0. Let $t_{c,i}$ be the interval between the time that p enters LA_i and the time that the next call arrives.

Let $f_c(t)$ and $g_m(t)$ be the density function of t_c and t_{M_i}, respectively. Note that $E[t_c] = \frac{1}{\lambda_c}$ and $E[t_{M_i}] = \frac{1}{\lambda_m}$. And then,

$$f_c(t) = \lambda_c e^{-\lambda_c t}, \quad g_m(t) = \lambda_m e^{-\lambda_m t}.$$

From the memoryless property of the exponential distribution, $t_{c,i}$ and t_m have the same exponential distribution as t_c and t_{M_i}, respectively. The probability $\alpha(K)$ of the MT K LA boundaries crossing is derived as follows.

$$\alpha(K) = Pr[t_m + t_{M_1} + \cdots + t_{M_{k-1}} < t_c \le t_m + t_{M_1} + \cdots + t_{M_K}]$$

$$= Pr[t_c > t_m] * \left(\prod_{i=1}^{K-1} Pr[t_{c,i} > t_{M_i}] \right) * Pr[t_{c,K} \le t_{M_K}]$$

$$= \frac{\lambda_m}{\lambda_m + \lambda_c} \left(\prod_{i=1}^{K-1} \frac{\lambda_m}{\lambda_m + \lambda_c} \right) \frac{\lambda_c}{\lambda_m + \lambda_c} = \frac{\lambda_c}{\lambda_m + \lambda_c} \left(\frac{\lambda_m}{\lambda_m + \lambda_c} \right)^K. \quad (4)$$

Substituting (4) into (3), n_{HLR} is calculated as follows.

$$n_{HLR} = \sum_{K=1}^{\infty} K\alpha(K) = \sum_{K=1}^{\infty} K \left(\frac{\lambda_c}{\lambda_m + \lambda_c} \right) \left(\frac{\lambda_m}{\lambda_m + \lambda_c} \right)^K = \frac{\lambda_m}{\lambda_c}. \quad (5)$$

The average number of VLR location updates. Deriving the average number of VLR location updates between two call arrivals is the most difficult in the

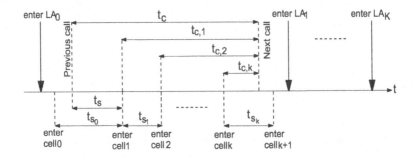

Fig. 4. Timing diagram for $\epsilon_1(k)$

analysis. The calculation of the average number of VLR location updates needs to be concerned with the movement among both PAs and LAs into account. Suppose that the MT p resides in the LA LA_0, when the previous call arrived. The average number of VLR location updates per call arrival, denoted by n_{VLR}, can be expressed as follows,

$$n_{VLR} = \sum_{K=0}^{\infty} n_{VLR_K} \cdot \alpha(K), \tag{6}$$

where n_{VLR_K} is the average number of VLRs when the MT p receives the next call in arbitrary LA LA_K $(K = 0, 1, 2, ...)$.

Since the size of an LA is fixed while PA is changed by the value of threshold d, n_{VLR_K} has also various values by the size of the PA. Let d be the pre-defined movement threshold and ϵ be the probability of the MT movement among both PAs and LAs. From [14], n_{VLR_K} is given by,

$$n_{VLR_K} = \sum_{l=1}^{\infty} l \sum_{j=ld}^{(l+1)d-1} \epsilon(j), \quad K \geq 0. \tag{7}$$

In order to calculate the value of n_{VLR_K}, it is necessary to obtain the following four probabilities which can describe the movement of an MT among both PAs and LAs since the MT p does not move out a PA or crosses some PAs and LA's between two calls. The four probabilities are given by

1. $\epsilon_1(k)$: The probability that there are k cell boundaries crossing within the LA_0, where the previous phone call arrived when the MT receives the next phone call in the same LA. In this case, $K = 0$, i.e., there is no LA boundary crossing.
2. $\epsilon_2(k)$: The probability that there are k cell boundaries crossing within LA_0 when the MT enters LA_1. In the case, $K > 0$, i.e., there are LA boundaries crossing.
3. $\epsilon_3(k)$: The probability that there are k cell boundaries crossing within LA_i during period t_{M_i} $(1 \leq i \leq K - 1, K > 0)$.

4. $\epsilon_4(k)$: The probability that there are k cell boundaries crossing after entering the last LA_K ($K > 0$) until the next call arrival.

We proceed to the calculation of these four probabilities. We assume that the cell residence time follows the Gamma distribution. Assume that the probability density function of the cell residence time has Laplace-Stieltjes transform $f_m(s)$ with mean $\frac{1}{\lambda_s}$ and variance ν.

$$f_m(s) = \left(\frac{\lambda_s \gamma}{s + \lambda_s \gamma}\right)^\gamma, \quad \gamma = \frac{1}{\nu \lambda_s^2}. \tag{8}$$

[9] introduces the solution for the probabilities $\epsilon_1(k)$, $\epsilon_2(k)$, $\epsilon_3(k)$, and $\epsilon_4(k)$ in a special case. From using time diagram shown in Fig.4, we can obtain the general solution for each probability.

$$\begin{cases} \epsilon_1(k) = \frac{\lambda_s}{\lambda_c}[1 - f_m(\lambda_c)]^2[f_m(\lambda_c)]^{k-1}, k = 1, 2, 3... \\ \epsilon_2(k) = [1 - f_m(\lambda_m)][f_m(\lambda_m)]^k, k = 1, 2, 3... \\ \epsilon_3(k) = [1 - f_m(\lambda_m)][f_m(\lambda_m)]^k, k = 1, 2, 3... \\ \epsilon_4(k) = \frac{\lambda_s}{\lambda_c}[1 - f_m(\lambda_c)]^2[f_m(\lambda_c)]^{k-1}, k = 1, 2, 3... \end{cases}$$

Substituting the each probability into eq.(7), n_{VLR_K} is given by

$$n_{VLR_K} = K\frac{[f_m(\lambda_m)]^d}{1 - [f_m(\lambda_m)]^d} + \frac{\lambda_s}{\lambda_c}[1 - f_m(\lambda_c)]\frac{[f_m(\lambda_c)]^{d-1}}{1 - [f_m(\lambda_c)]^d} \tag{9}$$

Substituting eq.(9) into eq.(6), the average number of VLR location updates per call arrival is given by,

$$\begin{aligned} n_{VLR} &= \sum_{K=0}^{\infty} n_{VLR_K} \cdot \alpha(K) \\ &= \sum_{K=0}^{\infty} \left(\left\{ \begin{matrix} K\frac{[f_m(\lambda_m)]^d}{1 - [f_m(\lambda_m)]^d} + \\ \frac{\lambda_s}{\lambda_c}[1 - f_m(\lambda_c)]\frac{[f_m(\lambda_c)]^{d-1}}{1 - [f_m(\lambda_c)]^d} \end{matrix} \right\} * \left\{ \frac{\lambda_c}{\lambda_m + \lambda_c}(\frac{\lambda_m}{\lambda_m + \lambda_c})^K \right\} \right) \\ &= \frac{\lambda_m}{\lambda_c}\frac{[f_m(\lambda_m)]^d}{1 - [f_m(\lambda_m)]^d} + \frac{\lambda_s}{\lambda_c}[1 - f_m(\lambda_c)]\frac{[f_m(\lambda_c)]^{d-1}}{1 - [f_m(\lambda_c)]^d}. \end{aligned} \tag{10}$$

To sum up, we have the dynamic location update cost between two call intervals as follows:

$$C_{DU}(d) = HU * \frac{\lambda_m}{\lambda_c} + VU * \left(\begin{matrix} \frac{\lambda_m}{\lambda_c}\frac{[f_m(\lambda_m)]^d}{1 - [f_m(\lambda_m)]^d} + \\ \frac{\lambda_s}{\lambda_c}[1 - f_m(\lambda_c)]\frac{[f_m(\lambda_c)]^{d-1}}{1 - [f_m(\lambda_c)]^d} \end{matrix} \right) \tag{11}$$

3.2   Call Delivery Cost with Caching

Call delivery involves in call setup between the calling MSC and the called MSC and paging the cell location of an MT in an LA. Let P_k denote the probability that the cached location information for the called MT is correct. P_k is defined the *cache hit ratio*. Alternatively, at steady state, P_k denotes the probability that the MT has not moved out an LA since the last call. Consider the previous section in Fig.3 to derive P_k. From our assumption of section 3, the LA_i residence times t_{M_i} $(0 \leq i \leq K)$ and t_m for an MT are an exponentially distributed with mean $\frac{1}{\lambda_m}$ and the call arrival interval t_c to the MT is a Poisson process with rate λ_c. Thus, we have

$$P_k = Pr[t_c \leq t_m] = \int_{t_m=0}^{\infty} \int_{t_c=0}^{t_c=t_m} \lambda_c e^{-\lambda_c t_c} \lambda_m e^{-\lambda_m t_m} dt_c dt_m = \frac{\lambda_c}{\lambda_c + \lambda_m}. \quad (12)$$

If the cache information is correct, the cost of call setup is smaller than that of without caching. However, if the cache information becomes invalid, the cost of call setup with caching is greater than that of without caching. Let DC be the cost for performing a call setup when the cached location entry is correct. Let SC be the cost for performing a call setup when the cached location entry is invalid. Under dynamic location management, the performance of call delivery may depends on the size of a paging area. The call delivery cost for the cache hit, denoted by $C_H(d)$, and the call delivery cost for the cache invalid, denoted by $C_B(d)$, are given by

$$C_H(d) = DC + C_p(d), \quad (13)$$
$$C_B(d) = SC + C_p(d), \quad (14)$$

where $C_p(d)$ is the expected paging cost per call arrival. From the equation (1), the expected paging cost per call is given by

$$C_p(d) = P * PA(d) = P * (1 + 3d(d-1)), \quad (15)$$

where P is the cost for performing the polling a cell.

The location information of an MT has to be cached at an MSC only if the MT changes its LA less frequently than it receives calls from that MSC. In order to determine which MT's location information to cache, we use the system parameters called *Local-Call-to-Mobility Ratio* (LCMR) in caching the location information. LCMR is the ratio between the number of calls originating from an MSC and the number of times the MT changes its service area as seen by that MSC. That is the small value of LCMR $(=\frac{\lambda_c}{\lambda_m})$ means the high mobility that the MT has, and vice versa. The location information of an MT is cached at an MSC, if the LCMR maintained for the MT at the MSC is larger than a threshold derived from the link and database access cost of the network. A call delivery cost saving with the caching scheme is achieved by caching location information if

$$P_k C_H(d) + (1 - P_k)(C_H(d) + C_B(d)) < C_B(d), \quad (16)$$

Simplifing the above equation (16),

$$P_k > \frac{C_H(d)}{C_B(d)}. \quad (17)$$

If the cache hit ratio, P_k, is larger than a cost saving, $\frac{C_H(d)}{C_B(d)}$, the system will cache the MT's location information. Consequently, the mean call delivery cost denoted by $C_{DC}(d)$ can be expressed.

$$C_{DC}(d) = P_k C_H(d) + (1 - P_k)(C_H(d) + C_B(d)). \qquad (18)$$

To sum up, the expected total cost from (11) and (18) denoted by $TC_{DC}(d)$ is given by

$$TC_{DC}(d) = C_{DU}(d) + C_{DC}(d)$$

$$= HU * \frac{\lambda_m}{\lambda_c} + VU * \left(\begin{array}{l} \frac{\lambda_m}{\lambda_c} \frac{[f_m(\lambda_m)]^d}{1-[f_m(\lambda_m)]^d} + \\ \frac{\lambda_s}{\lambda_c}[1 - f_m(\lambda_c)] \frac{[f_m(\lambda_c)]^{d-1}}{1-[f_m(\lambda_c)]^d} \end{array} \right)$$

$$+ P_k C_H(d) + (1 - P_k)(C_H(d) + C_B(d)), \qquad (19)$$

where $d \ (\geq 1)$.

4   Optimal Paging Area

In this section, we try to obtain the optimal paging area through minimizing the total cost. The total cost has a different value through the size of a paging area determined by the threshold d. Note d is a positive integer. We have

$$\text{Minimize}[TC_{DC}(d)]. \qquad (20)$$

If we take d as a real number, functions $C_{DU}(d)$ and $C_{DC}(d)$ are twice differentiable. Derive the first derivative and the second derivatives of $C_{DU}(d)$ and $C_{DC}(d)$, and arrange them. We have

$$C'_{DU}(d) < 0, \quad C''_{DU}(d) > 0, \quad C'_{DC}(d) > 0, \quad C''_{DC}(d) > 0.$$

That is, C_{DU} is a decreasing and convex function and C_{DC} is an increasing and convex function. Since the function $TC_{DC}(d)$ is convex, the value of d is the unique solution to minimize total cost, $TC_{DC}(d)$, if it satisfies the following differential condition,

$$TC'_{DC}(d) = C'_{DU}(d) + C'_{DC}(d) = 0. \qquad (21)$$

For the purpose of determining the threshold d in various mobility patterns, we use the system parameter called *Local-Call-to-Mobility-Ratio* (LCMR). That is the ratio between the number of calls originating from an MSC and the number of location updates of a called MT as seen by that MSC. That is the small value of LCMR $(=\frac{\lambda_c}{\lambda_m})$ means the high mobility that the MT has, and vice versa. Note that the mean LA residence time $(=\frac{1}{\lambda_m})$ shall be larger than the mean cell residence time $(=\frac{1}{\lambda_s})$.

It is known that the size of a paging area is greatly affected by VU and P. The effect of the VLR location update cost VU and the polling cost P on the

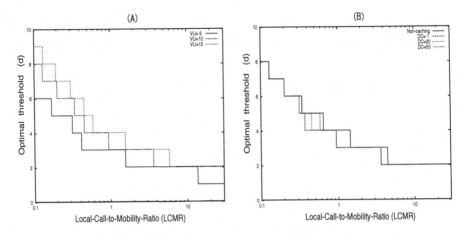

Fig. 5. Optimal threshold d with $P = 1$

threshold d is shown in Fig.5.(A). Three VU values, 5, 10, and 15 are considered with $P = 1$ and other parameters are set to $HU = 200$, $DC = 20$ and $SC = 200$. As the LCMR increases from 0.1 to 30, the value of d decreases like a stairway. Intuitively, the high LCMR will cause a large threshold d, that means increasing the size of a paging area according to decrease the value of LCMR. It is also shown that an increase in VU may cause an increase in the size of a paging area.

Fig.5.(B) shows the effect of caching in the dynamic movement-based caching scheme on the size of a paging area. Three DC values, 1, 20, and 50 are considered with $SC = 200$ and other parameters are set to $P = 1$, $VU = 10$, and $HU = 200$. The optimal paging area with caching is smaller than that of without caching. A decrease in the value of DC causes an smaller the value of d between $LCMR = 0.3$ and $LCMR = 5$. It means that the caching scheme has a most effect on the dynamic movement-based location updates between $LCMR = 0.3$ and $LCMR = 5$. Otherwise, the higher LCMR ($LCMR \leq 0.3$) or the lower LCMR ($LCMR \geq 5$), the caching scheme has a limited effect on the size of a paging area.

5 Performance Study

We compare the total cost of several location managements such as dynamic location management with caching, dynamic location management without caching, and static location management without caching. To the purpose of the performance comparison, we derive the total cost of the static location update without caching denoted by $TC_{SNC}(r)$ is given by

$$TC_{SNC}(r) = HU * \frac{\lambda_m}{\lambda_c} + SC + P * (1 + 3r(r-1)), \tag{22}$$

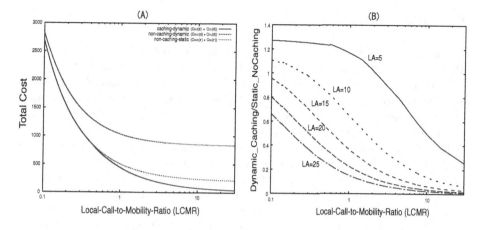

Fig. 6. Cost comparison of location management schemes

where r is the radius of LA from a center cell to the LA's boundary. The total cost of the dynamic movement-based location update without caching denoted by $TC_{DNC}(d)$ is given by

$$TC_{DNC}(d) = HU * \frac{\lambda_m}{\lambda_c} + VU * \left\{ \begin{array}{l} \frac{\lambda_m}{\lambda_c} \frac{[f_m(\lambda_m)]^d}{1-[f_m(\lambda_m)]^d} + \\ \frac{\lambda_s}{\lambda_c}[1 - f_m(\lambda_c)] \frac{[f_m(\lambda_c)]^{d-1}}{1-[f_m(\lambda_c)]^d} \end{array} \right\}$$
$$+SC + P * (1 + 3d(d-1)) \tag{23}$$

In HLR/VLR architectures, the HLR location update cost is larger than the VLR location update cost (i.e., $HU \geq VU$), the call setup cost for the correct cached data is smaller than the call setup cost for the invalid cached data. (i.e., $SC \geq DC$), and the polling cost P is the smallest. For the purpose of demonstration, we set to the parameters which are the value of $P = 1$, $VU = 10$, $HU = 200$. $DC = 20$ for caching scheme and $SC = 200$ for non-caching scheme are set. The radius of LA (r) is set to 15 cells for the static management scheme.

From Fig.6.(A), the total cost of the dynamic location update schemes is smaller than the static location update schemes. And the dynamic movement-based caching scheme has the best cost performance within the location management schemes. Specially, if the value of LCMR is bigger, this means a mobile user has a low mobility, the cached information has a more effect on the dynamic location management scheme, therefore the total cost can be greatly reduced by caching.

Fig.6.(B) shows the ratio of total cost $\frac{dynamic-caching}{static-noncaching}$ changing the radius of LA from $r = 5$ to $r = 25$. As the served LA by a VLR is bigger and bigger and the MT has a low mobility, the proposed scheme is a better performance compared with the static location management without caching scheme. Since the paging area can be dynamically changed by the MT mobility and incoming calls patterns, that area make a balance between the location update cost and the call delivery cost.

6   Conclusion

In this paper, we propose *dynamic location management scheme with caching* in PCS networks with practical HLR/VLR architectures. To evaluate the performance of the scheme, we establish an analytical model. The model successfully handles the additional complexity problems created by dynamically changing the paging area (PA) while the location area (LA) is fixed. The model is applied to obtain the formulas to evaluate the cost for location updates and a call delivery with simplicity, and the formulas are easily used in the performance evaluation. By using the analytical model and formulas, we studied the effects of changing the parameters of performing location updates, call delivery, and Local-Call-to-Mobility Ratio (LCMR) on the system performance. And also, we determine the optimal size of a paging area, which minimizes the overall cost that is sum of location update cost and call delivery cost. Since the size of paging areas can be dynamically changed by an MT mobility pattern and the incoming calls of the MT, the system can make a balance of the load in own network. From our study, the obtained analytical formulations are simple and easy to be used, and our model can provide the good analysis method for the system design and implementation for wireless network.

References

1. A. Bar-Noy, I. Kessler, and M. Sidi: Mobile users: to update or not to update?. ACM-Baltzer J. Wireless Networks, vol.1, no.2, (1995) 175–186
2. R. Jain and Y. Lin: Performance modeling of an auxiliary user location strategy in a PCS network. ACM-Ballzer Wireless Networks, vol.1, no.2, (1995) 197–210
3. EIA/TIA. Cellular radio-telecommunications intersystem operations. Tech. Rep. IS-41 Revision B, EIA/TIA, (1991)
4. M. Mouly and M.B. Pautet: The GSM system for mobile communications. M.Mouly,49 rue Louise Bruneau, Palaiseau, France, (1992)
5. Joseph S.M. Ho and Ian F. Akyildiz: Dynamic Hierarchical Database Architecture for Location Mangement in PCS Networks. IEEE/ACM Trans. Networking. vol.5, (1997) 646–660
6. R. Jain, Y.B. Lin, and S. Mohan: A Caching Strategy to reduce network impacts of PCS. IEEE J. Selet. Areas Commun., vol.12, (1994)
7. K. Ratnam, I. Matta, and S. Rangarajan: Analysis of Caching-based Location Management in Personal Communication Networks. IEEE 7th International Conference on Network Protocols, (1999)
8. Jie Li, Hisao Kameda, and Keqin Li: Optimal Dynamic Mobility Management for PCS Networks. IEEE/ACM Trans. Networking, vol. 8, No. 3, (2000) 319–327
9. Jie Li, Yi Pan and Xiaohua Jia: Analysis of Dynamic Movement-based Location Update Scheme for PCS Networks. Proc. of ACM Symp on Applied Computing (ACM SAC'2001), USA, (2001) 368–372
10. S.Ross, Stochastic Processes, 2nd ed. New York, NY: Wiley, (1996)
11. A.R. Modarressi and R.A. Skoog: Signaling System 7: A Tutorial. IEEE Communications Magzine vol. 28, No. 7, (1990) 19 -35
12. D.C. Cox: Personal communications a viewpoint. IEEE Commun.Mag., (1990) 8-20

13. V.K. Garg and J.E. Wilkes: Wireless and Personal Communications Systems, Prentice-Hall, Inc. NJ, (1996)

14. I.F. Akyidiz, and J. Ho, and Y. Lin: Movement-Based Location Update and Selective Paging for PCS networks. IEEE/ACM Trans. Networking, vol.4, no.4, (1996) 629–638

15. J. Homa and S. Harris: Intelligent network requirements for personal communications services. IEEE Commun.Mag., (1992) 70–76

16. S. Mohan and R. Jain: Two user location strategies for personal communications services. IEEE Personal Commun.Mag., vol.1, (1994) 42–50

An Experimental Study on Query Processing Efficiency of Native-XML and XML-enabled Database Systems

Atakan Kurt[1] and Mustafa Atay[2]

[1] Fatih University, Computer Engineering Department
34900 Buyukcekmece, Istanbul, Turkey
akurt@fatih.edu.tr
[2] Wayne-State University, Computer Engineering Department
Detroit, Michigan, USA
matay@wayne.edu

Abstract. With XML becoming a standard for representing semi-structured documents on the web and a standard for data exchange between different systems, some database companies are adding XML support to their existing database systems, while some other companies coming out with pure or native database systems for XML. In this paper, we present an experimental study on the query processing efficiency of a native-XML database system and an XML-enabled database system on a selected set of queries including operations from text-processing, DML and relation algebra. The experiments are conducted on two well-known commercial database systems using the web interfaces based on HTTP. The cost metrics we used are CPU time, the numbers of physical and logical reads. The queries were run on identical machines for 3 different sizes of documents with and without indexing. A subset of experimental results is presented and overall results are discussed. Generally speaking the XML-enabled system performed better.

1 Introduction

XML – eXtensible Markup Language 1 is a standard for data representation and exchange on the Internet. XML documents are mostly semi-structured and can be stored and queried. Some important questions that arise in this context are:

Should new database systems be developed for management of XML documents or existing DBMSs extended with XML support?

How does the network sub-system and distributed environment affect the performance?

Will native-XML databases and query facilities replace traditional DBMSs by handling relational data as well in the future? Will there be a migration from relational to XML or vice versa?

How should XML documents be represented and stored in a database server for optimum efficiency? What types of models and methodology could be used to handle queries on XML documents?

S. Bhalla (Ed.): DNIS 2002, LNCS 2544, pp. 268–284, 2002.

Representing XML in native format and in relational database format, which method is more efficient under what conditions and on what types of queries? What kind of roles do the type, structure, content, size of documents and queries play in query processing?

How efficient are native-XML and XML-enabled databases on similar queries for large XML document sets?

In order to shed some light on these questions and provide some insights it is necessary to compare native-XML databases storing information in native format, with XML-enabled databases storing data in relational format. Hence we present an experimental study on the query processing efficiency of a native-XML and an XML-enabled system: Software AG's Tamino 2.3.1.1 as a native-XML database system, and Oracle's Oracle9i as a XML-enabled database system. We created 3 different sizes (containing 1, 2, and 3 million records) of large – up to ~700Mb - sample XML documents representing book records and loaded them into respective databases, executed 13 basic queries and measured efficiency in terms of selected cost metrics (CPU time, number of physical reads and, number of logical reads). The queries were run on two identical computers with and without index. The results from the experiments which involve only 2 systems cannot be generalized, but will be useful analyzing performance based on cost metrics, file size and content.

In Section 2 we cite relevant studies in benchmarking, and efficiency of XML queries and systems. In section 3 the native-XML and the XML-enabled databases and their query support for XML are briefly presented. In Section 4 we explain how experiments were designed and discuss the selected queries. Section 5 is reserved for a subset of experimental results. The overall results are discussed in the end of Section 5. Finally we summarize and conclude in Section 6.

2   Related Work

The XML Benchmark Project group 2 did a similar study with 14 kinds of XQuery 7 queries on a single user system on Monet XML 4. They used *running time* as the cost metric with no consideration of indexing.

A. Schmidt, M. Kersten, M. Windhouwer and F. Waas in 5 presented a data and execution model that allow for storage and retrieval of XML documents in a relational database. They measured the *load time* on Monet database server 4 with three different readily available XML documents on the web and *response time* for a set of 10 queries.

A general storage and retrieval method for XML documents using object-relational databases is described in 6. The authors used 10 simple queries and measured *processing time* after and before indexing in PostgreSQL. XQL was used as the XML query language.

In 3, 10 essential queries expressed in four different XML query languages: XML-QL, YATL, Lorel, and XQL. The first three languages come from database field and the last one from document-processing field. No experiment was conducted. This paper discusses expressiveness rather than efficiency.

```
<?xml version="1.0" encoding="UTF-8" standalone="yes"?>
<bib>
   <book year="1994">
      <title>TCP/IPIllustrated</title> <author><last>Stevens</last><first>W.</first></author>
      <publisher>Addison-Wesley</publisher>
      <price> 65.95</price>
   </book>
   <book year="1992">
      <title>Advanced Pro.</title> <author><last>Stevens</last><first>W.</first></author>
      <publisher>Addison-Wesley</publisher>
      <price>65.95</price>
   </book>
   <book year="1999">
      ...
   </book>
</bib>
```

Fig. 1. A Sample XML Document

In XMach-1 (XML Data Management Benchmark) project 8, both query and DML (Data Manipulation Language) operations are used for evaluating the performance of XML data management systems. 8 queries and 3 DML operations with XQuery are used in a scalable multi-user environment. The primary cost metric is *throughput* which is measured as *Xqps* (XML queries per second).

The XOO7 benchmark 15 is an XML version of the OO7 benchmark modified with relational, document and navigational queries for XML databases. They assert that the benchmark meets the four criteria: relevance, portability, scalability and simplicity. They implemented XOO7 and illustrate its applicability by using it to evaluate the performance of four XML management systems. In this study we primarily focused on the following points:

- Chose commercially available well-known systems,
- Run the same (or similar) query on an native-XML and XML-enabled systems
- Queries are tested with and without indices,
- Large sizes of xml documents used for realistic testing,
- The web-interface is used for storage, access, and querying where available.
- A wide range of queries including relational algebra operations, DML and text-search queries are employed.
- Unlike other studies we used *logical and physical disk reads* (accesses), as well as CPU time as a measure of performance.

3   Background: Native-XML versus XML-Enabled Databases

XML documents usually fall into two main categories: *data-centric* and *document-centric*. Dynamic web pages, such as online catalogs and address lists reflect data-centric properties. A user's manual, static web pages, on-line books are examples of document-centric XML data. They have irregular structures, or they are semi-structured with mixed content and the ordering of substructures is essential.

Databases storing and retrieving XML documents also fall into two main categories: XML-enabled and native-XML. In the discussions below we concentrate how each system approach to the query-processing. The discussions on storage models for XML data can't be discussed because of space limitations here.

3.1 XML-Enabled Databases

Relational/object-relational databases that have a limited degree of support for XML data are called *XML-enabled* database systems. These types of databases are traditionally used for data-centric applications. In most cases XML documents are first converted to relational form and then stored in the database. When the documents are queried, the data in the database is converted back to XML after query evaluation. The XML-enabling of a database is usually achieved by adding a web server, an XSLT translator, and other pieces software for handling XML documents. Below we discuss the XML-support in the XML-enabled system used in this study.

Oracle XDK: Oracle is a well-known DBMS and needs no introduction. We rather introduce the XML support, which is commonly abbreviated as XDK (XML Development Kit). XDK provides the tools for supporting XML including the XML Parsers, XSL Processors, XML Class Generator, XML Transviewer Beans, XML Schema Processor, and XML SQL Utility 12.

We used Oracle's XSQL Servlet for running queries in this study. The XSQL Servlet enables users to generate dynamic web content from the database and customize its presentation. The servlet firstly uses the XML SQL Utility and the XML Parser for Java to process the SQL queries embedded within a special XSQL XML file with the extension .xsql, secondly query the database using SQL, thirdly obtain the database results, and fourthly transform the data into any format including XML using XSL style sheets if required and lastly send it back to client. 13. The following is a sample XSQL query:

Consider documents shown in Fig. 1 and the DTD in Fig. 2. To select all the authors whose last names start with 'A' from a database called 'bib' in response to a URL request like *http://localhost/authors_a.xsql* one might create an XSQL page below:

```
<?xml version="1.0"?>
<xsql:query connection="bib" xmlns:xsql="urn:oracle-xsql">
SELECT *
FROM Author
WHERE last like 'A%'
</xsql:query>
```

3.2 Native-XML Databases

Databases that store and retrieve XML documents in structures especially crafted for efficient storage and access, generally as indexed text, are called *native-XML*. Many methods of storage and access for XML documents have been proposed for native storage mainly based on labelled-directed graphs. The term *native* means that documents are stored in data structures especially designed for XML data, not in the form of relations as in traditional DBMSs. These databases usually have limited support for relational data as well. The power of these databases supposedly comes from storing document in the *native form* and taking advantage of meta-data (DTD) in finding parts of documents more efficiently. Native-XML databases keep the document order of elements, CDATA sections, processing instructions, and comments, while XML-enabled databases usually do not, even though they can do so with a little overhead.

Tamino marketed by Software AG is one of the big players in the native-XML database arena 10. Software AG is ranked the leader in the XML and Virtual DBMS market in a report by International Data Corporation 11.

Tamino in its documentation is defined as a system that *generally* stores data as XML documents. No detailed information was available about the data structures and methods used in the system. XML Store and X-Machine provide internal storage and retrieval of XML objects. X-Node acts as an interface between external applications and data sources. SQL store and SQL Engine provides internal storage and retrieval of SQL data. Data Map keeps track of where documents are stored and how they can be retrieved. Tamino manager is web-based tool for administering Tamino servers. Tamino uses HTTP protocol for data exchange and uses X-Query as the query language.

X-Query: X-Query is the standard query language in Tamino for performing queries on XML objects and is based on the early XPath specifications of the W3C. XPath provides a data model and expression syntax for addressing parts of XML documents 10.

If, for example, we have a database 'mydb' on our local machine, and the database contains a collection called 'bib' that in turn contains the schema 'book' conforming to the DTD given in Figure 2, then we could type the following URL in the address line of a browser:

```
http://localhost/tamino/mydb/bib/book?_XQL=/book/author[last~='A*']
```

to return documents belonging to the schema 'book' and satisfying the node selection condition expressed by the clause */book/author[last~='A*']*, which selects the authors whose last names start with 'A'.

To select the last names regardless of whether they belong to authors or editors, we write the following query:

```
// last
```

4   Experiment Design

Documents used in the experiments, the cost metrics, the selected queries and indexing are discussed in this section.

4.1   Sample Documents

The book DTDs are widespread and used in similar studies with minor differences. We have chosen a non-recursive book DTD given in Fig. 2. One criticism about the book-DTD and data is that it is quite relational or structured, rather than textual or semi-structured. XML documents we generated by a program in these experiments have the following characteristics

- The publishing years of the books vary randomly between 1950 and 2001.
- The book titles consist of 15 random upper letters including the space character.
- Each book can have either *one or two authors*, or *one or two editors* but not both. 90% of books have authors, and 10% editors.
- The last and first names of authors/editors consist of 10 random upper letters including the space character.
- Affiliations and publishers are generated in the form of "AffiliationN" and "PublisherN" respectively where N is a random number between 0 and 3000.
- The book prices vary between 10.00 and 110.00.

```
<?xml version="1.0"?>
<!DOCTYPE bib [
<!ELEMENT bib (book* )>
<!ELEMENT book (title, (author+ | editor+ ), pub-
lisher, price )>
<!ATTLIST book year CDATA  #REQUIRED >
<!ELEMENT author (last, first )>
<!ELEMENT editor (last, first, affiliation )>
<!ELEMENT title (#PCDATA )>
<!ELEMENT last (#PCDATA )>
<!ELEMENT first (#PCDATA )>
<!ELEMENT affiliation (#PCDATA )>
<!ELEMENT publisher (#PCDATA )>
<!ELEMENT price (#PCDATA )>
]>
```

Fig. 2. The Book DTD

The data in Tamino is stored in an XML schema as one large document containing all the records. The corresponding relational database in Oracle contains 3 tables (books, author and editor) shown below. We skip the discussion on how we obtained relational database schema from the DTD [16][17][18]. However the number of tables, the schema of each table, the number of tuples in the tables, the number of joins and the complexity of the SQL queries has a direct affect on the performance [14].

Book (bookid, year, title, publisher, price)
Author (authorid, parentid, last, first)
Editor (editorid, parentid, first, last, affiliation)

Three documents, containing 1, 2, and 3 million book records, are generated by a Java program: Each set consists of 2 data files: One is the XML document in "Tamino Mass Load" format, and the other is the corresponding data file Oracle's SQL Loader. We worked with up to 746 MB of XML document in Tamino and up to 354 MB of corresponding data (the difference comes from the lack of tag fields in the input file format of Oracle) in Oracle. We used Tamino's *Mass Loader Facility* for loading documents directly not using HTTP 10. In Oracle, we used the SQL*Loader which is also used for mass loading. Each query is executed only twice, once for indexed data, once for un-indexed data.

4.2 Cost Metrics

The experiments were conducted on two identical computers with Intel Pentium III CPUs clocked at 733 MHz, 256 MBs of main memory and 15 GBs of hard disk. The operating system was Windows 2000 on both computers. The version of native-XML database was Tamino 2.3.1.1. The version of XML facility of Oracle9i Application Server was XSQL Servlet 1.0.0.0. The cost metrics used in related work was discussed before. Although different metrics were used in measuring query performance in the literature, most studies focused on processing or running time of query to measure the overall response time in general. It should be noted that, in an environment where servers and clients communicate through other programs and protocols, response time would be a measure of not solely of the database, but of all the software comprising the system including the operating system and the network. This, in turn, makes it hard to isolate the query processing time of database from other parameters involved in the whole process. Therefore we focus on the system resource consumption.

In our experiments we measured *the CPU time (T), the number of logical reads (LR)* and *the number of physical reads (PR)*. We believe a better and more exact measure could be achieved by using these metrics. First of all these metrics are at the lowers level of query processing compared to *response time* from the application/user's point of view. Since data is stored on disks, the basic efficiency measure of query processing would be physical reads. Logical read is important for processing data in buffers and main memory. It measures how good the buffer management is, and gives an idea about how efficiently the algorithms are designed.

The physical and logical reads in Tamino is available through System Management Hub of Tamino Manager, CPU time for Tamino is measured using Windows 200 Task Manager window. In Oracle, metrics were measured using SQL Trace and TKPROF facility. Although running SQL Trace adds some overhead, it is negligible.

4.3 Queries

To choose an appropriate set of queries for the experiments, we considered the types of queries used in data-centric and document-centric applications. Basic relational algebra operations in data-centric applications and basic text processing operations of searching, matching, sorting in document-centric applications are known and important types of queries. Indexing is an important factor in efficient evaluation of queries. Other operations include basic DML and aggregations. We determined 13 different queries covering almost all basic operations. The criteria used in choosing the queries are: (i) All basic operations should be covered as much as possible (ii) Queries should be simple (only one operation if possible) (iii) Different types (relational operators, string/text-functions, document-structure) of operations should be tested.

One point we considered in designing queries is the following: Given that the two systems store and process documents differently, it is intuitive that they will have their strengths and weaknesses in different areas or for different types of queries. Below we list the queries used in this study. Some operations are not supported by both systems, or by one of them:

- **Exact (String) Match:** This query tests the database ability to handle simple string lookups with a complete specified path 5.
- **Full–Text Search:** Full-text search of XML query languages are actually efficient for document-centric XML databases. Although our database has a data-centric characteristic, we wanted to test this challenging ability of XML query languages with a data-centric XML document in our experiment.
- **Sorting:** When processing large size of databases such as ours, sorting the results or immediate results have major impact on efficiency.
- **Aggregation:** There are two queries from this group in our study, because Tamino supports only *count* and *sum*.
- **Selection:** We chose 3 queries with selection: selection with a *comparison operator,* with logical *and,* and with logical *or.* The comparison operator > is used for seeing the effect of indexing on a numerical field. *or/and* are used for testing to see whether the query optimizer takes necessary steps in re-expressing the query before processing. Traditionally *ors* should be somehow eliminated or avoided.
- **Join:** This query tests the database's ability to handle large (intermediate) results. Join is one relational algebra operation that requires special attention.
- **Set Operations:** Tamino supports only two operations: union and intersection.
- **DML Operations:** Update and delete operations are supported by both systems. Insert is used during initial mass loading of documents.

4.4 Indexing

In general, indexing increases the loading time (insertion) and update, and decreases the response time in query processing. Tamino allows two types of indexing on text fields: Text indexing and standard indexing. Both can be built on the same field/element. The text indexing is utilized in full-text-search (the *contains* operator ~=). Creating this type of index naturally takes much longer than standard indices. The standard indexing is used for short strings and numbers. Indices are created on elements *year, title, publisher* and *price* in Tamino, since those are the only fields used with comparison operators. The only field that has a text index is *first* name field of element *author*. The primary/foreign keys are index by default in Oracle. The other indexed fields are *year*, *title*, *publisher*, *price* of book table, and *last* name of *author* table on Oracle side.

5 Experimental Results

In this section we present results for only a subset of queries from the experiment because of space limitations. Please see 14 for a full presentation of all 13 different queries and detailed discussions. For each query we give the description, X-Query and XSQL versions of the query, and the experimental results depicted as charts. Remember T for the CPU time in seconds, LR for the no. of logical reads, PR for the no. of physical reads, T-UI for Tamino on Unindexed data, T-I for Tamino on Indexed data, O-UI for Oracle on Unindexed data and O-I for Oracle on Indexed data. The legend used in Figure 3 applies to all other figures in this section.

5.1 Exact Match Query

Description: Return the publisher of the book with the title "MPVKEAWIXLHHMHE".
In X-Query: ...bib/book?_xql=/book[title='MPVKEAWIXLHHMHE']/publisher
In SQL: Select publisher From book Where title=' MPVKEAWIXLHHMHE';

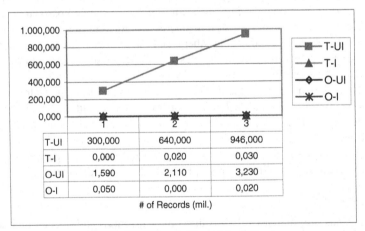

	1	2	3
T-UI	300,000	640,000	946,000
T-I	0,000	0,020	0,030
O-UI	1,590	2,110	3,230
O-I	0,050	0,000	0,020

\# of Records (mil.)

Fig. 3. CPU Time in Exact Match Query

The results are shown in Figures 3, 4, and 5. As seen in the charts, without index, Oracle was much faster than Tamino in "Exact Match" query. Tamino requires twice the number of physical reads more that of Oracle. On the other hand Tamino requires about 1500 times more logical reads than that of Oracle.

Query processing efficiency of Tamino changes considerably after indexing. Oracle and Tamino have approximately the same performance with index. Indexing improves efficiency dramatically, but Tamino still requires multiple times more logical reads than Oracle does. Without the index Oracle needs to check only a field in a table in linear fashion, while Tamino requires scanning of subparts of documents to do the same.

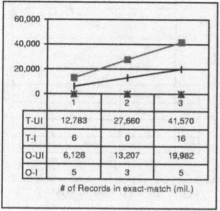

Fig. 4. Physical Reads in Exact Match

	1	2	3
T-UI	10.133.999	20.507.074	31.118.081
T-I	76	76	76
O-UI	12.948	13.459	20.276
O-I	6	5	9

# of Records in exact-match (mil.)

Fig. 5. Logical Reads in Exact Match

5.2 The Count Query

Description: Return the number of all books.
                  X-Query: ...bib/book?_xql=count(/book)
SQL: Select count(bookid) from book

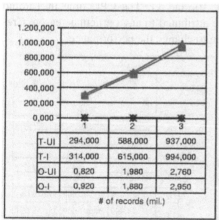

Fig. 6. CPU (seconds) in COUNT

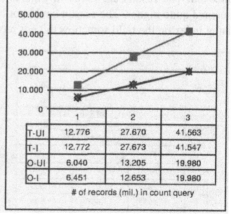

Fig. 7. Physical Reads in COUNT

The results are given in Figures 6, 7, and 8. The SQL query counts the bookids (primary key) in Oracle, while '\book' and 'ino:id'' (which is the most efficient method to access the records) in Tamino, but the performance was poor. Indexing doesn't affect query performance due to the fact that the sum function requires scanning of all records in the table or document.

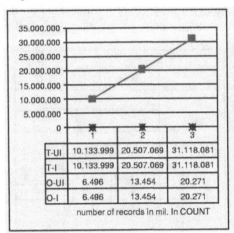

	1	2	3
T-UI	10.133.999	20.507.069	31.118.081
T-I	10.133.999	20.507.069	31.118.081
O-UI	6.496	13.454	20.271
O-I	6.496	13.454	20.271

number of records in mil. In COUNT

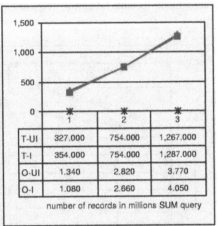

	1	2	3
T-UI	327.000	754.000	1,267.000
T-I	354.000	754.000	1,287.000
O-UI	1.340	2.820	3.770
O-I	1.080	2.660	4.050

number of records in millions SUM query

Fig. 8. The Logical Reads in COUNT   **Fig. 9.** The CPU Time in SUM

5.3 The Sum Query

Description   : Return the sum of prices of all the books.
X-Query   :   ...bib/book?_xql=sum(/book/price)
SQL   : Select sum(price) from book;

The sum function requires the linear scan of a table. If the field is indexed, then the sum can be computed without going to the table. In this experiment the price field was indexed. The results are given in Figures 9, 10, and 11. The CPU time in Tamino seemed quite higher. The reason could not be attributed to any particular reason. Creating index on the field somehow did not seem to change the performance.

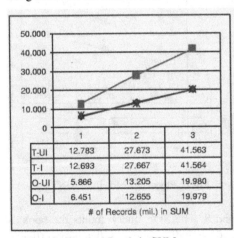

	1	2	3
T-UI	12.783	27.673	41.563
T-I	12.693	27.667	41.564
O-UI	5.866	13.205	19.980
O-I	6.451	12.655	19.979

# of Records (mil.) in SUM

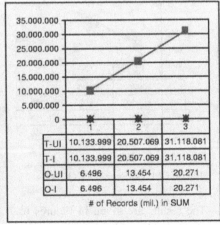

	1	2	3
T-UI	10.133.999	20.507.069	31.118.081
T-I	10.133.999	20.507.069	31.118.081
O-UI	6.496	13.454	20.271
O-I	6.496	13.454	20.271

# of Records (mil.) in SUM

Fig. 10. Physical Reads in SUM   **Fig. 11.** Logical Reads in SUM

5.4   The Full-Text Search Query

Description: Return the first names of all the authors whose first names contain 'CH'
X-Query: ...bib/book?_xql=/book/author/first[.~='*CH*']
SQL: Select first From author Where first like '%CH%';

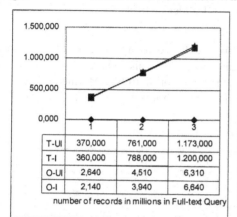

	1	2	3
T-UI	370,000	761,000	1.173,000
T-I	360,000	788,000	1.200,000
O-UI	2,640	4,510	6,310
O-I	2,140	3,940	6,640

number of records in millions in Full-text Query

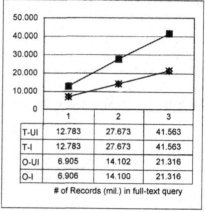

	1	2	3
T-UI	12.783	27.673	41.563
T-I	12.783	27.673	41.563
O-UI	6.905	14.102	21.316
O-I	6.906	14.100	21.316

# of Records (mil.) in full-text query

Fig. 12. CPU Time in Full-text Search   **Fig. 13.** Physical Reads in Full-text

The results are shown in Figures 12, 13, and 14. Although we used the 'text index', which is recommended for full text search in the Tamino documentation, the Tamino's performance did not improve after indexing. This could be due to the fact that the data was data-centric. So the advantages of full-text index were not reflected. The number of logical and physical reads were not affected by indexing. On the other hand, indexing did not have a considerable effect in this query on Oracle either.

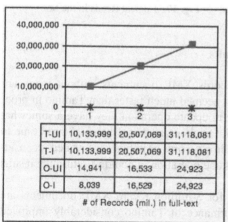

	1	2	3
T-UI	10,133,999	20,507,069	31,118,081
T-I	10,133,999	20,507,069	31,118,081
O-UI	14,941	16,533	24,923
O-I	8,039	16,529	24,923

# of Records (mil.) in full-text

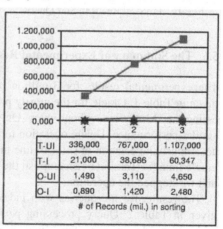

	1	2	3
T-UI	336,000	767,000	1.107,000
T-I	21,000	38,686	60,347
O-UI	1,490	3,110	4,650
O-I	0,890	1,420	2,480

# of Records (mil.) in sorting

Fig. 14. Logical Reads in Full-text Search   **Fig. 15.** CPU Time in the Sort

5.5 The Sort Query

Description: Select titles of the books which are published in 2001, listed alphabetically.
X-Query: ...bib/book?_xql=/book[@year=2001] sortby (./title)/title
SQL: Select title From book Where year=2001 Order by title;

The results are shown in Figures 15, 16, and 17. After indexing, the efficiency of Tamino improved very dramatically in the sort query. This is because the index already has the field in sorted order. Without index, a sort must be performed in order to answer the query. Oracle was faster than Tamino with indexing as well. Oracle's efficiency increased twice with index.

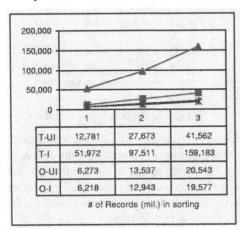

	1	2	3
T-UI	12,781	27,673	41,562
T-I	51,972	97,511	159,183
O-UI	6,273	13,537	20,543
O-I	6,218	12,943	19,577

# of Records (mil.) in sorting

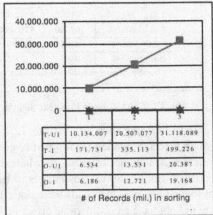

	1	2	3
T-UI	10.134.007	20.507.077	31.118.089
T-I	171.731	335.113	499.226
O-UI	6.534	13.531	20.387
O-I	6.186	12.721	19.168

# of Records (mil.) in sorting

Fig. 16. Physical Reads in Sort Query   **Fig. 17.** Logical Reads in the Sort

5.6 The Summary of Experimental Results

The experimental results for 3-million records XML documents without index are given in Table 1. Oracle for the mostly part seemed much faster than Tamino in processing the 13 queries without index. Only in update operation they have a somewhat similar performance. Delete operation took Oracle more than 4 hours elapsed time to accomplish the deletion of 0.1% of one million records. Although we waited a considerable time for Tamino to accomplish the same operation, it couldn't return the results and we stopped the operation.

The results for the queries with index for 3-million record XML documents are given in Table 2. Query processing performance of Tamino considerably improved with index. On 'exact match', 'logical and', and 'join' queries Tamino and Oracle have performed about the same. Although indexing caused performance improvement on Tamino, on 'query with comparison', 'union', 'logical or' queries, Oracle was about 10 times faster than Tamino. On 'sorting' query, Oracle was even faster than Tamino. Queries using aggregation functions 'count' and 'sum' are not affected by indexing which was expected. Although we created a text-search index, the perform-ance of full-text search query was not affected with index. Using this type of index on a short string field may be the reason for it. The text-search index might have been optimized for long strings containing potentially many pages of text. Performance of 'update' operation is not affected by indexing. We were able to execute the 'delete' operation on both systems after indexing. Before indexing the deletion took too long to execute. Indexing improved the performance of both systems in the deletion operation. However, Oracle was approximately 6 times faster in deletion operation than Tamino.

Table 1. Results for 3 million records without index

Query	Tamino LR	Oracle LR	Tamino T	Oracle T
Exact Match	31118081	20276	946.000	3.230
Count	31118081	20271	937.000	2.760
Sum	31118081	20271	1267.000	3.770
Selection (>)	31118081	24092	1180.000	4.600
Selection (and)	31118081	20273	1092.000	3.640
Selection (or)	31118081	24153	1139.000	5.950
Full-Text	31118081	24923	1173.000	6.310
Sorting	31118089	20387	1107.000	4.650
Join	31118081	16217791	985.000	75.640
Union	38215971	18020170	1295.000	86.220
Intersection	38215971	36040643	1245.000	170.200
Update	132	6	0.000	0.010

Table 2. CPU Time and Logical Records for 3-million records with Index

Query	Tamino LR	Oracle LR	Tamino T	Oracle T
Exact Match	76	9	0.030	0.020
Count	31118081	20271	994.000	2.950
Sum	31118081	20271	1287.000	4.050
Selection (>)	461929	25468	28.651	2.670
Selection (and)	485	153	0.120	0.050
Selection (or)	470154	26516	30.173	3.110
Full-text	31118081	24923	1200.000	6.640
Sorting	499226	19168	60.347	2.480
Join	8028	5047	1.012	0.280
Union	923805	442004	61.999	9.150
Intersecion	501	451662	0.060	12.340
Update	220	18	0.040	0.010
Delete	91665	13213	5.658	0.760

There is not a considerable difference between Oracle's and Tamino's physical read numbers. We specified the same size of buffer pool area on both systems. The 20 MB of buffer pool was assigned for operations of 1-million record data file and 50 MB of buffer pool was assigned for 2 and 3-million record data files. There is an ab-normal difference between Tamino's and Oracle's LR as shown in Table 1. In most queries, LR in Tamino was multiple times bigger than LR in Oracle. That might be the key to the performance gap between the two systems with or without index. It seems Tamino may have not used the buffer pool efficiently. This could be one improvement in this particular software.

Oracle's performance degrades in the join, union, and intersection queries. All of these queries performed join operations on two tables. When we write a query that returns the whole XML documents in Tamino, the same query in Oracle requires joining of all corresponding tables. Let's consider 1- million record data file: There are 1 million tuples in book table, more than 1,5 million tuples in author table and 100 thousands tuples in editor table. Joining those tables result in a huge temporary table because of the cross-product operation. We tried it and we waited for a considerably long time and we couldn't get any response. That's another reason we divided intersection query into sub-queries each of which includes joining only two tables. This is one query where native-XML systems can beat XML-enabled systems because they store the XML document in native form which means retrieving whole document should be easy.

We determined that Tamino's data retrieval performance is increased after indexing. But, on the other hand, data-storing performance is decreased extremely. Oracle's SQL*Loader seemed as an efficient tool for data loading. It provides high performance when storing large amount of data into Oracle. It looked faster than Tamino's Mass Loader Facility. Although Tamino has developed Mass Loader Facility for efficient loading, we determined that after 500 thousands books/records were loaded, it slowed down considerably. Table 3 shows the spent time measured during data loading of 2 and 3-millions record data files with indexing. The elapsed time parameters were taken from log files of both facilities.

Table 3. Elapsed Times of Indexed Loading

File Size	2 Mil. Records	3 Mil. Records
Oracle SQL*Loader	3953 sec	5916 sec
Tamino Mass Loader	112499 sec	138844 sec

6   Conclusions

We ran 13 selected queries with and without index on a native-XML database and an XML-enabled database for 3 sets of large data-centric XML documents to measure the query processing efficiency in terms of CPU time, logical and physical disk accesses. The experimental results for some queries are discussed in the previous section individually. Overall the XML-enabled database seemed faster than the native-XML database especially when columns were not indexed. In general the native- XML database's performance approached to the XML-enabled database's performance, when the columns were indexed. The query processing in the XML-enabled database was multiple times faster than the native- XML database. Although the findings are insightful, one should be careful about generalizing the results. Remember that the XML document used in the experiment were data-centric. For document-centric data, the native-XML system could be expected to do better. The data-oriented queries can be expected to execute faster on the XML-enabled system, while text/document-oriented queries should execute faster on the native systems in general. The performance depends on many parameters including but not limited to the type of operations and queries (text operations versus relational operators), the type and size of data used in the experiment (data-centric versus document-centric or structured versus semi-structured), the environment in which the experiment conducted (the disk I/O subsystem, memory sub-system, CPU, network and internet sub-systems), indexing (standard indexing versus full-text indexing), the size of buffer pool, algorithms and data structures used in each system. Further study and experimentation is needed to shed some light on these issues. The results could be used to improve where and how to improve processing the queries used in the experiments.

References

1. W3 Consortium *Extensible Markup Language (XML) http://www.w3.org/TR/REC-xml*, W3C Recommendation 6 October 2000
2. A.R. Schmidt, et al., The XML Benchmark Project. INS-R0103, Amsterdam, Netherlands, April 30, 2001.
3. M. Fernandez, J. Simeon, P. Wadler. XML Query Languages: Experiences and Exemplars, Summer 1999
4. P. A. Boncz and M. L. Kersten. MIL primitives for Querying a Fragmented World. The VLDB Journal, 8(2):101-119, 1999.
5. A.R. Schmidt, et all., Efficient Relational Storage and Retrieval of XML Documents. In International Workshop on the Web and Databases (In conjuction with ACM SIGMOD), pages 47-52, Dallas, TX, USA, 2000.
6. T. Shimura, M. Yoshikawa, and S. Uemura. Storage and Retrieval of XML Documents Using Object-Relational Databases. In Database and Expert Systems Applications, pages 206-217. Springer, 1999.
7. D. Chamberlin, D. Florescu, J. Robbie, J. S,meon, and M. Stefanescu. *Xquery: A Query Language for XML,* Feb 2001, http://www.w3.org/TR/xquery.
8. T. Böhme, E. Rahm. Xmach-1:A Benchmark for XML Data Management.
9. P. Cotton, D. Fallside, A. Malhotra. *Position Paper on XML Query*. W3C Query Languages Workshop, December 1998.
10. Software AG. Tamino Documentation. 2001. http://www.softwareag.com/tamino/
11. Reston, VA, June 25, 2001. http://www.idc.com
12. B. Wait, Oracle Corporation. *About Oracle XML Products.* November 1999 http://otn.oracle.com/tech/xml/info/htdocs/otnwp/about_oracle_xml_products.htm
13. B. Wait, Oracle Corporation. *Customizing Data Presentation.* November 1999 http://otn.oracle.com/tech/xml/info/htdocs/otnwp/xml_custom_presentation.htm
14. Mustafa Atay, Query Processing Efficiency in Native-XML and XML-enabled Databases, Aug 2001 Fatih University, Istanbul, Turkey, MS Thesis.
15. S. Bressan, G. Dobbie, Z. Lacroix, M. L. Lee, Y. Guang Li, U. Nambiar, B. Wadhwa: XOO7: Applying OO7 Benchmark to XML Query Processing Tools, Proceedings of the 10th ACM CIKM , Atlanta, Georgia, November 2001.

16. P. Bohannon, J. Freire, P. Roy, J. Simeon: From XML,Schema to Relations: A Cost-based Approach to XML Storage. ICDE 2002
17. J. Shanmugasundaram, K. Tufte, C. Zhang, G. He, D.,J. DeWitt, J. F. Naughton: Relational Databases for Querying XML, Documents: Limitations and Opportunities. VLDB 1999: 302-314
18. D. Florescu, D. Kossmann: Storing and Querying XML Data using an RDMBS. IEEE Data Engineering Bulletin 22(3): 27-34 (1999)

Author Index

Altenschmidt, C.   103
Andres, Frédéric   64
Atay, Mustafa   268

Barbera, Francesco   161
Biskup, J.   103
Boldyreff, Cornelia   88

Carlson, C. Robert   15
Casati, Fabio   213
Cheng, Zixue   201

Dayal, Umeshwar   213
Dyreson, Curtis E.   29

Feng, Jianhua   74
Ferri, Fernando   161

Godard, Jérôme   64

Han, Dongsoo   43
Han, Sang Yong   147
Hirano, Kotaro   179
Hong, Gun Ho   147

Jambalsuren, Mungunsukh   201
Jia, Xiaohua   253
Jin, Qun   225

Kameda, Hisao   253
Kazuhide, Koide   239
Keeni, Glenn Mansfield   239
Kim, Hongsoog   43
Kim, Jaehyoun   15
Kitsuregawa, Masaru   173, 188
Kunii, Tosiyasu L.   58
Kurt, Atakan   268

Lavery, Janet   88
Lee, Hun   147
Li, Jie   253

Maarek, Yoelle   133

Norio, Shiratori   239

Ohura, Yusuke   173
Ono, Kinji   64

Peres, Yardena   133
Pramudiono, Iko   173
Pyo, Chang Woo   253

Rao, S. Srinivasa   188
Reddy, P. Krishna   188
Ricci, Fabrizio L.   161

Shan, Ming-Chien   213
Shim, Jaeyong   43
Sifer, Mark   133
Song, Ha Yoon   147
Sottile, Pier Angelo   161
Sowa, Tomoyuki   179
Sreekanth, P.   188

Takizawa, Shuichi   225
Toyoda, Masashi   173

Wiederhold, Gio   1

Xing, Chunxiao   74

Zhang, Shuohao   29
Zhang, Zhiqiang   74
Zhou, Lizhu   74

Lecture Notes in Computer Science

For information about Vols. 1–2465

please contact your bookseller or Springer-Verlag

Vol. 2466: M. Beetz, J. Hertzberg, M. Ghallab, M.E. Pollack (Eds.), Advances in Plan-Based Control of Robotic Agents. Proceedings, 2001. VIII, 291 pages. 2002. (Subseries LNAI).

Vol. 2467: B. Christianson, B. Crispo, J.A. Malcolm, M. Roe (Eds.), Security Protocols. Proceedings, 2001. IX, 241 pages. 2002.

Vol. 2468: J. Plaice, P.G. Kropf, P. Schulthess, J. Slonim (Eds.) (Eds.), Distributed Communities on the Web. Proceedings, 2002. XI, 305 pages. 2002.

Vol. 2469: W. Damm, E.-R. Olderog (Eds.), Formal Techniques in Real-Time and Fault-Tolerant Systems. Proceedings, 2002. X, 455 pages. 2002.

Vol. 2470: P. Van Hentenryck (Ed.), Principles and Practice of Constraint Programming – CP 2002. Proceedings, 2002. XVI, 794 pages. 2002.

Vol. 2471: J. Bradfield (Ed.), Computer Science Logic. Proceedings, 2002. XII, 613 pages. 2002.

Vol. 2473: A. Gomez-Perez, V.R. Benjamins, Knowledge Engineering and Knowledge Management. Proceedings, 2002. XI, 402 pages. 2002. (Subseries LNAI).

Vol. 2474: D. Kranzlmüller, P. Kacsuk, J. Dongarra, J. Volkert (Eds.), Recent Advances in Parallel Virtual Machine and Message Passing Interface. Proceedings, 2002. XVI, 462 pages. 2002.

Vol. 2475: J.J. Alpigini, J.F. Peters, A. Skowron, N. Zhong (Eds.), Rough Sets and Current Trends in Computing. Proceedings, 2002. XV, 640 pages. 2002. (Subseries LNAI).

Vol. 2476: A.H.F. Laender, A.L. Oliveira (Eds.), String Processing and Information Retrieval. Proceedings, 2002. XI, 337 pages. 2002.

Vol. 2477: M.V. Hermenegildo, G. Puebla (Eds.), Static Analysis. Proceedings, 2002. XI, 527 pages. 2002.

Vol. 2478: M.J. Egenhofer, D.M. Mark (Eds.), Geographic Information Science. Proceedings, 2002. X, 363 pages. 2002.

Vol. 2479: M. Jarke, J. Koehler, G. Lakemeyer (Eds.), KI 2002: Advances in Artificial Intelligence. Proceedings, 2002. XIII, 327 pages. (Subseries LNAI).

Vol. 2480: Y. Han, S. Tai, D. Wikarski (Eds.), Engineering and Deployment of Cooperative Information Systems. Proceedings, 2002. XIII, 564 pages. 2002.

Vol. 2483: J.D.P. Rolim, S. Vadhan (Eds.), Randomization and Approximation Techniques in Computer Science. Proceedings, 2002. VIII, 275 pages. 2002.

Vol. 2484: P. Adriaans, H. Fernau, M. van Zaanen (Eds.), Grammatical Inference: Algorithms and Applications. Proceedings, 2002. IX, 315 pages. 2002. (Subseries LNAI).

Vol. 2485: A. Bondavalli, P. Thevenod-Fosse (Eds.), Dependable Computing EDCC-4. Proceedings, 2002. XIII, 283 pages. 2002.

Vol. 2486: M. Marinaro, R. Tagliaferri (Eds.), Neural Nets. Proceedings, 2002. IX, 253 pages. 2002.

Vol. 2487: D. Batory, C. Consel, W. Taha (Eds.), Generative Programming and Component Engineering. Proceedings, 2002. VIII, 335 pages. 2002.

Vol. 2488: T. Dohi, R. Kikinis (Eds), Medical Image Computing and Computer-Assisted Intervention – MICCAI 2002. Proceedings, Part I. XXIX, 807 pages. 2002.

Vol. 2489: T. Dohi, R. Kikinis (Eds), Medical Image Computing and Computer-Assisted Intervention – MICCAI 2002. Proceedings, Part II. XXIX, 693 pages. 2002.

Vol. 2490: A.B. Chaudhri, R. Unland, C. Djeraba, W. Lindner (Eds.), XML-Based Data Management and Multimedia Engineering – EDBT 2002. Proceedings, 2002. XII, 652 pages. 2002.

Vol. 2491: A. Sangiovanni-Vincentelli, J. Sifakis (Eds.), Embedded Software. Proceedings, 2002. IX, 423 pages. 2002.

Vol. 2492: F.J. Perales, E.R. Hancock (Eds.), Articulated Motion and Deformable Objects. Proceedings, 2002. X, 257 pages. 2002.

Vol. 2493: S. Bandini, B. Chopard, M. Tomassini (Eds.), Cellular Automata. Proceedings, 2002. XI, 369 pages. 2002.

Vol. 2495: C. George, H. Miao (Eds.), Formal Methods and Software Engineering. Proceedings, 2002. XI, 626 pages. 2002.

Vol. 2496: K.C. Almeroth, M. Hasan (Eds.), Management of Multimedia in the Internet. Proceedings, 2002. XI, 355 pages. 2002.

Vol. 2497: E. Gregori, G. Anastasi, S. Basagni (Eds.), Advanced Lectures on Networking. XI, 195 pages. 2002.

Vol. 2498: G. Borriello, L.E. Holmquist (Eds.), UbiComp 2002: Ubiquitous Computing. Proceedings, 2002. XV, 380 pages. 2002.

Vol. 2499: S.D. Richardson (Ed.), Machine Translation: From Research to Real Users. Proceedings, 2002. XXI, 254 pages. 2002. (Subseries LNAI).

Vol. 2501: D. Zheng (Ed.), Advances in Cryptology – ASIACRYPT 2002. Proceedings, 2002. XIII, 578 pages. 2002.

Vol. 2502: D. Gollmann, G. Karjoth, M. Waidner (Eds.), Computer Security – ESORICS 2002. Proceedings, 2002. X, 281 pages. 2002.

Vol. 2503: S. Spaccapietra, S.T. March, Y. Kambayashi (Eds.), Conceptual Modeling – ER 2002. Proceedings, 2002. XX, 480 pages. 2002.

Vol. 2504: M.T. Escrig, F. Toledo, E. Golobardes (Eds.), Topics in Artificial Intelligence. Proceedings, 2002. XI, 432 pages. 2002. (Subseries LNAI).

Vol. 2506: M. Feridun, P. Kropf, G. Babin (Eds.), Management Technologies for E-Commerce and E-Business Applications. Proceedings, 2002. IX, 209 pages. 2002.

Vol. 2507: G. Bittencourt, G.L. Ramalho (Eds.), Advances in Artificial Intelligence. Proceedings, 2002. XIII, 418 pages. 2002. (Subseries LNAI).

Vol. 2508: D. Malkhi (Ed.), Distributed Computing. Proceedings, 2002. X, 371 pages. 2002.

Vol. 2509: C.S. Calude, M.J. Dinneen, F. Peper (Eds.), Unconventional Models in Computation. Proceedings, 2002. VIII, 331 pages. 2002.

Vol. 2510: H. Shafazand, A Min Tjoa (Eds.), EurAsia-ICT 2002: Information and Communication Technology. Proceedings, 2002. XXIII, 1020 pages. 2002.

Vol. 2511: B. Stiller, M. Smirnow, M. Karsten, P. Reichl (Eds.), From QoS Provisioning to QoS Charging. Proceedings, 2002. XIV, 348 pages. 2002.

Vol. 2512: C. Bussler, R. Hull, S. McIlraith, M.E. Orlowska, B. Pernici, J. Yang (Eds.), Web Services, E-Business, and the Semantic Web. Proceedings, 2002. XI, 277 pages. 2002.

Vol. 2513: R. Deng, S. Qing, F. Bao, J. Zhou (Eds.), Information and Communications Security. Proceedings, 2002. XII, 496 pages. 2002.

Vol. 2514: M. Baaz, A. Voronkov (Eds.), Logic for Programming, Artificial Intelligence, and Reasoning. Proceedings, 2002. XIII, 465 pages. 2002. (Subseries LNAI).

Vol. 2515: F. Boavida, E. Monteiro, J. Orvalho (Eds.), Protocols and Systems for Interactive Distributed Multimedia. Proceedings, 2002. XIV, 372 pages. 2002.

Vol. 2516: A. Wespi, G. Vigna, L. Deri (Eds.), Recent Advances in Intrusion Detection. Proceedings, 2002. X, 327 pages. 2002.

Vol. 2517: M.D. Aagaard, J.W. O'Leary (Eds.), Formal Methods in Computer-Aided Design. Proceedings, 2002. XI, 399 pages. 2002.

Vol. 2518: P. Bose, P. Morin (Eds.), Algorithms and Computation. Proceedings, 2002. XIII, 656 pages. 2002.

Vol. 2519: R. Meersman, Z. Tari, et al. (Eds.), On the Move to Meaningful Internet Systems 2002: CoopIS, DOA, and ODBASE. Proceedings, 2002. XXIII, 1367 pages. 2002.

Vol. 2521: A. Karmouch, T. Magedanz, J. Delgado (Eds.), Mobile Agents for Telecommunication Applications. Proceedings, 2002. XII, 317 pages. 2002.

Vol. 2522: T. Andreasen, A. Motro, H. Christiansen, H. Legind Larsen (Eds.), Flexible Query Answering. Proceedings, 2002. XI, 386 pages. 2002. (Subseries LNAI).

Vol. 2525: H.H. Bülthoff, S.-Whan Lee, T.A. Poggio, C. Wallraven (Eds.), Biologically Motivated Computer Vision. Proceedings, 2002. XIV, 662 pages. 2002.

Vol. 2526: A. Colosimo, A. Giuliani, P. Sirabella (Eds.), Medical Data Analysis. Proceedings, 2002. IX, 222 pages. 2002.

Vol. 2527: F.J. Garijo, J.C. Riquelme, M. Toro (Eds.), Advances in Artificial Intelligence – IBERAMIA 2002. Proceedings, 2002. XVIII, 955 pages. 2002. (Subseries LNAI).

Vol. 2528: M.T. Goodrich, S.G. Kobourov (Eds.), Graph Drawing. Proceedings, 2002. XIII, 384 pages. 2002.

Vol. 2529: D.A. Peled, M.Y. Vardi (Eds.), Formal Techniques for Networked and Distributed Sytems – FORTE 2002. Proceedings, 2002. XI, 371 pages. 2002.

Vol. 2532: Y.-C. Chen, L.-W. Chang, C.-T. Hsu (Eds.), Advances in Multimedia Information Processing – PCM 2002. Proceedings, 2002. XXI, 1255 pages. 2002.

Vol. 2533: N. Cesa-Bianchi, M. Numao, R. Reischuk (Eds.), Algorithmic Learning Theory. Proceedings, 2002. XI, 415 pages. 2002. (Subseries LNAI).

Vol. 2534: S. Lange, K. Satoh, C.H. Smith (Ed.), Discovery Science. Proceedings, 2002. XIII, 464 pages. 2002.

Vol. 2535: N. Suri (Ed.), Mobile Agents. Proceedings, 2002. X, 203 pages. 2002.

Vol. 2536: M. Parashar (Ed.), Grid Computing – GRID 2002. Proceedings, 2002. XI, 318 pages. 2002.

Vol. 2537: D.G. Feitelson, L. Rudolph, U. Schwiegelshohn (Eds.), Job Scheduling Strategies for Parallel Processing. Proceedings, 2002. VII, 237 pages. 2002.

Vol. 2538: B. König-Ries, K. Makki, S.A.M. Makki, N. Pissinou, P. Scheuermann (Eds.), Developing an Infrastructure for Mobile and Wireless Systems. Proceedings 2001. X, 183 pages. 2002.

Vol. 2540: W.I. Grosky, F. Plášil (Eds.), SOFSEM 2002: Theory and Practice of Informatics. Proceedings, 2002. X, 289 pages. 2002.

Vol. 2541: T. Barkowsky, Mental Representation and Processing of Geographic Knowledge. X, 174 pages. 2002. (Subseries LNAI).

Vol. 2544: S. Bhalla (Ed.), Databases in Networked Information Systems. Proceedings 2002. X, 285 pages. 2002.

Vol. 2545: P. Forbrig, Q, Limbourg, B. Urban, J. Vanderdonckt (Eds.), Interactive Systems. Proceedings 2002. X, 269 pages. 2002.

Vol. 2546: J. Sterbenz, O. Takada, C. Tschudin, B. Plattner (Eds.), Active Networks. Proceedings, 2002. XIV, 267 pages. 2002.

Vol. 2548: J. Hernández, Ana Moreira (Eds.), Object-Oriented Technology. Proceedings, 2002. VIII, 223 pages. 2002.

Vol. 2549: J. Cortadella, A. Yakovlev, G. Rozenberg (Eds.), Concurrency and Hardware Design. XI, 345 pages. 2002.

Vol. 2550: A. Jean-Marie (Ed.), Advances in Computing Science – ASIAN 2002. Proceedings, 2002. X, 233 pages. 2002.

Vol. 2551: A. Menezes, P. Sarkar (Eds.), Progress in Cryptology – INDOCRYPT 2002. Proceedings, 2002. XI, 437 pages. 2002.

Vol. 2555: E.-P. Lim, S. Foo, C. Khoo, H. Chen, E. Fox, S. Urs, T. Costantino (Eds.), Digital Libraries: People, Knowledge, and Technology. Proceedings, 2002. XVII, 535 pages. 2002.

Vol. 2556: M. Agrawal, A. Seth (Eds.), FST TCS 2002: Foundations of Software Technology and Theoretical Computer Science. Proceedings, 2002. XI, 361 pages. 2002.

Vol. 2557: B. McKay, J. Slaney (Eds.), AI 2002: Advances in Artificial Intelligence. Proceedings, 2002. XV, 730 pages. 2002. (Subseries LNAI).

Vol. 2559: M. Oivo, S. Komi-Sirviö (Eds.), Product Focused Software Process Improvement. Proceedings, 2002. XV, 646 pages. 2002.

Vol. 2561: H.C.M. de Swart (Ed.), Relational Methods in Computer Science. Proceedings, 2001. X, 315 pages. 2002.

Vol. 2569: D. Gollmann, G. Karjoth, M. Waidner (Eds.), Computer Security – ESORICS 2002. Proceedings, 2002. XIII, 648 pages. 2002. (Subseries LNAI).